ARIS AND PHILLIPS HISPAI

THE POEM OF FERNÁN GONZÁLEZ

(Poema de Fernán González)

Edited and Translated with an Introduction and Commentary by

Peter Such and Richard Rabone

Aris & Phillips is an imprint of Oxbow Books

Published in the United Kingdom in 2015 by
OXBOW BOOKS
10 Hythe Bridge Street, Oxford OX1 2EW

and in the United States by
OXBOW BOOKS
908 Darby Road, Havertown, PA 19083

Hardback Edition: ISBN 978-0-90834-200-9
Paperback Edition: ISBN 978-0-90834-201-6

A CIP record for this book is available from the British Library

For a complete list of Aris & Phillips titles, please contact:

UNITED KINGDOM	UNITED STATES OF AMERICA
Oxbow Books	Oxbow Books
Telephone (01865) 241249	Telephone (800) 791-9354
Fax (01865) 794449	Fax (610) 853-9146
Email: oxbow@oxbowbooks.com	Email: queries@casemateacademic.com
www.oxbowbooks.com	www.casemateacademic.com/oxbow

Oxbow Books is part of the Casemate group

Front cover: Ruins of the monastery of San Pedro de Arlanza.

Printed and bound in Great Britain by
Marston Book Services Ltd, Oxfordshire

To friends and colleagues at the Instituto Fernando III el Santo,
Priego de Córdoba

CONTENTS

ACKNOWLEDGEMENTS

We have a great debt of gratitude to Jonathan Thacker for his encouragement and guidance, and also to Clare Litt, Sarah Ommanney and Tara Evans at Oxbow for their helpfulness and efficiency.

We are also grateful to Heather O'Brien, who drew the maps, and to Professor Eric Naylor, who kindly read a draft of the introduction and made a number of valuable suggestions.

We must also express our deep thanks to Sylvia, who has shared her marriage with Fernán González for the past two years, and to Katie, *sine qua non*.

P. T. S.
M. R. K. R.

MAP OF THE COUNTY OF CASTILE AFTER 932 AS DEPICTED IN THE *POEMA DE FERNÁN GONZÁLEZ*

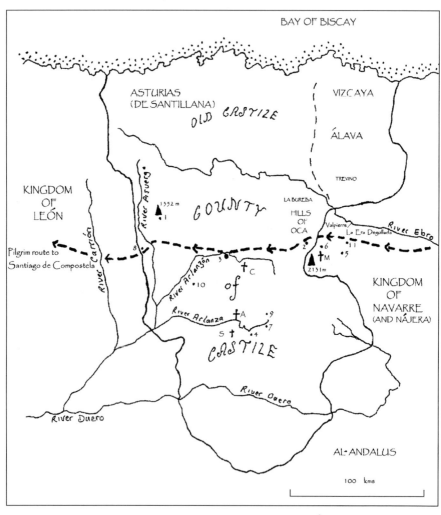

Settlements

1 Amaya
2 Belorado
3 Burgos
4 Carazo
5 Castroviejo
6 Cirueña
7 Hacinas
8 Itero del Castillo
9 Lara
10 Muñó
11 Nájera

Monasteries †

A San Pedro de Arlanza
S Santo Domingo de Silos
M San Millán de la Cogolla
C San Pedro de Cardeña

MAP OF THE IBERIAN PENINSULA IN 1252

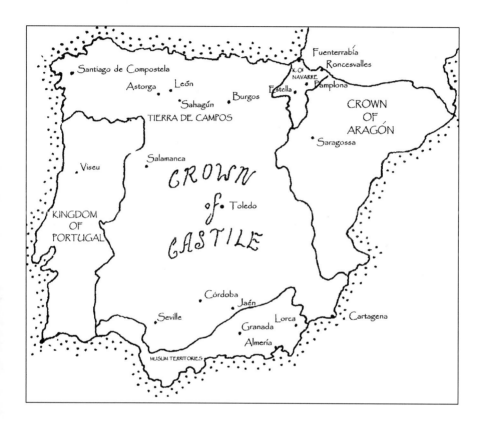

FROM THE ISLAMIC INVASION TO THE REIGN

OF ALFONSO X: A CHRONOLOGY

Events in Spain	International events	Literary and historical works
711 Beginning of the Islamic invasion of the Iberian Peninsula; battle of Guadalete		
c. **718** Establishment of Christian kingdom in Asturias		
722 Pelagius wins victory over Muslims at Covadonga		
	732 Charles Martel defeats Muslims at Poitiers	
	750 Umayyad caliphate overthrown by Abbasid dynasty	
756 Abd al-Rahman I establishes independent emirate in Córdoba		
	778 Charlemagne's expedition into Spain; his rearguard is defeated at Roncesvalles	
	800 Coronation of Charlemagne as emperor in Rome	
824 Establishment of independent kingdom of Pamplona		
c. **830** Discovery of remains of St James (Santiago)		
866–910 Reign of Alfonso III of Asturias; the Christians push southwards to the Duero		
		c. **881** *Chronicle of Albelda*
		c. **883** *Prophetic Chronicle*
c. **910** Birth of Fernán González	**910** Foundation of the Order of Cluny	
		c. **911** *Chronicle of Alfonso III*
912–929 Abd al-Rahman III emir		
929–961 Abd al-Rahman III first independent caliph of Córdoba		
931–951 Reign of Ramiro II of León		

Events in Spain	International events	Literary and historical works
932–970 Fernán González count of Castile (dies in 970)		
939 Christian victory at Simancas		
944–945 Fernán González imprisoned by Ramiro II		
985–997 Devastating raids by al-Mansur, including León in 988 and Santiago de Compostela in 997		
		c. **1000** *Chronicle of Sampiro* (bishop of Astorga); covering 866–982
1031 Caliphate of Córdoba breaks into taifa kingdoms		
1037 Castile and León united by Fernando I, great-grandson of Fernán González		
1085 Capture of Toledo by Alfonso VI of Castile and León		
1086 Arrival in al-Andalus of the Almoravids, who win victory at Zalaca (Sagrajas)		
1094 Capture of Valencia by the Cid		
	1095 Pope Urban II proclaims the First Crusade at Clermont	*c.* **1095** *Song of Roland*
	1099 Fall of Jerusalem to crusaders	
1118 Capture of Saragossa by Alfonso 'the Battler' of Aragón		
		c. **1135** Compilation of the *Codex Calixtinus*
c. **1145** Almohads come to power in al-Andalus		
	1147–1148 Second Crusade	
1157 Death of Alfonso VII: León and Castile divided		
		c. **1160** *Lais* of Marie de France
	1170 Contract for the marriage between Eleanor (daughter of Henry II of England and Eleanor of Aquitaine) and Alfonso VIII of Castile	*c.* **1170–1190** Works of Chrétien de Troyes

Events in Spain	International events	Literary and historical works
1177 Henry II of England pronounces on frontier dispute between Castile and Navarre		
		c. **1180** *Chronicle of Nájera*
	1187 Saladin captures Jerusalem	
1188 Alfonso IX summons *Cortes* in León; in Carrión de los Condes Alfonso IX of León swears vassalage to Alfonso VIII of Castile		
		Probably *c.* **1190** *Historia Roderici* (*History of Rodrigo*), recounting the deeds of El Cid
	1191 Third Crusade and capture of Acre	
1195 Alfonso VIII of Castile suffers heavy defeat at Alarcos		
1197 Berenguela of Castile marries Alfonso IX of León (marriage dissolved in 1204)		
	1204 Crusaders sack Constantinople and establish Latin Empire	
		c. **1205** *Razón de amor* (*Speech about Love*)
		c. **1207** *Poema de Mio Cid* (*Poem of My Cid*)
c. **1208** Establishment of *studium generale* at Palencia by Alfonso VIII		**Between 1205 and 1220** *Libro de Alexandre* (*Book of Alexander*)
	1210–1229 Albigensian crusades in southern France	
1212 Alfonso VIII wins crucial victory at Las Navas de Tolosa		
	1215 Fourth Lateran Council held at Rome by Innocent III	
1217 Fernando III named king of Castile	**1217–1221** Fifth Crusade captures, and then loses, Damietta in Egypt	
1218 Establishment of *studium generale* at Salamanca by Alfonso IX		
1221 Birth of Alfonso X		

Events in Spain	International events	Literary and historical works
1226 Construction of Toledo Cathedral begins		
	1228–1229 Crusade of Frederick II of Sicily; Frederick gains crown of Jerusalem	**Between 1228 and 1246** *La vida de San Millán de la Cogolla* (*Life of San Millán de la Cogolla*) by Gonzalo de Berceo
1230 Final union of Castile and León under Fernando III		*c.* **1230** *Romance of the Rose* (Part 1)
1236 Conquest of Córdoba by Fernando III, followed by fall of Valencia (1238) and Murcia (1243)		
1238 Establishment of the Nasrid dynasty in Granada		*c.* **1238** *Chronicle of the World* by Bishop Lucas of Tuy
		c. **1239** *Latin Chronicle of the Kings of Castile*, probably by Bishop Juan de Osma
	1244 Jerusalem falls to Muslims; in Morocco the Marinids make Fes their capital – the beginning of the Marinid dynasty	
		c. **1245** *De rebus Hispaniae* (*On the Affairs of Spain*), by Archbishop Rodrigo Jiménez de Rada
1248 Conquest of Seville, the culmination of Fernando III's achievements	**1248–1250** Seventh Crusade: Louis IX of France captures Damietta and is himself captured a year later	
		1250 *Verses on Julia Rómula or the City of Seville*, by Guillermo Pérez de la Calzada
1252 Death of Fernando III and beginning of reign of Alfonso X	**1252–1254** Alphonse de Poitiers regent of France	
1253 Death of Thibault I of Navarre; Alfonso begins preparations for an African expedition		**1253–1255** Probable date of composition of the *Poem of Fernán González*
1254 Anglo-Castilian treaty on Gascony		
1254–1255 Alfonso visits León and Castile and holds *Cortes* in Burgos		

Events in Spain	International events	Literary and historical works
		From 1256 Drawing up of the *Siete Partidas de la Ley* (*Seven Divisions of the Law*)
1260 Prince Enrique forms alliance with Aragón against Alfonso		**From *c.* 1260** *Estoria de España* (*History of Spain*) by Alfonso X
	1269 Marinids defeat Caliph of Marrakech, putting an end to Almohad empire	
	1270 Louis IX of France dies on crusade in Tunis	
1275 Expedition against Salé in Morocco		*c.* **1275** *Romance of the Rose* (Part 2)
1282 Marinid army enters Spain in support of Mohammed II of Granada		
1284 Alfonso is deposed at the *Cortes* of Valladolid; Death of Alfonso X		
	1291 Fall of Acre to Muslims	

THE DYNASTY OF THE COUNTS OF CASTILE
IN THE EARLY TENTH CENTURY

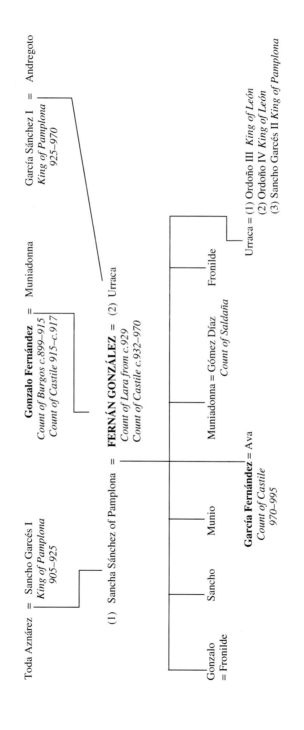

THE RULERS OF CASTILE (HOUSE OF BURGUNDY) 1126–1284

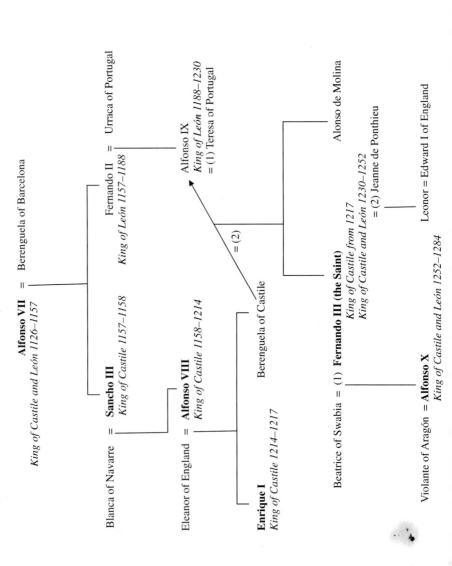

Alfonso VII = Berenguela of Barcelona
King of Castile and León 1126–1157

Fernando II = Urraca of Portugal
King of León 1157–1188

Alfonso IX
King of León 1188–1230
= (1) Teresa of Portugal

Alonso de Molina

Blanca of Navarre = **Sancho III**
King of Castile 1157–1158

Eleanor of England = **Alfonso VIII**
King of Castile 1158–1214

Berenguela of Castile

= (2)

Fernando III (the Saint)
King of Castile from 1217
King of Castile and León 1230–1252
= (2) Jeanne de Ponthieu

Leonor = Edward I of England

Enrique I
King of Castile 1214–1217

Beatrice of Swabia = (1) **Fernando III (the Saint)**

Violante of Aragón = **Alfonso X**
King of Castile and León 1252–1284

INTRODUCTION

1. The tale of Fernán González

(i) The figure of Fernán González: the intertwining of fact and legend

The visitor to Burgos who approaches from the south, crossing the River Arlanzón and entering the city's historic centre on foot, will almost certainly pass through the *Arco* (or *Puerta*) *de Santa María*, a sixteenth-century gateway built to honour Spain's king, the Holy Roman Emperor Charles V. The principal group of sculptures, dominating the entry to the city, represent Charles himself in the company of five of the great figures of Castilian history and legend. Among them, in the upper rank and at Charles' right hand, stands Fernán González; he is an imposing figure, sword aloft and wearing what might almost be taken for a crown.

Some fifty kilometres south east of Burgos are to be found the partly restored ruins of the monastery of San Pedro de Arlanza, set in the attractive wooded valley of the River Arlanza. Standing high on the side of the valley, the remains of the original hermitage from which the monastery had grown still dominate the scene. The monastic buildings, begun in the mid-eleventh century, had been magnificent in their day, but the nineteenth century saw them subjected to a series of disasters and the loss of almost all of their artistic treasures. One sculpture which has survived dominates the Renaissance façade of the main gateway. It represents the mounted figure of Fernán González with the bodies of vanquished foes lying at his horse's feet. What is perhaps most striking about this sculpture (which probably dates from the early seventeenth century) is that the hero's pose seems to be modelled on that commonly associated with Santiago, the slayer of Moors.

These two subjects reflect several features of what had become – and, in many respects, remains – the popular image of Fernán González: a fearsome warrior who gave his people protection from their enemies (both Muslim and Christian), and a wise and respected lord who enabled them to live in security and harmony. His presence among the great figures of early Castilian history is explained by the part that he was generally accepted to have played in achieving independence for Castile and freeing it from dominance by the kingdom of León. Perhaps above all he came to be seen a man of the people, and into the twentieth century some writers continued to

This statue of Fernán González is one of a group of six which occupy the central part of the Arco or Puerta de Santa María in Burgos. This gateway, conceived as a triumphal arch, was built between 1536 and 1553 and replaced a previous construction of the thirteenth and fourteenth centuries. It was dedicated to the Emperor Charles V, whose statue occupies a central position, and the other four figures that accompany him represent Count Diego Rodríguez Porcelos (founder of Ubierna and Burgos in 884), the legendary two judges of Castile, Laín Calvo and Nuño Rasura (see note to line 163b) and Rodrigo Díaz de Vivar, the Cid.

present him as not just a model of heroic grandeur and piety but also as the very expression of the spirit of the land and nation of Castile.[1]

In all of this fact and legend had become intertwined, and in the course of this introduction we shall examine the process by which this transformation took place and the rich tradition which provided the context

---

[1] A good example is Fray Justo Pérez de Urbel's eulogy of the hero and his achievements: '[t]he people were irrevocably bound to him, and he was the perfect personification of the people: of its desires, of its aspirations, of its struggle, of its ideal, of its faith. He carried Gothic blood in his veins, but he wished to still its impulses so as to allow the most profound essence of the nation to triumph. In him the Gothic was joined to what was most radically Spanish and it is this that will ensure the grandeur and the permanence of his works. ... His merit is to have understood Castile and to have turned himself into the spokesman for its aspirations of long ago' (1945, 2.622–623). Here and elsewhere in the Introduction and the Notes, except where we have indicated otherwise, translations from texts originally written in languages other than English are our own.

for the composition in the mid-thirteenth century of the *Poema de Fernán González*. We shall look closely both at the historical circumstances which inspired the *Poema* and at the art of the poet who created this complex, highly original and in some ways enigmatic work. This is a demanding poem; it can appear confusing and repetitive and sadly it survives in an incomplete form. Perhaps contrary to its appearance on an initial reading, it is skilfully constructed; moreover, it is rich in allusions which can require the reader to respond on a number of different levels. In what follows we hope to be able to show not only why the *Poema de Fernán González* has much to tell us about the history and culture of its age but also why it merits close study as an outstanding example of the poet's craft.

(ii) The manuscript of the Poema de Fernán González *and evidence of its missing content*

The *Poema de Fernán González* was composed (by an unknown author) in the mid-thirteenth century, but it has survived largely thanks to a single manuscript held by the Royal Monastery of El Escorial (ms. b-IV-21; ff. 136r–191r). It is written on good quality paper and bound in leather as the last of five works, probably added in after the others without great concern for its formal appearance. During the process of binding, in the late sixteenth century or the early seventeenth century, the words 'El conde Fernán Gonçález' ('Count Fernán González') were added as a title. It seems that the copying of the poem was carried out between 1470 and 1480 by three different scribes, perhaps as a formal exercise and probably in a notary's office, using a cursive gothic script and without any kind of decoration.[2] It is evident, moreover, that these copyists had no understanding at all of the poem's metre and that they had very little interest in the text that they were copying or in its accurate transmission, even given that they may have been working from a copy which was already in itself inaccurate. The first page is relatively neatly copied, but subsequently there are numerous crossings out, blottings, abbreviations, careless omissions and other errors, with the difficulties for the reader being compounded by the careless work of the binder, whose inaccurate cutting, either vertically or horizontally, resulted in the loss of several lines of text. Most seriously of all, the text of the poem

[2] See the detailed study by Geary to accompany his paleographic edition (1987) and also the helpful analysis of the manuscript by López Guil (2001, 11–15). José Manuel Ruiz Asencio (1989, 102–103) points out that the manuscript was probably copied and left lying in a fairly public environment, a circumstance which would explain the unrelated annotations made on it in a number of different hands.

is unfinished. Indeed, it ends abruptly in the middle of a folio, and López Guil (2001, 14) suggests convincingly that the scribe had simply decided, for whatever reason, not to copy any more.

Other fragments of the *Poema* exist: a tile, inscribed with three stanzas, which dates from about 1300; a copy of stanzas 158–170 and 195–207 made by Fray Gonzalo de Arredondo y Alvarado who was abbot of the monastery of Arlanza in the late sixteenth century and the early seventeenth century; stanzas 171–174, cited by Gonzalo Argote de Molina in his *Discurso sobre la poesía castellana* (*Discourse on Spanish Poetry*) which was composed in the late sixteenth century; and stanzas 158–165, included by Fray Prudencio de Sandoval in a work that came to be known as the *Historia de los cinco obispos* (*History of the Five Bishops*) of 1615.

Where we can find most help in the task of completing our knowledge of the content of the *Poema de Fernán González*, however, is in the *Estoria de España* (*History of Spain*), also known as the *Primera Crónica General* (*First General Chronicle*), compiled under Alfonso X in the second half of the thirteenth century. This compendious work includes in prosified form, at times reproduced almost verbatim, much of the text of the *Poema*, dispensing with its introductory section but including what seems to be the conclusion that the fifteenth-century copyist was so frustratingly to omit. It is this prose source that has been used in our edition (and in a number of others) to complement the existing text of the poem. A fuller version of the prose narrative, including some material which does not appear in the *Estoria de España*, is to be found in the Portuguese *Crónica geral de Espanha* (*General Chronicle of Spain*) of 1344.

(iii) The account of the hero's deeds in the Poema de Fernán González *and its relationship with historical fact*
Fernán González lived from about 910 to 970 and it was almost three centuries after his death, that is to say soon after 1250, that the *Poema* was composed as an enduring celebration of his triumphs. It will already be evident that in the thirteenth century there was a close and ill-defined relationship between fictional narrative and what we might now view as history. This was an age in which the existence of an account in written form was generally regarded as evidence for the reliability of its content.[3] In the light of such a belief it

---

[3] The author of the *Libro de Alexandre* discusses the reliability of his material on precisely this basis in, for example, lines 2115a and 2305b (see Such and Rabone 2009). Our poet's contemporary Gonzalo de Berceo, likewise, repeatedly refers to his written sources,

is not surprising that the compilers of the *Estoria de España* should have incorporated into their work, almost in its entirety, the *Poema*'s version of Fernán González's life and achievements, with significant consequences for how these were to be viewed for centuries to come. At the same time, however, we might be prompted to consider how the *Poema*'s author viewed his role as a poet and how he in turn went about the selection of his material. What kind of person that author was and the circumstances under which he wrote are matters that we shall consider at a later point, but it seems helpful at this stage to look briefly at the nature of the *Poema*'s content. In broad outline, this can be summarized as follows:

Stanzas

1–13   The poet invokes God's aid and goes on to describe the Christian character of Spain and the threat posed by Islam.

14–114   We are given an account of the qualities and deeds of the Goths, their Christian faith, how Spain fell into Muslim hands and how its people sought God's aid.

115–169   The poet recounts the deeds of the early heroes of Christian Spain and in particular of Castile in its struggle against its enemies, and then gives a eulogy of Castile. He describes the background to the election of the Two Judges and goes on to tell us of his hero's lineage.

170–191   We are told of the origins of Fernán González, of his childhood and his emergence as a leader and of his determination to free Castile from Muslim domination.

192–225   Fernán González captures Carazo and Christians and Muslims prepare for battle near Lara.

226–250   Fernando encounters the hermit at San Pedro de Arlanza, receives hospitality and promises to endow the monastery and eventually be buried there. He returns to his troops and tells them of his experience.

251–282   The Christians, with God's assistance and to al-Mansur's dismay, achieve victory; Fernando uses his booty to endow San Pedro de Arlanza.

283–329   A dispute with King Sancho of Navarre ends in victory for the Castilians at La Era Degollada, where Sancho is killed.

330–382   The Castilians are attacked by French troops led by the Count of Toulouse and Poitou, an ally of Sancho of Navarre; the French count is killed but he is paid great honour.

383–391   The Muslims (under al-Mansur) launch another attack.

particularly in telling of supernatural events, in order to lend authority to his account.

The ruins of the Benedictine monastery of San Pedro de Arlanza, which occupies a central position in the Poema de Fernán González, *are situated about 45 kilometres south east of the city of Burgos. Work on the present monastery church began in 1080 and it still retains important features of what was one of Castile's most striking Romanesque churches, including its twelfth-century tower, its cloister and various monastic buildings. This building was on a much grander scale than the small hermitage to which, according to the* Poema, *the Count made his crucial visits and which, much enlarged and elaborated over the centuries, is visible in the top right-hand part of the photograph. After the seizure of monastic property by the Spanish state in 1840, San Pedro de Arlanza was abandoned and fell into disrepair, but the ruins that can be visited today are nevertheless quite extensive.*

392–434   Fernando revisits the hermitage, receives assurance from Saints Pelagius (San Pelayo) and Aemilianus (San Millán), and returns to explain to his troops the importance of what he has heard.

435–565   Fernando goes on to harangue his troops, who engage in a fierce battle against the Muslims at Hacinas; with supernatural assistance, the Christians eventually gain victory.

566–570   The bodies of the dead are taken to San Pedro de Arlanza, and Fernán González announces that he too will be buried in the monastery.

571–582   Fernán González is summoned to the Cortes (or Parliament) in

León, where he is persuaded by King Sancho Ordóñez to sell him a
and a hawk (which are not paid for at the time).

583–611 Fernando is tricked by Teresa; Teresa is sister of King Sancho
Navarre (who was killed by the Count at La Era Degollada) and wife of King
Sancho of León. As a result of Teresa's deception, Fernando is captured by
King García of Navarre and imprisoned, to the great sorrow of the people of
Castile.

612–643 Fernando is visited in prison by a pilgrim from Lombardy, who then
persuades Princess Sancha, niece of King Sancho and Queen Teresa, to help
the Count to escape from prison – which she does. He promises to marry her.

644–659 Fernando and Sancha, fleeing towards Castile, overcome and kill
a lecherous archpriest who was out hunting and sought to take advantage of
them.

660–691 The Castilians decide to make a stone statue of the Count and set
off with it to free him; they meet him and Sancha on the way and they all return
to Burgos, where Fernando and Sancha marry. The people of Castile rejoice.

692–705 Castile is attacked by the Navarrese; King García of Navarre is
captured and imprisoned.

706–720 (including missing text, reflected in the chronicles, equivalent
to about 13 stanzas) Sancha persuades Fernando to free her brother, King
García. Meanwhile, the Muslims, led (according to the chronicle) by King
Abd al-Rahman III, launch an attack on León and Fernando goes to the aid
of King Sancho Ordóñez.

721–737 Fernando's troops rout the Muslims but he meets only hostility
in León, especially from the Queen, sister of King García of Navarre; the
Castilians return home.

738–742 Fernando requests payment for the horse and the hawk but King
Sancho Ordóñez continues to delay in meeting his obligation.

743–760 While the Count is away, the Navarrese invade Castile. When he
returns, he defeats the invading army in the battle of Valpierre.

(Missing text, reflected in the *Estoria de España*, probably equivalent to
about another 80 stanzas):

After the defeat of the Navarrese, Fernando is again summoned to Cortes in
León. He asks his followers for advice (lecturing them on the importance
of good counsellors), goes to León, asks the King for payment for the horse
and hawk and is promptly imprisoned. He escapes with the aid of his wife
who visits him in prison, dresses him in her clothes and remains behind in

ncho Ordóñez forgives the Countess. The Count again
for the horse and hawk, and raids the lands of León. The
is owed, with interest, has now become so great a sum that
is obliged to cede independence to Castile in lieu of payment.
ing to the longer text which appears in the 1344 Portuguese *Crónica*
Espanha, when the king of León fails to meet his commitment the
Castilians devastate his territories. Open warfare looms until, helped by the
mediation of the abbot of Sahagún, the clergy and nobility of León persuade
King Sancho that he must offer Castile its freedom. They then approach the
Count who, after consulting his people, agrees to the deal, more as an act of
service to God than out of any affection for King Sancho. Great rejoicing follows.

It has also been suggested that the full form of the poem would have
continued after the liberation of Castile up to the death of Fernán González,
thus giving it the appearance of a rhymed chronicle (see Lacarra 1979, 14).

The relationship between the tale of Fernán González as told in the *Poema*
and what is generally considered to be historical fact is summed up quite
neatly by an analysis of its content which lists the following as some of the
episodes to be defined as legend rather than history:

> his upbringing by the charcoal burner, the taking of Carazo, the attack on
> al-Mansur with all its anachronisms, the hunt for the boar and Pelayo's
> prophecies, the supposed battle of Lara, the Navarrese attack with the death
> of King Sancho in La Era Degollada, the intervention and death of the Count
> of Toulouse and Poitou, the imaginary battle of Hacinas, the appearance of
> the Apostle Santiago, the purchase of the horse and the hawk by King Sancho
> Ordóñez who did not exist, the trick which led to the imprisonment of the
> Count in Cirueña, the journey of the Count from Lombardy, the freeing of
> Fernán González by Princess Sancha, the episode of the lustful archpriest, the
> new war with Navarre with the capture of King García, the entry of the Moors
> through Sahagún, the third Navarrese war with the battle of Valpierre and the
> death in it of King García, doña Sancha's trick to set her husband free from
> the prison in León, and finally, as the culmination of it all, the most important
> and decisive act in the entire poem: the independence of Castile when the king
> of León could not pay the debt that he had contracted over the horse and the
> hawk. (Martínez Díez 1989, 72)

It follows from this that the *Poema* is very far from providing a faithful
account of historical events. As we shall see, it does embody a significant

core of historical truth and it also contains a wealth of detail which gives it the appearance of fact and, in short, makes it credible. Nevertheless, the celebration of an epic hero such as Fernán González will never be the same thing as an accurate narrative of deeds and achievements and it would never occur to the author of such a poem that his task should be to preserve such a historical record. Nor, indeed, could we consider as historically accurate any of the accounts which had come down to him and on which he based his narrative. 'Epic', wrote one of the great students of thirteenth-century Spanish literature, 'has its roots in a vaguely historical compost' (Smith 1972, xx), and in this the *Poema de Fernán González* is no exception. We hope, however, to show that the roots of this poem are to be found not just in the tenth century but also in periods a good deal closer to its composition.

(iv) The epic, 'popular' and 'learned'
Throughout this study, repeated reference will be made to 'epic tradition'. By 'epic' in the context of medieval Castilian poetry we understand a narrative in verse on a heroic subject. A much quoted description of the content of epic is 'the pursuit of honour through risk' (Bowra 1952, 5). Its world (see Smith 1972, xii–xiv) is likely to be a predominantly masculine one in which military prowess and the qualities of leadership play a fundamental role. Such poems often communicate a strong sense of national destiny and there is a marked sense of a common bond between the hero of the poem and the work's audience. Epic poems thus often celebrate the heroic deeds of an earlier age, which are held up before their public as examples for emulation. The epic hero has to overcome a series of trials in which he demonstrates outstanding qualities, and he may well receive some form of divine guidance; this other-worldly element lends to him and his people a sense of both grandeur and predetermined mission. Such poems are likely to be characterized by their idealism and by their emotive power.

We will also make allusion to a division between 'learned' and 'popular' epic and to the distinction which has conventionally been drawn in discussion of medieval Castilian literature between 'popular' and 'learned' elements, and to works of 'oral' and 'written' origin. This division is neatly expressed by Colin Smith (1972, xiv–xv):

> Before proceeding further, a distinction should be made between learned epic written for a limited circle of cultivated readers (of which the *Aeneid* and Renaissance epics are examples), and the epic which sprang from a more popular oral tradition and still bears the traces of performance (*e.g.* Homer and

medieval vernacular epic). One cannot call the medieval variety of the latter unreservedly 'popular', for in the written form in which it survives for us it is a rather highly developed genre, coherent and assured in its techniques, not wholly devoid of learned elements and courtly tone. None the less one has the conviction that the written genre depends on earlier, more popular material, and that even the written genre is still popular in the sense of being 'for all the people'. Its public, so far as we can judge, was at first that of the knightly or military-feudal caste, later a lower-class public also, but in any event a very different society from that of Augustan Rome and that of Renaissance Europe.

The earliest epics in Spanish were almost certainly oral compositions, created and performed by *juglares* or minstrels. In most cases, both the minstrels and a large part of their public are likely to have been illiterate, and the poems were not written down, except in very rare cases when they were probably dictated. It may well be, in part at least, for this reason that so few Spanish epic poems have survived: only three texts in what are considered to be the traditional epic metres, of which one is a brief fragment. Evidence that there were other well-known epic poems, now lost, seems to be furnished by both the chronicles which made extensive use of them and ballads that derived from them; but the contrast between the wealth of French epic material that has survived and the paucity of Spanish manuscripts is nevertheless a stark one.

The sharp division between the art of the *juglar* and that of the cleric was first proclaimed with great enthusiasm by the author of the early thirteenth-century *Libro de Alexandre* (see section 3(i), below). It should emerge in the course of this study that, through his pride in his new creation, this poet exaggerated the clarity of the distinction between his composition and those of the *juglares*, and that he has led many others to do so, too. He has, however, given us a helpful point of reference when we allude to the 'learned' origin of a poem, for he relates his work closely to the art of literary composition as taught in the schools and universities: by 'learned' we do not necessarily mean that a work is the product of advanced study of literary theory or of a high level of scholarship, but we do mean that an individual has studied grammar – the art of writing – and has also acquired the ability to read Latin and, where written material exists, Castilian. The author of the *Libro de Alexandre* sets a very high standard in terms of learning. The author of the *Poema de Fernán González* does not seek to match him in this, but he does draw on several different written sources and shows knowledge of the teachings of the grammarians. In this sense the *Poema* is a 'learned' work, but, particularly in terms of its evident debt to epic tradition, it can be said to contain many elements that are of 'popular' origin.

In a very helpful recent study, Matthew Bailey has emphasized the extent to which we might expect the composition of the *Poema* to have been characterized by a mixture of orality and writing. He points to evidence which makes it clear that, when the *Poema* was set down in its known form, the process of composition 'involved the oral dictation by the author to a scribe or scribes for initial transcription onto wax tablets, followed by a process of editing, before making a fair copy on parchment' (2010, 6). Thus, even in the elaboration of what we may view as a 'learned' poem, there is an important element of oral composition and the characteristics of improvised speech play an important part. We shall return at a later point (see section 3, below) to examine the use made in the *Poema* of stylistic features commonly associated with oral composition.

(v) The Poema de Fernán González *and epic tradition*

It has been widely assumed that the *Poema* was quite closely based on an earlier epic poem, generally termed the *Cantar de Fernán González*. It is not uncommon for scholars to state without question (and sometimes without explanation) that the *Poema* is a reworking of this older work. The clearest summary of the evidence for the existence of such an epic poem is given by Alan Deyermond in his study of the lost literature of medieval Spain (1995, 63–67); taking due account of the arguments of the scholars who have expressed scepticism about the antiquity of this oral tradition, Deyermond concludes (p. 64) that it would be difficult to explain the development of the literary tradition dealing with Fernán González without postulating the existence of the lost epic. It has been suggested, for example, that significant evidence for the existence of this epic is to be found in chronicles of the fourteenth century, notably the 1344 Portuguese *Crónica geral de Espanha*, and in ballad tradition. Both of these show the Castilian count taunting the Leonese King Sancho, and the Castilians and the Leonese on the verge of coming into open conflict, neither of which developments would have been in keeping with the depiction of Fernán González's conduct found in the *Poema*. The 1344 chronicle and the ballads also reflect minor differences from the story told in the *Poema* (including a different version of Fernando's childhood), but it is the extended conclusion which emphasizes the hostility between the King and his Count and between a people in search of independence and their oppressors; it is argued that such a portrait of a rebellious and angry hero is representative of the world of popular epic (see for example Victorio 2010, 15), but likely to have been considered inappropriate by both the pious author of the *Poema* and the compilers of the Alfonsine chronicle.

We need to consider, however, how much is really known about the growth of the legend of Fernán González and how, when and for what reasons the tales of his exploits garnered such fame and acquired the features with which they were most closely associated in the period of the *Poema*'s composition. Before making any assumptions about the antiquity of the account on which its author drew, it is vital that we look closely at the evidence that we actually possess with regard to when the corpus of legend surrounding the Count may have developed. We do know that the most famous of the ballads dealing with this topic probably derives from a fourteenth-century epic, now lost (Menéndez Pidal 1899, 433), and the author of an article on the continuing influence of the oral tradition in propagating the tale of Fernán González points out that 'the time of great popularity of the *Cantar de Fernán González*' corresponds to the early fourteenth century, over fifty years after the composition of the *Poema* (Avalle-Arce 1972, 70). It is, of course, very difficult to say with certainty when, and how, an oral tradition began, but, although there is some evidence from the late twelfth century for the circulation of stories about the illustrious count, the earliest really significant evidence for the existence of an epic poem dealing with his achievements appears to date from the mid-thirteenth century (Dutton 1961), not long, indeed, before the *Poema* was composed.

Some scholars consider that there is convincing evidence indicating the existence of a rich oral tradition celebrating the deeds of Fernán González which stretches back long before the mid-thirteenth century. The *Poema* contains numerous elements commonly associated with popular tradition, including an abundance of folkloric motifs which play a fundamental part in its narrative (although we must beware of assuming any kind of incompatibility between such features and scholarly or courtly authorship). Some studies have sought to emphasize the *Poema*'s popular origins, in such a way that it comes to be seen as the culmination of, or perhaps an important link in, an unbroken chain by which information about the noble Count's deeds has been passed down over the centuries. Thus, for example, we read that the *Poema* is 'a song of the people' (West 1983, 2) and are told of Fernán González that 'such a heroic character could only be kept alive in the minds of the people by the songs of the minstrels sung in courts, taverns and public squares and the legends passed from parent to child by the hearth' (West 1983, 3). More significantly, the great and immensely influential scholar Ramón Menéndez Pidal saw the epic in its origin as having an essentially informative or news-bearing function, arguing that it 'is born as a tale which provides information about great deeds committed in a people which lacks histories, chronicles or annals, and its vigour decreases as historiography is born and gains in strength' (1951, xxiii). Menéndez Pidal did not hesitate to see the *Poema de Fernán González* as representative of an oral tradition and published its text as evidence for the existence of an earlier epic poem on which it had been based (1951, 34–180). This view has been widely accepted; as just one example, we read in the introduction to Alonso Zamora Vicente's edition of the *Poema* the statement that we can find 'disguised, concealed beneath the monorhythmic metre of the monk from Arlanza, the breath of the ancient epic' (1978, xxiii). Some aspects of Menéndez Pidal's approach have, however, been seriously questioned – notably in the important study by René Cotrait (1977) – and in addition much valuable work has been done on the *Poema*'s scholarly origins and on the features which distinguish it as the work of a learned individual.

In this short study we intend to examine the existing evidence for how the tale of Fernán González was transmitted to our poet, looking closely at those features of the *Poema* which can be considered 'learned' and those which might be associated with oral composition, and exploring the process by which he used the material at his disposal to create a distinctive and powerful poem composed with a very specific purpose. We hope to show that he is a knowledgeable and skilful individual who has very clear points of his own to make about his nation's past and about the age in which he lives. It seems likely that the author of the *Poema de Fernán González* drew in part on an oral tradition, although few would go so far as Emilio Alarcos Llorach, who wrote that 'the monk from Arlanza who composed it invented nothing and did not adorn oral tradition with anything of his own' (1965, 10). However, we shall argue that to describe this poet's creation as essentially a 'reworking' – as many scholars are inclined to do – is also an inaccuracy which, in the eyes of the modern reader at least, does the *Poema* an injustice. We shall attempt to demonstrate that the *Poema* is a distinctive and carefully thought out work which embodies and expresses powerfully the values and preoccupations of its own age, the mid-thirteenth century.

It will already have become apparent that it is essential to distinguish very clearly between the historical figure of the celebrated Count and the figure of legend that is presented in the *Poema* and in the chronicles of the thirteenth and fourteenth centuries, and so it is with the life of Fernán González and the events of the second and third quarters of the tenth century that we now propose to start.

2. Inventing the past: a tenth-century hero in a thirteenth-century context

(i) The recovery of Christian Spain, the rise of the kingdom of León and the emergence of the county of Castile

In spite of the rapid success of the Islamic conquest of the Iberian Peninsula in the second decade of the eighth century, the Muslim conquerors never succeeded in eradicating Christian resistance in the Basque country and the Cantabrian mountains in the far north. In spite of periodic raids, the Umayyad rulers based in Córdoba were unable to break down the independence of these territories, which steadily gained in strength. Castile, whose name indeed designates a land of castles, had already at the beginning of the tenth century developed considerably from its original heartland. This heartland (in fact a Basque-speaking region) had reached to the coast of the Bay of Biscay and corresponded approximately to the modern Basque province of Vizcaya, bordering to the east on what was to become the county of Álava. The region's early development had been the result of a long-term process of migration southwards into depopulated territory, a plateau crossed by a number of fertile river valleys. By the second half of the ninth century this process had received a new impetus, for organized repopulation had taken place driven by a number of locally based magnates or counts. Such figures belonged to families which exercised considerable power, granting privileges and concessions to the inhabitants of new communities and also, for example, making extensive donations to monasteries in order that they in turn would encourage further population. By 912 the establishment of a series of new settlements saw a new development of considerable strategic importance as the boundary between Christian and Muslim Spain was extended to the River Duero along the whole of its length.

In this dangerous frontier territory, the Castilian counts exercised a high level of autonomy. However, it was further to the west that the centre of power in Christian Spain was really to be found. After the Muslim invasion in 711 and the subsequent period of conquest, the first Christian uprising against the conquering people (see note to line 115a) is said to have taken place between 716 and 719 and to have been led by Pelayo, an Asturian nobleman. Joined by marriage to the family who ruled Cantabria to the east, Pelayo's lineage was to produce the Christian rulers who steadily extended and consolidated their authority across the north of the peninsula, from Galicia to Castile. By the early ninth century they had established their capital in Oviedo, in the heart of Asturias, and begun to present themselves in both secular and ecclesiastical matters as the heirs to the authority of the Visigothic kings. The development of the cult of Saint James from the early ninth century gave the Asturians what seemed to be a celestial protector in their struggle with the Muslims. Steadily the process of resettlement and reconquest saw the area of Christian population extend southwards, initially along the valleys of the rivers that flowed down from the mountains of the north to become tributaries of the Duero. Oviedo was now quite remote from the critical border territories and by 910 the royal capital had moved southwards, onto the plateau, to the old Roman city of León.

Following a period of conflict among various elements of the royal family, the throne of León passed in 932 to King Ramiro II, who set about imposing control initially by brutal treatment of several of his relatives and subsequently by instituting radical changes in the composition of his court. It seems that until Ramiro came to the throne the area known as Castile, part of the kingdom of León, had been divided up to be governed as more or less autonomous units by several individuals who each held the title of 'count', and that he promptly removed all of them from office (including the last count of Álava). In their place he appointed the young Fernán González, who as Count of Castile was now responsible for an extensive area, in many respects autonomous, but most definitely subordinate to the authority of the king of León.[4]

Ramiro II of León reigned until 951. He was a strong and effective ruler who imposed a firm control on his kingdom with limited military resources and in spite of ambitious and at times rebellious nobles, not to mention the external threat to his kingdom posed by the Muslim forces of Abd al-Rahman III. Abd al-Rahman, who had proclaimed himself caliph in 929, carried out *aceifas* or punitive raids on several targets in the north, but combined forces under the Leonese king inflicted on him an immense defeat at Simancas in 939. It is perhaps surprising that no Leonese epic tradition seems to have existed to celebrate this great achievement on Ramiro's part. Ramiro on his death left two sons by different wives, a situation which predictably led to

---

[4] For a clear and succinct summary of the history of the kingdom of León and Castile in this period, see Collins (2012, 138–165; 238–256).

further conflict within the kingdom of León. Ordoño III ruled from 951 to 956, Sancho I (known as 'the Fat') from 956 to 966, and Ordoño IV (known as 'the Bad') for a short intervening period in 958 and 959. When Sancho died he was succeeded by his son Ramiro III (966–985). It was against this troubled political canvas that Fernán González played out the later stages of his career and it is Sancho I 'the Fat' who appears in the *Poema de Fernán González* depicted as the monarch whose incompetence obliges him to surrender control over the county of Castile.

At this point mention must be made of the independent kingdom of Pamplona, which during the course of the twelfth century was to come to be known as Navarre; it is as Navarre that it is known in the *Poema*. Pamplona was Castile's eastern neighbour and its first king ruled from 824. This first dynasty had close links, both politically and in terms of intermarriage, with the Islamised Banū Qasī clan. As we shall see below, their links with the rulers of al-Andalus were to continue to be significant. However it was members of a second Navarrese dynasty who were to be the contemporaries of Fernán González: Sancho Garcés, whose reign began in about 905, was the first of a line of kings who would rule Pamplona until 1076. He moved radically away from the approach of his predecessors and embarked on a policy of close military alliance with the kingdom of León. The increasing influence of the rulers of Pamplona was certainly to play its part in the political manoeuvres of the historical Count Fernán González. However, we shall see below that it was Navarre's relationship with Castile in the following two centuries that was to be more significant in shaping the content of the *Poema*.

(ii) The career and achievements of Fernán González

Against this background, then, Fernán González was born in about 905 into a family which had already, as the available evidence seems to suggest, produced a number of counts who played an important role in the development of the Castilian frontier area (Collins 2012, 251). The only thing that we know with certainty about Fernán González's childhood (though there has been much speculation based on the *Poema*) is that his family was closely associated with the region of Lara; this information comes in a document of 929 from the monastery of San Pedro de Arlanza, concerning a donation by Fernando's mother to a nearby convent.[5] The area around Lara figures prominently in the

---

[5] For a full and closely documented account of the life of Fernán González, see Martínez Díez (2005, 1.291–450). The following summary has benefited considerably from his clearly argued analysis.

Poema (see note to line 463a). We certainly know too that in 932 Fernando was installed as count of both Castile and neighbouring Álava. By 935, moreover, he was married to Sancha, who had been married to the previous count of Álava, and their marriage had already produced two sons, Gonzalo and Sancho. Through this marriage Fernando was also to find himself related to both King García Sánchez of Navarre and King Ramiro II of León.

Ramiro II was the first to break the existing truce with Abd al-Rahman III, but it was the latter, recently proclaimed as caliph, who embarked upon a major campaign in 934, setting off for the north with a vast and splendid force. He then celebrated a meeting with Toda Aznárez; this formidable lady was mother of the king of Pamplona, mother-in-law of both Fernán González and of Ramiro II, and indeed an aunt of Abd al-Rahman himself. Toda swore vassalage to the caliph. Abd al-Rahman then moved to sack Castile, desolating the lands around Burgos, moving along the Arlanzón and Arlanza valleys and infamously slaughtering the monks of Cardeña. At this stage, meeting resistance from both Fernán González and Ramiro and after an inconclusive skirmish with Ramiro's troops outside Osma, the Muslim army returned to Córdoba and Ramiro set in motion negotiations for a truce. Two years later the truce was broken and the Count found himself accompanying Ramiro on an expedition to Saragossa. On the whole, however, his principal concern was to assure the wellbeing of the county of Castile, which had suffered terrible devastation during the raid of 934.

It was in 939 that Abd al-Rahman launched an expedition on a vast scale against the heart of Ramiro's kingdom and in particular directed at the recently repopulated area known as the *tierra de campos*, which lay between Simancas and Zamora. Outside the castle of Portillo, 23 kilometres from Simancas, his force was met by that of Ramiro II, whom we know to have been accompanied by two of his counts, Fernán González and Asur Fernández, Count of Monzón, with their armies. After two days of battle with no clear outcome, Abd al-Rahman sought to withdraw from Simancas towards the Muslim fortress of Atienza where his army could occupy a more advantageous position. In a deep gorge on the river Tiermes, some 170 kilometres from Simancas, the second part of the battle was fought, a bloody slaughter as the retreating Muslims found themselves trapped. The booty taken by the Christian armies was immense.

The Castilian count had clearly played an important part in the battle, but the commander of the victorious forces had without doubt been Ramiro; and it was, of course, the King of León who negotiated the truce which followed. In

Over the Renaissance main gateway of San Pedro de Arlanza there is a statue representing Fernán González. Its most striking feature is the depiction of the hero in the pose commonly associated with Santiago Matamoros (Saint James the Slayer of Moors). The Poema *recounts how Santiago comes to the aid of the Count's army during the battle of Hacinas.*

the treaty document Fernando is conspicuous as the only one of the Christian counts to be listed together with the territory that he governed, evidence of the special position that he occupied. In the years which followed we see Fernán González commanding expeditions at Ramiro's behest and demonstrating 'total collaboration, submission and obedience' (Martínez Díez 2005, 1.374) towards his lord. In a document of 949 Fernando is the first of the counts to sign, evidence that in the kingdom of León no other nobleman could rival him in importance or in the favour that he enjoyed from the King.

In May 944 Fernando disappears temporarily from the documentation and in his place as count of Castile appears no less a figure than Prince Sancho, son of Ramiro II, who is replaced in turn three months later by Asur Fernández. By April of the following year, however, it is clear that Fernando is once again fully restored to his position as count. In the intervening period, he and Diego Muñoz, count of Saldaña, had both fallen from favour with Ramiro and been imprisoned (one in León and one in the fortress of Gordón, though it is not known which of them was held where). We have no evidence for what kind of intrigue or disagreement led to this period of imprisonment.

We do know that the two counts were only reconciled with Ramiro after swearing an oath but once again we have no evidence as to its content. The reconciliation was sealed with the marriage at the end of 944 of Ramiro's son Ordoño to Fernando's daughter Urraca.

Ramiro II, responding to a military need, had concentrated considerable power in the eastern regions of his kingdom in Fernán González's hands. When the Count overstepped the mark Ramiro did not hesitate to impose submission, but the evidence that we have suggests that on the whole their relationship had been a harmonious one. Ramiro's death in 951 effectively divided the Count's career in two, and the struggle for succession which followed opened the gates to intervention by the ruler of Pamplona into Leonese affairs and allowed Fernán González to pursue a relatively autonomous course in pursuit of more personal ambitions. Initially, on the accession to the throne of Ramiro's son Ordoño III, Fernando seems to have given him his full backing. Ordoño was, after all, his son-in-law. However, probably in mid-954, Fernando supported Ordoño's brother Sancho in his bid to take over the kingdom, a bid which was also supported by King García of Pamplona. The adoption of such a policy makes it clear that at this stage Fernán González's alliance with the king of Pamplona (later to become Navarre) was so strong that it outweighed even his allegiance to his own monarch. Ordoño defeated his brother's attempt to dethrone him. Although Ordoño expressed his anger towards the Count by formally repudiating his daughter Urraca, Fernando was promptly allowed to return to his previous position in Ordoño's service. The harmony of the relationship between king and count was never again in doubt, and there is a chronicle account of the assistance given by Ordoño to Fernán González in his successful defence of the castle of San Esteban de Gormaz against Muslim attack. In 956 the Count's prestige was such that Ordoño specifically requested that Abd al-Rahman include him in the terms of their truce.

Ordoño died in 956 and the Leonese throne passed peacefully to his brother Sancho, who we can imagine to have been firmly supported by his uncle King García of Pamplona and by Fernán González (who was also related to him through his wife Sancha, Ordoño's cousin). Sancho wasted little time in rejecting the existing truce with Abd al-Rahman, who unleashed punitive raids. Sancho, known as 'the Fat', was so obese as to have difficulty in mounting a horse and this clearly undermined his credibility as a warrior. Sancho 'the Fat' seems to have enjoyed little popularity with the Leonese (and Galician) nobility, and within a year he was replaced as king by his cousin Ordoño IV.

There is no evidence that Fernán González played any part in this process, but in the face of the new political situation he seems to have been reasonably quick to change his allegiance. It will have been as a reward for this offer of support that Ordoño IV took as his bride Fernando's daughter Urraca, the widow of Ordoño III. Unfortunately for the Castilian count, Ordoño IV's reign was to last for just a single year: Sancho had fled to Pamplona, whence his grandmother Toda had dispatched him to Córdoba for his obesity to be cured, taking advantage of her own family link with Abd al-Rahman. Sancho returned to depose Ordoño and to take over for a second time the throne of León, with support from Pamplona and, indeed, from Córdoba. Politically, Fernán González had made a wrong choice. He continued to give his support to Ordoño, who was now taking refuge in Asturias. Conflict with Sancho's ally, King García of Pamplona, almost inevitably ensued, and it is a late twelfth-century monastic chronicle, the *Crónica najerense* (*Chronicle of Nájera*), which reports Fernando's imprisonment by García, first in Cirueña and then in Pamplona. A Muslim chronicle also records Fernando's imprisonment in Pamplona – after a battle – and pays an indirect tribute to the Count's importance when it affirms that al-Hakam II, who had just succeeded to the caliphate in Córdoba, agreed to a truce with King García provided that the illustrious prisoner was handed over to him. Fortunately for Fernán González, García set the Count free instead.

It seems that Fernando's wife Sancha died in the summer of 963, some three years after his release from prison. By the time of her death, it would appear that only four of the children that Sancha had borne to Fernando still survived: García was to follow his father as count of Castile; the daughters were Fronilde, Muniadonna, who married the count of Saldaña, and Urraca, who had already had two royal marriages and probably by this time had celebrated a third – with Sancho Garcés II of Pamplona. The bonds of friendship between the royal family of Pamplona and the county of Castile were being tightened. Indeed, by May 964 we know that Fernando had remarried: his new wife, also called Urraca, was the daughter of King García and niece of Fernando's first wife, tightening the bonds of friendship still further. It is clear, moreover, that in the following years Fernán González was to do nothing that would threaten that friendship, though it is equally clear that during this period he remained the object of the intense hatred of his Muslim enemies who continued to direct frequent attacks at Castile. When Sancho I died in 966, the Count accepted without difficulty the accession to the throne of the five-year-old heir Ramiro III. It is known that in 967

Castile suffered a damaging Muslim raid and that the in following kingdom of León successfully sought a peace treaty with Córdoba. problems ensued for the monarchy in 968 with the arrival of an in Norman fleet off the coast of Galicia and by now there was a perceptible weakening in the power of the young king's government. We know very little of Fernán González's activities during this period, but by February 970 his son García Fernández is recorded as occupying the position of Count of Castile. Fernando died at some point in late 969 or early 970 and, at his own request, his remains were buried at the monastery of San Pedro de Arlanza, in the territory of Lara. As we shall see, this monastery was to play a major role in the subsequent development of his legend.

* * * * * *

We have pointed out that it is important to distinguish clearly between the Fernán González of history and the hero of legend, and this examination of the Count's career should serve to emphasize still further just how much of the content of the *Poema* is the product of later elaboration. Certain elements of what we might term the core of the *Poema* do, however, correspond to historical fact – in particular: Fernando's role as leader and protector of the Castilian people and as a warrior dedicated to defending them against a powerful Muslim enemy; his involvement in political dealings which led to him being imprisoned twice, once by the king of León and once by the king of Pamplona/Navarre; his marriage to Sancha, a member of the royal family of Pamplona/Navarre; and his burial at San Pedro de Arlanza. Fernán González would be remembered above all as the count who freed Castile from Leonese domination, but all the existing evidence indicates that, throughout his lifetime and beyond, the count of Castile remained firmly subordinate to the Leonese monarchy.[6] So history gave us just the core of the legend. We now need to look closely at how and why that legend may have developed as it did and at the circumstances which surrounded the composition of the *Poema de Fernán González* some 285 years after its hero's death.

(iii) After Fernán González: the age of al-Mansur, conflict among the Christian kingdoms and their eventual supremacy over the Muslims

The years following Fernán González's death saw the military supremacy of

---

[6] Martínez Díez (2005, 1.445–450). It could be argued that the principal difference brought about during Fernán González's lifetime was that from now on the role of count would be a hereditary one, but Castile was not alone in this.

Muslim Spain reinforced as one of the regents of the young caliph Hishām II seized power, imposed his authority on al-Andalus and proceeded to launch a series of devastating raids into the Christian north. This was Muhammed ibn Abī 'Āmir, later to be known as al-Mansur or Almanzor, 'the Glorious One'. This is the man who appears anachronistically in the *Poema de Fernán González* depicted as the Count's formidable Muslim enemy. Once al-Mansur died in 1002, however, it was not long before the caliphate, faced by insurrection and political unrest, crumbled into a number of minor small states and the balance of power gradually shifted definitively towards the Christian kingdoms. In the early stages they were too preoccupied with their internal divisions and rivalries to take full advantage of the situation. It was Navarre which was the first to push for dominance under Sancho III 'the Great' ('el Mayor'), and in 1029 Sancho seized control of Castile. However, on his death in 1035 his kingdom was partitioned by his four sons. One of these sons was Fernando, who had initially governed Castile as *comes* or count, in the same capacity as Fernán González a hundred years before. Initially he remained a vassal of his brother-in-law Vermudo III of León, but subsequently territorial disputes led to overt hostility. Fernando now brought about the crucial shift in the balance of power: firstly he defeated and killed Vermudo, thus uniting Castile and León under his rule as Fernando I, and then in 1054 he defeated and killed his brother, García III of Navarre, at Atapuerca near Burgos. This was a confrontation of great historical importance. For a major battle which results in a crucial victory for the Castilians over the Navarrese (and results in the death of the Navarrese monarch), Atapuerca offers the only real parallel to the events recounted in the *Poema*. It could well be, moreover, that in the *Poema* a single account of the battle is divided up to form the basis of two episodes (see notes to 695a and 703c) and in the second version the victor and the victim bear the names of the protagonists at Atapuerca: Fernando and García.

Navarre now became a tributary of Castile-León, which, on the assassination of García's son in 1076, annexed most of it, with the remainder falling to Navarre's eastern neighbour Aragón. Navarre had effectively ceased to exist, whilst Castile-León and Aragón went on to gain great wealth through exploitation and conquest of the Muslim kingdoms to the south. It was in the late eleventh century that Rodrigo Díaz de Vivar, through his successful campaigns against the invading Almoravids, achieved the fame that was to make him the hero of Spain's best known epic poem, the *Poema de Mio Cid* (*Poem of My Cid*).

*(iv) The twelfth century: the re-emergence of Navarre and rivalry
between Castile and León*

We now need to look ahead to 1134, when, on the death of Alfonso I of
Aragón, a great-great-grandson of Sancho III through an illegitimate lineage
was recognized in Pamplona as king of Navarre. This was García Ramírez
IV of Navarre, grandson of the Cid and known as 'the Restorer', who was
to rule until 1150. To the west, Alfonso VII ('the Emperor') ruled a united
León and Castile. He was a powerful and successful ruler and his death in
1157 was to signal the end of some forty years of triumphant progress on
the part of the Christian kingdoms. It was also to be marked by a critical
decision which was to have immense and long-lasting consequences: Alfonso
bequeathed Castile to his elder son Sancho and León to his younger son
Fernando. The delicate balance between them was disturbed when Sancho
died just over a year later, leaving his two-year-old son to rule as Alfonso
VIII. The Castilian monarchy was thus left in a highly vulnerable position,
which was aggravated by two of its great noble families, the Lara and the
Castro, who vied for power, the latter seeking support from Fernando II of
León. For almost seventy years the relationship between the two kingdoms
was one of intense rivalry and at times open hostility, not least between the
two cousins who ruled as Alfonso VIII of Castile and Alfonso IX of León.
This was a period when Castile, struggling initially to survive, steadily
carved out its identity, both political and cultural, and went on to achieve
immense triumphs in the name of Christianity. Finally, by 1230 a definitive
union with León was achieved in which the balance of political power would
remain firmly with Castile. Just as significantly, it was the culture and the
language of Castile which were to impose themselves firmly on this union.

On its way to these successes, the Castilian monarchy had to overcome
serious difficulties. These included two periods of royal minority: firstly
that of Alfonso VIII himself and then the years which followed his death,
the short and ill-fated rule of his son Enrique and the troubled period that
ensued as Alfonso's daughter Berenguela saw her own son established on
the throne as Fernando III. From early in Alfonso VIII's reign, conflict over
the frontier with Navarre simmered and not even the submission of the
dispute to arbitration by Henry II of England satisfied either party. Moreover,
the constant campaigning against the Muslims was far from being always
successful: the battle of Las Navas de Tolosa in 1212 was, of course, a
triumph, but first Alfonso had had to endure the disastrous defeat of Alarcos
in 1195. In neither of these battles did he receive support from León, and

in 1196 both León and Navarre actually joined in the attacks on Castile, a sign of the bitterness which at times existed among the Christian kingdoms. It was to put an end to such hostility and the consequent suffering that in 1197 Alfonso VIII married his daughter Berenguela to his cousin, Alfonso IX, thus incurring the wrath of the Pope who excommunicated the couple on grounds of consanguinity.

(v) The Plantagenets, the Castilian monarchy and an age of triumph

Yet this Castilian royal family were a formidable dynasty. In 1170, at the age of fifteen, Alfonso VIII married the nineteen-year-old Eleanor Plantagenet (known in Castile as Leonor), one of the eight children of Henry II of England and Eleanor of Aquitaine. Brought up among the nuns at Fontevraud, she certainly had first-hand experience of her mother's famous court in Poitou; and she almost certainly received from her half-sister Marie de Champagne an introduction to the work of the Provençal poets and, through them, to an international world of politics, history and myth (Salvador Martínez 2012, 52). She would have been aware, for example, of the power in northern Europe of the myth of King Arthur and she would have understood, therefore, how the Plantagenets exploited the supposed discovery in 1191 of the remains of this hero of the fifth and sixth centuries. She would have seen how they used it to provide prestige and, indeed, legitimacy for their own dynasty and a counterbalance to the legend of Charlemagne that was being similarly exploited by the French monarchy (see, for example, Flori 2004, 416). Indeed, it seems likely that Eleanor/Leonor brought to Castile a copy of Geoffrey of Monmouth's *Historia regum Britaniae* (*History of the Kings of Britain*), an important early text for the diffusion of the legend of King Arthur. We must not underestimate the mutual influence exercised by the royal courts, to the extent that '[t]he literary and political fortunes of Spain and southern France during the twelfth century can hardly be separated' (Salter 1973, 414). It seems highly plausible, then, that such lessons were absorbed in the Castilian court of the late twelfth century, particularly in the light of what we know of the roles of Alfonso VIII and Eleanor as patrons of the arts and of the welcome that they gave to poets and minstrels, among them those of Provence (see section 2(vi) below).[7]

---

[7] For discussion of the cultural implications of such dynastic ties and of the links between royal courts, see Salter (1973, 408–410), emphasizing how in the twelfth century royal marriages contributed to the rapid spread of romance themes, including those of Arthurian literature, and also of the ideas and principles of courtly love; she points to evidence, for example, that by about 1170 the deeds of the Arthurian knights were being celebrated south

Alfonso VIII and his grandson Fernando broke the power of Islam in the Iberian Peninsula and, with the series of conquests in the four decades which followed the triumph of Las Navas de Tolosa, they brought Castile immense territorial gains. They also succeeded in creating for their nation a new political and cultural identity, and we must not underestimate the role in this process played by Leonor and her daughter Berenguela, an extremely powerful figure who stamped her character firmly on the royal court until her death in 1246. This was, of course, the court in which Fernando's son and successor Alfonso X grew up and with whose values he was thoroughly imbued. During a period of over seventy years there was a strong sense of continuity and an equally powerful sense of purpose. If we are to see in the *Poema de Fernán González* the reflection of an oral tradition which bore witness to proud nationalist sentiment (see, for example, Dutton 1961, 202) it is to this period that we might well look for its development. For if these were days of glory for Castile, what that kingdom lacked was an equally glorious past. The Castilian monarchs and their advisers will have seen the task before them as filling a gap left by a 'lack of institutional pedigree' (Peña Pérez 2005, 46) and this they set out to achieve by creating a sense of belief in a past as magnificent as the present. In particular they looked back to the earliest days of the Castilian nation, and even before that, to the days of the noble Gothic people to whose qualities they believed themselves the heirs. To this purpose they were to make skilful use of the literary and intellectual ability available to them, including that of the scholars and poets of the royal court and, indeed, the considerable resources of the monastic communities.

(vi) The Castilian court: a centre of learning and literary creation
The Castilian royal court during the reigns of Alfonso VIII and Fernando III had to concern itself, of course, with the business of war. More and more, too, it had to deal with matters of administration, law and finance, and the need for the issue and recording of correspondence and documentation began to place a fresh emphasis on the written word; there was a rapidly growing requirement

---

of the Pyrenees (p. 409). There is also ample evidence of the great cultural importance of the Castilian court in the decades which followed Eleanor's marriage to Alfonso VIII: Sánchez Jiménez (2001) surveys the extensive literary production which is associated with the court of Alfonso VIII, including consideration of such major texts as the *Poema de Mio Cid* and the *Libro de Alexandre*, and Salvador Miguel (2000) similarly examines the importance of the stimulus given by the court of Fernando III to composition in a number of languages. For discussion of the role played by Eleanor/Leonor Plantagenet, see Cerda (2012, 638–640); Susong (2007); Romero (2014, 285–287).

for clerics skilled in the accurate use of written Latin and – increasingly – of Castilian, and some of these clerics will undoubtedly have been trained in the newly founded university at Palencia or at foreign universities such as Paris and Bologna. Even the Leonese chronicler Lucas de Tuy, perhaps because he wrote at the behest of Alfonso's daughter Berenguela, praised the Castilian monarch as 'another Solomon' for having built the new convent of Las Huelgas in Burgos, an important cultural as well as spiritual centre, and above all for establishing the new university in Palencia, bringing 'teachers of Theology and of the other liberal arts' (see Salvador Martínez 2012, 576–577). Strikingly too, Lucas de Tuy comments on the fact that Alfonso, towards the end of his lengthy reign, adopted the castle as the heraldic symbol of his kingdom, a further example of the King's determination to create for it a clearly defined identity.

The permanent court (the *curia ordinaria*), which accompanied the king on his constant travels, consisted of members of his family and a select group of advisers and officials, including, for example, some of the most prominent bishops of the kingdom. On rarer occasions – though these became increasingly frequent by the beginning of the reign of Alfonso X – there met the *curia extraordinaria*, by now attended also by members of the principal noble families, representatives of the towns, the diocesan bishops, the masters of the military orders and the abbots of the major monasteries. These are the *Cortes* or parliament, with a significant role to play in the *Poema de Fernán González* (see note to 571ab).

The royal court was attended by men of learning. It was also important in the development of a new, and in many senses international, culture. It promoted new values of courtly society, among them, for example, the principle of *mesura* (balanced, reasonable and prudent conduct), which is an essential virtue in courtly society (see, for example, Salter 1973, 416), as well as a quality whose importance is much emphasized in both moralizing and literary texts of the period (see Salvador Martínez 2010, 370ff. and our note to 30b). *Mesura* is highlighted by Alfonso X in his legal treatise *Las Siete Partidas* (*The Seven Divisions*) – see section 2,21,4 – as a quality that is essential in his knights. Moreover, the principle of *mesura* is central to the message of the *Libro de Alexandre* (*Book of Alexander*), a text which is almost certainly the product of the courtly world and undoubtedly a crucially important source for the *Poema de Fernán González*. The term *mesura* is used on several occasions in the *Poema*. This parallel could itself be a reflection of a debt to the earlier work; on the other hand it is entirely plausible that both poets were well aware of the great importance of this concept in courtly society.

Starting from a position in which Castile was marked by its cultural and intellectual impoverishment, the royal court was steadily transformed into a very important centre for culture and the arts. It provided the environment, for example, in which Diego García de Campos (royal chancellor in two periods for altogether some 23 years) composed in Latin his remarkable moralizing work *Planeta*; both the *Libro de Alexandre* and the *Poema de Fernán González* have been attributed to this erudite individual, though the argument seems unconvincing.[8] The royal court was also the intellectual background against which two major historical works were composed, again both in Latin: the *Chronica latina regum Castellae* (*Latin Chronicle of the Kings of Castile*), almost certainly compiled by Fernando III's chancellor, Juan de Osma, and the *De rebus Hispaniae* (*On the Affairs of Spain*) by the Archbishop of Toledo, Rodrigo Jiménez de Rada. Equally significant is the way in which the court of Castile (like that of Aragón) became home to a large number of poets of French origin. Both Alfonso and Fernando were renowned for the patronage that they extended to Gascon and Provençal troubadours (particularly in the case of Alfonso VIII, probably through Leonor's connection with the French court) and others composing in Galician-Portuguese (more common in the court of Fernando III). Alfonso X was to write in his *Setenario* of his father's personal interest in music and poetry, explaining that he took delight in 'men who sang, for he knew how to do so himself; and likewise ... in men of the court who were talented as singers and composers, and minstrels who were able to play instruments well; for he took great pleasure in this and knew who was playing well and who was not' (Vanderford 1984, 13). Not the least significant of the monarchs' achievements, moreover, was the emphasis that they seem personally to have placed on the development on the use of the Castilian language in official documentation, without which the appearance of literary texts such as the *Libro de Alexandre* and the *Poema de Fernán González* would have been inconceivable (Salvador Miguel 2000, 690; Wright 1996).

The combination of scholars, historians, poets and musicians who at various times were part of the Castilian court must have proved a heady mixture, particularly during a period when the monarchy was keen to exploit such resources in order to help in the creation of a new and lasting national

---

[8] See Hernando Pérez (2001). This attribution is based on a number of factors, including a detailed analysis of linguistic similarities between *Planeta*, the *Libro de Alexandre* and the *Poema de Fernán González*. It seems improbable, however, in view of the fact that Diego García died in about 1235, which implies an unrealistically early date for the composition of the *Poema*.

identity; during a period, indeed, that was marked by dramatic military successes and territorial advances. This was the world to whose values and traditions, both political and cultural, King Alfonso X 'the Learned' was heir, and it also determined the outlook and points of historical reference of the author of the *Poema de Fernán González*. In the course of this Introduction and of the notes to the text and translation we shall point to various details in the *Poema* that may plausibly be interpreted as containing allusions to episodes from recent Castilian history. There can be no doubt that our poet saw past events as paralleling and prefiguring those of the present and that he sought to communicate the clear and exhilarating message that the glories of the past were to be those of the present, too.

Indeed, it seems to have been almost certainly during the reigns of Alfonso VIII (in particular) and Fernando III that the legend of Fernán González had really taken shape.

(vii) The invention of a historical tradition
The development of the tale of Fernán González and of his role in achieving independence for Castile was, it appears, accompanied by the emergence of another legend related to the early days of the county: that of the two judges, Laín Calvo and Nuño Rasura (see note to 163b). It may be, too, that at more or the less the same time there was also a notable development related to the body of legend surrounding Castile's other great early hero, Rodrigo Díaz de Vivar, El Cid, in the form of the composition of the *Historia Roderici*, a Latin biography of the hero.[9] Indeed, in this case, the appearance of this and other works has been described as a kind 'literary boom' on the Burgos-born hero.[10] Fernán González died in 969 or 970, but it was about two centuries later, in a chronicle dating from the final quarter of the twelfth century, that he first appears presented as the man who won Castile its freedom from Leonese oppression. The chronicle in question is the *Crónica najerense*, probably composed at some point between 1173 and 1194 in the monastery of Santa María la Real de Nájera. This monastery bore close links with the Navarrese monarchy and several of the nation's kings (including García

---

[9] It has been argued that the *Historia Roderici*, like the *Crónica najerense*, which gives us our earliest evidence for the existence of important elements of the Fernán González legend, dates from the last quarter of the twelfth century. It is possible that the both works were composed in the same area and even that the biography of the Cid, like the *Crónica*, was composed in Nájera. See Montaner and Escobar (2001, 77–93). Some other scholars, however, are inclined to date the *Historia Roderici* as early as the first quarter of the twelfth century.
[10] See Montaner and Escobar (2001, 119).

Ramírez IV of Navarre, 'the Restorer') are buried there. It was an important monastic centre, standing on the road to Santiago; it had been Cluniac since 1079 and it possessed an extensive library. At the same time, the city of Nájera had a special link with Alfonso VIII of Castile: it remained loyal to him from 1162 to 1176 when the surrounding area was in Navarrese hands, and the Castilian court assembled there in 1185.

The first record of the existence of either of the famous judges, in this case Laín Calvo, is in the *Historia Roderici* where he appears as the first member of the line through which the Cid is descended. Nuño Rasura appears in the *Crónica najerense*, which lists him as the grandfather of Fernán González. It is in a series of accounts and chronicles composed in the second half of the twelfth century (see note to 163b), starting with the Navarrese *Liber regum* (*Book of Kings*; see note to 14c) that we find Laín and Nuño depicted as the two judges, with particular emphasis on their roles as the heads of the two illustrious lineages, and subsequently we find them appearing in the major history of Lucas de Tuy and, with appropriate elaboration, that of the archbishop of Toledo, Rodrigo Jiménez de Rada. From here their historical journey takes them through the *Poema de Fernán González* into Alfonso X's *Estoria de España*. They were by now fully accepted as playing a key part in the history of Castile, even though there was not a trace of solid evidence for their existence. As Javier Peña Pérez (2005, 60–61) points out, in his detailed and illuminating analysis of the development of these legends, it is worth emphasizing that this genealogy for Count Fernán González, clearly invented by the author of the *Crónica najerense*, appears in the very same paragraph which (to judge from all the known evidence) attributes to him for the first time the role of achieving for Castile independence from the kingdom of León.

The emphasis on lineage is critical, particularly given the Navarrese connection of Santa María de Nájera: it has been argued (see Peña Pérez 2005, 85–86) that, particularly in view of the doubts about the legitimacy of the Navarrese king García Ramírez, 'the Restorer', the newly established genealogies sought to show that, in terms of their historical prestige, the monarchies of the two kingdoms were equally impressive: that of Navarre was seen as descended from Laín Calvo and the Cid, that of Castile from Nuño Rasura and Fernán González. To this should be added the fact that the Cid, through the marriage of his daughter Cristina to the *infante* Ramiro, was not only grandfather of García Ramírez of Navarre but also a direct ancestor of Alfonso VIII of Castile, through whose veins thus flowed the blood of both of his nation's great epic heroes.

The *Crónica najerense*, then, establishes the distinguished ancestry of Fernán González as well as reporting the claim that he freed Castile from the yoke of Leonese domination; it records his marriage to Sancha and his involvement in the struggle between the two claimants to the throne, Sancho and Ordoño (including the latter's repudiation of his daughter Urraca). It also recounts his capture at Cirueña, his imprisonment and his liberation by Sancha. Although this account hinges on a confusingly anachronistic promise of marriage, the *Crónica* does seem to contain some sound historical detail (which in fact does not figure in the *Poema*). By this relatively early stage (that is, the late twelfth century) some key elements of the Count's story had clearly been assembled, but it also seems that substantial parts of the legend had yet to develop. It is also worth mentioning at this point the new emphasis which the *Crónica* placed on the decisive and legitimizing role of women, a theme which was again to appear in the *Poema de Fernán González* and one which clearly reflected concerns and principles particularly characteristic of the Castilian ruling dynasty of the twelfth and thirteenth centuries (see Martin 2009, and also the note to stanza 684).

From here the body of legend associated with Fernán González was taken up and elaborated by the historians of first León (Lucas de Tuy, who wrote in about 1236 at Berenguela's wish) and then Castile; the versions which then emerged were almost certainly inspired by the precisely directed policies of Berenguela, Alfonso VIII and Fernando III. The attitude of the Leonese Lucas de Tuy to Fernán González is one of disapproval: he shows him as a vassal in revolt against his rightful king; the Count's conduct is condemned by Lucas as 'tyrannical'; and in this account the offending nobleman is rightly punished by imprisonment. However, in Rodrigo Jiménez de Rada's *De rebus Hispaniae* (V, II), a work completed some seven years later and written with a strong Castilian emphasis, Fernán González has become a hero, whom God has set above other men, elected by the whole of the nation, who give thanks that they have been given a leader who has freed them from the burden of servitude, ensured that they will no longer be troubled by the kings of the Asturians (that is to say, of León), and struggled ceaselessly against the Muslims. There is also mention of the Count's generosity to the monastery of San Pedro de Arlanza and of his burial there.

The *De rebus Hispaniae* was completed just a decade before the composition of the *Poema de Fernán González*. In this text we find for the first time such extended praise for Fernán González's achievements, but even here there is no mention of how Castile was freed from its submission to León. There is no mention of the story of the horse and the hawk in connection with the Count until it appears in the *Poema de Fernán González* and from there it is incorporated into Alfonso X's *Estoria de España* and subsequent chronicle accounts. What must be emphasized at this point is that, before the chroniclers and historians of the twelfth and thirteenth centuries took up his story, almost certainly for a specific political purpose, there is no hard evidence that there existed a developed tradition concerning the part that the Count played in the liberation of Castile.

As we have seen (section 1(v), above) many scholars have assumed that the *Poema* was closely based on, indeed a reworking of, an earlier lost epic; some, for example, have argued that there is convincing evidence of a tradition related to the tale of the horse and the hawk going back to the Goths, although this theory is not now commonly accepted (see note to 576a–c and in particular the articles by Harvey (1976) and Harvey and Hook (1982)). There is much in the *Poema*, as we shall see, to point to a connection between at least some parts of this work and oral tradition, and some features of the Count's tale are likely to have ancient origins; but there is also good reason to associate a key stage in its development with that dynamic and creative period which embraced the reigns of Alfonso VIII and Fernando III and also, in important respects, the early years of that of Alfonso X 'the Learned'.

(viii) The monastery of San Pedro de Arlanza and its part in the development of a tradition

For what is almost the final piece in what may seem something of a jig-saw puzzle, we now need to look at the history of the monastery of San Pedro de Arlanza, which plays so prominent a part in the *Poema*, and in particular at the position in which it found itself in the mid-thirteenth century. Situated in the valley of the River Arlanza and near to the two important castles of Lara and Carazo, the monastery had grown from a small hermitage set high on the side of the valley. It preserved a series of diplomas dated from 912 to 925 which seemed to provide solid evidence for its very close connection with Fernán González and the earliest of which confirmed that it had been formally founded by him in 912. This date itself is enough to make us suspicious, as Fernando would only have been about seven years old at the time, and close scrutiny seems to show that none of these documents can be taken as reliable evidence (see Martínez Díez 2005, 1.292–294). That is to say, they are almost certainly later forgeries. What is beyond doubt, however, is that, like other similar communities in the area, San Pedro de

Fernán González's wish to be buried at the monastery of San Pedro de Arlanza is expressed in line 247c of the Poema *and in this respect the poet seems to have reflected historical fact. Fernando's remains were kept at the monastery until 1841 when they were transferred to the Collegiate Church in nearby Covarrubias, where his tomb can still be visited, together with those of his wife Sancha and three of their female descendants. The tomb which today contains the Count's remains actually dates from the fifth century, whilst its lid belongs to the nineteenth century.*

Arlanza quite rapidly became one of Castile's biggest landowners, benefiting from the generous donations of a series of counts. This generosity was less motivated by religious fervour than by the counts' desire to consolidate their political property: in some cases, for example, establishing a firm link with such a powerful ecclesiastical institution allowed a count to reinforce the power that he could exercise over an area (Álvarez Borge 1996, 106–107), and it will almost certainly be this motive which lay behind the donations that Fernán González was later to make to Arlanza and other monasteries. In the eleventh century the donations from such individuals reached exceptional proportions, but the monastery also benefited considerably from royal patronage, with Fernando I handing over to it smaller local monastic communities, towns and other properties. The wealth of Arlanza, like that of Cardeña, Silos, San Millán de la Cogolla, and Arlanza's close neighbour Covarrubias continued to grow throughout the eleventh century, but this highly prosperous situation was to come to an end.

By the late twelfth century and throughout the first half of the thirteenth century, the monasteries had to compete with other powerful interests for the income that was available. Arlanza became embroiled, for example, in increasingly bitter disputes with the bishops of Burgos and Osma, particularly with the latter over the *diezmos* or tithes from those of its lands which fell within the Bishop's diocese; and by the mid-thirteenth century it was having to cope with an increasing number of law-suits with landowners, both ecclesiastical and secular (Álvarez Borge 1996, 176–178). These were very different days, in which attitudes to property were changing rapidly and there was a new emphasis on a money economy and on the acquisition and retention of wealth. The relationship between the secular and the spiritual was changing apace (see, for example, Ruiz 2004, 151–154) and in practical terms this meant for the great monasteries a marked decrease in the donations that they received, accompanied by a new emphasis on boundaries, justification of ownership and litigation. The period of growth had ended in the early years of the thirteenth century and what mattered now was the increasingly difficult struggle to protect their existing wealth. There were also growing problems resulting from the pressure exerted by royal authority and by harsh fiscal demands. Arlanza, moreover, faced a particular pressure: in the final years of the twelfth century Alfonso VIII had founded the 'Hospital del rey', a hospice whose purpose was to provide aid to the poor and especially to pilgrims passing through Burgos. By 1212 this foundation had come under the jurisdiction of the abbess of the royal convent of Las Huelgas, which stood just outside the walls of Burgos. The considerable cost of endowing this hospice meant that the monarchy was obliged to transfer to it possessions and rights to income from other ecclesiastical landowners, and, together with Covarrubias, it was Arlanza that bore the brunt.

These were indeed difficult times and Arlanza continued to face stiff competition for income from rivals such as Silos and San Millán de la Cogolla. We have seen how much emphasis was placed by the mid-thirteenth century on the establishment of legitimacy of ownership. By now the three monasteries were clearly competing, for hard economical reasons, to make use of the figure of Fernán González and the prestige which he had by now acquired in both popular and learned tradition.[11] By the middle of the century Arlanza undoubtedly possessed a strong advantage in that it had already figured in the *De rebus Hispaniae* as having been founded by the Count

---

[11] See particularly Azcárate *et al.* (2006) for a clear and helpful analysis of the methods adopted by the three monasteries in their attempts to outdo their rivals.

and as his place of burial. It is impossible to assess the age of this tradition. On the other hand, it does seem that the falsified documentation associating the Count with the monastery's foundation was produced and added to the cartulary at some point in the third quarter of the twelfth century and probably quite early in the reign of Alfonso VIII (Azcárate *et al.* 2006, 372–373), and this dating would constitute further evidence for the development of the legend of Fernán González during that period. However, it was in the mid-thirteenth century that it became common practice for monasteries to seek from the royal chancery confirmation of their existing documentation, as an insurance against its deterioration or destruction. In 1254–1255 Arlanza requested that Alfonso X grant confirmation of the authenticity of the most significant parts of its archive, including the clearly falsified diploma of foundation. This incontrovertible confirmation of legitimacy and of so close a link with the great Castilian hero would be of inestimable value in the monastery's struggle for financial survival. Alfonso acceded to Arlanza's petition and the necessary confirmation was given; but it seems highly likely that the monastery was first able to produce some very detailed evidence in support of its claim and at the same time perform for Alfonso a very valuable service.

It is, of course, no coincidence that the monastery of Santo Domingo de Silos also managed to secure in 1255 the confirmation of its documentation. This included, together with an impressive collection of privileges of royal origin, another forged diploma claiming foundation by Fernán González in 919. There is clearly here an attempt to rival Arlanza's greatly prized link with the Count, and there is evidence, too, of the rivalry between the two monasteries in Gonzalo de Berceo's *Vida de Santo Domingo de Silos* (*Life of Saint Dominic of Silos*), when the poet is at pains to emphasize the superiority of the collection of relics which this monastery eventually acquired over that possessed by Arlanza (see Dutton 1978, stanzas 279–283).

Whilst Arlanza and Silos were successful in their petitions, the monastery of San Millán de la Cogolla would have to wait until 1289 to receive similar royal confirmation of their documentation (from the chancery of Alfonso's son, Sancho IV). In the case of this Riojan monastery, this documentation included what is now well known as the forgery of 'Los votos de San Millán' ('the Vows of San Millán'). According to this privilege, the victory over the Muslim forces won by Ramiro II and Fernán González was gained with supernatural assistance brought by Santiago and San Millán, and in gratitude the two leaders promised a generous annual tribute; the Count's vow is presented as being made on behalf of all the communities of Castile, including even Lara and all the territories depending on it (a claim which strikes very close to home for the monks of Arlanza). The essential details of the vow were incorporated into a Latin text composed in the monastery at some point in the 1220s and this in turn was a source for Gonzalo de Berceo in his *Vida de San Millán de la Cogolla* (*Life of San Millán de la Cogolla*), which likewise includes a list of communities bound to pay their tribute to the Riojan monastery, under pain of excommunication. In spite of the image that he projects of himself as a gentle cleric, Berceo was clearly no friend of Arlanza. The *Vida de San Millán de la Cogolla*, like the *Vida de Santo Domingo de Silos*, was written in the same metre as the *Poema de Fernán González* and stylistically the three works have a good deal in common; it is not difficult to see the *Poema* as in some degree a riposte to the work composed on behalf of San Millán de la Cogolla. It is not surprising, therefore, that in the Arlanza poem, unlike in Berceo's account, there is no sign of San Millán alongside Santiago in the skies above the crucial battle, and that the victor's generosity is now directed to the Monastery of San Pedro.

When the *Poema de Fernán González* was composed, and we can state with some certainty that this was early in the reign of Alfonso X, the strong connection between the Count and San Pedro de Arlanza was already well known. It is plausible that Arlanza commissioned the Poema as a response to attempts of its rival monasteries to undercut this prestigious position, drawing on the expertise of a member of its community or of a secular cleric; such an individual might have occupied a position in the monastery's service similar to that which Berceo himself held (possibly as a notary) at San Millán de la Cogolla. In the light of the central role played by Arlanza in the Poema's narrative, its close link with the work and with the background to its composition seems beyond doubt. In his recent study, Matthew Bailey (2010, 99–100) sees the monastic community of Arlanza as assimilating the story of Fernán González through readings and reflections and together reformulating the narrative to emphasize the hero's close connection to the monastery. However, it has been argued that the nature of the poet's geographical knowledge (and its limitations) suggest that he was not, in fact, a monk at Arlanza (Serrano 1943, 45). Nonetheless, the parallel with the position of the secular priest Berceo is offered here as a possible explanation, and such problematic details as those noted by Serrano may be convincingly explained by setting them in their dramatic context within the poem (see Hernando Pérez 2001, 116–117).

If the monastery's objective was to provide a written narrative to support its claim to a very close link with the illustrious Count, thus backing up the documentation for which it now sought royal confirmation, this was fully achieved. The tale of the Count as it appears in the *Poema* was, as we have seen, duly incorporated into King Alfonso's own history. We know that Alfonso was already collecting material for precisely this purpose in the early 1250s, and in this context it is well worth considering the parallel with a Latin poem, four hundred lines in length, which we know to have been submitted to Alfonso in 1250. This is the *Rithmi de Iulia Romula seu Ispalensi Urbe* (*Verses on Julia Rómula or the City of Seville*) composed in the monastery of San Zoilo de Carrión by Guillermo Pérez de la Calzada, ex-abbot of Sahagún. In his dedication of the poem to Alfonso as heir to the throne, the poet says that he is writing to offer his verses to the future monarch: 'Celsitudini uestre rithmos presentes offerro de urbe Ispalensi a me editos. ... Precipiat ergo Regia celsitudo, si placet, predictos rithmos cum hac epistola in cronicis annotari, ob memorie perpetue nutrimentum.' ('I offer to your majesty these verses on the city of Seville, which I have related. ... Therefore let your royal majesty, if such is your will, dispose that the aforementioned verses, together with this letter, should be included in the chronicles, to sustain a lasting memory.') The metre and rhyme-scheme of this Latin poem are very close indeed to those of the *Poema de Fernán González* and the other vernacular *cuaderna vía* poems and there are, moreover, marked stylistic similarities between the *Rithmi* and the *Poema* (Carande Herrero 1986, 13–15); the two works also share a kindred purpose: to win the favour of the heir to the throne and subsequently monarch by offering him a skilfully written account of the heroism displayed by the Castilian people, in the hope that it can be incorporated into the chronicles for which Alfonso was known already to be compiling material.

There would seem, then, to be much to support the argument that the *Poema de Fernán González* was composed specifically for submission to King Alfonso X. Moreover, its author certainly had a close connection with Arlanza but he also seems to have been well informed about Alfonso's political concerns and ambitions during the early years of his reign. One of the great qualities of the *Poema* is the skill with which it interweaves the specific concerns of Arlanza, Alfonso's own aspirations and the broader questions related to a nation's origins and identity. It is to the political situation of the 1250s that we now turn.

(ix) The reign of Alfonso X, the crisis of 1253–1255 and the African crusade: the background to the composition of the Poema de Fernán González

The final words that the dying Fernando III is recorded as saying to his son Alfonso X are cruel ones in the demand that they placed on him: 'I leave you as lord of all the land this side of the sea, which the Moors had won from Rodrigo of Spain; and it all remains under your lordship, either conquered or placed under tribute. If you are able to maintain it in this state in which I am leaving it to you, you are as good a king as I; and if you win for yourself more, you are better than I; and if you do less than this, you are not as good as I' (*Estoria de España*, chapter 1132: see Menéndez Pidal 1955, 2.772–773). In this way the new king, already on ascending to the throne in 1252 in succession to his immensely successful father, was effectively committed to a policy of continuing expansion.

Alfonso, aged 31 when he came to the throne of the Crown of Castile, had already fulfilled an important role in his father's campaigns against Muslim Spain, commanding the Christian armies in the conquest of Murcia and Cartagena and playing his full part in the taking of Seville. He possessed wide cultural interests and, as would be amply demonstrated by the immense scholarly and literary output produced under his direction, he was a man of great learning. He possessed a deep passion for the study of history and he showed a strong interest and profound personal involvement in the history of his own nation. He had a strong sense, too, of the importance and the nature of the state; not least, indeed, of the significance of his own role as sovereign, in his own words, 'coraçon, e alma del pueblo', ('the heart and soul of the people', *Partidas*, 2,1,5), and of the inviolability of royal authority. Alfonso was a ruler who wished to scrutinize, control and regulate his kingdom, and these tendencies were to become increasingly marked.[12] It is not surprising that such a man would wish to produce a clear written account of his nation's origin and of the qualities which, from the very outset, had characterized its people.

But how was that nation made up? Alfonso, although in principle ruler over a single Crown of Castile, did not reign over a fully unified kingdom. His full title was 'King of Castile, Toledo, León, Galicia, Seville, Córdoba, Murcia, Jaén and the Algarve', a list in which Toledo, as the seat of the

---

[12] See, for example, Linehan (2008, 116–118) for further discussion of this aspect of Alfonso's reign. Indeed, Linehan examines the development of Alfonso's absolutist tendencies and suggests that during the early years of his reign he developed into 'what would now be described as a control-freak ... preoccupied to an unhealthy degree with matters of detail and aspects of majesty' (p. 118).

ancient Visigothic monarchy, was set before León. The very grandeur of the title was a statement of power and prestige. Between Castile and León there were marked legal and institutional differences and in the latter the Leonese dialect continued to be extensively used. Castile possessed a strong sense of individual identity, seeing itself as the driving force behind the reconquest of vast areas of the Iberian Peninsula. It is clear that Alfonso X saw it as his task to bring together his dominions in a closely organized whole and was acutely aware that his duty was to the entirety of his people; arguably it is for this reason that in the *Poema de Fernán González*, at least in the version represented by the *Estoria de España*, although he wins great victories over the Navarrese and the Muslims and does at one point raid the lands of León, the Count is never seen to come directly into conflict with the Leonese monarch. Nevertheless, there can be no doubt that, having been brought up in a Castilian court for which León during several years remained a rival kingdom, it will have been above all with Castile's cultural traditions that Alfonso identified.

Until 1254 Alfonso remained in Seville dealing with the reorganization and repopulation of the recently conquered city and summoning an assembly (*Cortes*) in 1252 to deal with urgent economic problems. It was noticeable already that there was a marked shift in the group of noblemen surrounding the King, with the list now headed by his close friend Nuño González de Lara, a member of the old Castilian family intimately associated with the lands of Fernán González.[13] Alfonso, moreover, was from the outset evidently determined to leave his mark. There was an early dispute with the new king of Portugal over ownership of the Algarve (important as the basis of a campaign that the Spanish sovereign was already planning in North Africa) but thanks to papal intervention hostilities were avoided. However, in 1253 the death of Thibault I of Navarre, succeeded by his son Thibault II, brought about a situation which threatened serious conflict. Alfonso, clearly seeking to demonstrate his superiority among the rulers of the Peninsula and giving early evidence of imperial ambitions, prepared to invade Navarre.[14] Castilian troops massed on the Navarrese frontier. The tense and increasingly

---

[13] It has been suggested that Nuño González de Lara might have paid for the composition of the *Poema de Fernán González*, thus drawing attention to the distinguished past of the Lara family (see José Fradejas Lebrero 1989, 20). The poet will also have been well aware that to emphasize in this way the illustrious lineage of the royal favourite would be highly pleasing to Alfonso.

[14] For further discussion of Alfonso's imperial designs within the Peninsula and of how these go back to the reign of Fernando III, see González Jiménez (2006, 73–74).

complex situation which ensued was complicated by a rebellion of members of the Castilian nobility, notably Diego López de Haro, who severed his bonds of vassalage with the King; and one of the causes of this rebellion was concern at the rapid rise of Alfonso's close friend Nuño González de Lara.

The principal source of opposition to Alfonso's plans, however, came from Jaime I of Aragón, with whom Thibault II of Navarre signed an alliance in August 1254. Alfonso sought to isolate his enemies diplomatically, exploiting a dispute over Gascony, which had been the source of contention since forming part of the dowry of Eleanor (Leonor) of England on her marriage to Alfonso VIII. In 1205 Alfonso VIII had failed in his attempt to assert his control over the region, but now, almost fifty years later, his great-grandson Alfonso tried again, taking advantage of the decision of two Gascon noblemen to commit an act of rebellion against Henry III of England by becoming Alfonso's vassals. For a time there was a real threat that Castile would invade Gascony, but this threat did not materialize; Alfonso's real aim was to prepare the way for an invasion of Navarre and, with this much in mind, he was quick to sign a treaty with an English delegation in Toledo in March–April 1254. The terms were significant and among them, together with Alfonso's renunciation of all his rights to Gascony, were the following: the marriage of Edward the crown prince of England to Alfonso's sister Leonor and also that of a daughter of Henry III to one of Alfonso's brothers; agreement by Henry III to give military aid to Alfonso in the conflict with Navarre; and Henry's pledge to participate with Alfonso in an African Crusade. Although nothing is known of Henry's actual involvement in or contribution to the crusade, these other conditions were substantially fulfilled by both sides, and in October 1204 Prince Edward was warmly welcomed in Burgos, where he was knighted by Alfonso. The tension on the Navarrese frontier continued to mount and open conflict between Castile and Aragón only failed to materialize owing to internal difficulties within the two kingdoms.

It is surely highly tempting, then, to see the composition of the *Poema de Fernán González*, in which conflict with Navarre plays such a prominent part, as dating from the time when Castile did indeed seem to be preparing for an invasion of its eastern neighbour, a conflict on a scale far greater than any experienced between the two kingdoms during the time of Fernán González. The list of Castile's potential foes in line 436a, 'Aragón and Navarre and all the Poitevins', seems to point clearly in this direction. But why is such emphasis placed in the *Poema* on French involvement and what historically was the role of the Count of Poitou and Toulouse? Both questions should be easy to answer in the light of the events of 1253–1255. Certainly we know that French troops were being concentrated on the Navarrese frontier in late 1254, and, apart from its obvious concern over Alfonso's diplomatic manoeuvering, it is not surprising that France would be lending support to Thibault II: the Navarrese royal family was French, of the line of the counts of Navarre, and both Thibault and his father spent the greater part of their reigns in France. Thibault, indeed, was the son-in-law of King Louis IX.

The part played by the French count and his identification have given rise to considerable debate, particularly because of its importance for the dating of the *Poema*. It has been argued (Keller 1990, 92–105) that the source of this figure is Guillaume VII of Poitou and IX of Aquitaine (grandfather of Eleanor of Aquitaine); and the count of the *Poema* has also been identified with Philip III of France, who gave protection to Navarre in 1271 (Lacarra 1979, 28–31). Bearing in mind the involvement of French forces in the crisis of 1253–1255, there is surely a more obvious solution to this enigma. Alphonse de Poitiers, Count of Poitiers and Toulouse (see note to lines 331ab) was the brother of King Louis and regent of France during Louis' absence on Crusade until September 1254. He was, therefore, right at the centre of the crisis that occurred during that period; we know that he took significant precautionary measures both in Normandy and in Poitou (Ducluzeau 2006, 110–112) and we can reasonably assume that he was responsible for providing troops to support Navarre. He is evidently a figure important enough to merit the honorific treatment accorded to him in the *Poema*, and he is certainly, too, tied by 'kinship to the King' (331b). He was the great-grandson of Blanche of Navarre (*c.* 1181–1229), countess of Champagne, and thus a relative of Thibault II; but he was also related to the Castilian monarchy: as the son of Alfonso VIII's daughter Blanche of Castile, he was a cousin of Fernando III and uncle of Alfonso X. There is, then, enough evidence here to suggest that our poet may well have based the figure of the Count of Poitiers and Toulouse on King Louis' brother Alphonse.

* * * * * *

One final – and crucial – element of Alfonso's policies remains to be considered. We have already seen how his treaty with Henry III required Henry to participate in the planned African Crusade. There is every indication that this enterprise was close to the Castilian king's heart. He, as his father had done, cherished the idea of gaining a foothold in Morocco – now that Peninsular Islam had been overthrown – with the intention of eventually launching a campaign for the recovery of the Holy Land. Fernando had already begun to assemble a fleet in Seville and as early as October 1252 Alfonso was pressing on with the preparations, the African Crusade representing a fundamental objective in the early years of his reign.[15] In 1253 Pope Innocent IV proclaimed a crusade, conferring remission of sins on all those who participated, just as if they had made a pilgrimage to the Holy Land, and in May of the following year he praised Alfonso for having 'assumed the sign of the living cross against the Saracens of Africa' (O'Callaghan 2011, 15). We shall see below (section 4(vii)) how the idea of the Crusade runs through the *Poema*, binding together the campaigns of the Visigoths and Fernán González and, by implication, that of Alfonso X; and it must be borne in mind that it was Alfonso who was to be the first Spanish monarch to promote extensively the idea of the 'pueblo cruzado': the Castilian people who have devoted themselves to the battle on behalf of Christianity against the unbelievers.[16] The mention of the Marinids in line 387a has been used as evidence to date the *Poema*'s composition to 1264 at the very earliest, for it was in that year that the Marinid dynasty, from its base in Morocco, made its first intervention into the Iberian Peninsula (see Keller 1990, 99; Lacarra 1979, 30–31). This argument is surely unconvincing if the poet knew of the Marinids' presence, alongside the Almohads, as a potential enemy in Morocco.

* * * * * *

There seems, then, to be a strong case for asserting that the *Poema de Fernán González* reflects various aspects of the troubled but heady political situation of the time in which it was composed. Growing tension and the threat of war with Navarre, a kingdom closely identified with French interests and with the figure of the king's regent; anticipation of a crusade which would carry the fight against Islam into North Africa; dispute with members of the nobility and the need to assert firmly the authority of the monarch: all of these are unmistakably mirrored in the *Poema*'s narrative and they are accompanied by an awareness of great achievement on the part of the people of Castile and a powerful sense of national pride. At a time when conflict loomed, here was a picture of triumph over precisely the two enemies who must again be faced, and the new crusaders were set alongside the triumphant

---

[15] For an analysis of the Castilian king's objectives, Alfonso's preparations for the crusade and the eventual outcome, see O'Callaghan (2011, 1–16).

[16] See the important study of the correspondence between Alfonso's crusading ideal and the themes and language of the *Poema* in Luis Fernández Gallardo (2009).

warriors of a previous century. Moreover, the pride of the Castilians was sustained by a leader who commanded the respect and absolute obedience of his whole people, and such unflinching support – in spite of the hardship that it involved – provided the people of Alfonso's own kingdom with an ideal model. There are numerous reasons why the King would have been deeply pleased by the *Poema*, and it is no surprise that in 1254 and 1255 he confirmed the privileges and the concessions made to Arlanza, including the document of highly doubtful provenance giving evidence of the monastery's foundation by Fernán González.

This survey of Castilian history from the tenth to the thirteenth century has been a lengthy one, but we believe that it has contained a great deal that is relevant for a full understanding of the *Poema*. The tale of the tenth-century count, as assembled by a thirteenth-century cleric, reflects the poet's great pride in the growth of Castile from a small and vulnerable territory into the driving force behind a vast and powerful nation. He has drawn on both learned sources and also, undoubtedly, some oral accounts, and it can be confidently asserted that the resulting narrative reflects not just the achievements of Fernán González himself but also other important features of more recent Castilian history, including: the victory achieved over the Navarrese in the eleventh century by Fernando I, the man who really established Castile as an independent kingdom; the crusading triumphs of Alfonso VIII, whom the Castilians would have viewed as standing alone against his Islamic enemy, and also the immense territorial gains made by Fernando III; and the distinctive and crucial role played by the women of their dynasty, notably Queen Berenguela, whose force of character made possible Fernando's succession to the throne of Castile (and eventually to that of León as well). It is reasonable to assume that the author of the *Poema de Fernán González* was aware of such outstanding features of Castile's past and we have already noted that he was inclined to view past events as prefiguring and anticipating those of the present. We have seen, too, how the Castilian royal courts of the twelfth and thirteenth centuries were powerful cultural centres and how the monarchs were well aware of the value of literary creation as a means of cementing a strong spirit of national identity: in this context we can see the *Poema* as a foundation story, whose creation responds to the Castilians' growing confidence and sense of self-awareness. It should be stressed, too, that the Castilian rulers were equally conscious of the value of promoting the use of the Castilian language in order further to affirm that spirit of collective identity. Above all, it has become clear that there is a very close relationship between the narrative of the *Poema* and the events of the early years of the reign of Alfonso X and the principles and aspirations of the new monarch. This relationship will be examined more closely in section 4, below, but at this point it is appropriate to look at the nature of the *Poema* itself and in particular at the stylistic features which appear to relate it to different traditions and forms of composition.

3. *Men of learning and* juglares: *the art of the* mester de clerecía *and the use of stylistic features associated with oral poetry*

(i) The Libro de Alexandre *and the* mester de clerecía

There can be no doubt at all that, as regards both verse form and style, our poet took his lead in producing an extended written narrative in Castilian from the author of the *Libro de Alexandre*, a long, learned and complex poem composed at some point during the first two decades of the thirteenth century. The second stanza of the *Alexandre* sets out very clearly the artistic purpose of its author:

> The craft I bring is refined, it is no minstrel's work,
> a craft without fault, born of the clergy's learning:
> to compose rhyming verse in the four-line form,
> with counted syllables – an act of great mastery.

In the Spanish text of this stanza two key terms are introduced: *la quaderna vía*, the four-lined verse form; and *mester de clereçía* ('mester es sin pecado, ca es de clereçía'), a craft associated with the office of the priest and one which is also without (metrical) error. The regular and accurate syllable count is emphasized here as marking a firm contrast with the world of the 'popular' epic.[17]

The term *mester de clerecía* has come to be applied to a body of poetry from the thirteenth century and beyond which follows the artistic principles set out by the *Libro de Alexandre* and which includes both the corpus of the Riojan cleric Gonzalo de Berceo (*c.* 1197 to *c.* 1264) and the *Poema de Fernán González*. That is to say, the author of the *Poema* is consciously imitating the form and the style which were used in the earlier *clerecía* poems. We shall see below that he has indeed been extensively influenced by the *Alexandre*, and not just in matters of form and style, and he certainly also draws on Berceo's *Vida de San Millán de la Cogolla* and *Vida de Santo Domingo de Silos*. He

---

[17] See also the analysis of this stanza in Such and Rabone (2009, 2–3).

was writing within what was by now quite a clearly defined tradition and had already developed its own characteristic narrative style.

*(ii) Elements of oral narrative poetry incorporated in the work
of the* clerecía *poets: direct speech, direct address and features
of the spoken language*

The *Alexandre* poet, then, chooses to emphasize the distinction between his art and that of the performer of less learned works. However, he and the *mester de clerecía* poets who imitate him incorporate in their works not only many features which belong to the learned world of Latin composition as taught in the schools but also others which are characteristic of oral narrative poetry. Indeed, there is firm evidence that even the production of learned works will have involved dictation and thus an important element of vocalization (see Bailey 2010, 83). Among features considered typical of orally produced poetry is the extensive use of direct speech; over a third of the stanzas of the *Poema de Fernán González* include at least some element of either monologue or conversation, and this proportion is, of course, higher after the lengthy historical narrative with which the work opens. It is, moreover, essential that, as we read the text on the page, we bear in mind the skills of the actor which might accompany its delivery. To give just two examples: we can imagine how the performer would attempt to conjure up the character of Count Julian as in stanzas 44–46, warped, vengeful and grasping, he proposes his insidious plan to the Muslim leader; and the two encounters of Sancha with Fernán González in prison, particularly the second with its bawdy overtones and the Count's escape in his wife's clothes, could be exploited in performance to provide rare light-hearted moments. Furthermore, instances of the poet directly addressing his public, with such structures as 'First I shall tell you' (3a), 'you have surely heard tell' (42a), or 'this you may well believe' (134c), are legion. There can be no doubt that the poet has in mind oral delivery, probably accompanied by gesture and mime, but it must be taken into account that in this he is drawing on learned written sources (notably the *Alexandre*), as well as oral models. We might well expect to find our poet making use of linguistic features associated with the spoken language. This is the case, for example, with diminutives: see, for example, 'paneziello' (97c: 'the humble bread') and 'condeziello' (745b: 'a petty little count'); but their use is nevertheless quite limited, mostly being employed to provide rhyme words and usually in the same form, *-iello* – certainly they are less extensive or striking than in the works of Berceo. There are examples of the use of colourful popular sayings (such as 'his fate was the same as the ram that sought wool': 583d); common expressions expressing contempt ('I will not be worth a fig': 182d; 'nowhere worth a fig': 217c); or pithy moral sayings ('yet without him we have not the worth of a penny; | a man's good standing is lost in a moment': 667cd). However, these are probably less common and certainly less varied or striking than in either Berceo's poems or the *Libro de Alexandre*. Moreover, the natural imagery which abounds in the battle scenes of the *Poema* – 'like a ravenous lion' (490a), 'doing as a wolf does when set among the flocks' (501b), 'raging wilder than a serpent' (518a), blood 'which flowed in great rivers like a fount gushing forth' (502c) – would seem to be at least as conventional in learned epic as in popular narrative poetry.

(iii) Other features of oral-formulaic style: 'epic' epithets, 'pair phrases' and 'physical expressions'
Perhaps the three features most often cited as characteristic of Spanish oral-formulaic style are 'epic' epithets, various kinds of what might be called 'pair' or 'binary' phrases, and 'physical expressions' which involve the use of a redundant adverbial phrase. They are all conspicuous in the *Poema de Fernán González* and their presence has been taken as evidence of a close link with oral tradition. The first of these three features, the epic epithet, has been defined as a 'noun, adjective, adjectival phrase or relative clause limiting, or standing in opposition to or in place of, the name of the epic hero, and generally reserved for him alone' (Michael 1961, 33). Often this device is an extremely simple one, taking the form of a concise descriptive phrase. It is much used in the *Poema*, but by far the most common of its applications is to Fernán González himself: he is alluded to, for example as 'the good Count' (on numerous occasions, for example 312a, 318a, 324c, 330d), 'the Castilian count' or 'the Count of Castile' (as in 287a, 313c, 373a, 541a), 'cuerpo de grand valor', literally 'a body of great worth' (170d), 'a man of sharp wits' (226a), 'the fortune-favoured count' (249b), 'that man of great deeds' (284b), 'a man with no semblance of cruelty' (372a), 'his men's loyal leader' (488a), 'man well schooled' (246a) and 'the epitome of valour' (730a). The device can also be extended to all those around the hero, both supporters and foes: the Count's counsellor Gonzalo Díaz is 'a man of wisdom' (202a); the Castilian nobleman Nuño Laínez is rapidly summed up by three epithets: 'a man born with wisdom, | a fine knight in combat, and loyal to his lord' (661cd); in a kind of epithet common in oral tradition, the Asturian King Alfonso is described

as 'a man whose lance struck fear' (123c). And likewise, 'epic epithets' are applied not just to the Muslims (see below) but also to the Christians' most formidable enemy throughout the *Poema*, the Devil himself: a 'deadly foe' (for example, 6c, 217a), '[t]he Devil of old' (70c), 'the cinderous Devil' (588d).

Similar descriptive phrases are also applied, for example, to the lands of Castile, as in the account in stanza 747 of the attack by the king of Navarre who raids 'the Hills of Oca, a fine land of renown' and 'the Ubierna valley, with its rich stocks of bread' ('de pan bien abastada'). Attention has been drawn (Dutton 1961, 198–199) to the 'epic' epithet applied to Carazo in 192d ('una sierra muy alta, muy firme castellar': 'a difficult stronghold set high in the hills'). A very similar line occurs in Berceo's *Vida de Santo Domingo de Silos* and Dutton and others have viewed this as evidence of direct borrowing by both poets from the older popular epic.

Undoubtedly, the use of such concise descriptive phrases to sum up the essential nature of a person or a place is fundamental to our poet's technique, helping him to create an instant picture and to situate both characters and places within a clearly defined moral framework. They also have a very precise practical purpose, for they are ideally suited to the *cuaderna vía* verse form, constituting units which correspond neatly to a hemistich of seven syllables. The description of the two judges of Castile in stanza 165, for example, demonstrates very clearly how the use of four 'epic epithets' within a structure based on parallelism and symmetry is a very valuable aid to composition. Incidentally, it is also worth noting how here the symmetry of form relates to the poet's purpose in emphasizing the parallels between the two great lines of Castilian nobility whose blood was later to flow through the veins of the monarchs of Christian Spain.

> Don Nuño ovo nonbre,   omne de grand valor,
> vino de su linaje   el cond' batallador.
> El otro don Laíno,   el buen guerreador,
> vino de su linaje   el Çid Campeador.

> (The first was named Nuño, a man of great worth,
> and from his lineage came the Count, the battler;
> the second was Laíno, who was a fine warrior,
> and from his lineage came the Cid, the Champion.)

It is striking that the best known and most memorable of all the epithets cited here is the one that is applied to the Cid, 'el Çid Campeador'. Ian Michael, in his comparison of the use of the epic epithet in the *Poema de*

Mio Cid and the *Libro de Alexandre*, concludes that the learned *clerecía* poet of the *Alexandre* fails to handle the device with the subtlety and the dramatic impact with which it is employed in the *Poema de Mio Cid*, asking whether we 'merely see in the *Alexandre* the dead remains of what had previously been a flourishing epic convention' (1961, 41). It is worth considering how far the same point could be made with respect to the *Poema de Fernán González*, for very few of the epithets that its author employs stick in the mind as defining a character in a memorable or incisive way and they are not used in the essentially dynamic and dramatic way that Michael demonstrates for the *Poema de Mio Cid*. Nevertheless, it is undeniable that the epic epithet is a fundamental feature of the descriptive technique of our poet and, although often used in quite a simple way, it can certainly have the effect of establishing correspondences (and contrasts) between characters in a poem marked by black-and-white moral judgments. This is the case, for example, with Fernán González, repeatedly viewed as 'the good Count', and his predecessor in the fight against Islam, 'the good King Rodrigo' (as in 6b, 49a, 75a). Against them are set Mohammed 'of the evil faith' (7a), the 'unbelieving tribe(s)/people(s)' (for example in 15b, 238a, 253a, 518d), 'the renegade people(s)' (205a, 441a), and '[t]he accursed people' (392a). Here verbal parallels help to establish a close link between the enemy which defeats the Goths and the Muslim forces conquered by the Count, part of the process, as we shall see, by which the poet emphasizes the sense of continuity in the Christian struggle over the centuries.

It is also worth drawing attention to a particularly subtle example of the use of an epic epithet in line 684c when the people of Castile welcome Sancha with a formula which was famously applied to the hero of the *Poema de Mio Cid*: a phrase much associated with male heroes is directed to a female who has just acted in an important and assertive way. We have already pointed to the distinctive and at times pivotal role played by women in the Castilian history of the twelfth and thirteenth centuries and such a detail draws our attention to the crucial and highly significant nature of Sancha's actions. The use of epic epithets is, then, a conspicuous feature of the *juglar*'s craft and also of descriptive technique in the *Poema de Fernán González*. It would be difficult to argue that our learned poet handles the epic epithet in as varied a way as the author of the *Poema de Mio Cid*, but in his hands it is certainly more than 'the dead remains of a flourishing convention'.

* * * * * *

A second stylistic feature of the *Poema de Fernán González* that could be classified as typical of an 'oral-formulaic' narrative style is the very extensive use of phrases of different kinds built around pairs. If we accept the definition of a formula in this sense as 'a group of words which is regularly employed under the same metrical conditions to express a given essential idea' (Parry 1930, 80; discussed by Lord 1960, 30), and if we accept, too, that the use of such formulae is a fundamental feature of the art of composition and transmission of oral poetry, then there might seem to be ample evidence for the *Poema*'s direct debt to oral poetry. It has been calculated (Geary 1980, 25) that overall 17% of the language of the *Poema* is essentially formulaic, exactly the same figure, by the way, as for the *Libro de Alexandre*. Often the 'pair phrases' involve duplication, a pair of words where one would suffice, such as '[t]hey spoke and they claimed' (93a), 'disconsolate and wretched' (161c), 'joyful and contented' (680b, 727a), 'full of fury and rage' (733a), '(their) weeping and (their) wailing' (242d, 243a, 249d). Often they are inclusive pairs, commonly used to mean 'everyone' or 'everywhere', 'at all times' or perhaps 'nobody' or 'nowhere': 'young and old' (as in 65b, 184b, 189d, 281b, 379c, 574a, 670a), 'horsemen, foot soldiers' (62c), 'men on foot and horseback' (266a), 'the Moors and the Christians' (504d), 'the living and those yet to come' (697d), '[n]either Moor nor Christian' (50c), 'no Christian or Moor' (277c), 'neither town nor castle' (19b), 'no tower or rampart' (298b), 'through the night and the day' (90d), 'day and night', (114c). Attention has also been drawn (see, for example, West 1983, 122) to the frequency with which our poet builds a line around formulaic antithetical expressions, such as 'the joy that they felt was turned to weeping' (40d), 'their weeping and their wailing turned to joy' (249d) and 'they turned their former weeping to elation' (687d). The correspondence with the language of orally composed epic poetry seems clear, but it should be stressed that just as such features provide valuable aid to improvisation and in oral performance, they are also of considerable assistance in written composition. Given the nature of our poet's medium, a verse-form which imposed tight constraints and which, as we have already seen, lent itself to parallelism and symmetry, he will no doubt have found that such devices fitted easily into the narrative style which had already been developed by the author of the *Libro de Alexandre* and by Gonzalo de Berceo. Not only did they tend to provide a ready-made half-line unit or even a whole line, but the author of the *Poema de Fernán González* had at his disposal models which demonstrated very effectively how to exploit them. Indeed, we have here a particularly striking example of this in the way in which the antithesis in 249d gains force from the echo of 'weeping and wailing' already repeated in 242d and 243a. There is in these stanzas a clear sense of a formula not carelessly inserted but skilfully exploited; and it may be significant, too, that there is an almost exact parallel for the wording of 249d in line 2263b of the *Libro de Alexandre*.

* * * * * *

The use of 'physical phrases' is commonly associated with oral poetry, not least because of their likely connection with ritual gestures but also because of the powerful and direct emotive force that they sometimes achieve. Certainly, they are used in some memorable passages in the *Poema de Mio Cid* and there are also several examples of this device in the *Poema de Fernán González*, such as 'llorar de los ojos' (literally, 'weep from his/their eyes': 114b; cf. 394c), 'fincó los sus finojos' (literally, 'he knelt down on his knees': 394b), 'Bien se veién por ojos' (literally 'they could see each other well with their eyes': 252a) and 'Todos por una boca ... dixeron/ fablaron' (literally, 'they all through one mouth said/spoke': 281c; 448b). Again, the principal reason for the use of such formulae by our poet may be metrical convenience, but these were commonly used expressions – all with parallels, for example, in the *Libro de Alexandre* (such as 116b, 401b, 710d, 713c, 1416a, 1682c). Like the other linguistic features that we have just considered, they form part of the stylistic repertoire of the cleric just as much as of the *juglar* or minstrel. So too, if we find in the *Poema* features typical of epic such as the enumeration of the outstanding warriors in the Count's army (see stanzas 451–464), we must bear in mind that this is a feature just as much of the learned epic as of popular or improvised poetry.

* * * * * *

We have looked in this section at some stylistic characteristics to be found in the *Poema de Fernán González* which are often pointed to as evidence of the poet's debt to oral tradition and, indeed, of his extensive reliance on a now lost *Cantar de Fernán González*. We have seen, however, that he shares his debt to oral poetry with other *clerecía* poets, who, in terms of form and style, provided him with more direct models for imitation. There is no doubt that the *Poema* has features in common with works like the *Poema de Mio Cid*. However, the sharp division between the worlds of 'popular' and 'learned' has come to be markedly exaggerated: the author of the *Alexandre* may have distinguished between his craft and that of the *juglar*, but that does not mean that he and other *mester de clerecía* poets did not share some features of that art. Likewise, the appearance of features of oral poetry in the *Poema de Fernán González* does not constitute evidence that it depends closely on an epic that was the product of an oral tradition.

(iv) The Poema de Fernán González *and the world of learning*
It is worth at this point returning to look more closely at what is meant by describing the *mester de clerecía* poems as 'learned', a subject considered briefly above (section 1(iv)). What seems to be a scholar's itinerary in the *Libro de Alexandre* (with mentions of Paris and Bologna in stanzas 2582– 2583) might suggest that its author had some knowledge of the university world. It is also commonly accepted that Gonzalo de Berceo (and perhaps other *clerecía* poets) may well have studied in the University of Palencia which was founded by Alfonso VIII in the early years of the thirteenth century and whose teachers we know to have included teachers brought from Paris and Bologna (for a study of such French influences, see Dutton 1973). Among those teachers there were undoubtedly teachers of grammar and rhetoric and it would have been the former who were responsible for teaching the art of Latin composition. It is generally believed that the *cuaderna vía* verse form developed from the French alexandrine rather than Latin verse, whose hemistichs are of six rather than seven syllables (Dutton 1973, 83–85). It is also, however, generally accepted that the *clerecía* poets make extensive use of stylistic techniques associated originally with the art of composition in Latin, and we shall see examples of these below. It is interesting, moreover, to examine a text like the *Rithmi de Iulia Romula seu Ispalensi Urbe* (see above, section 2(viii)), with its hemistichs of 7 and 6 syllables and rhyming four-line stanzas, in order to see a close Latin parallel to the *cuaderna vía* verse form. Certainly the suggestion that the *mester de clerecía* originated among scholars sent to study law in preparation for a career as a notary or administrator is a highly plausible one, for in the initial stages of their studies they would have learned the art of composition in Latin based on the study of the classical authors. It is, without doubt, in such a programme of study that the *Libro de Alexandre* has its roots. It is an erudite and artistically self-conscious work, in which the importance of the liberal arts is brought to the fore and scholarship and artistry themselves play a major thematic role. The text of the poem, in its construction and in the direct comments made on the author's technique (for example with regard to the carefully calculated use of the digression), leaves no doubt as

to the work's link with the teaching of the grammarians; and the teaching of the schools on the elaboration and ornamentation of a text (for example through the use of the so-called 'colours' of rhetoric) is also reflected in a wealth of stylistic details.

Although, as we shall see, the *Poema de Fernán González* draws on a variety of sources, written and almost certainly oral, and, like the *Libro de Alexandre*, very successfully binds them together in a carefully constructed whole, it is not characterized by either the complexity of construction or the conspicuous emphasis on learning and artistry that were fundamental to its predecessor. We do not find in the *Poema*, for example, the long descriptive digressions which are so prominent a feature of the *Libro de Alexandre*. Nevertheless, in the *Poema*'s construction we do find evidence of similar stylistic concerns, for example in the handling of the digression in praise of Spain and especially Castile in stanzas 145–159. In introducing the digression the poet states clearly his reason for doing so: 'Therefore do I tell you, that you may see it clearly: | the land in which you live is a finer land than others' (145ab). He shows concern that he should not be seen to err by making his digression too long: 'I wish to leave this matter; I have told you enough; | I wish to say no more, lest I lapse into error' (153ab). And he makes the same point again on concluding: 'With this, I wish to put an end to this account, | for I fear that to continue might put me at fault' (159ab). By the end of the twelfth century the emphasis on brevity was considered one of the most important of the precepts of the grammarians (see, for example, Rico 1985, 141–142), and, like both the author of the *Alexandre* and Gonzalo de Berceo, our poet has this firmly in his mind.[18] There are several other points at which the concern to avoid verbosity becomes apparent in the *Poema* (see, for example, 270a, 329a, 431ab and also 127ab when the poet insists on the need for the account on which he is about to embark). It could certainly be that there is a direct reflection here of what has been learned in the classroom of the grammarians, but we should also bear in mind that the author of the *Poema de Fernán González* had at his disposal a number of stylistic models. It is evident that he had access to and knew in detail the *Libro de Alexandre*, and José Hernando Pérez's important study (2001, 126–141) demonstrates that both of these vernacular poems share both stylistic concerns and very close verbal parallels with each other, and also with

---

[18] For Berceo, see, for example, *Los Milagros de Nuestra Señora*, the opening of 'El milagro de Teófilo', stanza 749 (704) (see Dutton 1971, 211), where the poet says that to err in this respect would be to 'sin' ('peccar'); this is the same term used by the *Alexandre* poet for the kind of error that must be avoided in the *mester de clerecía*.

Diego García de Campos' *Planeta* (see section 2(vi) above). Our poet was, in short, working within an already well developed literary tradition.

We should look briefly at some of the stylistic features in the *Poema* which seem to correspond to the teachings of the grammarians. There are, apart from the section in praise of Spain and Castile (in fact based largely on a passage from Lucas de Tuy's *Chronicon Mundi*), very few descriptive passages. One is the account of the Wheel of Fortune (stanzas 441–444) which forms part of the Count's harangue to his troops. Built around a series of antitheses and making full use of repetition, parallelism and symmetry in form (including an example of chiasmus in d), stanza 442 is a very good example of our poet's art:

> It is not called Fortune for remaining in one state,
> with one man always rich and another always poor;
> Fortune is quick to reverse these two states:
> it makes the poor man rich and the rich man needy.

It is also an excellent example of the art of the rhetorician as the Count goes on to argue how those who in the past have suffered cruel defeat will now emerge as victors. It should also be pointed out, however, how a very similar passage is placed by the *Alexandre* poet in the mouth of the defeated Darius (1652–1655), with a return to the same theme in a memorable moralizing passage (1805ff.), and again in the description of Alexander's tent (2532). There are close verbal and stylistic parallels between the passages which appear in the two poems and it seems that here, as in many other respects, the *Poema de Fernán González* was drawing directly and consciously on the earlier poem. The Wheel of Fortune is placed in a Christianized context by both *clerecía* poets (see stanza 443 of the *Poema*) and as such it was a topic which could serve preachers as the basis of a moral lesson. This is exactly how it is exploited by the *Alexandre* poet – to lead into a lengthy and powerful critique of human failings; on the other hand, what is probably most striking in the *Poema de Fernán González* is the restrained and concise use that its author makes of the device.

Another descriptive topic which is recommended in the treatises of the grammarians is the *locus amoenus* or depiction of a place of beauty. It is quite common for such descriptive digressions to be included, set in an ironic context, as the scene where a bloody conflict is about to take place, and the *Alexandre* offers a very good example of this in stanzas 935–940 which describes the idyllic scene of a spreading laurel and an orchard set on a low hill constantly watered by a fountain; a place of beauty indeed.

The author of the *Poema* also includes two brief descriptions of the natural setting for a battle: the first is depicted very briefly in 313b as 'a beautiful meadow'; the second (in stanza 754) is also marked by its conciseness but the emphasis is a very different one:

> The two armies clashed in a deep-sided valley,
> a fine place for hunting for rabbit and hare;
> they gather there much grain to make the red dye,
> and the torrent of the Ebro does rage at its foot.

Instead of a gentle hill there is a deep valley and the cool stream is replaced by the waters of an angry river. The detail of the red dye suggests powerfully the blood which is to flow and the image of the hunt picks up a metaphor which is fundamental to the meaning of the poem. There is little sense here that the poet had in mind a literary convention or the need to follow the teachings of the grammarians, but rather that he had an instinctive grasp of how to use detail to powerful dramatic effect.

Much has been made of the presence in the work of the *clerecía* poets of devices of stylistic ornament recommended by the literary theorists.[19] We have already looked briefly at the use in battle scenes of the natural imagery conventional in learned epic. It must be emphasized that there are many direct parallels, for example, in the *Libro de Alexandre*; but we should also bear in mind that those images of wolves and lambs, lions and serpents have many possible biblical sources, as indeed have those of rivers of blood, the echoing of mountains and the quaking of hills and valleys, or the image of the beast used for the Devil (see Revelation 20:10). Sometimes there are specific biblical sources for the *Poema*'s images: for example, that of the wheat and the chaff in 49d (see Matthew 3:12); and probably too that of the clap of thunder in 593a (see Revelation 4:5 and 10:3). In such cases the presence of metaphors and similes is certainly not necessarily evidence that the poet is following the prescriptions of literary theorists. In the same way, what can be defined as an example of metonymy, such as 'una lança dudada' (literally, 'a lance that struck fear': 123c) or 'cuerpo de grand valor' (literally, 'a body of great worth': 170d) can also be categorized as epic epithets typical of popular narrative poetry (see section 3(iii), above). And when in stanza 344ab we find a simile in which the Count's men contrast his constant restlessness with the forces of Nature,

---

[19] See, for example, the emphasis on 'rhetorical' features in the introduction to Itzíar López Guil's edition of the *Poema* (2001, 49ff.).

> We see winds that rage fiercely tire and fade,
> and we can watch the angry sea grow calm

it is striking to see that its inclusion has been directly prompted, albeit with a marked change of emphasis, by a passage in the *Alexandre* (2274–2278) in which the hero's followers comment on the energy which leads him to struggle endlessly to outdo Nature's powers. In short, then, although in his deployment of imagery our poet makes use of a variety of stylistic models, there is so far very little evidence to suggest that he is consciously putting into practice the teachings of the grammarians.

Without doubt the author of the *Poema de Fernán González*, as an aid to composition, makes extensive use of different linguistic devices involving different forms of repetition and parallelism which could be classified as figures of diction or 'colours'. The very form of duplication which we looked at above as typical of oral formulaic style, such as 'Por lloro nin por llanto' ('In their weeping and wailing': 243a) or 'recabdé tu mensaje e cunplí tu mandado' ('I carried out your message and fulfilled your command': 48c), could be classified as *interpretatio*, essentially repetition of an idea in different words as a form of amplification.

Balance and parallelism are fundamental to our poet's use of his medium; for example, when in 607bc he emphasizes the force of the Castilians' lament in a series of parallel phrases bound together by the repetition of forms of 'mucho' and also 'roto':

> mucho vestido negro,   rota mucha capiella,
> rascadas muchas fruentes,   rota mucha mexiella;

> (many black clothes of mourning, many hoods ripped in grief,
> many brows being clawed at and cheeks that were scratched;)

Our poet quite often employs verbal repetition to achieve an effect of intensity or dramatic power as in the Christians' prayer in stanzas 105–113, with its recurrent use of 'libreste' ('You freed') and other second person singular verbs. Sometimes repetition extends to a substantial proportion of a line, as in 328cd where the effect is to emphasize the relentless force of the conflict:

> daban e resçebían   mucha buena lançada,
> daban e resçebían   mucha buena porrada.

> (many fine lance thrusts were given and received,
> and they gave and received many more struck by clubs.)

There are also more subtle forms of repetition, such as in 80cd, where the verb 'tornar' is not only used to end one line and begin the next but also employed in two different senses:

a los dueños primeros   les sería tornada;
tornaron en el canpo   ellos otra vegada.

(to the land's first lords she was to be restored;
and to the field once more they now returned.)

To good effect, too, the poet's praise of Fernán González in battle (542cd) is lent force by parallelism of structure combined with the use of two words similar in form:

nunca podrié ser malo   el que con él se viesse;
mejor devrié ser d'otro   el que con él visquiesse.

(none who met him could ever be inclined towards evil,
and any man who lived with him must be of finer nature.)

At times, moreover, it becomes apparent that the poet relishes the opportunity for word-play and for sound effects, as in the bitterness achieved by near repetition in 585d: 'una carta ditada con un falso ditado' ('a letter dictated with a mendacious dictation'); in the alliteration of 368d: '¡Sal, sal acá al canpo! Cata a don Fernando!' ('Out, out, to the field! Come look upon Fernando!'); and in 740d the sense of joyful mockery as Sancho fails to pay his debt: 'plaçié l' de voluntad del plaço que passava' ('and deep was his elation at how late it became').

Our poet's verse form naturally lends itself to the use of antithesis, which can include the use of chiasmus, as in 'los pobres eran ricos e los ricos menguados' ('the poor were made rich and the rich brought low': 97d). In 680ab the effect of the contrast is heightened by the use of two pairs of synonyms set directly against each other:

La dueña, que estava   triste e desmayada,
fue con aquestas nuevas   alegre e pagada;

(The lady, whose mood was of sadness and despair,
grew joyful and contented on hearing this news;)

Or more simply, in 650ab careful placement of words at the end of a line gives a heightened sense of contrast:

El falso descreído, lleno de crüeldat,
más que si fuessen canes non ovo pïedat;

(The false unbeliever, who was brimful of cruelty –
had they been dogs he might have shown them more pity;)

Skilfully, too, in the description of the Wheel of Fortune, two different words formed from the same root are contrasted with powerful effect: 'el que suel' ser vençido será el vençedor' ('the one accustomed to defeat will be the victor': 443d).

Our poet is certainly not unique in his use of such techniques, but from this brief study it should be clear that he exploits very effectively the characteristic features of his learned medium. He works adeptly within the conventions of the *cuaderna vía* verse form, which by the mid-thirteenth century were well established; as we have already shown, this is in no sense incompatible with the extensive exploitation of stylistic features commonly associated with oral composition. He does not seek, as does the author of the *Libro de Alexandre*, to impress by his knowledge of literary technique; and it is, perhaps, surprising that he does not exploit the descriptive digression which is such a prominent aspect of the *Alexandre*. Rather, as we have seen, his descriptive technique is based on the use of telling details, concisely expressed, usually with the aim of setting people or places within a clear moral framework and within the context of the poem as a whole. One of the most striking characteristics of the *Poema de Fernán González* is its pace and the speed, almost overwhelming at times, with which we are moved on from one episode to the next. Its author was undoubtedly a man of learning, and he makes extensive use of stylistic features associated with the linguistic teachings of the grammarians who taught in the schools and universities. These are fundamental to the way in which he exploits his medium, but there are in the *Poema* many echoes of the language of epic and popular poetry. There are also at one point, it must be added, echoes of the more refined world of courtly love and of terminology that belongs to the language of the Provençal troubadours (see note to 636a and also section 3(vi), below). It is precisely in the way in which diverse elements are woven together that the strength and the originality of the *Poema* lie.

(v) The construction of the Poema: *features of folk narrative?*
Before moving on to consider the *Poema*'s themes and how they relate to the historical and social developments which lay behind it, it will be helpful to

look briefly at how it is constructed and at some other aspects of its origins. Without doubt our starting point has to be the significance of the number three in its structure, which has been analysed in considerable detail by Jean Paul Keller (1990, 11–21). Keller points to the opening invocation to the Holy Trinity and to the fact that the *Poema* consists of three main sections: the history of the Gothic, Asturian and Leonese kings up to the advent of Fernán González; the narrative of the Count's military victories over the Moors and over the kingdom of Navarre; and the third section, beginning with the first mention of the Leonese monarch Sancho I, which is centred around the winning of independence for Castile. Keller argues that each of these main sections is in turn subdivided into three elements and then goes on (1990, 13) to examine how throughout the poem the number three is repeatedly used as a 'surface decoration':

> FG is said to be one of three brothers, which was not true. There were three hermits in the chapel discovered by FG on his boar hunt. Of the three, one would have been enough for only one, Pelayo, speaks. He foretells, among other things, difficulties within three days. To encourage his men to fight in the first battle against the Moslems, the hero said that the enemy was not worth three beans, that thirty wolves (the Castilians) would kill thirty thousand sheep (the enemy). In this battle, our hero faced the foe with three hundred horsemen. The second battle with Almanzor's forces was also full of the number three. The hero divided his army into three parts of three, six and six thousand men respectively. They attacked from three quarters, and would not have fled if the thirty thousand enemy troops had been three times as many. The battle lasted three days and pursuit ended on the third day, and FG completed a threesome of kings killed. There were three battles against Navarre of which the last is merely a filler, with no apparent purpose other than to complete another threesome.

Keller goes on to suggest two consequences for this emphasis on the number three: firstly that there was a resulting need for the poet to draw on a range of disparate sources in order to increase the number of threes available to him; and secondly that such a preconceived structure shackled him to such an extent as to reduce his work's dramatic power. His essential argument – that adherence to a predetermined plan has a significant effect on the structure of the *Poema* – is a plausible one, and could be seen as an explanation for the way in which one episode appears to follow another at a relentless pace. It could also explain some cases of duplication in the poem's construction, for example the way in which a single episode from the chronicles has been elaborated into two separate accounts of the defeat of Navarrese kings (see note to 703c). We shall see, too, how our poet has drawn in turn from a number of different sources in the course of elaborating his narrative. Perhaps Keller overstates the case, but there can be no doubt that the author of the *Poema de Fernán González* does tend consistently to use ternary structures and to use the number three in various other ways in the course of his narrative. It is not surprising that a cleric deeply practised in the exegesis of the Scriptures should make so much of this numerical symbolism, but others have given a different explanation for the prominence in the *Poema* of the number three.

Beverly West, for example, argues that the poet's repeated emphasis on the number three 'reflects not a conscious, deliberate effort of elaborate poetic structure and ornamentation, but the most basic, naive, and uncontaminated law of folk narrative' (1983, 129–30). West goes far beyond this in highlighting episodes or details in the *Poema* which seem to have their roots in folkloric motifs. There are a large number of elements of the *Poema* which she considers to be among these, for example: the tale of the hero's birth, infancy and return into the community; the hunt and prophecy episode, involving the separation, initiation and return of the hero who has undergone a symbolic death and resurrection; many features of the description of the battle of Hacinas (see below); the two episodes involving the Count's imprisonment and liberation by Sancha, constituting a process of initiation for the heroine and both involving a very high concentration of folk motifs, 'much greater than one would expect to find in Spanish epic' (1983, 156); and the horse and hawk episode leading to the liberation of Castile, which could be based on an Oriental tale (1983, 72; for parallels in Arab histories, see also our note to 576a–c). That there are numerous such elements in our poet's work that embody folkloric motifs, there can be no doubt; but we certainly cannot make the automatic assumption that they are evidence of a popular origin, that is to say based essentially on oral tradition, for what he writes.

We might consider, for example, the account of the origins of Castile in stanza 173, where the founding of the kingdom takes place in three stages: 'A poor municipality they turned into a county; | the county they later made the head of a kingdom'. There is a parallel to this in the *Aeneid*'s version of the founding of Rome, again full of threes: according to Jupiter's prophecy (*Aeneid* 1.257–296), Aeneas will rule in Latium for 3 years; Ascanius, his son, will rule for 30, and move the throne to Alba Longa, whence their descendants will then rule for 300 years; then Romulus will found Rome, the third stage of development in the seat of their power (Latium-Alba Longa-Rome). Our point is not that there is any question of direct borrowing here, but rather that a parallel detail may be found in a poem of undoubtedly learned origins and authorship. The kind of folkloric features that have been mentioned above are as common in 'learned' texts as in popular epic and they do not provide evidence for the existence of an epic tradition behind a work of 'learned' origin like the *Poema de Fernán González*. Deyermond and Chaplin, at the end of their study of the use of folk-motifs in medieval Spanish texts, conclude that 'since so much of the content of Spanish epics is folk-motif, and so much of the rest is ecclesiastical (some, of course, falls into both categories), it becomes even harder to accept the *neotradicionalista* view that the typical Spanish epic was composed by a *juglar* at the time of the events or very soon afterwards, that it is historically accurate, and that its interests are entirely secular' (1972, 52). Certainly, the evidence that we have considered so far does not provide the basis of a convincing argument that the *Poema* is underpinned by an account of the hero's life which is of great antiquity, nor that such accounts as existed were characterized by any real sense of historical accuracy; and, on the other hand, it is beyond doubt that the monastic and educational world of the mid-thirteenth century played a critical role in the work's genesis. This is an appropriate point at which to suggest how our poet may have set about his task.

(vi) The creation of the Poema*: drawing together the materials*

When he embarked on the task of compiling his account of the life and achievements of Fernán González, set within the context of Christian Spain's struggle against Islam, Castile's rise to dominance, and the ambitions and enterprises of his own king, our poet had at his disposal a variety of resources. In his mind he will have had a very limited amount of vaguely historical knowledge about the Count's life. He will have known that he was a successful warrior and champion of his people against the Islamic invaders and that he helped to win independence for Castile; that he was imprisoned by the kings of both León and Pamplona/Navarre and that his (first) wife, Sancha, was daughter of the ruler of Pamplona/Navarre. He was also acutely aware of the importance of Fernán González's relationship with the monastery of San Pedro de Arlanza, and he seems to have known that the wife of Sancho I of León was called Teresa, even though he falsely links her to the kings of Pamplona/Navarre. He will also have been acquainted with various aspects of local legend associated with the Count, and crucially he will have had access to monastic archives giving him the names of his hero's contemporaries and lieutenants. There is little more solid historical fact than this in the *Poema*.

It seems certain that by the time of the *Poema*'s composition there were tales already in existence dealing with the imprisonment and freeing of the Count (on two occasions) and also recounting the episode of the horse and the hawk and the independence of Castile. These elements, it is generally agreed, are essentially novelesque in tone; apart from short skirmishes, the skill of the warrior plays no part in them. There are well-known parallels in epic for the Count's colourful liberation: Fernán González's escape dressed as a women recalls Achilles dressed in a nun's clothes to escape detection; and the motif of the woman who sets free an imprisoned hero has numerous parallels in French epic (Cotrait 1977, 67–68), which could have fired our poet's imagination. The Castilian court was richly supplied with both performers and poets providing entertainment in a number of languages (see section 2(vi), above) and it should be borne in mind that Spanish audiences undoubtedly had experience of the performances of French *jongleurs* along the road to Santiago which ran through our poet's homeland. It is quite possible, then, that our poet had some knowledge of French epic, but for narratives which place particular emphasis on the figure of the lady who plays a prominent and assertive role we might also look to the courtly romance. It is not certain that the existence of a wealth of folk-motifs in the *Poema* is evidence of reliance on an earlier popular epic: the imagery and some of the themes of the episodes of the *Poema* are quite close to those which characterize *romans courtois*, such as the works of Chrétien de Troyes, whose Arthurian romances drew extensively on Celtic themes and imagery. We make no suggestion here of a direct borrowing, but it would be well worth examining further the parallels between the *Poema* and a courtly romance like *Erec et Enide*; the French poem examines the relationship between husband and wife within the chivalric world and a significant part of the poem centres around the test in which Enide proves her worth, with the emphasis falling eventually on her decision to play an active rather than passive role. The image of the hunt (at whose use in the *Poema* we shall look more closely in section 4(ix)) is important in the French poem, as is that of the sparrow-hawk that the knights seek to win; and both of these motifs, along with the theme of the trials endured by lovers in adversity, are of fundamental importance in the world of the courtly narrative.[20] Chrétien

---

[20] A good example of their treatment is in the *Lais* of Marie de France, composed during

wrote in the last third of the twelfth century and his patron was Marie de Champagne, daughter of Eleanor of Aquitaine and half-sister of Eleanor (Leonor), wife of Alfonso VIII. It has already been pointed out that the court of Alfonso VIII (particularly under the influence of Leonor) and later that of Fernando III were frequented by numerous French poets. It could well be in just such an environment that, as part of the developing interest in the story of Fernán González, there was elaborated the tale of the loyalty and initiative displayed by the lady who, after overcoming a series of trials, was to become the Count's wife. This could help to explain the striking emphasis in this section of the *Poema* on the part played by a wife and partner in authority. The role often played in the French romance by the horses and hawks as chivalric symbols and in relationship with the process of courtship could possibly shed new light on the significance of these items in the *Poema*. There are numerous other examples of the use in the *Poema* of the language and imagery of courtly love: Sancha is presented initially as a '[l]ady with no pity, or proper understanding' (624a), the archetypal cold courtly lady; the image of the pilgrim, closely associated with the relationship between Sancha and the Count (notably in the account of his liberation from prison in León) is one much used by courtly love poets, as can be seen, for example, in the *Roman de la Rose*, in which it is a central element; the count introduced in stanza 614 (another pilgrim) is from Lombardy, a region associated with courtly love (see note to 614a), and his role in convincing Sancha can be associated with the stage of supplication, the first part of the courtly love process (López Guil 2001, 83); the scene of the Count's captivity becomes the prison of love and his cruel suffering (seen in 620c) is unambiguously depicted as that of the courtly lover (637a); Sancha talks of 'buen amor' ('true love', a term which here is equivalent to *fin' amors*, the refined love of the devoted courtly lover, though in this case it is the lady rather than the lover who expresses it); Sancha describes how she has been overcome by the charms of the 'entendedor' (a word which was used to denote a particular stage in a courtly relationship); and the image of the lover swearing homage to his lady is likewise fundamental to the language of the troubadour. It might seem confusing that the author of the *Poema* is using the image of

the late twelfth century. Although the emphasis in Marie's poems is very different from the heroic tone of the *Poema de Fernán González*, it is worth listing some of the motifs that they share: the hunt (in several of the *Lais*), a chapel in the woods, the death of a hermit, a donation to an abbey, imprisonment, a lady who takes the initiative in love and another who plays a prominent part in saving her lover, a noble child entrusted to others, and the hawk and palfrey as a symbol of power.

prison at the same time in the context of the trials of a courtly lover and also to denote a spiritual death from which the Count and his people are to be restored. This double meaning might be less surprising if we see him as building this part of his poem around a courtly text which already existed. There is no doubt that our poet had come into contact with the work of poets of the courtly world or knew their work (either in a Castilian form or in French, Provençal, or just possibly Galician Portuguese), and it is at least possible that he had access to a courtly romance on which he drew in composing some parts of the final section of his poem. If this is the case, we could be dealing essentially not with a lost 'popular' epic but with a lost courtly romance.

It is generally agreed that the author of the *Poema de Fernán González* had access to several learned sources, among them the *Liber regum* (*Book of Kings*), a chronicle of Aragonese origin (see note to 14c), which, in compiling the first section of the *Poema*, he supplemented with material taken from other works including the *Chronicon Mundi* (*Chronicle of the World*) composed by Lucas de Tuy. He was possibly also acquainted with Rodrigo Jiménez de Rada's *De rebus Hispaniae* (*On the Affairs of Spain*) and of the works of Saint Isidore at least the *Historia Gothorum* (*History of the Goths*). He also knew the *Historia Turpini* (also known as the *Pseudo-Turpin Chronicle*; see note to 134b) and the *Crónica najerense* (the *Chronicle of Nájera*; see notes to 163b, 695a and 703c). That is to say, in elaborating his poem he seems to have had access to a range of the most important historical sources available to Castilian scholars of his age. In addition, of course, he had an extensive biblical knowledge, of which he made ample use, and, as we have seen, he also had access to some of the most important vernacular Castilian poems written in the first half of the thirteenth century: the *Libro de Alexandre* and a number of works by Gonzalo de Berceo. Equipped with this impressive array of scholarship, he set about establishing the political and religious context within which to set the achievements of his hero, and it is to the creation of this historical framework, with its clear implications for the events of both the age of the Count and that of the poet himself, that he devotes the first clearly defined section of the *Poema*, taking us up to stanza 170, the point at which Fernán González himself appears on the scene.

As we have seen, the poet seems to have had at his disposal some kind of narrative dealing with the 'historical core' of his work: the Count's infamous period(s) of imprisonment, also mentioned in the *Crónica najerense*, and the question of independence, with Fernando's disputes with the Leonese monarchy also being mentioned by Lucas de Tuy and Rodrigo Jiménez de Rada. This section clearly begins at stanza 571 in our text. What remained for the poet now was to establish clearly Fernán González's credentials as a warrior, a Christian hero and the defender of his people. At the same time he had to ensure that the Count's career was clearly seen to be intertwined with the prosperity of the monastery of San Pedro de Arlanza and that this holy community could be demonstrated to have played a crucial part in his triumph. Clearly the poet had models on which to draw in his account of his hero's great victories and we have seen how scholars have tended to view his poem as a reworking of a lost epic. We have also seen that there are clear stylistic echoes of the world of popular epic – and, for example, that the poet's descriptive technique, based on sharply defined judgments and concisely expressed visual details, has much in common with that of orally composed poetry. On the other hand, there is convincing evidence that, in order to enhance the stature of the Count as a warrior representing all of Christendom in a struggle against the dark powers of Islam, it was to the greatest of the warriors of antiquity that he first looked: he found the ideal model for his hero in the protagonist of the *Libro de Alexandre*.

For a public closely associated with the Arlanzón valley, the setting of the *Poema de Fernán González* is undeniably a recognisably local one – recognition of which may well have helped create a sense of historical reality – and the Count's triumphs are set within a closely defined area. The great battle against Abd al-Rahman III, which took place outside the walls of Simancas on the banks of the Duero, has, for example, been moved to Hacinas (see note to 392ab), close to the monasteries of Arlanza and Silos, where it is certain that no such conflict has occurred. What our poet does seem to have known, however, was that the great conflict lasted for two days without resolution but was followed by a lengthy pursuit of the enemy (though in reality this was a matter of several days). Other episodes such as the capture of Carazo (see note to stanza 171) have a setting which is convincing enough, but clearly cannot have occurred there, at least in the way in which they are recounted in the *Poema*. Moreover, the battles against the kingdom of Pamplona/Navarre never took place but, as has already been suggested, the hostility that they imply is a reflection of the political situation at the time that the poem was composed (with perhaps echoes, too, of a famous eleventh-century triumph). We would search in vain for sources which could relate many of the events recounted in the *Poema* to those of the Count's own day, for they are often essentially a fiction, based upon a literary source but given a sense of historical reality by a wealth of recognizable geographical detail and, for example, the use of names and details which were available to the poet in the documentation and correspondence to which he had access.

Scholars have long been aware of the obvious debt of the *Poema de Fernán González* to the *Libro de Alexandre*. There are numerous detailed verbal parallels and the similarities between the narrative formulae that figure in the two texts have led to the suggestion that both works were written by the same author. This belief is fundamental to the argument of Hernando Pérez's study (2001), in the course of which he adduces a wealth of specific verbal parallels between the two texts (see, for example, pp. 126–141). We shall examine here just one brief verbal parallel and the way in which the borrowed material has been exploited: a line which some scholars have labelled formulaic, and evidence of a direct borrowing from oral tradition – 'en los pueblos paganos fazié grand mortandat' ('he inflicted much slaughter on the pagan troops': 506b); in fact this line appears in a very similar form in the *Alexandre* (for example in 984c). In the *Poema de Fernán González* variations of the phrase 'fazer grand mortandat' ('to inflict great slaughter') are used seven times in the course of quite a short section of text describing the battle at Hacinas, which also contains other evident borrowings from the *Alexandre* (see below); but it is, moreover, a reflection of the poet's careful and deliberate artistry that the heavy use of this phrase during the description of the battle is anticipated by a precise verbal parallel in Pelayo's prophecy about how it will be fought (408b).[21] Our poet does not just make extensive use of the earlier poem but manipulates it with great skill.

We now wish to look briefly at some examples of how both in substantial sections and also with regard to specific details, elements of the *Poema* may have been suggested by the *Alexandre*. To adapt and elaborate a source in this way was, of course, seen as an essential part of the medieval poet's art, and, indeed, this is precisely what the *Alexandre* poet had done with his own principal source, the *Alexandreis*, a learned school text which could itself have been known to the author of the *Poema*. It has been pointed out, for example (see Deyermond 1960, 37), that Nuño Laíno's accusation in 342c that the Count is guilty of *codiçia* (greed) is not appropriate to the account that has been given of his actions and motives, but is rather a direct allusion to the fatal flaw which marks the character of Alexander in the *Alexandre*. More than this, of course, it comes in the course of a lengthy passage (stanzas

---

[21] For a different interpretation of this evidence, see West (1983, 142–143; 148–149).

336–358), full of verbal reminiscences of the earlier poem, in which the hero's exhausted followers plead for his campaigning to stop and in return are convinced that they must continue to give him their unconditional support. The Count's reply not only uses Alexander's own reasoning but even alludes to him directly in terms which make the borrowing unmistakeable (see note to stanza 354). It could not be more apparent that our poet, in depicting the heroism and restless energy of Fernán González, has Alexander firmly in mind, to the extent that he imbues the medieval count with the desire for glory and undying fame which marked the hero of antiquity.

There are numerous other significant borrowings which help to shape our poet's narrative; for example the correspondence with King Sancho (289–299) which echoes that of Alexander with Darius, in each case the powerful opponent dismissing the hero as mad to take on such a conflict, and in each poem identical words are used – 'de seso menguado' ('much lacking in sense': *Poema* 297a; *Alexandre* 781a). Just as the *Libro de Alexandre* places great emphasis on its hero's skills as an orator, repeatedly convincing his men of the need to continue their campaigning, so too Fernán González is shown delivering powerful harangues to his troops. More precisely, through the *Alexandre* there runs a thread of advice to adopt a cautious approach being given by Alexander's counsellors (usually the unfortunate Parmenion), advice which is promptly rejected. In stanzas 200–225 of the *Poema* the debate follows exactly the same course: the Count asks his followers for advice and it is Gonzalo Díaz who advises caution, thus incurring a stern rebuke from his lord who proceeds to harangue his troops about the need for direct and valiant action. The way in which the character and actions of the hero of the *Poema* are conceived, and many of his experiences, mirror closely the case of Alexander: for example, the dismay and determination of the young Fernán González on learning of the Castilians' suffering at the hands of a foreign people seems to be a reflection of the anguish felt by Alexander when, still a child, he learns of how the Greeks are held in subjection by the rulers of Babylon. Alexander summons a scholar to display his learning by explaining to his troops the workings of an eclipse and thus allaying their fears. Conveniently, the apparition of the serpent gives the Count (in 476–483) a similar opportunity to put his own men's minds at rest, albeit with a rather less learned explanation. Alexander was memorably confronted by a formidable giant in battle; so is Fernán González (stanza 491). If Alexander's horse famously died beneath him in battle, then it is appropriate that the Count's steed should suffer the same fate (down to the gruesome details of the hanging entrails – see note to 496d). We may perhaps wonder why so much is made of the honour paid to the Count of Poitou after his death in battle. The answer surely lies in our poet's attempt to depict Fernán González showing the same generosity to a defeated foe as does Alexander towards Darius and his family; indeed, the French regent (see note to 331ab) may well have been introduced precisely as a figure sufficiently illustrious to merit such treatment. There are many more parallels, which extend to close details of wording and imagery; indeed, it is worth noting just how many of the linguistic features of the *Poema*'s battle scenes can also be found in the *Alexandre*, often involving close verbal parallels (see, for example, Hernando Pérez 2001, 300–330). The picture of the Muslim troops as like Satan coming up from hell seems to evoke the vision of the infernal council which gathers as a prelude to Alexander's death. Finally, the importance of the Arlanza episodes for our poet seems clear, but it might even be suggested that in the back of his mind here was Alexander's famous visit to the shrine of Ammon (*Alexandre* 1167ff.).

In section 3(iv), above, we looked at examples of stylistic techniques which the *Poema de Fernán González* shares with other *mester de clerecía* poems. The evidence that we have given here points clearly to the powerful influence of a particular learned source, the *Libro de Alexandre*, on what our poet saw as appropriate for inclusion in his portrait of a hero and on the way in which that portrait was presented. There has certainly been no attempt here to argue that the language, style and themes of orally composed epic play no part in the *Poema de Fernán González*. Its poet had few models for composition in the vernacular, which was, of course, essentially the spoken word. There can be no doubt that he was familiar with the language of oral poetry and that this will have been in his mind as he composed. On the other hand, we have tried to show that the *Poema* is unlikely to be essentially a reworking of a lost epic, as has often been claimed. Almost certainly there lay behind it an oral tradition, though probably not ancient but developed during the previous century. This would have been known to the poet in either an oral or a written form, or both, and the sophisticated art of the court troubadours may have played a part in its elaboration. Without doubt the poet also made use of several written sources which included both chronicles and other *cuaderna vía* poems, notably the *Libro de Alexandre*, on which he relied to a considerable extent. The essence of his artistry lies in the way in which he combined these disparate materials to form a poem which embodied not just a plea on behalf of the monastery for which he worked but also a commentary on the events of his own day. We shall examine the nature of that commentary in the final section of this introduction.

4. Kingship and the social order, conquest and crusade: the themes of the Poema de Fernán González

(i) The portrait of the hero

The *Poema de Fernán González* is, first and foremost, a celebration of a great Castilian hero. So close is the identification of the hero and his nation that to a significant extent the poem is in fact a celebration of Castile itself. It is appropriate, therefore, to start by establishing the characteristics of the Count as he appears in the *Poema*.

The poet's view of his hero is, as we have seen above (see section 3(iii)), summed up clearly and concisely in the series of epithets that are applied to him: 'the good Count', 'the ablest of men', 'the fortune-favoured count', 'that man of great deeds', 'a man with no cruelty in him', 'his men's loyal leader', 'a man well schooled', and 'the epitome of valour, | a lord of fine conduct, distinguished in learning'. In case all of this should create a misleadingly gentle picture, he is also closely associated with animal imagery emphasizing his ferocity in battle: he is described as 'raging wilder than a serpent' (518a), as 'doing as a wolf does when set among the flocks' (501b) and in stanza 490 he appears as the most fearsome of opponents:

> He raged through the lines like a ravenous lion,
> and felt a great passion to conquer or die;
> everywhere he went, he left the field soaked in blood,
> passing over many souls to the hideous beast.

He is also repeatedly, as we shall see, identified with the imagery of the hunt, including two of its most important symbols: the horse and the hawk.

This initial portrait seems to be full of contradictions, but it is, on the whole, borne out by what we see of the Count's conduct as it is depicted throughout the *Poema*. At the heart of this apparent inconsistency is the contrast between the hero's quiet piety, purity of heart and acceptance of God's will (and that of the Church), and the ferocity he shows when defending his people or when confronted by the infidel. Just such a combination of pious devotion and the winning of worldly renown through military force lay at the heart of the notion of chivalry and of the crusading ideal.[22] Repeatedly

---

[22] See, for example, Maurice Keen (1984, 55) who states that by the end of the twelfth century '[t]he crusade has become a great chivalrous adventure, in which the service of God and the quest for earthly renown and reward have become so interlaced that it is no longer practical to seek to unravel the strands'. Where Fernán González seems to differ from this model is that, although he ultimately achieves great fame, he has not sought it (except in the sense of striving to set a fine example to others), and the material gain that he has pursued has

Fernán González's Muslim foes are described as 'unbelieving people(s)' (as in 15b or 513a) or '[t]he accursed people' (392a) and it is as such that they are dispatched to the Devil for punishment. The hero's first words in the poem, on hearing of Castile's state of oppression, take the form of a prayer to Christ for assistance in bringing liberation. The Count accepts that his people may have erred and asks for forgiveness on their behalf. He is wise and caring; unlike Alexander, he is not driven by pride and greed, but he does understand very clearly the importance of setting a fine example through valour and noble conduct: as he explains to his troops, 'but fine deeds remain, and these will live on, | in which those yct to come find their example' (352cd). He is an outstanding orator who repeatedly inspires his men and carries them with him at times of danger. If he feels that his men are weakening he does not hesitate to drive them on with cruel taunts and bitter words (697–698). But he is an inspiration in life and battle, and as he urges on his troops against the Muslims, the poet comments (542) that:

> I know no man in the world who listened to the Count
> and could have felt any fear, in the slightest respect;
> none who met him could ever be inclined towards evil,
> and any man who lived with him must be of finer nature.

When he seems to be facing death he shows exemplary courage, seeking to die rather than to live defeated (549–550) and his real concern is that Castile should not be left without a lord, soon to fall into the hands of a cruel Muslim conqueror. Fernán González is a fearless warrior indeed, but the one occasion on which he feels terror (413a) is when confronted by the apparition of Pelayo. With the exception of his outburst caused by his betrayal and capture (601–603), his attitude to all holy men and all representatives of the Church is one of quiet humility. When he first enters the hermitage as a hunter (230–232) he immediately lays aside all violent intent and prays to the Virgin for protection and pardon for his errors. On his next visit he again shows great piety and keeps his vigil, at one with God. He is an outstanding example of the chivalric ideal, of the knight who places himself at God's service. He is exemplary, too, in his generosity to San Pedro de Arlanza, and in the way in which he keeps his word by having himself – and his followers – buried in the monastery. Faultless to the point of explicit association with Christ, the Count seems incapable of weakness or any baseness of motive. Significantly, we are told (212) that he would not accept victory gained by deceit:

---

been for Castile rather than for himself.

To win by deceit is the worst of all things:
he who falls thus will fall into great error;
the Saviour died for his fight against deceit;
better to be deceived than a deceiver.

In the light of this, indeed, it would be difficult to see him later in the poem as the wilful deceiver of King Sancho of León: when the Count enters into the deal with Sancho over the horse and the hawk, it is presented as being in a spirit of generosity ('My lord, I would not sell them; but order them be taken. | I have no wish to sell you them; but give you them, I will': 577cd). What is subsequently agreed on, in a deal initiated by King Sancho rather than Fernán González, is a legitimate contract which is set out in precise legal terms. It is only towards the end of the poem that there is any sense that Sancho may have been deliberately ensnared, with the Count now pleased that Sancho is taking such a long time to pay. It is as though there is an unresolved contradiction here which derives from the poet's reluctance to present his hero as the originator of a deception, whilst this is precisely the role in which he has eventually to place him.

In short, Fernán González is presented throughout almost all the poem as an idealized figure. He is a hero to whom a king would be thoroughly contented to see himself compared. Unlike other famous heroes of medieval epic such as Alexander and Roland, he does not have a serious flaw which leads to his downfall; he is proud, but never arrogant and he wishes for conquest and gain not for himself but on behalf of his people and of Christianity. There are touches of humanity in his characterization (such as his quiet resignation when faced by death and his tearful separation from the count who has visited him in prison), but on the whole he is far from being portrayed as a distinctive and memorable individual. Rather, he is a character created to embody the strengths and achievements of a whole nation. To depict him as a rounded individual is, of course, not our poet's purpose, but it is worth, for example, looking at the development of his relationship with Sancha, where we might expect to see a more tender, intimate side of the hero's personality.

(ii) Sancha: a heroine in a masculine world of conflict

When Princess Sancha is approached by the Lombard count (stanzas 621ff.), she finds herself criticized as the cause of all of the problems that have beset Fernán González and his people. We have already seen (see section 3(vi), above) how as a '[l]ady with no pity, or proper understanding' (624a) she is already endowed with the characteristics of the heartless courtly lady whose hardness inflicts suffering on her suitor, and how in her encounter with the Count in his prison their relationship continues to be conducted in terms explicitly linked to the poetry of courtly love. Moreover, we have suggested that there could well be a link here with the world of courtly romance, with its narratives in which are worked out complex social questions like the relationship between love, marriage and duty. What is surely surprising here, particularly in the context of a poem so dominated by the values of a very masculine world, is the way in which Sancha takes the initiative in going to the prison, immediately declaring her love, proposing marriage, leading her husband-to-be out of the prison, carrying him part of the way, deceiving the lecherous archpriest and playing a major part in the latter's death. Her later exploit in freeing the Count again by means of a change of clothes could well be part of the same story (see note to stanza 599), used as the basis of a separate episode. Somewhat curiously, in response to this extraordinary strength of character, all that Fernando can manage is to recognize that this will be his salvation and agree to marry her. It is Sancha's hands that the Castilian people kiss in a gesture of loyalty, and it is to her that they apply the epic epithet associated with the greatest Castilian hero of all (see note to stanza 684). There may well be an allusion here to the prominent role of the women of the Castilian royal family and particularly Alfonso X's grandmother Berenguela and the critical act of homage that she received from the people of Castile in 1217, an episode of whose great importance we know that Alfonso was well aware (see note to stanza 684). As for the Count himself, he is warmly welcomed back by his people but in this episode roles seem to have been reversed and the valiant warrior has been completely overshadowed – both as a lover and also, indeed, as a hero. There could not be a greater contrast here with the depiction in the *Poema de Mio Cid* of Rodrigo Díaz's relationship with his wife and family, in which the hero's role is that of the confident protector who bids them watch him fight from the security of Valencia's battlements.

(iii) Castile and the Castilians: a chosen people
Although, naturally enough, he is mentioned in the *Poema*'s opening stanzas, Fernán González plays no part until the end of the long introductory section which constitutes about a fifth of the whole work. During this time the real protagonist has been Christian Spain, or, to be more precise, Castile. Alfonso X came to the throne in 1252 as the ruler of a large part of Christian Spain which was known as the Crown of Castile. He had, in particular, however, inherited the proud historical tradition of the kingdom of Castile, which was

now extending its cultural identity throughout the remainder of Alfonso's territories. The *Poema*, as we shall see, places great importance on the unity and harmony enjoyed by the state under a firm and successful monarch, but throughout it there is also an overwhelming emphasis on the role of the old kingdom of Castile and, indeed, of the poet's own homeland north of the river Duero. Perhaps the aim was to remind the King, who had spent the first years of his reign in the newly won territories of the south, that he should not neglect the northern lands where the reconquest had had its origins. Perhaps it was to relate the *Poema*'s content to a political message which had long been evolving among the scholars, propagandists and poets of the Castilian court. Certainly, Castile, closely identified with its heroic and virtuous leader, is here presented as the champion of Christianity against Islam and as the core from which the triumphant new Christian Spain had sprung. Already in the Spain of the Visigoths (themselves described in line 24c as 'singled out from among the whole world') the poet tells us that this region was held to be 'highly prized Castile'; and, he continues, 'the like of this province could nowhere else be found' (57cd). Against the Muslim invaders it was a bastion (87), which was defended by mountains and could only be approached by means of a well guarded mountain pass, such that eventually, 'nowhere worth a fig was there left in all Spain, | except the ancient land of Old Castile' (217cd). It was from Castile that the mighty Charlemagne was repulsed, just as later it was principally against Castile that al-Mansur was to direct his onslaughts. The poet's message about the origins of the triumphs of his own age is expressed with absolute clarity. While Spain is a land of unrivalled qualities, it is those of the original Castilian territories (the lands governed by the illustrious Count) which have made possible such great achievement (stanzas 157–158):

> But of all of Spain it is Castile that bears the palm,
> for it was of all the others the beginning and the strength
> and always of the Lord it stood in proper faith and fear,
> such that the Creator's will became to make it grow.

> Moreover, Old Castile, in my understanding,
> outmatches all others, for it was the foundation,
> and though of few people, their conquests were great;
> well can you see it in where all of this has led.

The poet points to conquest based on military power and Christian devotion, precisely the same qualities that stand out in the portrait of Fernán González. The essence of Castile's achievement lies in growth from 'a tiny little corner'

(171a), 'a small municipality' (172a), equipped with fine warriors, whose unswerving concern is to 'to raise up their lord to the highest of standing' (173b). By the time that the poet wrote, of course, the lord of Castile was the ruler of a vast territory that extended 'from sea to sea' (2d), a phrase repeated for emphasis in line 19a, and thus the *Poema* could be composed in praise of Castile, of the count who achieved so much in its name, and at the same time of the mighty king who now sought to carry on his conquests. Just as was the case with Alfonso's triumphant father and great-grandfather, Fernando III and Alfonso VIII, we are told of Fernán González that 'he brought wide new lands within the boundaries of Castile' (175c). The Count's success is viewed in terms of territorial expansion – terms which might well remind us of how Fernando is said to have declared that the kingship of his son Alfonso X should be judged.

Fernán González is, then, closely identified with the welfare and destiny of Castile. The first words that we hear him speak (179–182) are a prayer for help in enabling the Castilians to escape from their life of cruel oppression suffered at the hands of the Moors. He goes on to plead for divine aid in his struggle on behalf of his people, accepting that they may have erred (188), and this plea becomes one for not just freedom from oppression but also for vengeance (186b). In battle, Fernando, with his cry of 'Castile' and with his heartfelt cries of encouragement (as in 222a), is naturally enough identified very closely with his people and also with the cause of Christianity (see, for example, the intertwining of all three in stanza 274 and the association of the Count and his troops with crusaders in lines 283a and 474c). When Sancha is praised for freeing Fernando from prison she is told (686ab) that 'You have freed Castile from the depths of captivity, | and done a great mercy to all Christendom's lands', for the Count's importance as a Christian leader in fact extends far beyond the territories which in the first half of the tenth century were occupied by Castile.

In the repeated emphasis on liberation from servitude there are clear overtones of the liberation of the Jewish people from Babylonian captivity, the Count thus being cast in the role of a the leader of a chosen people. The biblical parallels become explicit at times, as in stanza 270 when Fernando appears as David against al-Mansur's Goliath. The interdependence of the leader and his people are heavily emphasized. Thus, when it seems that they have unwittingly ignored his call for help, the Castilians, tormented by a sense of their guilt, 'felt terribly distressed and in grief | at how they were all fallen so deeply into error' (322cd). The Count prays for help in defending his people against 'all the land of Africa' (403c) and, when it seems that the battle against the Muslims is going badly, he fears the loss of Castile and all of Spain through the sin of himself and others (553). Fernando's capture through trickery by the King of Navarre is the cause of a bitter lament by the people of Castile and their prayer (as in 609–610) gives striking evidence of the nature of his role and importance:

> We Castilians are taken with great fury for God,
> because of His desire that we suffer such oppression;
> we have incurred the anger of all those in Spain,
> and once again Castile has become a tiny hut.

> To none other are we able to address our lament
> except to the Creator, who must hear us;
> with the Count we thought that we would leave this hardship,
> but instead we have only just come into it.

On this occasion the Count has been captured by the people of Navarre, but the 'oppression' to which his people are now returned is that inflicted by all their enemies – just as the freedom achieved from subservience to León at the end of the poem (and first mentioned in another prayer in 572cd) relates equally to that being sought from Muslim domination at its beginning. No longer able to play their God-given role at the head of other Christian peoples, the Castilians now see themselves as prey to a number of adversaries, both Christian and Muslim. Perhaps most interestingly, however, the figure of the leader is directly identified with gain or loss of territory, a point which will certainly not have been lost on a thirteenth-century Castilian monarch and particularly on one whose eyes were firmly set on overseas crusade and on territorial conquest.

(iv) The Crown of Castile under Alfonso X: king and state, loyalty and treachery

In the legal works of Alfonso X, increasing emphasis was placed on the concept of the state, which Alfonso believed to emerge from human nature itself.[23] The term 'tierra' ('land') was specifically used to designate the

---

[23] See O'Callaghan (1993, 17–30) for a very helpful discussion of Alfonso's theory of the state and of his concept of the role of the monarch. Key background Alfonsine texts here are the *Espéculo* (Alfonso X 1990) and the *Siete Partidas,* particularly Book 2; the *Partidas* are most easily consulted in the English translation by Samuel Parsons Scott which has been edited in five volumes (Parsons Scott and Burns 2001).

kingdom and Alfonso distinguished clearly between the feudal relationship between a lord and his vassals and the particular bond which existed between the king as natural lord and those who dwelt in his land. The king and his people both had a natural duty to love, protect and extend that land, and any failure to do so was automatically condemned as treason. It was the duty of every individual to defend their monarch (*Espéculo*, 3,5,10; *Siete Partidas*, 2,13,26 and 2,19,2), but Alfonso also had a very clearly defined idea of his own role as a man set on earth by God to give justice to his people (*Siete Partidas*, 2,1,5–6; 2,10,2). As Vicar of God, the king, whom Christ had caused to be born of a royal lineage, was the intermediary between God and the people (*Siete Partidas*, 2,1,5). It was his role to protect his whole people against harm and against any external enemy (*Espéculo*, 2,1,5; *Siete Partidas*, 2,10,1–3). His relationship with his subjects was so close that their suffering would cause him pain as if they were part of his own body (*Partidas*, 2,1,5–6; 2,10,2) and in return the people should honour and revere him, desire his welfare and set great store by his good reputation (*Partidas*, 2,13,1–7); above all it was the king's duty to love God and serve him by offering his protection to churches and their priests (*Partidas*, 2,2,1–4).

This is a picture which is immediately recognizable in the *Poema*, with its heavy emphasis on the relationship between the Count and his people and the mutual affection and duty which binds them together. The *Espéculo* was probably promulgated at Palencia in May 1255 and the *Siete Partidas* were drawn up between 1256 and 1265, but these two legal works are referred to here as representative of the highly developed thinking about the state and kingship which was current in Alfonso's court at the time of the composition of the *Poema de Fernán González*. We see in the *Espéculo* and the *Siete Partidas* and also in the *Poema* how ruler and vassals are bound together by a mutual duty closely linked to the provision of physical protection and to the furthering of the well-being of the state. The Castilian count, of course, is presented in every sense as possessing the lineage, the qualities and devotion of his people befitting a king, and in this sense his personal attributes are already such as to be able to transform his county into a kingdom. For monarch and count alike, together with their vassals, service is clearly seen in terms of the defence of the kingdom's physical integrity and, indeed, of its extension. The kingdom, of course, for Alfonso meant the territory of the Crown of Castile, which was already vast, but in the *Poema* it is represented by the county of Castile, so closely identified with the figure of Fernán González. Thus, from the outset the Count is defined as the ideal lord, one in whom all his people take pleasure and in whom they can place absolute trust:

> The Castilians came up to set eyes on their lord,
> and all men, young and old, took pleasure in him;
> they set the whole county beneath his authority;
> no finer lord could all the world have offered. (184)

In the *Poema*, Castile is a land which from the start was destined to lead and which could never contemplate subservience; its people are presented as possessing a natural nobility of character, in such a way that the young Fernando, in his prayer for divine assistance for the Castilians, proclaims that: 'I hold it wrong for lords to be as serfs' (188d); and, in just the same way, at a later point in the poem it is made clear that it is naturally wrong to keep the Count imprisoned (617d), as he, like the nation whose spirit he embodies, has a much finer destiny. Thus Fernando's prayer (185–190) shows us just how he sees his role and the task before him. As both lord to the people of Castile and God's vassal he has a well defined responsibility:

> This is the mercy I would ask of You, my Lord,
> that since I am Your vassal, You not fail me;
> with You I believe, Lord, that I will make such conquests
> that Castile will be able to escape her oppression. (190)

The reply that Fernando receives before the battle of Hacinas (409a–c) takes up and rewards this declaration:

> The Creator on high has still more to tell you:
> that you are His vassal and He is your Lord;
> with the Christian troops, you will fight for love of Him …

It is clear that only with God's help can the goal of freeing Castile from oppression be attained and it is equally apparent that conquest is what the leader must be able to offer to his people. At times this conquest takes the form of the wealth of booty taken in battle, as in stanzas 277ff., but the Count does not neglect his responsibility towards the Church, commanding that one fifth of what has been taken (the amount which would normally constitute a king's share) is given to San Pedro de Arlanza.

We have seen how for Alfonso X the bond between lord and vassals involves very strong mutual responsibilities and how in the *Poema* this obligation is represented in terms of a duty for the Count to protect and further the interests of his land and its inhabitants. Repeatedly in the *Poema* the Count emphasizes his strong desire to do right by all of his people (see, for example, his wish in stanza 556 to pay every one of them great honour by exacting vengeance for all those fallen in battle). We also see how, as intermediary between God and his vassals, Fernán González delivers powerful battle harangues urging his men to fight on in God's name, interprets for them a series of prodigies that have filled them with fear (the disappearing horseman, the serpent and the ways of Fortune), and, before the battle of Hacinas, explains the message of imminent triumph given to him by the two saintly messengers. Not surprisingly, scholarship is among the qualities considered by Alfonso to be important in a ruler, and Fernán González, characterized as a 'man well schooled' (246a), shows on these occasions, if not a high level of learning, sufficient wit to prevent the harm caused by ignorance and superstition.

Alfonso also underlines in the *Siete Partidas* (2,9,6) the need for both wisdom and discretion in his noblemen ('los ricos omes'), for he will require them to give him counsel; this role on their part is certainly reflected in the *Poema*, as in stanzas 201ff., when the Count requests advice, even though he pays little heed to that which is given, and it is heavily emphasized in his lengthy speech in the reconstructed text which precedes his attendance at the *Cortes* and second period of imprisonment.

In a broader sense, the Count's vassals pledge to serve him as their lord. The homage sworn by the Castilians to the stone effigy (663–664) could not be clearer in its implications:

> As if it were the Count, let us also kiss its hand,
> let us place it in a cart that we carry before us;
> for love of the good Count, we shall make it our lord,
> and we shall swear to it a pledge, and do it homage.

> The standard of Castile let us place in its hand,
> and if that does not flee, then neither shall we;
> may we never come back to Castile without the Count;
> any man who turns sooner, let us hold him a traitor.

In the stone or rock (= *petrus*) there may well also be an allusion to the Church (Deyermond 1990, 61). This image also undoubtedly represents a kingship (albeit in the form of a count) which is unflinching and utterly dependable, a firm and enduring support of the people of Castile. It is up to the Castilians to reciprocate by in turn remaining just as constant. We have looked briefly at Alfonso X's theory of kingship, and it should be emphasized that this was related closely to a current of ideas common to the

Europe of the mid-thirteenth century and based on a combination of Roman law and Aristotelian theory (see O'Callaghan 1993, 30). According to these principles, the king and the people were bonded together in an unbreakable unity, which we can surely see here as symbolized by the people's homage to the rock. What the people must not do, the poet tells us with absolute clarity, is to fail to support their ruler, and this is a point to which attention is repeatedly drawn elsewhere in the *Poema*. Just as the law codes specify that not to support a king in battle is to commit an act of treachery (see O'Callaghan 1993, 29), in stanza 447 the Count proclaims the same message by establishing a parallel with the man who betrayed Christ Himself.

> Any one of you who flees the battlefield
> or gives himself up for prison, fearing death,
> let one who does such deeds be held a traitor,
> and lie in Hell with Judas, when he dies.

Likewise, the devotion of the Castilians to the physical defence of their lord is shown in lines 264a–c:

> They put all their strength in protecting their lord,
> and death could bring them neither pain nor sorrow;
> the great debt they owed took away all fear of death;

Furthermore, their objective in battle is to bring their leader glory and make him outstanding among the men of Spain. By doing this, they will win even greater glory for themselves (224). The idea of such all-consuming duty to king and lord – God's earthly representative – as a debt of ancient origin recurs often in the *Poema* (see also, for example, stanzas 215–216).

On the other hand, a preoccupation with the threat of treachery is not apparent only in the *Poema de Fernán González*; it is prominent, too, in a number of powerful passages in the *Libro de Alexandre*, such as stanza 1911, where we find a form of the same ritual curse used against the traitor as in the *Poema*'s stanza 447. There can be no doubt that the emphasis on the unswerving loyalty of every individual to his sovereign will have been particularly important in the years when we believe the *Poema* to have been composed. In 1254–1255, as has been seen above, there were already conflicts within Alfonso's kingdom. Among those set against the King was Diego López de Haro, who for many years had been a key figure in the administration of Alfonso's father and who now severed his bonds of vassalage with Alfonso. Diego took refuge in Navarre, and other important nobles, together with Alfonso's brother Enrique, signed an agreement with Jaime I of Aragón. As we have seen, the poet lists Castile's foreign enemies at the time of the hostilities with Navarre as Aragón, Navarre and Poitou (line 436a). In fact in 1255 hostilities broke out in both Andalucía and Vizcaya, whilst Alfonso followed events from Burgos. The rebellion was subdued and peace was signed with Jaime I in 1256, but for Alfonso X, a monarch who placed such emphasis on the harmonious nature of the state under his own incontestable authority, so serious a revolt, coupled with the increasing possibility of an international war, will probably have caused no small concern. It is certainly possible that our poet, in placing great emphasis on the debt of loyalty owed to the king, has firmly in mind the danger posed by just such divisions.

(v) Fernán González: a model and inspiration for a thirteenth-century monarch in a time of conflict
It would also seem highly likely, as has already been suggested, that the conflicts with the kings of Pamplona/Navarre, supported by the French as described in the *Poema*, are in part at least a direct reflection of the events of the early years of Alfonso X's reign: they are essentially a form of propaganda, demonstrating the military superiority of the Castilians – and the personal standing of their monarch – at a time when war seemed imminent. There is a curious parallel, indeed, between the tenth-century count's other-worldly encounters and the miracle described by Pero Marín, abbot of Santo Domingo de Silos, in chapter XVIII of his vernacular account of the life and deeds of Saint Dominic (*Los miráculos romançados*; see Anton 1988, 43ff.). This tells of how King Alfonso, in early 1255, made a five-day stay at Silos. Deeply troubled by the conflicts in Vizcaya and with Navarre and Aragón, the King prayed all night before the sanctuary of the saint, who appeared to him assuring him that within three months all these problems would be satisfactorily resolved provided that Alfonso held firm. We are told that the King promised a substantial donation to the monastery if the prophecy came true. The account goes on to tell of how the rebellion was subsequently subdued and the monarchs of both Navarre and Aragón rapidly sought peace. The grateful Castilian monarch seems indeed to have rewarded the monastery with the grant of a privilege to receive a locally paid tax. It is difficult to know who is borrowing from whom here, but it is clear that the heavenly reassurance and support received by the Count in the *Poema* could equally be seen as a promise of divine assistance for Alfonso at a time when

both members of his own nobility and hostile kingdoms appeared to pose him a serious threat.

On the other hand whilst, as is well known, Fernán González suffered a period of imprisonment at the hands of the King of Pamplona, there was no significant tenth-century conflict between Castile and her eastern neighbour such as the one depicted in the *Poema*. The poet does, however, attribute the outbreak of hostilities to the raids on Castilian territories by the troops of King Sancho (284–285). Such raids, frequently performed in times of hostility, devastating the lands and carrying off people and livestock, were a thoroughly unpleasant fact of life in the tenth century and remained so during the wars of the thirteenth century. This is a very good example of a situation in which it was the feudal lord's duty and above all that of the king to protect his people, both in the tenth century and in the age of Alfonso X; it was the responsibility of both king and lord to act against their hostile neighbours. Moreover, the poet also places in the Count's mouth a further accusation against the monarchs of Navarre (292):

> To do harm to Castile and destroy the Castilians,
> you entered into friendship with the pagan nations
> and waged evil war on the people of Christ,
> for they did not wish to succumb to your rule.

This criticism becomes even more explicit in the account in the *Estoria de España* which is based on the *Poema*, for here we are told that the king of Pamplona/Navarre assembles 'great forces made up of his own people and of others, both Gascons and Moors' (quoted by Deyermond 1990, 63). These two versions of the Count's words have a range of possible associations (see note to 292b). However, there can be no doubt with regard to their significance: firstly they help to identify closely together all the enemies against which Castile has to struggle, representing them all as separate parts of a hostile and oppressive force; and secondly they blacken the picture of the Navarrese, who are here portrayed as treacherous and dangerous and lying at the centre of a web of foes.

(vi) Castile and León

The case of León is, of course, very different, for at the time when the *Poema* was composed it was not an enemy power but an important part of Alfonso X's own kingdom. The versions of Castile's liberation which are reflected in the later chronicles do recount open hostility, with Castilians and Leonese on the brink of a full-scale confrontation, and this more aggressive tone is reflected in ballad tradition. However, such elements are incompatible with our poet's approach to the depiction of his hero throughout his narrative and also with the purposes of Alfonso's *Estoria de España*. The poet does not lose sight of the point that Fernán González is not actually a king but a count, and Sancho's vassal at that. The account from the *Estoria de España* does show the Castilians raiding the lands of León, but only once Sancho has proved unable to pay his debt; and an understanding is promptly reached. The Count, even when instructed by Sancho to give up the county of Castile, protests firmly that the Castilians are fair-minded and respectful of the law (see the text to fill the lacuna after stanza 760):

> The King of León has sent me a written instruction that I cede to him the county, and I am willing to do so, for it would not be right to keep it from him by force, as a result of which he would have cause to make criticism of me and all those who came after me if I reacted otherwise. Moreover, I am not a man to seize land for myself, and that is not the manner in which Castilians are accustomed to act.

The highly scrupulous attitude expressed here seems to relate closely to the concept of the harmonious state centred on the role of the king as God's representative which is repeatedly and heavily emphasized in the legal works of Alfonso X; just as Alfonso repeatedly condemns any act which goes against the king's interests and highlights the responsibility of every individual always to speak truth to his sovereign (see, for example, *Partidas* 2,13,5), there can be no doubt that the poet condemns entirely any act of treachery towards the monarch and that his hero is expected to pay his lord due honour and respect. It would be impossible, then, however firm may be his belief in the inevitability and importance of Castilian independence, for him to represent Fernán González as either tricking or taking up arms directly against his lord and king.

Apart from its brief appearance as one of the Gothic 'provinces', León is not actually mentioned until the final third of the poem. Even then, the burning hostility which meets the Count when he obediently attends the Leonese *Cortes* originates with Queen Teresa, who is of Navarrese origin and is seeking vengeance for the death of her brother. As we have seen, it is not Fernán González who suggests the sale of the horse and the hawk (577–578); indeed, he offers to make a gift of them. It is the ingenuous King Sancho who is responsible for ensnaring himself in a deal that will lead him to lose part of his kingdom. The Count continues to act in good faith, lending much-needed military support to Sancho against the marauding Muslims. Although he does refuse the aid of the Leonese knights in a gesture which has heavy historical overtones (see note to line 723c), the fury that is directed at him instead of gratitude seems out of place; but once again the source of the hostility is unequivocally identified (stanza 734) as Navarrese:

> The Queen of León, a native of Navarre,
> to the Castilians was the deadliest of foes;
> they had killed her brother, and she wished them great ill;
> she thought of nothing but of seeking all their deaths.

In gaining their independence, the Castilians are winning a political, rather than military, victory. There is, in fact, no struggle or conflict in the poem between the people of Castile and those of León and they are at no time explicitly depicted as adversaries. On the other hand, in terms of moral – and military – stature, the ineffectual and rather child-like Leonese monarch is far from being the equal of the good Count of Castile; the Leonese cannot match the great military achievements of the Castilians; and, when independence is finally brought about, it is closely identified with the freedom from oppression by the Muslims that from the outset of his career Fernán González had sought to achieve for his people.

(vii) Christianity and Islam: the ruler's duty

This, indeed, is how our poet very skilfully combines two crucial elements of his narrative: on the one hand, his subject was the man identified above all with the achievement of bringing Castile to independence; on the other, the most powerful of his themes – and his principal preoccupation – were the ruler's deep responsibility to the Church and the continuing struggle in the Peninsula and beyond between Christianity and Islam, viewed as a profound conflict between good and evil.

We have already seen (section 2(viii), above) how behind the composition of the *Poema de Fernán González* there is sound evidence to discern specific practical motives related to the financial wellbeing of San Pedro de Arlanza. These, together with the celebration of the monastery as Fernando's final resting place (see stanzas 247 and 569–570), were clearly in the poet's mind; and they correspond, too, to the Alfonsine conviction that it was the ruler's duty to care for the Church and its representatives. Underpinning the narrative of the *Poema*, however, there is also an extensive web of biblical allusions, which has been analyzed in detail by Alan Deyermond (1990). Deyermond points out that Old Testament allusions are more frequent in the early part of the *Poema* whilst those to the New Testament are more commonly associated with the figure of Fernán González himself. He points, for example, to an analogy between the fall of the Visigoths (with Roderic deceived by the Devil, 'the deadly foe', as in stanza 6) and the error by Adam and Eve which leads to their expulsion from Eden; to parallels with Isaiah and Micah in Count Julian's advice to turn weapons into agricultural implements (see note to stanza 50); to similarities between the Muslim conquest of Spain and the Babylonians' capture of Jerusalem; to the parallels between the role of Pelayo as deliverer of his people (stanzas 115–116) and God's designation of a series of individuals for this purpose as in Judges 1:1–2, 2:16, 3:15, 6:11–14 and I Samuel 16:19. Deyermond also argues convincingly that there are several very close parallels between Fernán González's initial imprisonment as depicted in the *Poema* and biblical accounts of Christ's crucifixion (see note to 599), reinforced by other details such as the lance wound described in 321b. There seems to be little doubt that our poet intends to present the Castilians as a chosen people, condemned to endure a lengthy period of suffering, but eventually brought to freedom from the oppression that they had endured under the Moors (and, by extension, under their Leonese neighbours as well) through the sacrifice of brave warriors led by Fernán González.

Repeatedly we are reminded that it is the Devil who lies behind the ills that have afflicted the peoples of Christian Spain (see, for example, 32bc, 40b, 101a, 217a, 584a). If Mohammed himself is described as being 'of the evil faith' and preaching 'many evil claims' (7a/d), the Moors are also directly associated with the powers of evil ('they were uglier than Satan with all of his coven | when he comes out from Hell, caked in dirt and in soot': 388cd).[24] Their inhuman and sadistic treatment of Christian prisoners as described in the *Poema* (see stanzas 89ff.) bears out this image of profound evil. The suffering which was to precede the eventual defeat of the Devil was foreseen by the prophets (stanzas 10–12), and the poet places in his hero's mouth a reminder of the promises that God made through Isaiah not to abandon those who serve him (see note to 402a). Indeed, the notion of service to God is central to the *Poema*; as the monk Pelayo tells the Count (409a–c):

---

[24] For an analysis of how this process of demonization of Muslims was common in the art of Christian Spain and of how Romanesque art was used as a powerful tool of propaganda against Islam in the period of reconquest and during the Crusades, see Monteira Arias (2012).

> The Creator on high has still more to tell you:
> that you are His vassal and He is your Lord;
> with the Christian troops, you will fight for love of Him ...

That service, moreover, is conceived in very specific terms. Certainly duty demands that economic support be given to the Church and its representatives, and in this Fernán González shows himself to be exemplary. However, what the good Count embodies above all else is the placing of knightly skills at the Lord's service within what has been described as 'a divinely sanctioned social order which is structured, not surprisingly, around the twin pillars of Church and military power' (Weiss 2006, 154). The beating of weapons and armour into tools for farming is presented as a perverse and destructive error, for what matters is the courage and military skill necessary to crush the infidel.

We repeatedly see in the *Poema* both the Castilian people as a whole (105–113) and Fernán González as an individual (as in 185–190, his first act as count; 394ff.; 548ff.) come to God in prayer to ask for help. So too in stanza 38 we see how the picture of the Gothic Golden Age rests on the idea of a Church well provided for and able to encourage the people in their faith:

> The churches were all of them set in careful order
> and possessed rich supplies of both oil and wax;
> of tributes and tithes loyal payment was given,
> and all of the people deeply rooted in their faith.

Of the emphasis placed on the role of the Church there can be no doubt, and of Castile, we are told (157c) that 'always of the Lord it stood in proper faith and fear'. However, more than faith was needed. The idea of martyrdom is introduced very early in the *Poema* when in stanza 13 we are told of the many Spaniards who died for their Christian belief, and three stanzas later the poet tells us that:

> Many kings and counts and many men of power,
> popes and archbishops, bishops and abbots,
> gave their lives for this law – this you must believe –
> and so in Heaven have their full inheritance.

Martyrdom, moreover, was also associated with the Crusade, for as early as the mid-ninth century the principle had been established that those who died in a holy war should be ranked as martyrs and if they died armed in battle their sins would be remitted. Thus in the *Poema* we see how Roderic's Goths fighting against the Muslim invaders 'washed away their sins' (77c) and are termed 'cruzados' or 'crusaders' (79d). Elsewhere, Fernán González's troops during the battle of Hacinas are also described in this way (as in 467a, 473d, 474c, 486b), and it is particularly striking that the divine reinforcements brought by Santiago and Pelayo likewise appear in the guise of crusaders ('all clad in white armour', for 'they are angels of the Lord, | each one of them carrying a cross on his pennant': 411bc; see also 558d and 560d). The Count himself is the epitome of the *miles Christi*, the crusader determined to win victory for Christendom or to die for his faith (see, for example, stanzas 446, or 554–556, where he is also confident that he will be reunited with all of his fallen warriors in paradise). In the sequence of conflicts with the Muslim invaders that is represented in the *Poema de Fernán González*, the battles fought by the Goths, by Pelayo and by the heroic Count himself all prefigure and point the way towards one final conflict, one soon to be fought by the Castilian crusaders under Alfonso X. We have seen how Alfonso cherished the desire to carry out such a conquest, extending still further the territorial gains made by his father and his great-grandfather and giving further evidence of the Castilian qualities epitomized by the great Count, and how preparations for this were underway during the early years of his reign. It is not surprising, then, that time and time again the poet alludes to Africa as the homeland of Islam. We hear, for instance, of how under King Roderic '[o]ur power extends far into African lands, | for which the unbelievers pay us tribute' (60ab), and we can imagine that this is the situation that Alfonso expects to recreate. Significantly, we hear that al-Mansur after his defeat returned to Morocco, not to his actual base in Córdoba (385), and from there brought support including Marinids and Almohads (387). The Count laments that 'all the land of Africa' has come upon him (403c), and in battle al-Mansur and his followers are repeatedly associated with Africa (as in 429c, 491a, 533c, 544a, 545c, 546a). In the tale of a Castilian hero triumphant in his campaigns over an Islamic – and, as presented here, essentially African – foe, there is a powerful message of encouragement for King Alfonso and for those loyal supporters and allies who are going to make up his crusading army. The Castilians, with the anticipated assistance of the English troops of Henry III, following the treaty of March–April 1254, were preparing for a great and heroic crusade. Success for the enterprise seemed assured, for the time of suffering which God had permitted (see note to 81d) was drawing to an end, and the land lost by the Goths waited to be recovered: 'what you then lost', the crusaders are told in line 68d, 'you can now win again'. We know that Alfonso attached great importance to the reading or performance to his knights of accounts of great deeds of arms, for it is stated clearly in the *Siete Partidas* (2,21,20; see Parsons Scott and Burns, 2001: 2.429) that this should be done 'in order that, hearing them, their minds and hearts might be enlarged and strengthened by the performance of good actions, and to awaken a desire to attain to what others had accomplished, or to surpass their efforts'. Fernán González's harangue to his troops in stanzas 209–224 calls upon them to take up the heroic struggle of their Visigothic predecessors against the unbeliever and cast away their fear as they fight to win glory for both their lord and themselves. The ensuing battle sees them inspired by his words to victory. In short, to borrow a point made by Joseph Duggan about the *Poema de Mio Cid* (1989, 20), we would suggest that in just this context the *Poema de Fernán González* will have posed a rhetorical question: 'if the illustrious count could win such victories against overwhelming odds and thus perform such heroic service to Castile and to Christianity, why can't you?'

(viii) Interpreting the Poema

Early in this introduction we described the *Poema de Fernán González* as a demanding text. Its complexity is in part the consequence of the way in which it combines material, themes and stylistic features from a variety of texts, in some cases superimposing quite different layers of meaning in a single passage or episode, as we have seen, for example, in the case of the prison in which the Count is held by the Navarrese. We have argued too that the *Poema* is rich in historical associations, less with events from the lifetime of the Count and much more with those of the age in which it was composed. We have made some suggestions for links with earlier events in Castilian history, but much more significant are surely the parallels with the initial years of Alfonso's reign. We believe that the imprint of Alfonso's concept of kingship, the preparations for conflict with Navarre and, above all, those for the African Crusade, is clearly visible in the *Poema*, along with the evident influence of its author's association with San Pedro de Arlanza. Indeed, there would seem to be little doubt that our poet was reasonably well informed about the political developments of his age. We hope, therefore, that we have established clearly that he sought to blend together his source materials in such a way as to reinforce very effectively his own message about the nature, values and objectives of contemporary Castile. The most notable of those materials seem to have been the *Liber regum* and other historical sources used in the first section, the *Libro de Alexandre*, which formed the basis of the second, and the various predominantly novelesque materials which constitute the core of the third. Certainly the poet's narrative style and descriptive technique seem to be much influenced by those of the *juglar*, but, given the degree to which he has chosen, shaped and carefully intertwined his materials, it is surely very difficult to see his work as essentially the 'reworking' of a lost epic.[25]

(ix) Binding the poem together: the image of the hunt

Finally, it is appropriate now to examine one final illustration of how the author of the *Poema de Fernán González* combined both a range of different themes and material taken from a variety of sources. This is the image of the hunt, which runs throughout the *Poema*. Hunting on horseback and usually using a bird of prey such as a hawk or falcon was, of course, immensely popular with the nobility of medieval Europe. Hunting with birds of prey was a passion of King Alfonso, to which he is believed to have devoted one of a number of works on hunting; we have already seen that in his account in the *Siete Partidas* (2,5,20) of the abilities essential to a king, he explains the importance of hunting, which he describes as 'the art and skill of waging war and gaining victory, about which it is the duty of kings to be well informed'. The hunt appears in the *Poema* in a number of contexts. In stanza 754 its identification with the bloody business of war becomes transparent in the description of the place of battle:

> The two armies clashed in a deep-sided valley,
> a fine place for hunting for rabbit and hare;
> they gather there much grain to make the red dye,
> and the torrent of the Ebro does rage at its foot.

It has been argued that, given this identification between the hunt and war, in the deal between the Count and King Sancho the uncontrollably escalating cost of the horse and hawk represents the 'unpayable debt to war' and that 'the problem this transaction attempts to resolve is not how to enforce the rule of law, but how to legalize and give justification to the inevitability of violence' (Weiss 2006, 176). We would suggest that, rather than the exercise of violence, what these items represent here are chivalric virtues and skills properly used. We have pointed (see note to 576a–c) to parallels

---

[25] Again, Duggan (1989, 77) expresses very neatly the purpose of the author of the *Poema de Mio Cid* in terms which are directly applicable to the *Poema de Fernán González*: '... in receiving, transforming and giving a new slant to his material, its poet used themes and invented outcomes that he knew would please his audience'. In this case, it is highly likely that the most important figure in that audience was King Alfonso himself.

in both literature and the visual arts which associate the bearing of a hawk with power, success and ownership. It is because Sancho lacks the personal qualities which are necessary for him to merit the horse and the hawk that he has to attempt to buy them and it is likewise through his personal inadequacies that the deal is doomed to bring him disaster. In a similar way the lustful archpriest, who carries a hawk, rides a mule and hunts with dogs, is a grotesque parody of the noble knight, showing himself unable to control his sexual appetite just as King Sancho cannot keep his envy within bounds (a clear example of an individual lacking in the crucial courtly quality of *mesura*). If the hunter's conduct does not merit the state to which he aspires and he becomes the victim, that is exactly what he deserves.

Two more aspects of the image of the hunt merit attention. The first is its very common association with the pursuit and winning of the courtly lady (there are many examples, including in Chrétien de Troyes' *Erec et Enide* and in two of Marie de France's *lais*, *Guigemar* and *Lanval*, in the second of which the hawk – together with a palfrey – is used as a symbol of power and of success in love). There is no link of this kind explicitly established in the *Poema*, but it may be significant that Sancha is first mentioned immediately after the deal for the horse and the hawk is struck and that her relationship with the Count seems to be intertwined with his trials and eventual triumph in the final episodes. Finally, of course, we must bear in mind the early and fundamental episode in which Fernán González pursues the boar into the hermitage and demonstrates his natural piety (230):

> When Fernando set eyes on a place of such honour,
> he left the boar unharmed, and would not kill it:
> 'Lord,' he said, 'feared by the winds and the sea,
> if I have here erred You must grant me Your pardon.'

Here the hunter knows when it is right to lay down his arms. The Count is a man of great military skill, power and innate nobility – a point which is reinforced by his association with the image of the horse and the hawk – but he understands fully that he must recognize his duty to the Church. This sense of service, as we have seen, is central to the *Poema*, and the respect shown on this occasion is to be amply repaid. The poet establishes a telling contrast almost 370 stanzas later when he describes the conduct of King García when it is the turn of the Count, now the victim of the hunt, to take refuge in a church: 'King García had the church firmly surrounded', we are told; 'he would not hold off, even though it was sacred' (597ab).

It is reasonable to assume that the poet would expect us to be alert to such parallels; indeed, to establish a complex pattern of associations and links, carefully worked into the body of his narrative, is a fundamental feature of his craft. In a number of contexts verbal echoes occur throughout the poem, heavily laden with significance. We have seen how they are used to connect events which have occurred at various stages in Castile's development, and how Pelayo's prophecy is linked to the actual events of the battle of Hacinas by precise verbal echoes; and similarly, for example, when Fernán González is imprisoned the wording of the Castilians' lament takes us back to Castile's state before the emergence of their hero (see note to stanza 609).[26] It is in just this way, such as to require our close attention and sensitivity to echoes and parallels, that the image of the hunt is used at different points and in different ways in the poem, with a range of connotations, in order to comment on various aspects of character and theme. This, we hope we have been able to show, is evidence of the complex nature of our poet's art and of the skill with which the *Poema de Fernán González* has been forged.

5. Note on the Spanish text

The single surviving manuscript of the *Poema de Fernán González* has caused many problems for editors. In addition to the numerous omissions, some minor, some of substantial passages, there are many points at which the text is unclear. In addition, the three late fifteenth-century copyists, probably already working from a version containing significant inaccuracies, seem to have had little understanding of the verse form used by the poet. In the case of details as well as of the major missing sections, therefore, editors have found themselves striving to reconstruct the wording of the original thirteenth-century text. In attempting to do this, we have been guided by two fundamental assumptions: that the original respected consistently the principle of metrical regularity (with every line consisting of two hemistichs of seven syllables) and that there is consonantal rhyme throughout each stanza. It is assumed that apocopation was heavily used but that, out of use by the fifteenth century, this feature will not have been preserved by the copyists. Inevitably, there will be some lines

---

[26] For another parallel between two apparently minor details which serves to establish a significant link between two events, see the two allusions to the pass of Cize in 138b and 332d. This feature of medieval narrative has been described by Eugène Vinaver (1971, 68ff.) as 'the poetry of interlace'; Vinaver (p. 83) argues that the author would assume not only that the reader's memory is infallible, 'but that the exercise of such a memory is in itself a pleasurable pursuit which carries with it its own reward'.

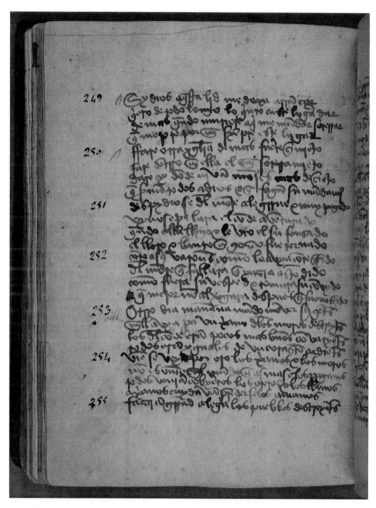

The Poema de Fernán González, *though composed in the mid-thirteenth century, eventually survived through just one manuscript which is housed at the Royal Library of the Monastery of San Lorenzo de El Escorial. The text of the* Poema *is just one of five works which make up Manuscript b-IV-21. It was copied between 1460 and 1480 and, unlike the other works in the volume, has no form of decoration. It seems to be the work of three different copyists and it suffers from many formal defects, such as crossings out and omissions by the copyists, and carelessness on the part of the binder, which have caused the loss of a significant part of the text.*

We would like to thank la Real Biblioteca del Monasterio de San Lorenzo del Escorial for their kind permission to reproduce their material.

which do not conform; one example is the first hemistich of line 22c – though López Guil (2001, 145) offers a good example of the complex solutions that editors can find to such problems.

The numbering of the stanzas presents a difficulty which could prove something of an irritant for students of the poem, as this is an area in which editors have signally failed to agree. The existing manuscript does not indicate stanza divisions (or indeed the division of lines into hemistichs). Occasionally, for example, where there appears to be a unit of, say, 5 or 6 lines, it is difficult to tell whether this corresponds to one stanza or two. This is the case, for example, in what, on account of the incompatibility in rhyme, we have taken as stanzas 271–272, whilst some editors have taken this as a single stanza:

271   Foía Almozor a guis' de algarivo,
      diziendo: '¡Ay, Mafómat! mal' ora en ti fío.
      Non vale tres arvejas todo tu poderío;
      ....

272   ....
      ....
      Todo mi grand poder es muerto e cativo;
      pues ellos muertos son, ¿por qué finco yo vivo?'[27]

Some editors, such as Victorio (2010) and Hernando Pérez (2001) have included verse reconstructions of the missing sections. We have opted not to attempt this but have included the text and translation of the equivalent sections from Alfonso X's *Estoria de España*, which has been used as the basis for such reconstructions. In order to facilitate comparison, we have made an allowance in the numbering of our stanzas to bring us roughly into line with Juan Victorio's edition. In the case of short omissions in the text, such as individual lines, we have only included a reconstruction if this seems to be both clear and generally agreed. In such cases we did not feel that it would be necessary or helpful to the reader to include an indication that this had been done.

Our aim has been to present a text which, whilst reflecting the original as closely as possible, is clear to read. With this intention, we have made a number of adjustments in spelling, among them the following:

- we have used modern accentuation;
- the use of b and v has been modernized when it seems that this will help

---

[27] Bailey (2010, 87–89) shows how these two stanzas, though combined in some editions, are essentially separate, each focusing on 'a separate centre of interest'.

comprehension (we have rejected, for example, *vuen* in 32d, *avastadas* in 38b, *vuscar* in 226c, and *vestión* in 417d);

- where appropriate the use of *j* and *y* in the manuscript has been regularized as *i*, as in vyen (bien) in 69a;
- *nn* has been replaced by *ñ* and *rr* has been replaced by *r* at the beginning of words;
- apocopation has been indicated by an apostrophe, making clearer such forms as *cadun* as *cad' un'* (466d); object and reflexive pronouns, often subject to apocopation, have usually been written as a separate word, as in 'furtó l' un pobreziello' (177c), '[t]ornó s' el mensajero' (299a); contractions such as *dellos* (1c) and *deste* (5a) have also been written with an apostrophe (*d'ellos, d'este*);
- to avoid ambiguity, we have spelt the present tense singular forms of *haber* with an *h* (*he, has, ha*);
- it would not have been appropriate to regularize all spelling, but we have, for example, harmonized the three forms of *faz/haz/az* (all occurring in close proximity in the battle scenes) as *az*.

The text of the passages taken from the *Estoria de España* follows closely the principles used by Menéndez Pidal, Marden and others, with minor adjustments in spelling and accentuation.

6. The translation

Before embarking on his allotted task, every translator is, above all else, a reader. Each new text will demand readjustment of the path to be picked through the universalizing dichotomies – such warring contraries as metaphrase and paraphrase, domestication and foreignization – that litter translation theory, for which the translator must first reflect on the identifying characteristics and interpretative possibilities of the text set before him, as well as the likely needs and expectations of the reader of the translation. It is to an elucidation of some of these, and an illustration of how they have marked our practice, that we turn in this final section.

The most consistently relevant issue to any translation of poetry is surely that of form. By now it will be clear that the *Poema de Fernán González* owes a substantial debt to the *Libro de Alexandre*, the founding stone of the *mester de clerecía*, in which four-line form the *Poema* is also composed. Accordingly, we have also found that many of the strategies adopted when translating the *Alexandre* suggest themselves here as appropriate for a version of the kindred stanzas of the *Poema*. As for the *Alexandre*, we make no effort to reproduce the rhyme of the original: the practicalities of Spanish accidence make the language far more susceptible of consistent rhyme than is English, as many other translators in this series have noted, and we have felt that to plot a rhyming course through a poem of this length runs the risk of sounding curiously antiquated to the modern ear, which would not have been the effect of the original. Instead, we have focused our formal efforts on the poem's rhythm: the 'counted syllables' which the *Alexandre* poet noted from the outset as fundamental to the *mester* (see section 3(i), above), and which lend the stanzas of the *Poema* a sense of regularity which it is important to convey. However, as there is no ready English metre whose characteristics are established as similar to, or intentionally imitating, those of the *mester*, as dactylic hexameter once had heroic verse, we have chosen to avoid any misleading connotations that another, familiar English metre would bring with it. Rather it is the effect of regularity that has been uppermost in our considerations: measuring length with the ear rather than the eye, as befits the important role played by orality in the *Poema*'s composition (see section 1(iv), above), all lines are kept to between ten and fifteen of those defining 'counted syllables', and arranged such that the natural stresses should draw the reader through the lines to the end of the stanza, in a way that we hope is also suitable for reading aloud.

Among the other issues surrounding this text that have caused most comment is that of its formulaic composition (see section 3(iii), above). The text contains many phrases, epithets, and useful half-lines which become familiar as they are re-used throughout the poem, and we have felt it important that the reader of the translation have a similar experience. However, this has not been a matter of mechanically re-inserting the same English phrase wherever its Spanish equivalent is found. For example, in the *Poema*'s frequent representation of the Moors as a faithless people, this is not a case of one repeated formula, but of several variations on the theme, which are deployed as equivalents as the poet sees fit, or as is most metrically convenient (see section 3(iii), above); to render each variation by a rigid English equivalence would be to misrepresent the flexibility of these formulae as a tool for composition, and we have thus allowed a similarly restricted licence in the English versions used, in order that those lines run as smoothly as they may. However, not every example of what may be termed formulaic repetition is of this type, and we have felt that more isolated repetitions than the epithets of the ubiquitous Moors often demand a stricter adherence in the English, lest their effect be lost without that tremendous frequency of occurrence to reinforce it. Thus, for example, to allow similar licence in rendering the grief of Fernán González's followers in stanzas 242–249 would be to traduce the Spanish, obscuring an important general truth regarding the poem's composition, as well as lessening the effectiveness of the transformation in line 249d, where that grief is recalled in the same terms as those used in 242d and 243a, but now turns to joy on their leader's arrival. We have tended to hold that the truest reflection of these more intricate examples requires the adduction of parallel (and ideally, in this case, alliterative) English terms; the Spanish 'lloro' and 'llanto' that mark those followers' grief are thus repeatedly rendered in this section by 'weeping' and 'wailing'.

This example also begins to indicate that such instances of repetition cannot always be simply labelled formulaic, but may influence the reader's interpretation of certain lines. We have tried to be alert to possible instances of such significant repetition, which do not always occur in close proximity in the text, and to ensure that our English versions show similar resemblance, without which these echoes are lost. At the extreme, such echoes may be as little as a single word: the use of the word 'cabaña', a small mountain shack, to describe a Castile now fallen on ill fortune in 609d is not itself remarkable, but picks up on the use of the same word in 181a when Fernán González identifies his future creation of a thriving Castile with its people's departure from those 'cabañas'; the sense, then, is of a return to an earlier and harsher state of affairs, of Fortune's wheel returning to its previous low position, and this shift is reflected in the lexis, which we retain by translating both instances identically, as 'hut'. Similarly, Santiago's words to Fernán González in 557d, as he brings a heavenly band of allies to the battle, are not merely an announcement of their arrival, but a virtual repetition of those spoken by Pelayo at 407c: our attention is being drawn here to the fact that their arrival is the fulfilment of a prophecy, that the aid which they bring was long since planned. Indeed, the prophecy had promised much Christian slaughter of the Moors, in a phrase ('grand mortandat farás': 408b) which is repeated often during the long battle scene, and thus perhaps serves to keep this prophecy in the reader's mind. That same stanza, however, warns that the victory will come at a great cost; that cost is the motivation behind the Count's despairing lament at 549–556 that he is forsaken by God, but the prophecy would hold that events are unfolding according to a divine plan that will nonetheless lead to Fernando's victory, of which plan he here seems unmindful. The relevance of the prophecy to the later battle scene is thus of interpretative significance, and suggested in the original only by these verbal reminiscences; we have felt it important that the reader of the translation have the same opportunities for interpretation, and thus render the recurring formula by a single English equivalent ('to inflict great slaughter'), while using the same formulation for the two hemistichs that refer to the arrival of the celestial warriors ('you gain many men this day': 407c and 557d).

All this implies a text which makes significant demands on its reader's memory, but such demands are not restricted to other passages within the *Poema*. It is difficult to reproduce in translation the effect of allusions to other medieval works, since those works have no recognizable equivalent in English; such references are outlined in the notes to relevant lines. However, a final word may be said about references to the Bible. Scholars have long noted the *Poema*'s debt to various biblical passages; these too are detailed in the notes, but where possible we have also sought at times to ensure that the translation reflects the allusion present in the Spanish: thus, for example, Isaiah 2:4 and Micah 4:3, both reading 'and they shall beat their swords into plowshares', lie behind our rendering of line 51c, 'and beat them into ploughshares so as to sow the grain' (see also note to stanza 50). In doing this, for our English Bible we have generally turned to the Authorized Version, and it is appropriate that we turn to it again in closing this discussion, as our poet so often did to his Vulgate. In their preface to that most celebrated of translations, the translators of the King James Bible wrote: '[t]ranslation it is that openeth the window, to let in the light; that breaketh the shell, that we may eat the kernel'. Our aim in this translation has been something similar: to shed some light on the *Poema de Fernán González*, that the English version may facilitate greater access to the kernel that lies on the facing page.

A note on names: in the majority of cases, we have preserved hispanicized forms of the names of people and places which appear in the *Poema*. However, it has on some occasions seemed perverse to maintain this practice with figures such as Saint Peter, who have such familiar currency in English; in such cases we have used the standard English form, for the sake of simplicity, following the conviction that consistency in these matters would come at some cost, as the alien form is unexpected and upsets the reader's smooth progress.

SELECT BIBLIOGRAPHY

1. Editions

Geary, John S., ed., 1987. *Historia del Conde Fernán González: A Facsimile and Paleographic Edition with Commentary and Concordance* (Madison: Hispanic Seminary of Medieval Studies).

Hernando Pérez, José, ed., 2001. *Poema de Fernán González e Hispano Diego García* (Salamanca: Publicaciones Universidad Pontificia).

Lihani, John, ed., 1991. *Poema de Fernán González: edición, prólogo y notas* (East Lansing: Colleagues Press).

López Guil, Itzíar, ed., 2001. *Libro de Fernán Gonçález* (Madrid: Biblioteca Nueva).

Marden, C. Carroll, ed., 1904. *Poema de Fernán Gonçález: texto crítico con introducción, notas y glosario* (Baltimore and Madrid: John Hopkins Press and Librería de M. Murillo).

Menéndez Pidal, Ramón, ed., 1951. *Reliquias de la poesía épica española* (Madrid: Gredos). [The text of the *Poema de Fernán González* comes on pp. 34–180.]

Ruiz Asencio, José Manuel, ed., 1989. '*Poema de Fernán González*: transcripción y versión', in José María Peña de San Martín, *et al.*, eds, *El Poema de Fernán González: edición facsímil del manuscrito depositado en el Monasterio de El Escorial* (Burgos: Excmo. Ayuntamiento de Burgos), pp. 105–273.

Serrano, Luciano, ed., 1943. *Poema de Fernán González* (Madrid: Junta del Milenario de Castilla).

Victorio, Juan, ed., 2010. *Poema de Fernán González*, 5th edn (Madrid: Cátedra).

Zamora Vicente, Alonso, ed., 1978. *Poema de Fernán González*, 5th edn (Madrid: Espasa-Calpe).

There is also a modern Spanish version:

Alarcos Llorach, Emilio, 1965. *Poema de Fernán González*, 2nd edn (Madrid: Castalia, Odres Nuevos).

2. Historical and cultural background to the career of Fernán González and to the composition of the **Poema de Fernán González**

Alfonso X, [1985]. *Las Siete Partidas del Sabio Rey don Alonso el nono [sic], nuevamente Glosadas por el Licenciado Gregorio Lopez del Consejo Real de Indias de su Magestad*, 3 vols. (Madrid: Boletín Oficial del Estado).

Alfonso X, 1990. *Espéculo: texto jurídico atribuido al Rey de Castilla Don Alfonso X, el Sabio*, ed. Robert A. MacDonald (Madison: Hispanic Seminary of Medieval Studies).

Allaigre, Claude Édouard, 1978. 'Des rapports de l'histoire, de la légende et de la chanson de geste: le saint moine-ermite du Poema de Fernán González', in *Les genres littéraires et leurs rapports avec l'histoire: Actes du XIVe Congrès de la Société des Hispanistes Français* (Nice: Société des Hispanistes Français).

Álvarez Borge, Ignacio, 1996. *Poder y relaciones sociales en Castilla en la Edad Media: los territorios entre el Arlanzón y el Duero en los siglos X al XIV* ([Valladolid]: Junta de Castilla y León, Consejería de Educación y Cultura).

Álvarez Borge, Ignacio, 2003. *La Plena Edad Media: siglos XII–XIII* (Madrid: Editorial Síntesis).

Anton, Karl-Heinz, ed., 1988. *Los 'Miraculos romançados' de Pero Marín: edición crítica, introducción e índices* (Silos: Abadía de Silos).

Azcárate, Pilar, Julio Escalona, Cristina Jular and Miguel Larrañaga, 2006. 'Volver a nacer: historia e identidad en los monasterios de Arlanza, San Millán y Silos (siglos XII–XIII)', *Cahiers d'études hispaniques médiévales* 29, 359–394.

Cadiñanos López-Quintana, Aniano, 2002. *Los orígenes de Castilla (una interpretación)* (Burgos: Editorial La Olmeda).

Carande Herrero, Rocío, ed., 1986. *Un poema latino a Sevilla: Versos de Julia Rómula o la urbe Hispalense de Guillermo Pérez de la Calzada (1250)* (Sevilla: Servicio de Publicaciones del Exc. Ayuntamiento de Sevilla).

Castets, Ferdinand, ed., 1880. *Turpini historia Karoli Magni et Rotholandi* (Montpellier: Publications de la société pour l'etude des langues romanes).

Castro, Américo, 1958. *Santiago de España* (Buenos Aires: Emecé).

Cerda, José Manuel, 2012. 'Leonor Plantagenet y la consolidación castellana en el reinado de Alfonso VIII', *Anuario de Estudios Medievales* 42, 629–652.

Chalon, Louis, 1970. 'L'histoire de la monarchie asturienne, de Pelayo à Alphonse II le Chaste, dans le *Poema de Fernán González*', *Marche Romane* 20, 61–67.

Collins, Roger, 1995. *Early Medieval Spain: Unity in Diversity, 400–1000*, 2nd edn (Basingstoke and London: Macmillan).

Collins, Roger, 2004. *Visigothic Spain, 409–711* (Malden, MA and Oxford: Blackwell).

Collins, Roger, 2012. *Caliphs and Kings: Spain 796–1031* (Malden, MA and Oxford: Wiley-Blackwell).

Cotrait, René, 1977. *Histoire et poésie: le comte Fernán González. Recherches sur la tradition gonzalienne dans l'historiographie et la littérature des origines au Poema. I: La genèse de la légende* (Grenoble: Imprimerie Allier).

Ducluzeau, Robert, 2006. *Alphonse de Poitiers: frère préféré de Saint Louis* (La Crèche: Geste).

Estévez Sola, Juan A., trans., 2003. *Crónica najerense* (Madrid: Akal).

Fernández Valverde, Juan, trans., 1989. *Rodrigo Jiménez de Rada: Historia de los hechos de España* (Madrid: Alianza).

Fernández Valverde, Juan, 2001. 'Tito Livio mozárabe', *Exemplaria* (Huelva) 5, 131–134.

Flori, Jean, 2004. *Aliénor d'Aquitaine: la Reine insoumise* (Paris: Éditions Payot et Rivages).

Forey, Alan J., 1973. 'The Crusading Vows of the English King Henry III', *Durham University Journal* 65, 229–247.

García Arancón, M. Raquel, 1985. *Teobaldo II de Navarra 1253–1270: gobierno de la monarquía y recursos financieros* (Navarra: Gobierno de Navarra, Departamento de Educación y Cultura).

García González, Juan José, 2008a. *Castilla en tiempos de Fernán González* (Burgos: Dossoles).

García González, Juan José, ed., 2008b. *Historia de Castilla de Atapuerca a Fuensaldaña* (Madrid: La Esfera de los Libros).

González Jiménez, Manuel, 2004. *Alfonso X el Sabio* (Barcelona: Ariel).

González Jiménez, Manuel, 2006. *Fernando III el Santo* (Sevilla: Fundación José Manuel Lara).

González Jiménez, Manuel and María Antonia Carmona Ruiz, 2012. *Documentación e itinerario de Alfonso X el Sabio* (Sevilla: Secretariado de Publicaciones de la Universidad de Sevilla).

Gozalbes Cravioto, Enrique, 2011. 'El *Comes Iulianus* (Conde Julián de Ceuta), entre la historia y la literatura', *Al Qantir* 11, 3–35.

León-Sotelo Casado, María del Carmen, 1980. 'Formación y primera expansión del dominio monástico de San Pedro de Arlanza, siglo X', *En la España medieval* 1, 223–236.

León-Sotelo Casado, María del Carmen, 1984. 'El dominio monástico de San Pedro de Arlanza durante la plena y baja Edad Media', *En la España medieval* 4, 499–512.

Linehan, Peter, 1993. *History and the Historians of Medieval Spain* (Oxford: Clarendon Press).

Linehan, Peter, 2008. *Spain, 1157–1300: A Partible Inheritance* (Malden, MA and Oxford: Blackwell).

Livermore, Harold, 1971. *The Origins of Spain and Portugal* (London: George Allen and Unwin).

Lomax, Derek W., 1978. *The Reconquest of Spain* (London and New York: Longman).

MacKay, Angus, 1977. *Spain in the Middle Ages: From Frontier to Empire, 1000–1500* (London and Basingstoke: Macmillan).

Martin, Georges, 2009. 'Mujeres de la *Najerense*', *e-Spania* (online), 7, June 2009. Online at: http://e-spania.revues.org/17990 [posted online 1 March 2010; accessed 1 July 2012].

Martín Duque, Ángel J., 1990. 'La fundación del primer burgo navarro: Estella', *Príncipe de Viana* 190, 317–327.

Martínez Díez, Gonzalo, 1989. 'Fernán González en la Historia', in José María Peña de San Martín, *et al.*, eds, *El Poema de Fernán González: edición facsímil del manuscrito depositado en el Monasterio de El Escorial* (Burgos: Excmo. Ayuntamiento de Burgos), pp. 37–78.

Martínez Díez, Gonzalo, 2005. *El Condado de Castilla (711–1038): la historia frente a la leyenda*, 2 vols. (Valladolid and Madrid: Junta de Castilla y León, Consejería de Educación y Cultura).

Menéndez Pidal, Ramón, ed., 1955. *Primera Crónica General de España*, 2 vols. (Madrid: Gredos).

Menéndez Pidal, Ramón, 1975. *Poesía juglaresca y juglares: aspectos de la historia literaria y cultural de España*, 7th edn (Madrid: Espasa-Calpe).

Monteira Arias, Inés, 2012. *El enemigo imaginado: la escultura románica hispana y la lucha contra el Islam* (Toulouse: Méridiennes. CNRS-Université de Toulouse le Mirail).

O'Callaghan, Joseph F., 1993. *The Learned King: The Reign of Alfonso X of Castile* (Philadelphia: University of Pennsylvania Press).

O'Callaghan, Joseph F., trans., 2002. *The Latin Chronicle of the Kings of Castile* (Tempe, Arizona: Arizona Center for Medieval and Renaissance Studies).

O'Callaghan, Joseph F., 2003. *Reconquest and Crusade in Medieval Spain* (Philadelphia: University of Pennsylvania Press).

O'Callaghan, Joseph F., 2011. *The Gibraltar Crusade: Castile and the Battle for the Strait* (Philadelphia: University of Pennsylvania Press).

Peña Pérez, F. Javier, 2005. *El surgimiento de una nación: Castilla en su historia y en sus mitos* (Barcelona: Crítica).

Pérez de Urbel, Fray Justo, 1944. 'Historia y leyenda en el Poema de Fernán González', *Escorial* 14, 319–351.

Pérez de Urbel, Fray Justo, 1945. *Historia del condado de Castilla*, 3 vols. (Madrid: Consejo Superior de Investigaciones Científicas).

Pick, Lucy K., 2004. *Conflict and Coexistence: Archbishop Rodrigo and the Muslims and Jews of Medieval Spain* (Ann Arbor: The University of Michigan Press).

Procter, Evelyn S., 1980. *Curia and Cortes in León and Castile 1072–1295* (Cambridge: Cambridge University Press).

Puyol, Julio, ed., 1926, repr. 2007. *Crónica de España por Lucas, Obispo de Tuy: primera edición del texto romanceado, conforme a un códice de la Academia* (Valladolid: Maxtor).

Reilly, Bernard F., 1993. *The Medieval Spains* (Cambridge: Cambridge University Press).

Rico, Francisco, 1985. 'La clerecía del mester', *Hispanic Review* 53, 127–150.

Romero, Miguel, 2014. *Leonor de Inglaterra, Reina de Castilla* (Madrid: Nowtilus).

Salvador Martínez, H., 2010. *Alfonso X, the Learned: A Biography* (Leiden: Brill).

Salvador Martínez, H., 2012. *Berenguela la Grande y su época 1180–1246* (Madrid: Ediciones Polifemo).

Salvador Miguel, Nicasio, 2000. 'La actividad literaria en la corte de Fernando III', in Manuel González Jiménez, ed., *Sevilla 1248: Congreso Internacional Conmemorativo del 750 Aniversario de la Conquista de la Ciudad de Sevilla por Fernando III, Rey de Castilla y León* (Madrid: Editorial Centro de Estudios Ramón Areces), pp. 685–702.

Sánchez Jiménez, Antonio, 2001. *La literatura en la corte de Alfonso VIII de Castilla* (unpublished thesis, Universidad de Salamanca). Online at: http:// es.scribd.com/doc/45873148/Sanchez-Jimenez-Antonio-La-literatura-en-la-corte-de-Alfonso-VIII-de-Castilla [accessed 30 November 2012].

Serra Ruiz, Rafael, 1965. *Honor, honra e injuria en el derecho medieval español* (Murcia: Universidad de Murcia).

Serrano y Sanz, M., 1919. 'Crónicon Villarense (Liber Regum)', *Boletín de la real academia española* 6, 192–220.

Vanderford, Kenneth H., ed., 1984. *Setenario* (Barcelona: Crítica).

Whitehill, Walter Muir, ed., 1944. *Liber Sancti Jacobi:* Codex Calixtinus, Vol. 1 (Santiago de Compostela: Seminario de Estudios Gallegos).

Wright, Roger, 1996. 'Latin and Romance in the Castilian Chancery (1180–1230)', *Bulletin of Hispanic Studies* 73, 115–128.

3. Books and articles on the Poema de Fernán González *and related texts*

Armistead, Samuel G., 1961. 'La perspectiva histórica del "Poema de Fernán González"', *Papeles de Son Armadans* 21, 9–18.

Avalle-Arce, Juan Bautista, 1972. 'El *Poema de Fernán González*: clerecía y juglaría', *Philological Quarterly* 51, 60–73.

Bailey, Matthew, 1993. *The* Poema del Cid *and the* Poema de Fernán González*: The Transformation of an Epic Tradition* (Madison: Hispanic Seminary of Medieval Studies).

Bailey, Matthew, 2010. *The Poetics of Speech in the Medieval Spanish Epic* (Toronto: University of Toronto Press).

Coates, Geraldine (see also Hazbun, Geraldine), 2008. 'Endings Lost and Found in the *Poema de Fernán González*', *Hispanic Research Journal* 9, 203–217.

Deyermond, Alan, 1960. 'Una nota sobre el *Poema de Fernán González*', *Hispanófila* 8, 35–37.

Deyermond, Alan, 1968. *Epic Poetry and the Clergy: Studies on the* Mocedades de Rodrigo (London: Tamesis).

Deyermond, Alan, 1990. 'Uses of the Bible in the *Poema de Fernán González*', in David Hook and Barry Taylor, eds, *Cultures in Contact in Medieval Spain: Historical and Literary Essays Presented to L. P. Harvey* (London: King's College Medieval Studies), pp. 47–70.

Deyermond, Alan and Margaret Chaplin, 1972. 'Folk-Motifs in the Medieval Spanish Epic', *Philological Quarterly* 51, 36–53.

Díaz-Mas, Paloma, ed., 2006. *Romancero* (Barcelona: Crítica).

Duggan, Joseph J., 1989. *The* Cantar de mio Cid*: Poetic Creation in its Economic and Social Contexts* (Cambridge: Cambridge University Press).

Dutton, Brian, 1961. 'Gonzalo de Berceo and the *Cantares de Gesta*', *Bulletin of Hispanic Studies* 38, 197–205.

Dutton, Brian, ed., 1967. *La "Vida de San Millán de la Cogolla" de Gonzalo de Berceo. Estudio y edición crítica* (London: Tamesis).

Dutton, Brian, ed., 1971. *Gonzalo de Berceo, Obras completas II: Los Milagros de Nuestra Señora. Estudio y edición crítica* (London: Tamesis).

Dutton, Brian, 1973. 'French Influences in the Spanish *mester de clerecía*', in Brian Dutton, J. Woodrow Hassell, Jr. and John E. Keller, eds, *Medieval Studies in Honor of Robert White Linker* (Madrid: Castalia), pp. 73–93.

Dutton, Brian, ed., 1975. *Gonzalo de Berceo, Obras completas III: El duelo de la Virgen, Los himnos, Los loores de Nuestra Señora, Los signos del Juicio Final. Estudio y edición crítica* (London: Tamesis).

Dutton, Brian, ed., 1978. *Gonzalo de Berceo, Obras completas IV: La vida de Santo Domingo de Silos. Estudio y edición crítica* (London: Tamesis).

Entwistle, William J., 1924. 'The Liberation of Castile', *Modern Language Review* 19, 471–472.

Fernández Gallardo, Luis, 2009. 'La idea de "cruzada" en el *Poema de Fernán González*', *eHumanista* 12, 1–32.

Fradejas Lebrero, José, 1989. 'Significado e intención del Poema de Fernán González', in José María Peña de San Martín, *et al.*, eds, *El Poema de Fernán González: edición facsímil del manuscrito depositado en el Monasterio de El Escorial* (Burgos: Excmo. Ayuntamiento de Burgos), pp. 13–36.

Geary, John Steven, 1980. *Formulaic Diction in the* Poema de Fernán González *and the* Mocedades de Rodrigo (Madrid: José Porrúa Turanzas).

González-Blanco García, Elena, 2010. *La cuaderna vía española en su marco panrománico* (Madrid: Fundación Universitaria Española).

Harvey, L. P., 1976. 'Fernán González's Horse', in A. D. Deyermond, ed., *Medieval Hispanic Studies Presented to Rita Hamilton* (London: Tamesis), pp. 77–86.

Harvey, L. P. and David Hook, 1982. 'The Affair of the Horse and the Hawk in the "Poema de Fernán González"', *Modern Language Review* 77, 840–847.

Hazbun, Geraldine (see also Coates, Geraldine), 2011. 'Female Foundations in the *Libro de Alexandre* and *Poema de Fernán González*', in Xon de Ros and Geraldine Hazbun, eds, *A Companion to Spanish Women's Studies* (Woodbridge: Tamesis), pp. 25–40.

Irizarry, Estelle, 1983. 'Echoes of the Amazon Myth in Medieval Spanish Literature', in Beth Miller, ed., *Women in Hispanic Literature: Icons and Fallen Idols* (Berkeley, Los Angeles and London: University of California Press), pp. 53–66.

Keller, Jean Paul, 1990. *The Poet's Myth of Fernán González* (Potomac, Maryland: Scripta Humanistica).

Lacarra, María Eugenia, 1979. 'El significado histórico del *Poema de Fernán González*', *Studi Ispanici* 4, 9–41.

Lacarra, María Eugenia, 1980. *El Poema de Mio Cid: realidad histórica e ideología* (Madrid: José Porrúa Turanzas).

Leroux Gravatt, Michelle, 2007. 'The *Arenga* in the Literature of Medieval Spain' (unpublished thesis, University of North Carolina at Chapel Hill). Online at: http://dc.lib.unc.edu/cdm/ref/collection/etd/id/812 [accessed 1 October 2012].

López Guil, Itzíar, 1999. 'El amor en el *Poema de Fernán Gonçález*', in Vicente González Martín, ed., *Amor y erotismo en la literatura* (Salamanca: Caja Duero), pp. 529–536.

Lugones, Néstor A., 1977. '"Commo voz de pauon" en el *Libro de Alexandre* y en el *Poema de Fernán González*', *Meridiano* 70 (Austin, Texas) 4, 25–33.

Menéndez Pidal, Ramón, 1899. 'Notas para el romancero del conde Fernán González', in *Homenaje a Menéndez y Pelayo en el año vigésimo de su profesorado*, vol. 1 (Madrid: Librería General de Victoriano Suárez), pp. 429–507.

Menéndez Pidal, Ramón, 1969. *La España del Cid*, 7th edn, 2 vols. (Madrid: Espasa-Calpe).

Michael, Ian, 1961. 'A Comparison of the Use of Epic Epithets in the *Poema de Mio Cid* and the *Libro de Alexandre*', *Bulletin of Hispanic Studies* 38, 32–41.

Montaner, Alberto and Ángel Escobar, 2001. 'Estudio preliminar: el *Carmen Campidoctoris* y la materia cidiana', in *Carmen Campidoctoris o Poema Latino del Campeador: estudio preliminar, edición, traducción y comentario* (Madrid: Sociedad Estatal España Nuevo Milenio), pp. 13–120.

Montgomery, Thomas, 1998. *Medieval Spanish Epic: Mythic Roots and Ritual Language* (University Park, Pennsylvania: Penn State University Press).

Muñoz Cortés, Manuel, 1946. Review of *Poema de Fernán González*, ed. Alonso Zamora Vicente, *Revista de Filología Española* 30, 211–214.

Nepaulsingh, Colbert I, 1986. *Towards a History of Literary Composition in Medieval Spain* (Toronto, Buffalo and London: University of Toronto Press).

Paredes Núñez, Juan, 2010. *El Cancionero Profano de Alfonso X el Sabio: edición crítica con introducción, notas y glosario*, 2nd edn, *Verba*: Anexo 66 (Santiago de Compostela: Universidad de Santiago de Compostela).

Parsons Scott, Samuel, trans. and Robert I Burns, S. J., ed., 2001. *Las Siete Partidas*, 5 vols. (Philadelphia: University of Pennsylvania Press).

Pattison, David G., 2007. 'The Role of Women in Some Medieval Spanish Epic and Chronicle Texts', in Rhian Davies and Anny Brooksbank Jones, eds, *The Place of Argument: Essays in Honour of Nicholas G. Round* (Woodbridge: Tamesis), pp. 17–30.

Pitollet, Camille, 1902. 'Note au *Poema de Fernán González*', *Bulletin Hispanique* 4, 157–161.

Sánchez-Albornoz, Claudio, 1944. 'De Sidonia a Segoyuela', *Revista de Filología Hispánica* 6, 191–196.

Smith, Colin, ed., 1972. *Poema de mio Cid* (Oxford: Oxford University Press).

Smith, Colin, trans., 1988. *Christians and Moors in Spain*, vol. 1 (Oxford: Aris and Phillips).

Such, Peter and John Hodgkinson, trans., 1987. *The Poem of My Cid (Poema de Mio Cid)* (Oxford: Aris and Phillips).

Such, Peter and Richard Rabone, trans., 2009. *Book of Alexander (Libro de Alexandre)* (Oxford: Oxbow Books). Aris and Phillips Hispanic Classics.

Susong, Gilles, 2007. 'À propos du rôle des Plantagenêts dans la diffusion de la littérature Arthurienne: l'exemple d'Aliénor de Domfront, Reine de Castile (1161–1214)', *La légende arthurienne, racine et réceptions* 7–8, 20–25.

Toro-Garland, Fernando de, 1973. 'El Arcipreste, protagonista literario del medievo español. El caso del "mal arcipreste" del *Fernán Gonçález'*, in M. Criado de Val, ed., *El Arcipreste de Hita: El Libro, El Autor, La Tierra, La Época. Actas del I Congreso Internacional sobre el Arcipreste de Hita* (Barcelona: S.E.R.E.S.A.), pp. 327–336.

Uría Maqua, Isabel, 2000. *Panorama crítico del 'mester de clerecía'* (Madrid: Castalia).

Uría Maqua, Isabel, 2001. 'Ritmo, prosodia y sintaxis en la poética del mester de clerecía', *Revista de poética medieval* 7, 111–130.

Weiss, Julian, 2006. The Mester de Clerecía: *Intellectuals and Ideologies in Thirteenth-Century Castile* (Woodbridge: Tamesis).

West, Beverly, 1983. *Epic, Folk, and Christian Traditions in the* Poema de Fernán González (Madrid: José Porrúa Turanzas).

4. Other background studies

Abós Santabárbara, Ángel Luis, 2003. *La historia que nos enseñaron (1937–1975)* (Madrid: Foca).

Bowra, C. M., 1952. *Heroic Poetry* (London: Macmillan).

Boyd, Carolyn P., 1997. *Historia Patria: Politics, History, and National Identity in Spain, 1875–1975* (Princeton, New Jersey: Princeton University Press).

Burgess, Glyn S., trans., 1990. *The Song of Roland* (Harmondsworth: Penguin).

Curtius, Ernst Robert, trans. Willard R. Trask, 1953. *European Literature and the Latin Middle Ages* (London: Routledge and Keegan Paul).

Deyermond, Alan, 1995. *La literatura perdida de la Edad Media castellana: Catálogo y estudio. I: Épica y romances* (Salamanca: Ediciones Universidad de Salamanca).

Farmer, David H., 2004. *The Oxford Dictionary of Saints*, 5th edn (Oxford: Oxford University Press).

García Gallo, Alfonso, 1955. 'El carácter germánico de la épica y del derecho en la Edad Media española', *Anuario de Historia del Derecho Español* 25, 583–679.

García Gallo, Alfonso, 1984. 'Las versiones medievales de la independencia de Castilla', *Anuario de Historia del Derecho Español* 54, 253–294.

Hemming, T. D., ed., 1993. *La Chanson de Roland: The Text of Frederick Whitehead. Revised, with a New Introduction, Bibliography and Notes* (Bristol: Bristol Classical Press).

Hollander, Robert, 1977. 'Typology and Secular Literature: Some Medieval Problems and Examples', in Earl Miner, ed., Literary Uses of Typology from the Late Middle Ages to the Present (Princeton, New Jersey: Princeton University Press), pp. 3–19.

Keane, John, 2009. *The Life and Death of Democracy* (London, Sydney, New York and Toronto: Simon and Schuster).

Keen, Maurice, 1984. *Chivalry* (New Haven and London: Yale University Press).

Ladero Quesada, Miguel Ángel, 2004. *La formación medieval de España: Territorios. Regiones. Reinos* (Madrid: Alianza).

Lord, Albert B., 1960. *The Singer of Tales* (Cambridge, Massachusetts: Harvard University Press).

Menéndez Pidal, Gonzalo, 1986. *La España del siglo XIII leída en imágenes* (Madrid: Real Academia de la Historia).

Monsalvo Antón, Jose María, 2010. *Atlas histórico de la España medieval* (Madrid: Editorial Síntesis).

Murphy, James J., 1974, *Rhetoric in the Middle Ages: A History of Rhetorical Theory from Saint Augustine to the Renaissance* (Berkeley, Los Angeles and London: University of California Press).

Parry, Milman, 1930. 'Studies in the Epic Technique of Oral Verse-Making. I. Homer and Homeric Style', *Harvard Studies in Classical Philology* 41, 73–143.

Ruiz, Teofilo F., 2004. *From Heaven to Earth: The Reordering of Castilian Society, 1150–1350* (Princeton and Oxford: Princeton University Press).

Salter, Elizabeth, 1973. 'Courts and Courtly Love', in David Daiches and Anthony Thorlby, eds, *The Medieval World* (London: Aldus), pp. 407–444. Literature and Western Civilization.

Vinaver, Eugène, 1971. *The Rise of Romance* (Oxford: Clarendon Press).

Víñez Sánchez, Antonia, 1998. 'Pobres infanzones. La sátira social en dos escarnios de Gonçal' Eanes do Vinhal', in Javier Martín Castellanos, Fernando Velázquez Basanta and Joaquín Bustamante Costa, eds, *Estudios de la Universidad de Cádiz ofrecidos a la memoria del profesor Braulio Justel Calabozo* (Cádiz: Servicio de Publicaciones de la Universidad de Cádiz), pp. 231–239.

THE POEM OF FERNÁN GONZÁLEZ

POEMA DE FERNÁN GONZÁLEZ

1   En el nonbre del Padre   que fizo toda cosa,
      del que quiso nasçer   de la Virgen preçiosa,
      e del Spíritu Santo   que igual d'ellos posa,
      del conde de Castiella   quiero fer una prosa.

2   El Señor que crïó   la tierra e la mar,
      de las cosas passadas   que yo pueda contar,
      Él, que es buen maestro,   me deve demostrar
      cómmo s' cobró la tierra   toda de mar a mar.

3   Contar vos he primero   de cómmo la perdieron
      nuestros anteçessores: en quál coita visquieron;
      cóm' omnes deserdados   fuïdos andodieron;
      essa rabia llevaron   que ende non morieron.

4   Muchas coitas passaron   nuestros anteçessores,
      muchos malos espantos,   muchos malos sabores:
      sufrién frío e fanbre,   e muchos amargores;
      estos viçios d' agora   estonz' eran dolores.

5   En tanto, d'este tiempo   ir vos he yo contando
      cómmo fueron la tierra   perdiendo e cobrando
      ....
      fasta que todos fueron   al conde don Fernando;

6   cómmo es muy lüenga   desd' el tienpo antigo,
      cómmo se dio la tierra   al buen rey don Rodrigo,
      cóm' la ovo ganar   el mortal enemigo,
      de grand honor que era   tornó l' pobre mendigo.

7   Esto fizo Mafómat,   de la mala creençia,
      ....
      ....
      predicó por su boca   mucha mala sentençia.

8   Desque ovo Mafómat   a todos predicado,
      avién los coraçones   las gentes demudado.
      ....
      e la muerte de Cristo   avién la olvidado.

1   In the name of the Father, who created all things,
     of Him who willed His birth of the Virgin fair,
     and of the Holy Spirit, who dwells as their equal,
     I now wish to make a rhyme on the Count of Castile.*

2   The Lord, the Creator of the land and the sea,
     in order that I may tell of things that are past,
     must show to me now, fine teacher that He is,
     how the land was all regained, from sea to sea.*

3   First I shall tell you of how the land was lost
     by those who came before us, and in what pain they lived;
     of how they took to flight, having lost their fathers' lands,
     angered that that loss did not also bring their death.

4   Many were the sorrows our forefathers endured –
     many cruel terrors, and terrible suffering;
     they bore cold and hunger, and much bitter torment:
     what now brings us pleasure was then only pain.

5   Meanwhile, I shall begin to tell you of this time,
     and how the lands were lost, and then in turn regained,
     ....
     until all men looked as lord to Count Fernando.

6   I shall tell the long story that began in ancient times,
     how the land was passed on to the good King Rodrigo,*
     and how it came to be won by the King's deadly foe:
     once a man rich in honours, he was left a poor beggar.

7   This was done by Mohammed, of the evil faith,
     ....
     ....
     from his mouth he preached many evil claims.

8   Once they had all heard the preaching of Mohammed,
     the people all felt a great change in their hearts
     ....
     and Christ's death was forgotten from their minds.

9   Desque los españones   a Cristo conosçieron,
desque en la su ley   bautismo resçibieron,
nunca en otra ley   tornarse non quisieron;
mas por guarda d' aquesto   muchos males sufrieron.

10   Esta ley de los santos   qu' oyeron predicada,
por ella la su sangre   ovieron derramada;
apóstoles e mártires   – esta santa mesnada –
fueron por la verdat   metidos a espada.

11   Fueron las santas vírgines   en est' afirmamiento:
de varón non quisieron   ningún ayuntamiento;
de los viçios del mundo   non ovieron talento;
vençieron por aquesto   al bestión mascariento.

12   Los primeros profetas   esto profetizaron,
los santos confessores   esta ley predicaron,
ca en los otros dioses   verdad nunca fallaron;
San Juan lo afirmó   quando l' descabeçaron.

13   Muchos reyes e condes   e muchas potestades,
papas e arçobispos,   obispos e abades,
por esta ley murieron   – esto bien lo creades –;
por end' han en los çielos   todas sus heredades.

14   Tornemos nos al curso,   nuestra razón sigamos:
tornemos en España,   a do lo començamos
– com' el escrito diz,   nos ansí lo fablamos –,
en los reyes primeros   que godos los llamamos.

15   Venieron estos godos   de partes de Oriente
– Cristo los enbïó,   est' pueblo descreyente –;
del linax' de Magog   vino aquesta gente;
conquirieron el mundo,   esto sin fallimiente.

16   Non fueron estos godos   de comienço cristianos,
nin judíos d' Egito,   nin de ley de paganos.
Antes fueron gentiles,   unos pueblos loçanos;
eran por' en batalla   pueblos muy venturados.

9   Ever since the Spaniards had had knowledge of Christ
and had received baptism into His law,*
to no other law did they ever wish to turn;
but to keep to this they had to suffer many ills.

10   This law of the saints that the Spaniards heard preached,
in the name of that law they spilt their blood freely:
this saintly band, of apostles and martyrs,
were put to the sword, for the sake of the Truth.

11   On this the holy virgins were of firm accord:
they had no desire for union with men,
nor any inclination for the pleasures of the world;
in this way they vanquished the hideous Beast.*

12   This was the prophecy of the first prophets,
and this law was preached by the holy confessors,
for in no other gods did they ever find truth,
as Saint John confirmed, when he was beheaded.*

13   Many kings and counts and many men of power,
popes and archbishops, bishops and abbots,
gave their lives for this law – this you must believe –
and so in Heaven have their full inheritance.

14   Let us return to our course and take up our thread:
let us return to Spain, and to where our tale began
– as the written text says, so our account is told –*
with the first of the kings, whom we know as the Goths.

15   These Goths were come from the lands of the Orient
– they were sent by Christ, this unbelieving people –;
from the line of Magog was this race descended;
it is no lie to say they conquered all the world.*

16   These Goths did not have their roots in Christianity,
they were not Jews from Egypt, nor followed pagan law,
but rather they were gentiles, a people of nobility,
and a people who in battle had great fortune.

17   Toda tierra de Roma   venieron l' avastando,
       a los unos prendiendo,   a los otros matando,
       ....
       ....

18   Passaron a España   con el su grand poder,
       ....
       ....
       era en este tienpo   el pap' Alexandrer.

19   Escogieron España   toda de mar a mar;
       nin villa nin castiello   no s' pudo anparar;
       África e Turonia   ovieron por mandar;
       omnes fueron arteros   – Dios los quiso guïar –.

20   Fueron de Sancti Spíritus   los godos espirados;
       los malos argumentos   todos fueron fallados;
       conosçieron que eran   los ídolos pecados:
       quantos creián por ellos   eran mal engañados.

21   Demandaron maestros   por' façer s' entender
       en la fe de don Cristo   que avién de creer;
       los maestros, sepades,   fueron muy volunter;
       fizieron les la fe   toda bien entender.

22   Dixeron los maestros: 'Tod' esto non val' nada:
       bautizados non sodes   en el agua sagrada,
       la qual culpa e error   es erejia llamada;
       el alma de pecados   será luego lavada.'

23   Resçibieron los godos   el agua a bautismo;
       fueron luz e estrella   de tod' el cristianismo;
       alçaron cristiandat,   baxaron paganismo;
       el cond' Ferrán Gonçález   fizo aquesto mismo.

24   ....
       que fue muy leal miente   de sus omnes servido;
       fueron de tod' el mundo   pueblo muy escojido;
       quanto 'l mundo durare   non cadrán en olvido.

17   They wrought devastation through all of Rome's lands;
some they seized as captives, to others they brought death;
....
....

18   They crossed into Spain, with their powerful army,
....
....
this was during the era of Pope Alexander.*

19   Spain was their choice, which they took from sea to sea;
neither town nor castle could resist their attack;
Africa to Touraine was all under their command;*
they were men of cunning, whom it was God's will to guide.

20   The Goths were men inspired by the Holy Spirit,
who revealed as such all the evil arguments;
they came to see that idols were nothing but a sin,
and that those with faith in them were ill deceived.

21   They sent out for teachers to gain understanding
of the Christian faith, which was to be their own;
the teachers, I tell you, were most willing to go,
and in the faith they gave them full instruction.

22   So spoke the teachers: 'All this is worth nothing,
for in holy water you have not been baptized;
this fault and error is labelled as heresy;*
do it, and the soul will be cleansed at once of sins.'

23   The Goths did indeed receive the water in baptism;
they were the leading light and star of all Christendom;
they upheld Christianity, and renounced the pagan path,
precisely the actions of Count Fernán González.

Allusion → Parallels drawn

24   ....
who received most loyal service from his men;
they were singled out from among the whole world,*
and will not be forgotten while the world endures.

25   Quando los reyes godos   d'este mundo passaron,
fueron se a los çielos,   grand reino eredaron;
alçaron luego rey   los pueblos que quedaron,
com' diz la escritura,   don Çindus le llamaron.

26   Quando reinó don Çidnus,   un buen guerreador,
era San Eügenio   d' españones pastor.
En Toledo morava   est' santo confessor,
Isidro en Sevilla   arçobisp' e señor.

27   Finó se el rey Çidnus,   un natural señor;
a España e África   ovo en su valor;
dio les pastor muy bueno   luego el Crïador:
rey Vanva vino luego,   que fue tal o mejor.

28   Vanva, aqueste rey,   com' avedes oído,
venía de los godos,   pueblo muy escojido;
porque él non reinasse   andava escondido;
nonbre se puso Vanva   por non ser conosçido.

29   Buscándo l' por España,   ovieron lo fallar;
fizieron le por fuerça   aquel reino tomar.
Bien sabié que con yerbas   lo avién de matar;
por tanto de su grado   non quisiera reinar.

30   Rey fue muy derechero   e de muy grand natura,
muy franc' e muy ardit,   e de muy grand mesura;
leal e verdadero,   e de muy grand ventura.
¡Aquel que l' dio la muerte   no l' falesca rencura!

31   Partió todas las tierras,   ayuntó los 'bispados,
....
Estableçidos fueron   lugares señalados,
cómmo fuessen los términos   a ellos sojuzgados.

32   Fue toda esta cosa   puesta en buen estado;
pesaba con su vida   muy fuerte al pecado;
dio l' yervas e murió   Vanva aponçoñado.
¡En paraïso sea   tan buen rey eredado!

25　　　　When the kings of the Goths passed on from this world,
　　　　　a vast kingdom in Heaven was theirs to inherit;
　　　　　the peoples who remained behind at once chose a king:
　　　　　as the written text says, Reccesuinth was his name.*

26　　　　While Reccesuinth reigned, who was a fine warrior,
　　　　　Saint Eugenio was the pastor of the Spaniards.
　　　　　Toledo was the dwelling of this holy confessor
　　　　　and Isidore was lord and archbishop in Seville.*

27　　　　On the death of King Reccesuinth, natural lord
　　　　　who held Spain and Africa under his sway,
　　　　　the Creator then gave them the finest of shepherds:
　　　　　King Wamba succeeded him, as good a king or better.*

28　　　　This man King Wamba, as you have already heard,
　　　　　came from the Goths, a people chosen above others;
　　　　　he spent time in hiding, that he should not be made king,
　　　　　and called himself Wamba, that he might remain unknown.

29　　　　He was sought throughout Spain, and eventually found,
　　　　　and forcibly compelled to take on that kingdom.
　　　　　But Wamba well knew that he would meet his death by poison:
　　　　　that was the reason why he had no wish to reign.

30　　　　He was a king of great honour and born of fine stock,
　　　　　most noble and courageous and of the greatest prudence;*
　　　　　he was loyal and true, and blessed with great good fortune.
　　　　　May the one who killed him be never free of pain!

31　　　　He divided the land and marked out the bishoprics,
　　　　　...
　　　　　and all the boundaries were clearly demarcated,
　　　　　to make it clear which territories they governed.

32　　　　All of these things were now set in good order,
　　　　　but the King's life weighed heavy on the Devil;
　　　　　he gave Wamba a poison which ended that life.
　　　　　May paradise bring such a fine king his inheritance!

[handwritten marginal note:] Refrain. See belladry in other Nations

33　　　　Reinó después un rey,　Egica fue llamado;
　　　　　dos años, que non más,　visquió en el reinado.
　　　　　A cabo de dos años　del siglo fue sacado;
　　　　　non pesó al su pueblo,　que fue malo provado.

34　　　　Quando finó Egica,　a poca de sazón,
　　　　　fincó en Vautiçanos　toda la regïón.
　　　　　Fue niño de los godos,　poderoso varón,
　　　　　omne de grand esfuerço　e de grand coraçón.

35　　　　Finó se Vautiçanos,　reinó 'l rey don Rodrigo,
　　　　　avién en él los moros　un mortal enemigo;
　　　　　era de los cristianos　sonbra e grand abrigo;
　　　　　por culpa en que era,　no l' era Dios amigo.

36　　　　Éste fue d' allend' mar,　de grand parte señor;
　　　　　ganó los Montes Claros　el buen guerreador.
　　　　　...
　　　　　de cómmo se perdió,　esto es grand dolor.

37　　　　Era estonç' España　toda d' una creençia:
　　　　　al Fijo de la Virgen　fazían obediencia.
　　　　　Pesava al dïablo　con tanta reverençia;
　　　　　non avié entre ellos　envidia nin contiençia.

38　　　　Estavan las iglesias　todas bien ordenadas;
　　　　　de olio e de çera　estavan abastadas.
　　　　　Los diezmos e premiençias　leal mient' eran dadas;
　　　　　eran todas las gentes　en la fe arraigadas.

39　　　　Vesquién de su lazerio　todos los labradores;
　　　　　las grandes potestades　non eran robadores;
　　　　　guardavan bien sus pueblos　com' leales señores;
　　　　　vesquién de sus derechos　los grandes e menores.

40　　　　Estava la fazienda　toda en tal estado:
　　　　　avié con este bien　grand pesar el pecado.
　　　　　Revolvió atal cosa　el mal aventurado:
　　　　　el gozo que avía　en llanto fue tornado.

33   Next ruled a king by the name of Egica,*
       who lived as monarch for two years, but no more;
       at the end of two years he was taken from the earth,
       but his people did not grieve, for his wickedness was known.

34   When death came to Egica but a short time after,
       the whole land came to be ruled by Wittiza.*
       He was a child of the Goths, and a powerful lord,
       a man of great valour and stoutness of heart.

35   Wittiza's life ended with Rodrigo next to reign;
       and in him the Moors found a deadly foe:
       to the Christians he brought shade and great protection,
       but, through his guilt, the Lord was ill-disposed to him.*

36   Rodrigo went beyond the sea, lord of many lands,
       and won the Shining Mountains, fine warrior that he was. *
       ....
       how the land was lost is a matter of great pain.

37   At that time all Spain was of a single creed,
       and to the Virgin's Son it did obeisance.
       So great was their reverence it brought the Devil sorrow,
       for conflict and envy had no place among them.

38   The churches were all of them set in careful order
       and possessed rich supplies of both oil and wax;
       of tributes and tithes loyal payment was given,
       and all of the people deeply rooted in their faith.

39   The farmers all lived on the fruits of their toil,
       with none of their governors inclined towards theft;
       loyal lords were they, who cared well for their people;
       great men and lesser lived in line with their rights.

40   Such was the state in which men's affairs then stood;
       but this wellbeing was the Devil's great sorrow.
       Wretch that he was, he did then so contrive it
       that the joy that they felt was turned to weeping.

41   Fijos de Vautiçanos   non devieran nasçer,
      que éssos començaron   traïçión a fazer;
      volvió lo el dïablo,   metió y su poder;
      esto fu' el escomienço   de España perder.

42   El conde don Yllán,   bien avedes oído
      cóm' ovo por las parias   a Marruecos troçido;
      ovo en est' comedio   tal cosa conteçido
      por que ovo el reino   de ser todo destruido.

43   Fizo le la grand ira   a traïción volver:
      fabló con Vusarván,   que avié grand poder,
      dixo cómmo podría   cristianos confonder:
      no s' podrié nulla guisa   España defender.

44   Dixo aquestas oras   el conde don Yllán:
      'Digo yo la verdat,   amigo Vusarván:
      si non te doy España,   non coma yo más pan;
      si non, de mí non fíes   más que si fuesse can.'

45   Dixo: 'Trespassaré   much' aína la mar;
      faré al rey Rodrigo   sus caveros juntar;
      fazer les he las armas   en el fuego quemar,
      por que después non ayan   con que se manparar.

46   Quand' esto oviere fecho   sabrás de mi mandado;
      travessarás el mar   con todo tu fonsado.
      Commo será el pueblo   todo bien segurado,
      refez miente podrás   conquerir el reinado.'

47   Despidió s' de los moros,   luego passó la mar,
      ....
      Deviera s' el mesquino   con sus manos matar
      pues qu' en la mar irada   non s' pudo afogar.

48   Fue luego por' el rey   qual ora fue passado:
      'Omillo m',' dixo, 'rey,   el mi señor onrado;
      recabdé tu mensaje   e cunplí tu mandado;
      Evas aquí las parias   por que ovist' enbiado.'

41   No children of Wittiza should ever have been born,*
for they began to act in treacherous ways;
the Devil pulled the strings: on this he trained his power,
and this was the beginning of the ruin of Spain.

42   Of Count Julian, you have surely heard tell*
how he had crossed, in search of tribute, to Morocco;
at this point, there had occurred something so grave
that it would bring the whole kingdom to destruction.

43   Spurred by great anger, he made recourse to treason,
and spoke with the powerful Tāriq ibn Ziyad,*
telling of how he could confound the Christians
and how Spain would be defenceless against him.

44   Whereupon Count Julian spoke forth with these words:
'The truth do I say to you, Tāriq, my good friend –
should I not give you Spain, may I eat no more bread;
if I fail, may you trust me no more than a dog.'

45   He said: 'I shall go far beyond the bounds of the sea,
and force King Rodrigo to assemble his knights;
I shall have them all burn their weapons in the fire
so no means of self-defence will be left them.

46   Once this has been done, you will hear of my orders,
and with all your army cross over the sea;
as the people will all feel assured of their safety,
you will conquer the kingdom with consummate ease.'

47   He took leave of the Moors and at once crossed the sea,

        ....

At his own hands should the wretch have met death,
for in the angry sea he could not drown.

48   He went straight to the King, with no hint of delay,
and said, 'My King and honoured lord, I bow before you;
I carried out your message and fulfilled your command;
here you have the tributes which you sent for.'

49   Resçibió lo muy bien   el buen rey don Rodrigo,
       tomó lo por la mano   e asentó l' consigo.
       Diz: '¿Cómmo vos ha ido,   el mi leal amigo,
       d' aquello por que fustes,   si es paja o trigo?'

50   'Señor, si tú quisieres   mi consejo tomar,
       – ¡grado a Dios del çielo   que te fizo reinar! –
       nin moro nin cristiano   non te pued' contrallar.
       Las armas, ¿qué las quieres,   pues non has pelear?

51   Manda por tod' el reino   las armas desatar:
       d'ellas fagan açadas   pora viñas labrar
       e d'ellas fagan rejas   pora panes senbrar;
       cavallos e roçines   todos fagan arar.

52   Todos labren por pan,   peones e caveros,
       sienbren cuestas e valles   e todos los oteros;
       enriquescan tus reinos   de paz e de dineros,
       ca non has contra quien   poner otros fronteros.

53   Mas todos los varones   a sus tierras se vayan;
       ningunas armaduras   defiende que no trayan.
       Si esto non fizieren   en la tu ira cayan;
       si non las que araren   otras bestias non ayan.

54   Non has a los caveros   por que les dar soldadas;
       labren sus eredades,   vivan en sus posadas;
       con mulas e cavallos   fagan grandes aradas,
       qu' esso han mester ellos   que non otras espadas.'

55   Quand' ovo acabada   el conde su razón
       – mejor non la dixeran   quantos en mundo son –,
       ....
       ....

56   Enbïó don Rodrigo   luego sus mensajeros
       ....
       ....
       ....

49   Warmly did the good King Rodrigo receive him;
he took him by the hand and sat him at his side.
He said, 'How did you fare, my loyal friend,
with your errand? Did it prove to be wheat or chaff?'

50   'My lord, if your will should be to follow my advice
– thanks be to our Heavenly God, who brought you to the throne!
Neither Moor nor Christian can make a stand against you;
what need have you of arms, since you do not need to fight?*

51   Order the destruction of all weapons in the kingdom,
and that people turn them into hoes to tend the vines
and beat them into ploughshares so as to sow the grain;
let warhorses and nags alike all be used to plough.

52   Let foot soldiers and knights all labour for their bread,
sowing seeds in the valleys, on the slopes and all the hills;
may they enrich your kingdoms with peace and with wealth,
for you have no enemies for frontier troops to fight.

53   But let all the lords now go back to their lands
and forbid that they should wear any armour.
Should they not comply, let them fall upon your wrath,
and let them keep no beasts, save for those that pull the plough.

54   You have no cause to be paying the knights:
let them work on their lands, and live in their homes;
let them plough vast estates with their horses and mules,
for that is their need – not the blade of a sword.'

55   When the Count had come to the end of his speech
– better left unspoken by any man alive! –
....
....

56   Rodrigo without delay sent out his messengers
....
....
....

57 Era la corte toda en uno ayuntada:
  Aragón e Navarra, buena tierra provada,
  León e Portogal, Castiella la preçiada;
  non serié en el mundo tal provincia fallada.

58 Quando vio don Rodrigo que tenía sazón,
  ante toda la corte començó su razón:
  'Oítme, cavalleros, si Cristo vos perdon',

  ....

59 ¡Graçias a Dios del çielo que lo quiso fazer!
  En aquesto l' avemos mucho que gradeçer
  por que es toda Spaña en el nuestro poder,
  mal grado a los moros que la solién tener.

60 Avemos nos en África una buena partida:
  parias nos dan por ella la gente descreída.
  Mucho oro e plata, a la llena medida;
  bien somos ya seguros todos d'essa partida.

61 El conde, cavalleros, las pazes ha firmadas
  e por estos çient años las parias recabdadas;
  pueden vevir las gentes todas bien seguradas,
  non avrán ningún miedo, vivrán en sus posadas.

62 Pues que todos avemos tales seguridades,
  han vos a dar carrera por que en paz vivades,
  peones e caveros e todas potestades
  que viva cada uno en las sus eredades.

63 Lorigas, capelinas e todas brafoneras,
  las lanças e cochiellas, fierros e espalderas,
  espadas e ballestas e asconas monteras;
  metet las en el fuego, fazet grandes fogueras.

64 Faredes d'ellas fierros e d'ellas guarneçiones
  e rejas e açadas, picos e açadones,
  destralejas e fachas, segures e fachones,
  estas cosas atales con que labren peones.

57   Now the whole court had been gathered together:
        Aragón and Navarre, a land shown to be fine,
        León and Portugal, and highly prized Castile;
        the like of this province could nowhere else be found.*

58   When Rodrigo saw that the moment had come,
        before the whole court he began his address:
        'Hear me, my knights, may Christ grant you pardon,*

59   Thanks be to Heavenly God, who willed to make it so!
        In this matter we have much cause to thank Him,
        for the whole land of Spain now lies in our power,
        to the sorrow of the Moors, its rulers of old.*

60   Our power extends far into African lands,
        for which the unbelievers pay us tribute:
        much gold and silver, both in full measure;
        of that share we now all rest well assured.

61   The Count, my knights, has made a pact of peace
        for us to gain tribute for the next hundred years;
        our peoples can now live safe and secure,
        and they will live without fear in their homes.

62   Since we can all now enjoy such security,
        the chance to live at peace will now be yours;
        horsemen, foot soldiers, and all men who govern,
        let each of them dwell in the lands which he owns.

63   Your mail-coats, helmets, and all your arm- and leg-guards,
        your lances and blades, iron arms and shoulder-plates,
        your swords and your crossbows and spears for the chase:
        cast them in the fire, and make it blaze high.*

64   You will forge iron tools from them, turn them into harness,
        make ploughshares and hoes, craft mattocks and picks,
        hatchets and sickles, axes great and small,
        such as might be employed by a labourer's hand.

65   Por aquesta carrera   avremos pan assaz;
      los grandes e los chicos,   fasta 'l menor rapaz,
      vivrán por esta guisa   seguros e en paz:
      quiero que esto sea,   si a vos otros plaz'.

66   Aquesto que yo digo   sea luego conplido,
      assí commo yo mando   quiero sea tenido;
      el que armas traxiere   e le fuere sabido
      fagan le lo que fazen   al traidor enemigo.

67   Tod' aquel que quisiere   salir de mi mandado,
      si en toda España   fuere después fallado,
      mando que el su cuerpo   sea justiçïado
      e que l' den tal justiçia   com' a traidor provado.'

68   Fue fecha la barata   atal com' entendedes,
      volvió lo el dïablo   que tiende tales redes;
      trastornó el çimiento,   cayeron las paredes:
      lo que estonz' perdiestes   cobrar vos lo podedes.

69   Tenién lo a grand bien   los pueblos labradores;
      non sabién la traición   mesquinos pecadores;
      los qu' eran entendidos   e bien entendedores
      dezién: '¡Mal sieglo ayan   tales consejadores!'

70   Ovieron a fer todo   lo que el rey mandava:
      quien las armas tenía   luego las desatava;
      el dïablo antiguo   en esto s' trabajava
      por fer mal a cristianos   – nunca en al andava –.

71   Quando fueron las armas   desfechas e quemadas,
      fueron aquestas nuevas   a Marruecos passadas;
      las gentes africanas   fueron luego juntadas;
      al puerto de la mar   fueron luego llegadas.

72   Todos muy bien guisados   por a Spaña passar,
      quando fueron juntados   passaron allend' mar;
      arribaron al puerto   que dizen Gibraltar;
      non podrié ningún omne   cuántos eran asmar.

65 In this way we shall have bread enough to eat;
everyone, young and old, to the tiniest child,
will thus dwell in safety and live a life of peace;
so do I wish things to be, if you are willing.

66 Let what I order be promptly carried out
and my command be obeyed to the letter;
any man bearing arms, and of whom this is known,
let him be dealt with as a traitorous foe.

67 Any man who chooses to ignore my command,
should he then be discovered in any part of Spain,
I command that justice be meted out upon him,
and that he be punished as a proven traitor.'

68 Just as you see was the deceit brought to pass,
woven by the Devil who sets such snares;
the foundations were shaken, down crashed the walls:
what you then lost you can now win again.

69 This won full approval of those who worked the land;
wretched sinners, they knew nothing of its treachery;
those of understanding, who understood full well,
cried out: 'May such advisers meet an evil end!'

70 They were obliged to do all the King commanded:
any man possessed of arms at once destroyed them.
The Devil of old always worked with this intent:
to bring harm upon Christians; he had no other aim.

71 When the weapons had met with destruction and fire,
report of this deed then travelled to Morocco;
the peoples of Africa were assembled at once,
and came without delay to the port of the sea.

72 They came well equipped for the journey to Spain,
and, once they were gathered, crossed over the sea;
they landed at the port that men call Gibraltar;
no man alive could reckon up their number.

73   Todos estos paganos   que África mandavan
            contra los de Oropa   despechosos estavan;
            ....
            entraron en la tierra   do entrar non cuidavan.

74   Llegaron a Sevilla   la gente renegada:
            essa çibdat nin otras   non se les fizo nada.
            Era de mala guisa   la rueda trastornada;
            la cautiva d' España   era mal quebrantada.

75   El buen rey don Rodrigo,   a quien avié contido,
            mandó por tod' el reino   dar luego 'l apellido:
            el que con él non fuesse   ante del mes conplido
            el aver e el cuerpo   tovies' lo por perdido.

76   Las gentes quand' oyeron   pregones aquexados
            que d' averes e cuerpos   eran mal menazados,
            non eran y ningunos   pora fincar osados;
            fueron ante del tienpo   con el rëy juntados.

77   Quand' ovo don Rodrigo   sus poderes juntados
            – era poder sin guisa,   mas todos desarmados –,
            lidiar fueron con moros,   lavaron sus pecados,
            ca fue de los profetas   esto profetizado.

78   Tenía don Rodrigo   sienpre la delantera;
            salió contra los moros,   tovo les la carrera.
            Ayuntó s' en el canpo   que dizen Sangonera,
            çerca de Guadïana   en essa su rivera.

79   Fueron d' amas las partes   los golpes avivados;
            eran pora lidiar   todos escalentados.
            Fueron de la primera   los moros arrancados,
            cojieron se con todo   essora los cruzados.

80   Era la cosa puesta   e de Dios otorgada
            que serién los d' España   metidos a espada;
            a los dueños primeros   les sería tornada;
            tornaron en el canpo   ellos otra vegada.

73 All of these pagans who in Africa held sway*
bore a bitter hatred for the people of Europe;
....
they entered lands they had not thought to enter.

74 The renegade people went as far as Seville:*
like the other cities, it showed them no resistance.
In grim fashion had the wheel now spun round;
the hapless lands of Spain lay cruelly broken.

75 The good King Rodrigo, who had suffered all this,
at once bade the rallying call be sounded through his realm:
that any man who stood not by his side within a month
should consider his possessions and his life to be forfeit.

76 When the people heard such insistent proclamations
of the grave threat to both their lives and their estates,
there was none among them who dared remain behind
and all were with the King before the appointed day.

77 When King Rodrigo had assembled his forces
– it was a force of vast extent, but all unarmed –
they met the Moors in battle, and washed away their sins,
for this had already been foretold by the prophets.*

So what? - Brave - Stupid?

78 Rodrigo stood always in the first line of battle;
marching out to face the Moors, he made to block their path;
he drew up his troops in the field called Sangonera,*
which lay near the banks of the River Guadiana.

79 On both sides the blows were ferociously dealt,
their spirits all stoked to a frenzy for battle;
the Moors, from the outset, were driven in retreat;
even then the crusaders withdrew to regroup.

80 It had been so ordained and granted by God
that the Spaniards should be put to the sword;
to the land's first lords she was to be restored;*
and to the field once more they now returned.

81   Cuidavan los cristianos   ser bien asegurados,
que avién a los moros   en el canpo rancados.
Fueran se los paganos   essas oras tornados,
si non por quien non ayan   perdón de sus pecados.

82   Otro día mañana   los pueblos descreídos
todos fueron en canpo,   de sus armas guarnidos,
tañendo añafiles   e dando alaridos;
las tierras e los çielos   semejavan movidos.

83   Volvieron essas oras   un torneo pesado;
començaron el fecho   do lo avién dexado;
morieron los cristianos   todos, ¡ay mal pecado!
Del buen rey essas oras   non sopieron mandado.

84   En Viseo fallaron   después la sepultura,
do avié un pitafio   'scrito d'esta figura:
'Aquí yaz' don Rodrigo,   un rey de grand natura,
el que perdió la tierra   por su desaventura.'

85   Fueron, commo oyestes,   de los moros rancados;
muchos eran los muertos,   muchos los cativados;
fuién los que fincaron   maldiziendo sus fados;
fueron por tod' el mundo   luego estos mandados.

86   Pero, con todo esto,   buen consejo prendieron:
tomaron las reliquias,   todas quantas podieron;
alçaron s' en Castiella,   assí se defendieron;
los de las otras tierras   por espadas murieron.

87   Era Castiella la Vieja   un puerto bien çerrado;
non avié más entrada   de un solo forado;
tovieron castellanos   el puerto bien guardado
porque de toda Spaña   ésse ovo fincado.

88   Fincaron las Asturias,   un pequeño lugar:
los valles e montañas   que son cerca la mar.
Non podieron los moros por los puertos passar
e ovieron por tanto   las Asturias fincar.

81   The Christians believed that they were in safety
        and had worsted the Moors on the battlefield;
        at that moment, the pagans would have turned in flight
        but for Him from whom their sins deserve no pardon.*

82   Upon the next morning, the faithless peoples
        all took the battlefield, clad in full armour,
        to the shrieks of their horns and their own battle-cries:
        it seemed to shake the heavens and the earth.*

83   They returned at this point to a violent tourney,
        taking up the battle from where they had ceased;
        the Christians met death to a man, oh evil fate!
        But there was then no news of their good king.

84   In Viseu was later discovered his tomb,*
        with an epitaph inscribed on it as follows:
        'Here lies Rodrigo, a king of fine stock,
        whose misfortune it was to lose his land.'

85   As you have heard, they were routed by the Moors:
        many Christians died and many suffered prison;
        those that remained fled with curses on their fate;
        word of this was quick to reach around the world.

86   But despite all this they were wise in their counsel:
        they took in their possession every relic that they could,
        and took refuge in Castile so to make their defence;
        those from other lands met their deaths by the sword.

87   A well closed-off mountain-pass was Old Castile,*
        with but a single way by which to enter;
        the Castilians held the pass securely guarded,
        for this alone was left from all of Spain.

88   The Asturias did remain: it was a tiny place –*
        valleys and mountains which border the sea.
        The Moors were unable to cross through the passes,
        and so the Asturias had come to endure.

89   España la gentil   fue luego destruïda;
           eran señores d'ella   la gente descreída;
           los cristianos mesquinos   avién muy mala vida,
           nunca fue en cristianos   tan grand cuita venida.

90   Dentro en las iglesias   fazían establías;
           fazién en los altares   muchas fieras follías;
           robavan los tesoros   de las sacristanías;
           lloravan los cristianos   las noches e los días.

91   Quiero vos deçir cosa   que fizo retraer;
           prendién a los cristianos,   mandavan los cozer,
           ....
           por tal que les podiessen   mayor miedo meter.

92   Tenién a otros presos: dexavan los foír
           por que veién las penas   a los otros sofrir;
           avían por do ivan   las nuevas a decir,
           ....

93   Dezién e afirmavan   que los vieran cozer:
           cozían e asavan   los omnes por' comer;
           quantos que lo oían   ivan se a perder;
           non sabién, con grand miedo,   adónd' se asconder.

94   Assí ivan foyendo   de las gentes estrañas,
           ....
           Morieron de grand fanbre,   todos por las montañas,
           non diez, veinte nin treinta   mas muchas de conpañas.

95   Perdieron muchos d'ellos   de miedo los sentidos;
           matavan a las madres,   en braços a los fijos;
           non podién dar consejo   mugeres nin maridos;
           andavan del grand duelo   muchos enloqueçidos.

96   E los omnes mesquinos   que estavan alçados,
           del grand bien que ovieron   estavan muy menguados;
           querían más ser muertos   o seer soterrados
           que non vesquir tal vida   fanbrientos e lazrados.

89   Destruction came quick upon the noble lands of Spain,
over which the faithless people were now lords;
the wretched Christians led terrible lives:
never before had Christians been so tried.

90   They set up their stables within the churches' walls,
and many were their acts of wicked folly on the altars;
the sacristies' treasures were taken as plunder;
the Christians shed tears through the night and the day.

91   I wish to tell you something that brought them rebuke:
they seized the Christians captive and bade that they be cooked,

....

that they might cause them all the greater terror.

92   They had other prisoners that they allowed to flee,
for they had seen the torments suffered by the rest,
and wherever they went, they would carry that news;

....

93   They spoke and they claimed that they had seen them cooked,
men being cooked and roasted to be eaten;
all those who heard it were brought to despair
and knew not, in their terror, where to hide.

94   So did they flee from the alien people,

....

They died in great hunger, all up in the mountains –
not ten, twenty, thirty: vast companies of men.

95   Many in their terror lost hold of their senses;
mothers were slain with their children in their arms;
woman and husband alike could give no counsel;
so deep was their grief, it drove many from their wits.

96   And the wretched men who had fled into hiding
were much brought down from their prosperity of old;
they would have chosen death or have rather been interred
than live such a life full of hunger and hardship.

Los omnes d' otro tienpo   que fueran segurados
veíen se de nuevo   en la tierra tornados;
comién el paneziello   de sus fijos amados;
los pobres eran ricos   e los ricos menguados.

98   Dezién los malfadados: '¡En mal hora nasçimos!
Diera nos Dios España,   guardar non la sopimos;
si en grand coita somos   nos bien lo meresçimos;
por nuestro mal sentido   en grand yerro caímos.

99   Si nos atales fuéssemos   commo nuestros parientes,
non avrían poder   aquestas malas gentes;
ellos fueron los buenos   e nos menos valientes;
traen nos commo lobos   a corderos rezientes.

100   Nos a Dios falesçiendo,   ha nos Él faleçido,
lo que otros ganaron,   hemos lo nos perdido;
partiendo nos de Dios   ha se de nos partido,
tod' el bien de los godos   por end' es confondido.'

101   Diera Dios essas oras   grand poder al pecado:
fasta allend' el puerto   todo fue astragado.
Semeja fiera cosa   mas diz lo el ditado:
a San Martín de Torres   ovieron allegado.

102   Visquieron castellanos   grand tienpo mala vida
en tierra muy angosta   de viandas muy fallida;
lazrados muy grand tiempo   a la mayor medida,
veién s' en muy grand miedo   con la gent' descreída.

103   En todas estas coitas   pero que malandantes,
en la merçet de Cristo   eran enfïuzantes
que les avrié merçed   contra non bautizantes.
'Val' nos, Señor,' dixeron,   'ond' seamos cobrantes.'

104   Avían en tod' esto   de a Almozor dar
çient doncellas fermosas   que fuessen por casar;
avién las por Castiella   cada un' a buscar;
avién lo de cunplir   pero con grand pesar.

97 Those whose lives had been secure in a bygone age
    once again found themselves living from the land,
    eating the humble bread of their beloved children;
    the poor were made rich and the rich brought low.

All. equal (before God?)

98 These hapless men declared: 'Ill-starred was our fate!*
    God gave us Spain but we could not keep it safe;
    if we suffer great trials, we do well deserve it;
    through our ill sense are we fallen far in error.

99 Had we been the equal of those who came before us,
    those evil people would not now hold power;
    they were the better men and we of lesser worth;
    they are to us as wolves to new-born lambs.

100 As we had failed God, He has failed us;
    what had been won by others, we have lost;
    as we abandoned God, so has He us,
    and thus the fortune of the Goths is all undone.'

Have faith in God

101 God had then granted great power to the Devil,
    and all was brought to ruin, stretching right beyond the pass.
    It beggars belief, but the written text confirms it:*
    the Moors had now advanced as far as Saint Martin de Tours.

102 For a long time a harsh life faced the Castilians
    in a tiny scrap of land, where food was scarce;
    for a very long time, their hardship was extreme,
    and great was their terror of the faithless tribe.

103 Much as they suffered in all these misfortunes,
    they still held their faith in the mercy of Christ
    that he would show them mercy against the unbaptized.
    'Help us, Lord,' they said, 'to recover what is lost.'

104 Meanwhile, to al-Mansur they were compelled to give*
    a hundred handsome maidens, all still to wed,
    who had all to be found from the land of Castile;
    they had no choice but compliance, to their sorrow.

105   Duró les esta coita   muy fiera tenporada,
los cristianos mesquinos,   conpaña muy lazrada;
dezién: 'Señor, nos vala   la tu merçed sagrada,
ca valist' a San Pedro   dentro la mar irada.

106   Señor, que con los sabios   valist' a Catalina,
e de muerte libreste   a Ester la reïna,
e del dragón libreste   a la virgen Marina,
Tú da a nuestras llagas   conort' e medeçina.

107   Señor, Tú que libreste   a Davit del león,
matest' al filisteo,   un soberbio varón,
quitest' a los jodíos   del rey de Babilón,
saca e libra nos   de tan cruel presïón.

108   Libreste a Susana   de los falsos varones,
saqueste a Daniel   de entre los leones,
librest' a San Matheo   de los fieros dragones;
libra nos Tú, Señor,   de estas tentaciones.

109   Librest' a los tres niños   de los fuegos ardientes
quando los y metieron   los pueblos descreyentes;
cantaron en el forno   cantos muy convenientes;
otra vez los libreste   de bocas de serpientes.

110   San Juan Evangelista,   ante muchos varones,
yazían ant' él muertos   de yerbas dos ladrones;
bebió él muy grand vaso   d'essos mismos ponçones:
mayor mal no l' fizieron   que si comies' piñones.

111   Tú que assí tolliste   a las yervas poder,
que no l' pudieron daño   ninguno le fazer,
Señor, por tu mesura,   deves nos acorrer,
ca en Ti nos yaz' todo,   levantar o caer.

112   Señor, Tú que quesiste   del çielo desçender,
en seno de la Virgen   carne vera prender,
cara mient' nos conpreste,   al nuestro entender;
non nos quieras dexar   agor' ansí perder.

105   This time of their misfortune endured a bitter age
for those wretched Christians, a sorely-treated band:
'Lord,' they cried, 'may Your holy mercy protect us,
for You protected Saint Peter in the angry main.*

Biblical References

106   Lord, who with the sages gave Catherine protection,
saved Esther the queen from the threat of her death,
and freed the chaste Marina from the clutches of the dragon,
may You grant us comfort and healing to our wounds.*

107   You, Lord, who delivered David from the lion,*
brought death to the Philistine, a man of haughty pride,
and freedom to the Jews from the king of Babylon,
free us and deliver us from so cruel a prison.

108   You rescued Susanna from the slanderous men
and Daniel You delivered from within the lions' den;
You freed Saint Matthew from the ferocious dragons;
so may You free us, Lord, from these temptations.*

Prayer

109   You saved the three children from the fiery furnace
when the disbelieving peoples cast them there;
in the midst of the flames they sang such seemly songs
that You again saved them from the serpents' jaws.*

Deliver us

110   Saint John the Evangelist, before a great audience,
and with two men dead of poison at his feet,
drank a large glass of the very draught that killed them,
and it did him no more harm than eating pine nuts.*

111   You who thus took away the force of the poison,
so that it was powerless to do him any ill,
Lord, in Your mercy, You must come to our aid,
for on You depends our all: to rise up or to fall.

112   Lord, whose will it was to descend from Heaven
and take on living flesh in the Virgin's womb,
You paid a heavy price for us, as we understand;
do not now allow us to be lost in such a way.

113 Somos mucho errados e contra Ti pecamos,
pero cristianos somos e la tu ley guardamos;
el tu nonbre tenemos, por tuyos nos llamamos;
tu merçed atendemos, otra non esperamos.'

114 Duraron esta vida al Crïador rogando,
de llorar de sus ojos nunca se escapando,
sienpre días e noches su cuita recontando;
oyó les Jesu Cristo a quien 'staban llamando.

115 Dixo les por el ángel qu' a Pelayo buscassen,
que l' alçassen por rey e que a él catassen;
en manparar la tierra todos le ayudassen;
él les darié ayuda por que la anparassen.

116 Buscaron a Pelayo commo les fue mandado;
fallaron lo en cueva, fanbriento e lazrado;
besaron le las manos e dieron l' el reignado;
ovo lo resçebir, pero non de su grado.

117 Resçibió el reinado, mas a muy grand amidos;
tovieron se con él los pueblos por guaridos.
Sopieron estas nuevas los pueblos descreídos;
por' venir sobre ellos todos fueron movidos.

118 Do sopieron que era venieron lo a buscar;
començaron le luego la peña de lidiar;
allí quiso don Cristo grant miraglo mostrar;
bien creo que l' oyestes alguna vez contar.

119 Saetas e quadriellos quantas al rey tiravan
a él nin a sus gentes ningunas non llegavan;
tan iradas com' ivan tan iradas tornavan,
si non a ellos mismos a otros non matavan.

120 Quando vieron los moros atán fiera fazaña
que sus armas matavan a su misma conpaña,
desçercaron la cueva, salieron de montaña;
tenién que les avía el Crïador grand saña.

113 We are in great error and against You we have sinned,*
but we are Christian people and we keep to Your law;
we hold to Your name and proclaim ourselves as Yours;
we look to Your mercy, and we hope for no other.'

114 A lifetime they spent in entreating the Creator;
tears flowed from their eyes without a moment's respite;
day and night, there was ever sorrow on their lips;
and Christ, to whom they called out, heard their prayer.

115 He told them through the angel to seek out Pelayo,*
to make him their king, and to look to his command,
that they should all support him in defence of the land,
and he would give them help in its protection.

116 They sought out Pelayo, as they had been bidden,
and found him wretched with hunger in his cave;
they kissed his hands in service and made him their sovereign;
he accepted their offer, but unwillingly.

117 He accepted the kingdom, though against his desire,
and with him the people all felt well protected;
when this news reached the ears of the tribes of unbelievers,
they were all moved to fall upon the Christians.

118 They came to seek him out where they knew him to be,
and set upon his rocky defences at once;
by the will of Christ, a great miracle was seen there:
I fancy that you will have heard tell of it before.*

119 Of all the darts and arrows that they fired at the King
not one of them could reach him or his people;
though sped out with anger, just as angry they returned,
and thus the Moorish archers could only kill their own.

120 When the Moors observed this remarkable portent,
that their own company fell victim to their arms,
they broke off their siege and abandoned the mountains,
and thought themselves the objects of the wrath of the Creator.

121   Este rey don Pelayo,   siervo del Crïador,
        guardó tan bien la tierra   que non pudo mejor;
        fueron ansí perdiendo   cristianos el dolor
        pero non que perdiessen   miedo de Almoçor.

122   Finó el rey Pelayo   – ¡don Cristo le perdon'! –;
        reignó su fijo Vávilla,   que fue muy mal varón.
        Quiso Dios que mandasse   poco en la regïón,
        ca visquió rey un año   e más poca sazón.

123   Fija del rey Pelayo,   dueña muy enseñada,
        con señor de Cantabria   ovieron la casada;
        dixeron le Alfonso,   una lança dudada;
        ganó muy fiera tierra   toda con su espada.

124   Éste ganó Viseo,   que es en Portogal,
        después ganó a Braga,   reigno arçobispal,
        Astorga, Salamanca,   Çamora otro tal,
        ganó después Amaya   que es alto poyal.

125   Murió est' rey Alfonso,   señor aventurado,
        – ¡sea en paraíso   tan buen rey heredado! –;
        reignó su fijo Fabia   que fue malo provado;
        quiso Dios que visquiesse   poco en el reignado.

126   Después reignó Alfonso,   un rey de grand valor,
        el Casto que dixeron,   siervo del Crïador;
        visquieron en su tienpo   en paz e en sabor;
        éste fizo la iglesia   que s' diz San Salvador.

127   Hemos esta razón   por fuerça d' alongar:
        quiero en el rey Carlos   este cuento tomar;
        ovo al rey Alfonso   mandado de enbiar
        que venié a España   pora gela ganar.

128   Enbió el rey Alfonso   al rey Carlos mandado
        qu' en ser atributado   non era acordado;
        por dar parias por él   non querié el reignado;
        serié llamado torpe   en fer atal mercado.

121   This man, King Pelayo, vassal of the Creator,
        gave the land the best protection he was able;
        with this, the Christians slowly overcame their grief,
        though they had not lost their fear of al-Mansur.

122   On the death of King Pelayo – may Christ grant him pardon! –
        his son Fáfila acceded, a very evil man.*
        By God's will, his rule of that land was short-lived,
        for he lived as king a year, and little longer.

123   King Pelayo's daughter, a lady of great learning,
        had been married to the lord who held Cantabria:
        Alfonso was his name, a man whose lance struck fear,*
        who won vast new lands by the conquest of his sword.

124   Viseu fell to this man, on Portuguese soil,
        who then took Braga, the seat of the archbishop,
        Astorga and Salamanca, Zamora besides,
        and then the lofty peak we call Amaya.*

125   Death took King Alfonso, a man whom fortune blessed,
        – may paradise bring so fine a king his reward! –
        and his son reigned: Fruela, notoriously wicked;*
        by God's will, he did not live long to rule.

126   Then reigned Alfonso, a king of great worth,
        known as 'the Chaste', and the Creator's vassal;
        in his time men lived at peace and in comfort;
        it was he who built the church called San Salvador.*

127   Here we are obliged to prolong our account:
        I wish to turn this tale to the subject of King Charles,*
        for he had bid a message be sent to King Alfonso
        that he was on his way to Spain to claim the lands.

128   To King Charles, King Alfonso sent word in his turn
        that he would not consent to the payment of tribute,
        and wished not to reign at the cost of a ransom;
        he would be held a fool in accepting such a deal.

129   Dixo que más quería   com' estava estar
que el reigno d' España   a Françia sojuzgar;
que non se podrién d'esso   franceses alabar;
¡que más la querién ellos   en çinc' años ganar!

130   Carlos ovo consejo   sobre este mandado;
commo menester fuera   non fue bien consejado;
dieron le por consejo   el su pueblo famado
que venies' a España   con todo su fonsado.

131   Ayuntó sus poderes,   grandes e sin mesura;
movió pora Castiella,   tengo que fue locura;
al que lo consejó   nunca l' marre rencura,
ca fue essa venida   plaga de su ventura.

132   Sopo Bernald' del Carpio   que franceses passavan,
que a Fuente Rabía   todos y arribavan
por conquerir España,   segunt qu' ellos cuidavan
que ge la conquerrían;   mas non lo bien asmavan.

133   Ovo grandes poderes   Bernaldo d' ayuntar
e dessí enbió los   al puerto de la mar;
ovo l' todas sus gentes   el rey casto a dar;
non dexó esse puerto   al rey Carlos passar.

134   Mató y de franceses   reyes e potestades;
com' diz la escritura,   siete fueron, sepades;
muchos murieron y,   esto bien lo creades,
que nunca más tornaron   a las sus vezindades.

135   Tovo se por mal trecho   Carlos essa vegada;
quando vio que por y   le tollió la entrada,
movió s' con assaz gentes   e toda su mesnada;
al puerto de Marsilla   fizo luego tornada.

136   Quando fueron al puerto   los françeses llegados,
rendieron a Dios gracias   que los avié guiados;
folgaron e dormieron,   que eran muy cansados;
si essora s' tornaran   fueran bien venturados.

129 He said that he preferred to remain as he was
than submit the Spanish realm to French command,
that Frenchmen be not able to boast of such a deed;
well might they wish to take it in five years!*

130 Charles then took counsel regarding this message,
and was not well advised, as was his need;
such was the counsel of his people of renown:
that he should come to Spain with all his army.

131 He assembled his forces, great beyond reckoning,
and made for Castile – it was madness, I maintain –;
may he who advised him forever meet with rancour,
for that campaign was a plague upon his fortune.

132 Bernardo del Carpio heard the French were passing,
all coming to the place called Fuenterrabía,*
to take Spain by conquest, for this was their belief –
that they would take it; but they were in error.

133 Bernardo brought together an army great in numbers
and sent them on from there to reach the sea-port;
the Chaste King was to send him all his men as reinforcements;
this man did not permit it that King Charles should pass that port.

134 There, among the French, he slew kings and great lords;
as the written text says, I tell you they were seven;*
many men died there, this you may well believe,
nevermore to return to their homelands.

135 King Charles thought that this time his fortune was ill;
on seeing that his entry was barred to that place,
he marched with many troops, all his company of men,
and made a swift return to the port of Marseilles.*

136 Once the French troops were arrived at the port,
they offered thanks to God for having guided them;
wearied, they gave themselves to rest and to sleep;
to have then turned for home would have been their good fortune.

137 Ovieron su acuerdo de passar a España,
    ond' non se les fincasse nin torre nin cabaña;
    ....
    ....

138 Movieron los poderes con toda su mesnada:
    al puerto de Gitárea fizieron la tornada;
    ....
    ....

139 Los poderes de Françia, todos muy bien guarnidos,
    por los puertos de Aspa fueron luego torçidos;
    fueran de buen acuerdo si non fueran venidos,
    que nunca más tornaron a do fueron nasçidos.

140 Dexemos los françeses en España tornados,
    por conquerir la tierra todos bien aguisados;
    tornemos en Bernaldo de los fechos granados,
    que avié d' españones los poderes juntados.

141 Movió Bernald' del Carpio con toda su mesnada
    – si sobre moros fuesse era buena provada –
    movieron por' un agua muy fuert' e muy irada:
    Ebro l' dixeron sienpre, assí es oy llamada.

142 Fueron a Çaragoça, a los pueblos paganos;
    besó Bernald' del Carpio al rey Marsil las manos
    que dies' la delantera a pueblos castellanos
    contra los Doze Pares, essos pueblos loçanos.

143 Otorgó gela luego e dio gela de grado;
    nunca oyó Marsil otro nin tal mandado;
    movió Bernald' del Carpio con su pueblo dudado;
    de gentes castellanas era bien aguardado.

144 Tovo la delantera Bernaldo essa vez;
    con gentes españones, gentes de muy grand prez,
    vençieron essas oras a franceses refez;
    bien fue éssa más negra que la primera vez.

137 They took their decision to cross over into Spain,
   where not a tower or dwelling might resist them;
   ....
   ....

138 In their full strength, the armies set out on the march
   to make way once more to the mountain pass of Cize;*
   ....
   ....

139 The armies of the French, all heavily equipped,
   were quick to make way through the passes of Aspe;*
   they would have been well served had they never made that journey,
   for no more would they ever see the land of their birth.

140 Let us leave the French who had turned into Spain,
   all well prepared for the conquest of that land,
   and return to Bernardo, a man of great feats,
   who had yoked together all the Spanish forces.

141 Bernardo del Carpio set out, with all his men,
   – in combat with the Moors their skill was well proven –
   and crossed over a river in furious spate,
   known always as the Ebro, and still so today.

142 They marched to Zaragoza and the pagan peoples;
   Bernardo del Carpio kissed the hands of King Marsile,
   that he might entrust the vanguard to the troops of Castile,
   in the battle with those valiant men, the Twelve Peers.*

143 It was granted him at once and was willingly given;
   no other such request was ever heard by Marsile's ears;
   Bernardo marched out with his feared band of troops,
   heavily protected by the men of Castile.

144 Bernardo fought here in the very front line,
   with Spanish troops – men of great worth – at his side;
   this worsting of the French was easily achieved,
   this day far blacker than the first had been.

145   Por esso vos lo digo   que bien lo entendades:
        mejor que otras tierras   es la que vos morades;
        de todo bien conplida   en la que vos estades;
        decir vos he agora   quántas ha de bondades.

146   Tierra es muy tenprada,   sin grandes calenturas;
        non faze en ivierno   destenpradas frïuras;
        non es tierra en mundo   qu' haya tales pasturas,
        árboles pora fruta   siquier' de mil naturas.

147   Sobre todas las tierras   mejor es la montaña:
        de vacas e d' ovejas   non ha tierra tamaña;
        tantos ha y de puercos   que es fiera fazaña;
        sirven se muchas tierras   de las cosas d' España.

148   Es de lino e lana   tierra much' abastada,
        de çera sobre todas   buena tierra provada;
        non serié de aceite   en mundo tal fallada:
        Inglatierra nin Françia   d'esto es abondada.

149   Buena tierra de caça   e buena de venados,
        de río e de mar   muchos buenos pescados;
        quien los quiere rezientes,   quien los quiere salados,
        son d'estas cosas tales   pueblos muy abastados.

150   De panes e de vinos   tierra muy comunal:
        non fallarién en mundo   otra mejor nin tal;
        muchas de buenas fuentes,   mucho río cabdal,
        otras muchas mineras   de que fazen la sal.

151   Ha y sierras e valles   e mucha buena mata,
        toda llena de grana   pora fer escarlata;
        ha y venas de oro   – son de mejor barata –,
        e ha y muchas venas   de fierro e de plata.

152   Por lo qu' ella más val'   aún non lo dixiemos:
        de los buenos cavallos   mención non vos fiziemos;
        mejor tierra es de las   que quantas nunca viemos,
        nunca tales cavallos   en el mundo nos viemos.

145   Therefore do I tell you, that you may see it clearly:
the land in which you live is a finer land than others;*
that in which you dwell now is blessed with every good;
I will tell you now how many are its riches.

146   A most temperate land, without waves of great heat,
its winters stay free of too-sharp snaps of cold;
no land in the world is so suited for pasture,
and it has trees for any fruit – a thousand kinds.

147   Over all other lands, the finest is the mountain:
for cows and for sheep it is rich beyond compare;
so many pigs are kept there their number is a marvel;
and many lands are served by the produce of Spain.

148   It is a land well provided of linen and of wool,
and above all others it is known for its wax;
none other in the world could be found to match its oil:
neither France nor England have the equal of this wealth.

149   A land fine for hunting and fine too for game,
it has many fine fish in its rivers and seas;
whether fresh or salted, according to desire,
they are in rich supply for the people of Spain.

150   In breads and in wines this land is abundant:
none like it or better could be found in all the world;
it has many fine springs, many rivers stretching wide,
as well as many mines, which are the source of their salt.*

151   There are mountains, valleys, and much fine woodland,
all full of grain, to make the scarlet dye;*
there are veins lined with gold, whose value is higher,
and many more of iron and of silver.

152   Of her richest blessing we still have not spoken:
having made no mention of her quality of horse;*
of all that we have ever seen, this land is the best,
and never in the world did we see such fine steeds.

153   Dexar vos quiero d'esto,   assaz vos he contado;
           non quiero más dezir,   que podrié ser errado.
           Pero non olvidemos   al apóstol honrado,
           fijo del Zebedeo,   Santïago llamado.

154   Fuerte mient' quiso Dios   a España honrar
           quand' al santo apóstol   quiso y enbïar;
           d' Inglaterra e Françia   quiso la mejorar:
           sabet, non yaz' apóstol   en tod' aquel logar.

155   Onró le otra guisa   el preçioso Señor:
           fueron y muchos santos   muertos por su Señor;
           de morir a cochiello   non ovieron temor;
           muchas vírgenes santas,   mucho buen confessor.

156   Com' ella es mejor   de las sus vezindades,
           sodes mejores quantos   en España morades;
           omnes sodes sesudos,   mesura heredades;
           d'esto por tod' el mundo   muy grand preçio ganades.

157   Pero de tod' España   Castiella es mejor,
           porque fue de los otros   el comienço mayor;
           guardando e temiendo   sienpre a su Señor,
           quiso acreçentarla   ansí el Crïador.

158   Aún Castiella Vieja,   al mi entendimiento,
           mejor es que lo al,   por que fue el çimiento,
           ca conquirieron mucho,   maguer poco conviento;
           bien lo podedes ver   en el acabamiento.

159   Pues quiero me con tanto   d'esta razón dexar;
           temo si más dixesse   que podría errar;
           otrossí non vos quiero   la razón alongar:
           quiero en don Alfonso,   el casto rey, tornar.

160   Rey fue de grand sentido   e de muy grand valor,
           siervo fue e amigo   mucho del Crïador;
           fue se d' aqueste mundo   por' el otro mejor;
           fincó toda la tierra   essora sin señor.

153 I wish to leave this matter; I have told you enough;
I wish to say no more, lest I lapse into error;
but let us not pass over the honoured Apostle,
Zebedee's son, Santiago by name.*

154 It was God's will to pay Spain a great honour
when He chose to send her His Holy Apostle;
His wish was to set her above England and France:*
know that no apostle lies there, in either place.

155 Otherwise, too, the glorious Lord paid her honour:
many saints were killed there in the name of their Lord;
dying at the knife-blade did not cause them any fear,
those many holy virgins and confessors of great worth.

156 As Spain is a land finer than her neighbours,
so you who dwell in her are finer, too:
you are men of wisdom, who are born with good sense,
for which you gain great fame through all the world.

157 But of all of Spain it is Castile that bears the palm,*
for it was of all the others the beginning and the strength
and always of the Lord it stood in proper faith and fear,
such that the Creator's will became to make it grow.

158 Moreover, Old Castile, in my understanding,
outmatches all others, for it was the foundation,
and though of few people, their conquests were great;
well can you see it in where all of this has led.

159 With this, I wish to put an end to this account,
for I fear that to continue might put me at fault;
besides, I have no wish to drag out a long tale,
but rather to return to King Alfonso the Chaste.

160 A king of great good sense and inestimable worth,
he was both vassal and good friend of the Creator;
he departed from this world for the paradise beyond,
whereupon the whole land was left without a lord.

161   Eran en muy grand coita   españones caídos;
        duraron muy grand tienpo   todos desavenidos;
        com' omnes sin señor,   tristes e doloridos,
        dizién: 'Más nos valdría   nunca seer nasçidos.'

162   Quand' vieron castellanos   la cosa ansí ir,
        e pora alçar rey   no s' podién avenir,
        vieron que sin pastor   non podién bien vevir,
        posieron quien podiesse   los canes referir.

163   Todos los castellanos   en uno s' acordaron;
        dos omnes de grand guisa   por alcaldes alçaron;
        los pueblos castellanos   por ellos se guiaron;
        que non posieron rey   muy grand tienpo duraron.

164   Dezir he los alcaldes   quáles nonbres ovieron,
        d'ende en adelante   los que d'ellos venieron;
        muchas buenas batallas   con los moros fezieron;
        con su fiero esfuerço   grand tierra conquirieron.

165   Don Nuño ovo nonbre,   omne de grand valor,
        vino de su linaje   el cond' batallador.
        El otro don Laíno,   el buen guerreador,
        vino de su linaje   el Çid Campeador.

166   Fi de Nuño Rasura,   omne bien entendido,
        Gonçalo ovo nonbre,   omne muy atrevido;
        anparó bien la tierra   fizo quant' ha podido;
        éste fue referiendo   al pueblo descreído.

167   Ovo Gonçalo Núñez   tres fijuelos varones,
        todos tres de grand guisa   e grandes coraçones;
        éstos partieron tierra,   dieron l' a infançones;
        por do ellos partieron   y están los mojones.

168   Don Dïego Gonçález,   el ermano mayor,
        Rodrigo el mediano,   Fernando el menor;
        todos tres fueron buenos   mas Fernando mejor,
        ca quitó muy grand tierra   al moro Almozor.

161 The Spaniards were fallen into terrible strife,
and for a long time remained in disarray:
as men with no lord, they were disconsolate and wretched,
and said, 'It would be better had we never been born!'

162 When the Castilians saw this state of affairs,
and could reach no accord in naming their king,
they saw that with no pastor their lives would be troubled,
and elected men who could put the dogs to flight.

163 All the Castilians now became of one mind,
and set up as judges two men of great prudence;*
from them the peoples of Castile took their guidance,
and a long time passed till they named another king.

164 I must tell you of the judges and the names that they bore,
before moving on to talk of their descendants;
many great battles did they fight against the Moors,
winning vast new lands with remarkable courage.

165 The first was named Nuño, a man of great worth,
and from his lineage came the Count, the battler;
the second was Laíno, who was a fine warrior,
and from his lineage came the Cid, the Champion.*

166 Nuño Rasura's son, a man of much understanding,
bore the name of Gonzalo, a man of great daring;
he gave the land firm protection, doing all he was able,
and he began to drive the unbelievers in retreat.

167 This man Gonzalo Núñez was father to three sons;
all three were great of prudence and great-hearted;
they divided up the land among men of noble birth;*
where they made their divisions, the markers may be seen.

168 Diego González was the eldest of the brothers,
Rodrigo was the second, and Fernando the youngest;
all three were good men, but Fernando was best,
for he took much land from the Moor al-Mansur.

169 Finó se Don Dïego, cavallero loçano;
quedó toda la tierra en el otro ermano,
don Rodrigo por nonbre, que era el mediano;
señor fue muy grand tienpo del pueblo castellano.

170 Quando la ora vino puesta del Crïador,
fue se Rüy Gonçález por' el mundo mejor;
fincó toda la tierra al ermano menor,
don Fernando por nonbre, cuerpo de grand valor.

171 Estonç' era Castiella un pequeño rincón;
era de castellanos Montes d' Oca mojón
e de la otra parte Fitero el fondón;
moros tenién Caraço en aquesta sazón.

172 Era toda Castiella sólo un' alcaldía;
maguer que era pobre e de poca valía,
nunca de buenos omnes fue Castiella vazía;
de quáles ellos fueron paresçe oy en día.

173 Varones castellanos, éste fue su cuidado:
de llegar su señor al más alto estado.
D' un' alcaldía pobre fizieron la condado;
tornaron la después cabeça de reinado.

174 Ovo nonbre Fernando el conde de primero;
nunca fue en el mundo otro tal cavallero;
éste fue de los moros un mortal omiçero;
dizién le por sus lides el bueitre carniçero.

175 Fizo grandes batallas con la gent' descreída
e les fizo lazrar a la mayor medida;
ensanchó en Castiella una muy grant partida;
ovo en el su tienpo mucha sangre vertida.

176 El conde don Fernando, con muy poca conpaña,
– en contar lo que fizo semejarié fazaña –
mantovo sienpre guerra con los reyes d' España;
non dava más por ellos que por una castaña.

169   Diego met his death, that valiant knight,
and the land all passed to the second of the brothers,
Rodrigo by name, who was the middle of the three;
he was lord for many years of the people of Castile.

170   When the hour came that the Creator had determined,
Ruy González departed for the paradise beyond
and the land all passed to the youngest of the brothers:
his name was Fernando, and his worth was great indeed.

171   Castile was no more then than a tiny little corner,
whose frontier was marked by the Hills of Oca
and the Plain of Itero, on the opposite side;
at that time Carazo was still held by the Moors.*

172   All of Castile was but a small municipality,
and though it was a poor land, possessed of little wealth,
the land of Castile never wanted for good men:
their character may still be seen today.

173   This was the concern of the men of Castile:
to raise up their lord to the highest of standing.
A poor municipality they turned into a county;
the county they later made the head of a kingdom.*

174   The first of the counts bore the name of Fernando:
the world has never seen the knight to match him;
to the Moors, this man was a deadly scourge,
known for his battles as a murderous vulture.

175   He fought great pitched battles with the unbelieving people,
on whom he wrought suffering in terrible measure;
he brought wide new lands within the boundaries of Castile;*
the years of his rule saw the spilling of much blood.

176   This man Count Fernando, with a tiny band of troops
– to give account of his deeds would seem invention –
kept up a constant war against the kings of Spain,
and cared for them no more than for a chestnut.

177   Enante que entremos   delant' en la razón,
dezir vos he del conde   quál fue su crïazón:
furtó l' un pobreziello   que labrava carbón;
tovo l' en la montaña   una muy grand sazón.

178   Quanto podié el amo   ganar de su mester,
tod' al su buen crïado   dava muy volunter;
de quál linaj' venía   fazié gel' entender;
avié quando l' oía   el moço grand plazer.

179   Quando iba el moço   las cosas entendiendo,
oyó cóm a Castiella   moros ivan corriendo.
'Valas me,' dixo, 'Cristo,   a Ti me encomiendo;
en coita es Castiella,   segunt que yo entiendo.

180   Señor, ya tienpo era,   si fuesse tu mesura,
que mudasses la rueda   qu' anda a la ventura;
assaz han castellanos   passada de rencura,
gentes nunca passaron   atán mala ventura.

181   Señor, ya tienpo era   de salir de cabañas,
que non so osso bravo   por' vevir en montañas;
tienpo es ya que sepan   de mí las mis conpañas
e yo sepa d'el mundo   e las cosas estrañas.

182   Castellanos perdieron   sonbra e grand abrigo
la ora que murió   mi ermano Rodrigo;
avién en él los moros   un mortal enemigo;
si yo d' aquí non salgo,   nunca valdré un figo.'

183   Salió de las montañas,   vino pora poblado,
con aquel pobreziello   que lo avié crïado;
aína fue sabido   por todo el condado;
non mayor gozo ovo   omne de madre nado.

184   Venién los castellanos   a su señor veer;
avién, chicos e grandes,   todos con él plazer,
metieron el condado   todo en su poder;
non podién en el mundo   mejor señor aver.

177   Before we embark upon the substance of our story,
       I shall tell you of the Count and of his childhood:
       he was stolen by a poor man, a worker of charcoal,*
       who kept him for a long time on the mountain.

178   Everything the master could gain from his profession
       he gifted most willingly to the noble youth he reared;
       he gave him to understand the bloodline that he came from,
       on hearing which the boy was greatly pleased.

179   As the boy came gradually to see how matters stood,
       he heard of how the Moors were bringing ruin on Castile.
       'Help me, Christ,' he said; 'I commend myself to You.
       A troubled time has fallen on Castile, as I have learned.

180   The time has come, Lord, if You should so judge it,
       for You to spin the wheel that turns at random;*
       bitterness enough have the Castilians endured;
       no people ever suffered such misfortune as them.

181   The time has come, Lord, for us to leave our huts behind,
       for I am no wild bear meant for mountain life;
       now is the time when my soldiers should hear of me,
       and I of the world, and of unfamiliar things.

182   The Castilians lost their shade and great protection
       at the hour of my brother Rodrigo's death;
       for the Moorish people he was a mortal foe;
       should I not set out, I will not be worth a fig.'

183   Leaving the mountains, he came into the city
       along with that poor fellow who had reared him;
       news of his arrival spread at once throughout the county;
       such joy was never felt by any man of woman born.

184   The Castilians came up to set eyes on their lord,
       and all men, young and old, took pleasure in him;
       they set the whole county beneath his authority;
       no finer lord could all the world have offered.

185   Quand' entendió que era   de Castiella señor,
alçó a Dios las manos,   rogó al Crïador:
'Señor, Tú me ayuda,   que so muy pecador,
que yo saque Castiella   del antigo dolor.

186   Da me, Señor, esfuerço,   seso e buen sentido,
que y tome vengança   del pueblo descreído
e cobren castellanos   algo de lo perdido
e te tengas de mí   en algo por servido.

187   Señor, ha luengo tienpo   que viven mala vida,
son mucho apremiados   de la gent' descreída;
Señor, Rey de los Reyes,   aya la tu ayuda,
que yo torne Castiella   a la buena medida.

188   Si por alguna culpa   cayemos en tu saña,
non sea sobre nos   esta pena tamaña,
ca yazemos cativos   de todos los d' España;
los señores ser siervos   tengo lo por fazaña.

189   Tú lo sabes, Señor,   qué vida enduramos;
non nos quieres oír,   maguer que te llamamos;
non sabemos con quexa   qué consejo prendamos;
Señor, grandes e chicos   tu merçed esperamos.

190   Señor, esta merçed   te querría pedir:
seyendo tu vassallo,   non me quieras fallir;
Señor, contigo cuedo   atanto conquerir
por que aya Castiella   de premia a salir.'

191   Fizo su oraçión   el moço bien conplida;
de coraçón la fizo,   bien le fuera oída.
Fizo grandes batallas   con la gent' descreída
mas nunca fue vençido   en toda la su vida.

192   Non quiso, maguer moço,   dar se ningún vagar;
començó a los moros   muy fuerte guerrear;
movió se con sus gentes,   a Caraço fue çercar:
una sierra muy alta,   muy firme castellar.

185   When he understood he was now lord of Castile,
he raised his hands to God the Creator in prayer:
'My Lord, grant Your aid to this terrible sinner,
that I might free Castile from her suffering of old.*

186   O Lord, grant me courage, and wisdom, and good sense,
that I may there take vengeance on the unbelieving people,
and the people of Castile recover something of their loss,
and You consider me to have rendered You some service.

187   For a long time, Lord, have they led a wretched life,
sore oppressed by the people of ill faith;
Lord, King of Kings, let me now receive Your aid
in restoring Castile to her rightful state.

188   If through any fault we have incurred your wrath,
let not so great a punishment befall us,
for we lie as captives of all of Spain's people,
and I hold it wrong for lords to be as serfs.

189   You know, my Lord, the life that we endure;
You do not wish to hear us, though we call You;
we know not in our sorrow the course that we should take;
young and old, we all hope for Your mercy, O Lord.

190   This is the mercy I would ask of You, my Lord,
that since I am Your vassal, You not fail me;
with You I believe, Lord, that I will make such conquests
that Castile will be able to escape her oppression.'*

191   The young man said his prayer just as he should:
he spoke from the heart, and the prayer was well received;
he fought great battles with the faithless people,
but he never met defeat in all his life.

192   Young though he was, he wished to make no delay,
and began a violent war against the Moors;
he marched with his troops and laid siege to Carazo,
a difficult stronghold set high in the hills.*

193   El conde castellano,   con todos sus varones,
conbatián las torres   a guisa d' infançones;
de dardos e d' asconas   peleavan peones;
fazién a Dios serviçio   de puros coraçones.

194   Non se podién los moros   por cosa defender;
enant' que Almozor   los pudiés' acorrer,
ovieron se los moros   por fuerça a vençer,
ovieron los cristianos   las torres en poder.

195   Llegó a Almozor   luego el apellido;
sopo cómmo avía   a Caraço perdido.
Dixo: 'Afirme so   del conde maltraído;
si d'él non he derecho   en mala fui nasçido.'

196   Enbïó por la tierra   a grand priessa troteros,
unos en pos de otros,   cartas e mensajeros,
que veniessen aína   peones e caveros,
sus reyes que veniessen   de todos delanteros.

197   Quando fueron con él   juntados sus varones,
reyes e ricos omnes   e muchos infançones;
si todos los contássemos,   caveros e peones,
serían más por cuenta   de cinco mil legiones.

198   Quand' ovo Almozor   su poder ayuntado,
movió pora Castiella   sañudo e irado;
avié muy fiera miente   al cond' amenazado
que non fincarié tierra   que non fuesse buscado.

199   Avié aquestas nuevas   el conde ya oído:
cóm' era Almozor   pora venir movido;
de toda Almería   traié el apellido;
mayor poder non viera   ningún omne nasçido.

200   Enbïó por Castiella   a priessa los mandados
que fuessen en Muñó   todos con él juntados;
fizo saber las nuevas   a sus adelantados:
cómmo de Almozor   eran desafïados.

193   The Count of Castile, with all of his knights,
made attacks, like noble lords, upon the towers,*
the foot soldiers fighting with darts and with spears;
pure of heart, they rendered up their service to God.

194   The Moors were unable to mount a defence,
and before al-Mansur could come to their aid,
the Moors had no choice but to yield in defeat,
and the Christians had the towers in their power.

195   Word sped quickly to the ears of al-Mansur,
and he learned of his loss of Carazo.
He said: 'I have been sorely maltreated by the Count;
should I gain no revenge then I was born a cursed man.'

196   He quickly sent envoys to go throughout the land,
one after another, both messengers and letters,
bidding foot soldiers and knights to come without delay,
and that his kings come at the head of all these men.

197   When his men were all assembled at his side,
kings and noblemen, and many men of rank,
if we counted them all, those who fought on horse and foot,
the reckoning of men would surpass five thousand legions.

198   When al-Mansur's forces were gathered together,
he set out for Castile in anger and in wrath;
dreadful were the threats he had issued to the Count,
that in no land would he not be hunted down.

199   The Count was already made aware of the news
that al-Mansur had now set out against him,
and brought with him the summons of all Almería:*
no man alive had ever seen an army of that size.

200   The Count made haste to send word through Castile
for all to be united in Muñó at his side;*
he sent report of the news to the governors of the land –
of the challenge then laid down by al-Mansur.

201   Fabló con sus vassallos   en qué acordarían;
    querié oír a todos   qué consejo l' darían:
    si querién ir a ellos   o les atenderían
    o quál serié la cosa   que por mejor ternían.

202   Fabló Gonçalo Díaz,   un sesudo varón:
    rogó que l' escuchassen,   que derié su razón:
    'Oít me,' diz, 'amigos,   si Cristo vos perdon':
    pora aver la lid   non tenemos sazón.

203   Si alguna carrera   podiéssemos fallar
    de guisa que s' podiesse   esta lid escusar,
    non devríamos tregua   nin pecho refusar,
    por do quier que s' pudiesse   al omne amansar.

204   En muchas otras cosas   se despiend' el aver;
    en el lidiar el omne   non puede estorçer:
    avrá cuerpo e alma   todo y a poner,
    que por oro nin plata   non lo puede aver.

205   Muchos son e sin guisa   los pueblos renegados:
    caveros e peones,   todos bien aguisados.
    Somos poca conpaña,   de armas muy menguados;
    seremos, si nos vençen,   todos descabeçados.

206   Si nos pleito podiéssemos   con Almozor tener
    que fincasse la lid   por dar o prometer,
    es el mejor consejo   que podemos aver;
    si otra cosa femos   podemos nos perder.

207   Todo el mi sentido   ya oído l' avedes;
    si yo fablé sin guisa   vos me lo perdonedes;
    dezit agora vos   lo que por bien tenedes;
    por Dios que lo mejor   al conde consejedes.'

208   Fue de Gonçalo Díaz   el conde despagado,
    ca non se tovo d'él   por bien aconsejado;
    maguer que fue sañudo,   no l' fabló desguisado
    mas contradixo l' todo   quanto avié fablado.

201	He spoke with his vassals and sought their opinion;
	he wished to hear all voices, and every man's advice:
	advance upon the enemy or wait for their attack,
	or which tactic it was that they judged to be best.

202	Gonzalo Díaz then spoke, who was a man of wisdom,*
	and begged their attention, for he would speak his mind,
	saying: 'Hear me, my friends, may Christ grant you pardon:
	this is an ill moment for us to go to battle.

203	If we could light upon some plan of action
	such that this battle might now be avoided,
	no truce or tribute ought we to refuse,
	nor any other means to calm his anger.

204	Many other things may be bought with our wealth,
	but on the battlefield a man has no escape:
	body and soul, he must put it all at stake there –
	what he cannot buy with any gold or silver.

205	The renegade people are many without reckoning:
	they have men on horse and foot, all fully armed;
	ours is but a small force and our equipment poor;
	should they beat us, they will hew off all our heads.*

206	If we could make a pact with al-Mansur,
	that our promise or our gift might halt the battle,
	this is the best possible counsel for us,
	for any other course may bring our ruin.

207	You have now heard in full how I am minded;
	forgive me if I spoke without due sense;
	it is now yours to say what you hold right;
	may God will you counsel the Count for the best!'

208	The Count was displeased with Gonzalo Díaz,
	for he did not think the man's advice was sound;
	yet, though in anger, he spoke not unkindly,
	but contradicted all that he had said.

209   'Por Dios,' dixo el conde,   'que m' querades oír:
quiero a don Gonçalo   a todo recudir;
todo quanto ha dicho   quiero contradezir,
ca tales cosas dixo   que sól' non son d' oír.

210   Dixo de lo primero   d' escusar el lidiar,
pero non puede omne   la muerte escusar;
el omne, pues que sabe   que non pued' escapar,
deve a la su carne   onrada muerte dar.

211   Por la tregua aver,   por algo que pechemos,
de señores que somos   vassallos nos faremos;
en vez que a Castiella   de su premia saquemos,
la premia en que era   doblar gela y emos.

212   Por engaño ganar   non ha cosa peor;
quien cayer' en est' fecho   cadrá en grand error;
por defender engaño   murió el Salvador;
más val' ser engañado   que non engañador.

213   Nuestros anteçessores   lealtat aguardaron;
sobre las otras tierras,   ellos la eredaron;
por ésta aguardar   las muertes olvidaron;
quanto sabor ovieron   por y lo acabaron.

214   Todavía s' guardaron   de malfecho fazer;
non les pudo ninguno   aquesto retraer;
eredat non quisieron,   pora menos valer,
qu' ellos non podiessen   enpeñar nin vender.

215   Este debdo levaron   nuestros anteçessores:
de todos los que biven   mejor guardar señores;
de morir ante qu' ellos   tenién se por debdores;
catand' esto, ganaron   el prez de los mejores.

216   Non deve otra cosa   y seer olvidada:
porqu' el señor fiziesse   cosa desaguisada,
ellos nunca l' ovieron   saña vieja alçada
mas sienpre lealtad   leal mientre pagada.

209　'By God,' said the Count, 'now lend me your ears!*
　　　Every word of Gonzalo's I wish to refute;
　　　all that he has said I desire to contradict,
　　　for he spoke such things as never should be heard.

210　Firstly he spoke of avoiding the battle,
　　　but avoidance of death is beyond any man;
　　　a man, since he knows that he cannot escape,
　　　must give his flesh a death that merits honour.

211　Through signing a truce and the payment of tribute,
　　　we shall make vassals of the lords we now are;
　　　instead of releasing Castile from oppression,
　　　we shall rather see that suffering double.

212　To win by deceit is the worst of all things:
　　　he who falls thus will fall into great error;
　　　the Saviour died for His fight against deceit;
　　　better to be deceived than a deceiver.

213　To loyalty our ancestors always held true;
　　　this was their inheritance, above the other lands,
　　　and that they might uphold it they paid no heed to death;
　　　all that they desired, through loyalty they achieved.

214　So too, they refrained from any evil deeds,
　　　and no-one could hold such a thing against them;
　　　they sought no inheritance to lower their worth,*
　　　that they would not be able to pledge or to sell.

215　This is the debt that our ancestors bore:
　　　that all who live pay their lords the finest service;
　　　they thought it their duty to die before their lords;*
　　　for keeping to this, they were esteemed as finer men.

216　One other point must be remembered in all this:
　　　that, had the lord done anything imprudent,
　　　they would never bear him a lingering grudge,
　　　but always their loyalty, loyally given.

217   Assí guisó la cosa   el mortal enemigo,
                quando perdió la tierra   el buen rey don Rodrigo,
                non quedó en España   quien valiesse un figo
                si non Castiella Vieja,   un lugar muy antigo.

218   Fueron nuestros abuelos   grant tienpo muy coitados,
                ca los tenién los moros   muy fuert' arrenconados;
                eran en poca tierra   muchos omnes juntados;
                de fanbre e de guerra   eran mucho lazrados.

219   Maguer mucho lazerio,   mucha coita sofricron,
                lo al sienpre ganaron,   lo suyo non perdieron;
                por miedo de la muerte   yerro nunca fezieron;
                todos sus adversarios   por aquí los vençieron.

220   ¿Cómmo se nos oviera   tod' esto olvidar?
                Lo que ellos ovieron   a nos es d' eredar;
                veniendo nos en miente   non podremos errar;
                puede nos tod' aquesto   de malfecho librar.

221   Dexemos los parientes,   a lo nuestro tornemos;
                por' ir a la batalla,   aquesso aguisemos.
                Por miedo de la muerte   la lid non escusemos:
                caer o levantar   y lo departiremos.

222   ¡Esforçad, castellanos,   non ayades pavor!
                Vençremos los poderes   del moro Almozor;
                sacaremos Castiella   de premia e d' error;
                él será el vençudo,   yo seré vençedor.

223   Maguer que muchos son,   non valen tres arvejas;
                ....
                más pueden tres leones   ....
                matarién treinta lobos   a treinta mill ovejas.

224   Amigos, d' una cosa   so yo bien sabidor:
                que vençremos sin duda   al moro Almozor;
                de todos los d' España   faredes m' el mejor;
                será grand la mi onra   e la vuestra mayor.'

217   And so the deadly foe devised his scheme
that, when the good King Rodrigo lost the land,
nowhere worth a fig was there left in all Spain,
except the ancient land of Old Castile.

218   For a long time our elders were sorely hard-pressed,
for the Moors had them backed square in a corner,
many men bottled up in a small piece of land,
enduring the ravages of hunger and war.

219   Despite their great suffering and the sorrow they bore,
they always won from others and never lost their own;
no fear of death ever led them to err,
and so they were able to vanquish their foes.

220   How could we come to forget all of this?
What they had is now ours to inherit;
if we keep it in mind, we cannot commit error,
and it can save us from any wrong act.

221   Let us leave our forebears and return to our lot,
and make our preparations for battle.
We must not shirk the conflict through any fear of death;
our rise or our fall we shall determine on the field.

222   Take heart, O Castilians, and cast off your fear!
We shall vanquish the forces of the Moor al-Mansur,
and rescue Castile from oppression and wrong;
he will be the vanquished and I shall be the victor.

223   Although they are many, they are worth not three peas,
....
three lions have more strength ....
thirty wolves would kill thirty thousand sheep.

224   My friends, on this one point I am quite convinced:
that the Moor al-Mansur we are sure to defeat;
of all men of Spain, you will make me the finest;
great will my fame be, and yours greater still.'

225   Quando ovo el conde   la razón acabada,
       con estos tales dichos   su gente conortada,
       movió se de Muñó,   con toda su mesnada,
       fueron se pora Lara   tomar otra posada.

226   El cond' Ferrán Gonçález,   cuerpo de buenas mañas,
       cavalgó su cavallo,   partió s' de sus conpañas;
       por' ir buscar el puerco,   metió s' por las montañas;
       falló l' en un arroyo   çerca de Las Quebañas.

227   Acojió se el puerco   a un ficro lugar
       do tenía su cueva   e solié albergar;
       non se osó el puerco   en cueva segurar;
       fuxo a un' ermita,   metió s' tras el altar.

228   Era essa ermita   d' una yedra techada,
       por que de toda ella   non paresçía nada;
       tres monjes y vevían   vida fuerte lazrada:
       San Pedro avié nonbre   essa casa sagrada.

229   Non pudo por la peña   el conde aguijar;
       sorrendó el cavallo,   ovo se d' apear;
       por do se metió 'l puerco,   metió s' por es' lugar,
       entró por la ermita,   llegó fasta 'l altar.

230   Quando vio don Fernando   tan onrado lugar,
       desanparó el puerco,   non lo quiso matar:
       'Señor,' diz, 'a quien temen   los vientos e la mar,
       si yo erré en esto   deves me perdonar.

231   A Ti me manifiesto,   Virgen Santa María,
       que d'esta santidat,   Señora, non sabía.
       Por y fazer enojo   aquí non entraría
       si non por dar ofrenda   o fazer romería.

232   Señor, Tú me perdona,   me val' e me ayuda
       contra la gent' pagana   que tanto m' es erguda;
       anpara a Castiella   de la gent' descreúda;
       si Tú non la anparas   tengo la por perduda.'

225   When the Count had arrived at the end of his speech,
bringing comfort to his men with such words as these,
he moved out from Muñó with all of his forces
and set out for Lara, to make a new camp.*

226   Count Fernán González, a man of sharp wits,
spurred on his mount to leave his companies behind;
he went up in the mountains, in pursuit of a boar,
and found it by a stream near Las Quebañas.*

227   The boar then took refuge in a desolate spot,
the site of its cave, where it used to find shelter;
the boar did not dare to seek safety in the cave,
but fled to a hermitage and hid behind the altar.

228   That hermitage bore a thick covering of ivy,
and so no trace of it was visible to the eye;
three monks lived out there a life of harsh privation;
San Pedro was the name of that holy house.*

229   The Count was unable to spur on up the crag;
he reined in his horse and was forced to dismount;
where the boar went before him, the Count made his way:
into the hermitage, right to the altar.

230   When Fernando set eyes on a place of such honour,
he left the boar unharmed, and would not kill it:
'Lord,' he said, 'feared by the winds and the sea,
if I have here erred You must grant me Your pardon.

231   Holy Virgin Mary, I make this vow to you,
that I knew nothing, my Lady, of this sacred place.
I would not have come here to cause an offence,
but only to give offerings, or walk the pilgrim path.

232   Lord, grant me Your pardon, Your aid, and support,
against the pagan peoples so opposed to me;
give Castile Your protection against the unbelievers,
for if You do not do so, I hold it as lost.'

233 Quando la oraçión el cond' ov' acabada,
   vino a él un monje de la pobre posada:
   Pelayo avié nonbre, vivié vida lazrada;
   salvó l' e preguntó l' quál era su andada.

234 Dixo que tras el puerco él era y venido,
   era de su mesnada redrado e partido;
   si por pecados fuesse de Almozor sabido,
   non fincaría tierra do escapasse vivo.

235 Recudió 'l monje, dixo: 'Ruego t' por Dios, amigo,
   si fuesse tu mesura, que ospedes conmigo:
   dar t' he yo pan de ordio, ca non tengo de trigo;
   sabrás cóm' has de fer contra 'l tu enemigo.'

236 El cond' Ferrán González, de todo bien conplido,
   del monje don Pelayo resçibió su convido;
   del ermitaño santo tovo s' por bien servido;
   mejor non albergara después que fue nasçido.

237 Dixo don fray Pelayo escontra su señor:
   'Fago te, el buen conde, de tanto sabidor,
   que quier' la tu fazienda guiar el Crïador;
   vençerás el poder del moro Almozor.

238 Farás grandes batallas en la gent' descreída,
   muchas serán las gentes a quien toldrás la vida;
   cobrarás de la tierra una buena partida;
   la sangre de los reyes por ti será vertida.

239 Non quiero más dezirte de toda tu andança;
   será de tod' el mundo temida la tu lança;
   quanto que te yo digo ten lo por segurança;
   dos vezes serás preso, creí me sin dubdança.

240 Antes de terçer día serás en grand cuitado,
   ca verás el tu pueblo todo muy espantado;
   verán un fuerte signo qual nunca vio omn' nado;
   el más loçano d'ellos será muy desmayado.

233   The Count having spoken the end of his prayer,
        a monk of that poor dwelling then approached him,
        Pelayo by name, who lived a life of privation;*
        he greeted him and asked what brought him there.

234   The Count said he was come upon the trail of the boar,
        but was detached and split off from his army;
        if, for his sins, al-Mansur should hear of him,
        no land would be left where he could flee with his life.

235   The monk replied and said, 'In God's name, my friend,
        should you approve it, then I beg you lodge with me:
        I will give you barley bread – I have none of wheat –
        and you will see what you must do against your foe.'

236   Count Fernán González, a most accomplished man,
        received the monk Pelayo's hospitality,
        and thought himself well treated by the saintly hermit:
        he had had no better lodgings since his birth.

237   Brother Pelayo spoke thus to his lord:
        'Of this, my good Count, I give you knowledge:
        the will of the Creator is to guide your campaign;
        you will conquer the armies of the Moor al-Mansur.

238   You will fight great battles with the unbelieving tribe,
        and many will be those whose lives you claim;
        you will regain a great portion of the land,
        and the blood of kings will be spilt by your hand.

239   I wish to tell you no more of your fortune,
        but your lance will strike fear in all the world;
        you may rest well assured of the truth of my words;
        you will twice see prison – do not doubt what I say.

240   Before the third day you will be deeply troubled,*
        for you will see your people in great terror;
        they will see such an omen as none ever born has seen,
        which will be daunting to the strongest among them.

241   Tú confortar los has   quanto mejor podieres,
dezir les has a todos   que semejan mugeres;
departir has el signo   quanto mejor sopieres;
perderán tod' el miedo   quand' gelo departieres.

242   Espídete agora   con lo que has oído;
aqueste lugar pobre   non l' eches en olvido;
fallarás el tu pueblo   triste e dolorido,
faziendo llor' e llanto   e dando apellido.

243   Por lloro nin por llanto   non fazen ningún tuerto,
ca piensan qu' eres preso   o que moros t' han muerto,
que quedan sin señor   e sin ningún confuerto;
coidavan con los moros   por ti salir a puerto.

244   Mas ruego te, amigo,   pido te lo de grado,
que, quand' ovieres tú   el canpo arrancado,
venga se te en mientes   d'est' convento laçrado
e non se te olvide   el pobre ospedado.

245   Señor, tres monjes somos,   assaz pobre convento;
la nuestra pobre vida   non ha nin par nin cuento;
si Dios non nos enbía   algún consolamiento
daremos a las sierpes   nuestro avitamiento.'

246   El conde dio l' respuesta,   com' omne enseñado;
dixo: 'Don fray Pelayo,   non ayades cuidado:
quanto que demandastes   ser vos ha otorgado;
conosçredes a dónde   diestes vuestr' ospedado.

247   Si Dios aquesta lid   me dexa arrancar,
quiero tod' el mío quinto   a este lugar dar;
demás, quando muriere,   aquí me soterrar,
que mejore por mí   sienpre este lugar.

248   Faré otra iglesia   de más fuerte çimiento,
faré dentro en ella   el mi soterramiento;
daré y donde vivan   de monjes más de ciento,
sirvan todos a Dios,   fagan su mandamiento.'

241   You must give them comfort as best you are able,
       and tell them all they are behaving like women;
       you must explain the omen as best you know how;
       at your explanation, they will shed all their fear.

242   Go on your way now with what you have heard,
       but be not unmindful of this humble place;
       you will find your people in sorrow and distress,
       weeping and wailing and crying out for you.

243   In their weeping and wailing they do not do wrong,
       for they think you captured, or murdered by Moors,
       and themselves now deprived of their lord and their comfort;
       they believed that you would save them from the Moors.

244   But I beg you, my friend, a request from the heart:
       that when on battle's field you have won victory,
       you spare a thought for this monastery's suffering,
       and do not forget our humble hospitality.

245   We are but three monks, lord, a poor enough brotherhood;
       our life's poverty has neither like nor telling;
       if God does not send us some form of consolation,
       we shall abandon our dwelling to the serpents.'

246   The Count gave his answer as a man well schooled,
       saying: 'Brother Pelayo, be not troubled by care,
       for everything you ask of me, you will be granted;
       you will know to whom you gave your hospitality.

247   If God should allow me to prevail in this battle,
       I wish to give my whole fifth share to this place,
       and then, at my death, to have my burial here,*
       that this place may always prosper by my hand.

248   I will build another church more firmly founded,
       and inside it I will have my resting-place;
       I will there make provisions for a hundred monks and more,
       that they may all serve God and obey His commands.'

249   Despidió se del monje   alegre e pagado,
        vino se pora Lara   el cond' aventurado;
        quando allá llegó   e le vio su fonsado,
        el lloro e el llanto   en gozo fue tornado.

250   Contó a sus varones   cómmo l' avié contido:
        del monje que fallara   que yazié escondido;
        cómmo fuera su uésped,   tomara su convido;
        mejor non albergara   después que fue nasçido.

251   Otro día mañana   mandó mover sus gentes
        – mil avié por cristiano   de moros descreyentes –;
        los del cond' eran pocos   mas buenos conbatientes;
        todos eran iguales,   d' un coraçón ardientes.

252   Bien se veién por ojos   los moros e cristianos:
        non es omn' en el mundo   que asmas' los paganos:
        todos venién cobiertos   los oteros e llanos,
        a cristianos cuidavan   prender se los a manos.

253   Fazién grand alegría   los pueblos descreídos;
        venién tañendo tronpas   e dando alaridos;
        davan los malfadados   atamaños roídos
        que los montes e valles   semejavan movidos.

254   El conde don Fernando   estava muy quexado:
        querié morir por verse   con los moros juntado;
        bien cuidava es' día   reignar y el pecado,
        que metió grand espanto   en el pueblo cruzado.

255   Uno de los del conde,   de la Puente Itero,
        tenié un buen cavallo,   fermoso e ligero,
        puso l' de las espuelas   por çima d' un otero,
        abrió s' con él la tierra   e somió s' el cavero.

[256–261]

El capítulo de cómo el conde esfuerçava sus compañas por el miedo que ovieron del cavallero que se sumió et de cómo lidió con Almançor yl' vençió

... Estonces fueron todos muy espantados et dixieron: 'Por nuestros peccados fue esto que assí contesció agora, et bien semeja que Dios nos ha desamparados. Et

249 Happy and much contented, he took leave of the monk,
and the fortune-favoured count rode back to Lara;
on reaching that place, when his army then saw him,
their weeping and their wailing turned to joy.*

250 He told his men his tale of what had happened:
of how he had found the monk who lay in hiding,'
become his guest, and received his hospitality;
he had had no better lodgings since his birth.

251 The next morning, he ordered his army move out,
one Christian for a thousand of the unbelieving Moors;
the Count's men were few, but in battle they were skilled,
and all alike they burned with one desire.

252 The Moors and the Christians looked each other in the eye;
no man alive could count the pagans' number:
the hillsides and plains were all covered by their force,
thinking soon to have the Christians in their hands.

253 The unbelieving peoples made a show of great joy,
playing horns as they marched, giving loud battle-cries;
the din was so great from those ill-fated wretches
that the mountains and the valleys seemed to tremble.

254 Count Fernando was filled with great anxiety,
as he was dying to join battle with the Moors;
he was convinced that day that the Devil there reigned,
striking grave terror in the people of the cross.

255 One among his men, from Puente Fitero,*
had a splendid mount, fleet of foot and handsome;
as he spurred it on past the crest of a hill,
the land gaped open and swallowed up the knight.

[256–261]
The chapter which tells how Count Fernán González spurred on his troops in the face of the fear that they suffered because of the knight who was swallowed up; and how he fought with al-Mansur and defeated him*
... Then they were all filled with terror and said: 'What has just happened is because of our sins and it indeed seems that God has forsaken us. We would have acted

fiziéramos mejor seso si nos oviéramos tornados, ca por ojo lo vemos que Dios quiere ayudar a los moros. Pues ¿cómo podremos nos ir contra ellos?' Díxoles estonces el Conde: 'Amigos, non lo fagades assí nin querades ganar en poco mal prez por siempre nin desmayedes sin feridas nin demostredes en vos tal covardía como ésta, ca departirvos quiero yo lo que muestra este signo et lo que quiere ser. Sabet que pues que vos fazedes somir la tierra ante vos que es tan dura et tan fuerte, ¿quáles cosas otras vos podrán sofrir? Et vos todos sodes omnes de alta guisa et veo agora vuestros coraçones enflaquecer contra yentes que non son si non como sombra. Et vos non devedes por esto aver ningún miedo, ca yo este día cobdiciava ver et ser en tal affruenta con Almançor en el campo, et agora veré de cómo los castellanos sabedes guardar señor.' Pues que el Conde ovo acabada su razón et esforçadas sus compañas como omne sesudo, mandó luego desbolver el su pendón et fue ferir en los moros muy esforçada mientre et iva llamando: '¡Castiella!'. Los castellanos otrossí fueron ferir aquella ora muy de rezio en los moros. Et fue y muy bueno Gustio Gonçález con sus dos fijos que tenié y consigo mancebiellos, et fazién muy grand daño en los moros. ...

262   ....
           quien con él s' encontrava   non se iva d'él sano;
           ....
           ....

263   Otrossí un ric' omne   que dezién don Velasco
           ....
           ....
           ....

264   Metién toda su fuerça   en guardar su señor,
           non avién de la muerte   nin pesar nin dolor;
           tollié les el grand depdo   de la muert' el pavor,
           non avié pora buenos   d'este mundo mejor.

265   Cómmo todos fizieron   refez es d' entender;
           tanto non fizo omne   con tan poco poder;
           semeja fiera cosa   pesada d' entender:
           trezientos cavalleros   tan grand pueblo vençer.

266   Caveros e peones   firme miente lidiavan,
           todos quanto podían   su señor aguardavan;
           quando dezié '¡Castiella!',   todos se esforçavan;
           los moros en tod' esto   las espaldas tornavan.

more wisely by turning back, for we can see clearly that the will of God is to aid the Moors. So how will it be possible for us to go against them?' Then the Count said to them: 'My friends, do not act in this way and do not seek to earn in little time ill fame that will last for ever, and do not lose heart without a blow being struck or show such cowardice as this, for I wish to explain to you what this sign shows us and what its meaning is. I tell you, since you cause the ground that is so firm and hard to give way before you, what other things can stand up to you? You are all men of noble nature and I can see now your hearts weakening in the face of people who are a shadow of you. You must feel no fear at this, for I this day longed to see and find myself in just such a combat with al-Mansur on the battlefield, and now I shall see just what support Castilians know how to give to your lord.' Once the Count had finished speaking and had given encouragement to his troops as a man of wisdom, he ordered his pennant be unfurled and went determinedly to strike the Moors, crying out as he went: 'Castile!'. The Castilians likewise then went heartily to battle with the Moors. Gustio González* with his two young sons that accompanied him fought well, and they inflicted great harm on the Moors. ...

262 ....
     any man who met him departed in ill health,
     ....
     ....

263 So too a nobleman known as Velasco*
     ....
     ....
                                                             *
     ....

264 They put all their strength in protecting their lord,
     and death could bring them neither pain nor sorrow;
     the great debt they owed took away all fear of death;
     for good men there was no better world than this.

265 How they all fared may be quickly understood:
     so much was never done with such small forces;
     it seems a marvel that should tax the understanding,
     for three hundred knights to beat an army so large.

266 Men on foot and horseback were steadfast in battle,
     and each did all he could in protecting his lord;
     when he cried out, 'Castile!', his men all took heart,
     while the Moors began to turn in retreat.

267   Fue les de una lid   el conde acuitando,
iva s' contra la tienda   d' Almozor acostando,

....

....

268   A Almozor llegaron   'questos malos roídos,
sabiendo cómmo eran   sus poderes vençidos:
eran muchos los muertos   e muchos los feridos;
avía de sus reyes   los mejores perdidos.

269   Demandó su cavallo   por lidiar con sus manos;
fueran y venturados   caveros castellanos
– muerto fuera o preso   de los pueblos cristianos –
mas non lo consejaron   los poderes paganos.

270   Por non vos detener   en otras ledanías:
fue Almozor vençido   con sus cavallerías;
allí fue demostrado   el poder del Mexías,
el conde fue David,   e Almozor Golías.

271   Foía Almozor   a guis' de algarivo,
diziendo: '¡Ay, Mafómat!   mal' ora en ti fío.
Non vale tres arvejas   todo tu poderío;

....

272   ....

....

Todo mi grand poder   es muerto e cativo;
pues ellos muertos son,   ¿por qué finco yo vivo?'

273   Fincaron en el canpo   muertos muchos gentíos,
de los que sanos eran   estonz' fueron vazíos;

....

....

274   Quando fueron vençidos   essos pueblos paganos,
fueron los vençedores   los pueblos castellanos;
el cond' Ferrán Gonçález,   con todos los cristianos,
fueron en su alcançe   por cuestas e por llanos.

267   The Count, in the battle, had the Moors on the rack,
coming ever closer to the tent of al-Mansur,

....

....

268   This terrible news reached the ears of al-Mansur,
who knew that it told of his forces' defeat:
the dead numbered many and many were the injured,
and from among his kings he had lost the very best.

269   He asked for his horse, to add his own hands to the fray;
the knights of Castile would have here had good fortune:
the Christian peoples would have captured or slain him;
but the pagan forces gave him different advice.

270   So as not to detain you with litanies more:
al-Mansur was defeated, along with his knights;
the power of the Messiah was clearly displayed there;
the Count's role was David, with al-Mansur, Goliath.

271   Just as a pariah, al-Mansur took to flight,
crying, 'Oh Muhammed! Ill-starred my faith in you!
All of your power has not the worth of three beans.

....

272

....

....

All my great army is captured or dead;
since they are dead, why am I left alive?'

273   Very many men were left dead on the field,
and their men still rude in health then numbered none;

....

....

274   When those pagan peoples had suffered defeat,
the peoples of Castile remained as victors;
Count Fernán González, with all of the Christians,
went in their pursuit across hills and plains.

275   Rendieron a Dios gracias   e a Santa María
        por que les dexó ver   tamaña maravilla;
        duró les el alçançe   quanto a medio día;
        enriqueçió s' por sienpre   la pobre alcaldía.

276   Quando fue Almozor   grand tierra alexado,
        fincó de los cristianos   el canpo bien poblado;
        cojieron sus averes   que Dios les avié dado;
        tan grand aver fallaron   que non serié contado.

277   Fallaron en las tiendas   sobejano tesoro,
        muchas copas e vasos   qu' eran de fino oro;
        nunca vio tal riqueza   nin cristiano nin moro;
        serién end' abondados   Alexánder e Poro.

278   Fallaron y maletas   e muchos de çurrones,
        llenos d' oro e plata,   que non de pepïones,
        muchas tiendas de seda   e muchos tendejones,
        espadas e lorigas   e muchas guarniçiones.

279   Fallaron de marfil   arquetas muy preçiadas,
        con tantas de noblezas   que non serién contadas;
        fueron pora San Pedro   las más d' aquellas dadas;
        están en su altar   oy día asentadas.

280   Tomaron d'esto todo   lo que sabor ovieron,
        más fincó de dos partes   que levar non podieron;
        las armas que fallaron   dexar non las quisieron.
        Con toda su ganançia   a San Pedro venieron.

281   Quand' fueron y llegados,   a Dios graçias rendieron;
        todos, chicos e grandes,   su oraçión fizieron.
        Todos por una boca   'Deo gratias' dixeron;
        cada uno sus joyas   al altar ofreçieron.

282   De toda su ganançia   que Dios les avié dado,
        mandó tomar el quinto   el cond' aventurado;
        qualquier cosa que l' copo   – ovo lo bien conprado –
        mandó lo dar al monje   que l' diera ospedado.

275   They gave thanks to God and the Blessed Virgin Mary
         for granting them the sight of such a miracle;
         they spent half a day in pursuit of the Moors,
         and the poor municipality was made forever rich.*

276   With al-Mansur now a good distance away,
         the field was left well peopled with Christians;
         they gathered their possessions, granted them by God,
         and found such great wealth as to be beyond tally.

277   They found in the tents an abundant treasure:
         many cups and goblets made of fine gold;
         such riches as no Christian or Moor had ever seen
         – it would have sufficed Alexander and Porus.*

278   Many cases they found there, along with many bags,
         filled with gold and silver – no sign of copper coins –,
         many silken pavilions and many tents of war,
         breastplates and swords and a great mass of armour.

279   They found caskets of ivory very great in value,
         with other noble objects impossible to count;
         to San Pedro de Arlanza were most of these given,
         where to this day they are displayed upon its altar.*

280   From this great hoard of wealth, they took as they desired;
         two thirds and more remained they could not carry;
         but the arms they had found they wished not to leave behind.
         They came to San Pedro, bringing all of their gains.

281   When they arrived there, they gave thanks to God,
         and all, both young and old, then made their prayer;
         all with one voice cried out, 'Thanks be to God';
         and each at the altar made an offering of his jewels.

282   From all of their gains, which were granted them by God,
         the blessed count ordered the fifth share be taken;
         anything that fell to him, which he had bought dear,
         he ordered be given to the monk who had lodged him.

283   El conde e sus gentes   e todos los cruzados
              a la çibdat de Burgos   fueron todos llegados;
              folgaron e dormieron,   que eran muy cansados;
              demandaron maestros   por sanar los llagados.

284   Dexemos éstos y,   qu' eran muy mal golpados;
              el cond' Ferrán Gonçález,   de los fechos granados,
              avía ya oídos   unos fuertes mandados
              que avién los navarros   a sus pueblos robados.

285   Mientra qu' el cond' estava   a Dios faziend' plazer,
              lidiando con los moros   con todo su poder,
              el rey de los navarros   ovo se a mover;
              cuidó toda Castiella   de robar e correr.

286   Quando los castellanos   oyeron los mandados,
              bien cuidavan que nunca   d'ellos serién vengados;
              dizién: 'En fuerte ora   fuemos mesquinos nados;
              de todos los del mundo   somos desafïados.'

287   El conde castellano,   quando l' ovo oído,
              por poco con pesar   non salió de sentido;
              mas commo león bravo   ansí dio un gemido;
              diz: 'Aun gelo demande   con mis armas guarnido.'

288   Avién los castellanos   d'esto fiero pesar,
              por que los confondía   quien los devié salvar.
              'Señor,' dixo el conde,   'quieras me ayudar,
              que pueda tal sovervia   aína arrancar.'

289   Enbïó 'l cond' al rey   don Sancho demandar
              si s' querié contra él   en algo mejorar,
              ca ferié su mesura   e el su bienestar;
              si fer non lo quisiesse,   mandó l' desafïar.

290   Llegó al rey don Sancho   aqueste mensajero:
              'Omillo m',' dixo, 'rey,   luego de lo primero;
              del conde de Castiella   so yo su mensajero;
              dezir t' he lo que dize,   fasta lo postrimero.

283   The Count and his people and all the crusaders
had all now arrived at the city of Burgos;*
wearied, they gave themselves to rest and to sleep,
and called for doctors to heal the wounded.

284   Let us now leave behind these badly injured men;
Count Fernán González, that man of great deeds,
had now heard report of a troubling event:
that the Navarrese had plundered from his people.

285   While the Count was acting to bring pleasure to God
by battling the Moors with all of his forces,
the king of the Navarrese launched an attack;*
his thought: to raid and ravage all Castile.

286   When the Castilians came to hear news of this,
they were convinced that they would never be avenged;
they said: 'An ill hour saw the birth of us wretches,
for we are issued challenges from all across the world.'

287   The Castilian count, when he had heard these words,
was near driven from his wits in his sorrow,
but like a wild lion he cried out with a roar:
'May I yet seek redress when I am decked in my arms!'

288   At this, the Castilians were deeply dismayed,
for he who should save them instead brought distress.
'Lord,' said the Count, 'may You grant me Your aid,
that I may root out such arrogance at once.'

289   The Count sent a message to ask of King Sancho*
if it was his wish to give the Count some redress,
for he would thus act rightly, and in his own best interests;
if this was not his will, the Count ordered he be challenged.

290   This messenger came before King Sancho, and said:
'My King, I prostrate myself before you at once;
I come to bear a message from the Count of Castile,
and I will tell you every word of what he says.

291   Sepas que ha de ti   el conde grand querella
que te lo gradesçría   si le sacasses d'ella,
ca traxist' a Castiella   grant tienpo a la pella,
dos vezes en el año   venist' a corrella.

292   Por fer mal a Castiella   e destruir castellanos,
feziste te amigo   de los pueblos paganos;
feziste guerra mala   a los pueblos cristianos
por que non querían   meter s' en las tus manos.

293   Ha de ti sobre todo   d'esto fiera rencura:
feziste otra cosa   que fue más desmesura,
ca, mientra él corría   allá Estremadura,
feziste le tal daño   que fue desapostura.

294   Si d' aquesta querella   le quisieres sacar,
de commo es derecho   ansí lo mejorar,
farías tu mesura   e el tu bienestar;
si esto non quisieres   manda te desafiar.'

295   Quand' ovo 'l mensajero   su razón acabada,
avié por lo que iva   la cosa recabdada,
fabló el rey e dixo   su razón a vegada:
'Non le mejoraré   valía d' una meaja.

296   Ermano, it al conde   e dezit l' el mandado,
de él me desfïar   so much' maravillado;
tan bien commo deviera   non fue aconsejado:
no s' puede bien fallar   d' aqueste tal mercado.

297   Mucho l' tengo por loco   e de seso menguado,
sól' por me desfïar   e de ser end' osado:
por que aquesta vez   ha los moros rancado,
por esta loçanía   ha esto començado.

298   Dezit le que aína   le iré yo a buscar;
en torre nin en çerca   no m' podrié escapar
que buscado non sea   fasta dentro en mar;
sabré por que m' osó   él a mí desfïar.'

291   Know that the Count has much grievance with you,
and would be grateful if you gave him redress,
for Castile has long suffered much at your hands,
as you came twice a year to lay waste to her lands.

292   To do harm to Castile and destroy the Castilians,
you entered into friendship with the pagan nations*
and waged evil war on the people of Christ,
for they did not wish to succumb to your rule.

293   Above all, he has this deep grievance against you,
for you did something else showing yet poorer judgment:
while he was campaigning in those frontier lands,*
you did him such harm as was worthy of shame.

294   If you wish to give him redress for this grievance,
and to make right the wrong, as you ought to do,
you would thus act rightly, and in your own best interests;
if this is not your will, then he orders you be challenged.'

295   When the messenger had come to the end of his speech
and had carried out the task on which he came,
the King spoke in turn, putting forth his own speech:
'I will not give him even a halfpenny in redress.

296   Brother, go now and bear this message to the Count:
I find it incredible that he should challenge me;
the counsel he received was not as sound as required:
he has no way of emerging from this deal in profit.

297   I hold him quite mad and much lacking in sense,
simply for his rashness in issuing me challenge;
because this time he has brought the Moors to defeat –
it is pride in this feat that has set him on this course.

298   Tell him I shall not hesitate to go and seek him out;
no tower or rampart could protect him from me,
such that I will not seek him to the depths of the sea;
I shall learn why he dared so much as challenge me.'

299   Tornó s' el mensajero   ya quanto espantado,
por que vïo al rey   fiera miente irado;
contó gelo al conde,   nada no l' fue çelado;
dixo l' cómmo l' avía   muy fuert' amenazado.

300   Mandó llamar el conde   a todos sus varones:
todos los ricos omnes,   todos los infançones,
tan bien a escuderos   commo a los peones;
querié de cada uno   saber sus coraçones.

301   Quando fueron juntados   começó de fablar;
qualquier se lo vería   que avié grand pesar:
'Ha menester, amigos,   de consejo tomar,
de guisa que podamos   tal fuerça rencurar.

302   Nunca a los navarros   mal non les meresçiemos,
nin tuerto nin sovervia   nos nunca les feziemos;
muchos fueron los tuertos   que d'ellos resçibiemos;
por' gelo demandar   nunca sazón toviemos.

303   Cuidé que se querían   contra nos mejorar,
que los tuertos e daños   querían emendar;
la querella qu' teniemos   quieren nos la doblar;
a mí e a vos otros   enbían desfïar.

304   Amigos, tal sobervia   ¡que non gela suframos!
¡Que nos venguemos d'ella   o todos y muramos,
ante que tanta cuita   e tal pesar veamos!
¡Por Dios, los mis vassallos,   nos los acometamos!

305   En los acometer   es nuestra mejoría:
por quanto ellos son   mayor cavallería,
nos non mostremos y   ninguna covardía;
en dudar nos por ellos   serié grand villanía.

306   Sepades qu' en la lid   non son todos iguales:
por çient lanças se vençen   las faziendas canpales;
más valen çien caveros,   todos d' un cuer iguales,
que non fazen trezientos   de los descomunales.

299   The messenger returned feeling no small fear
having seen such a savage show of anger from the King;
he told the Count his tale, keeping not a word back,
and spoke of the terrible threats made against him.

300   By order of the Count, his men were all summoned:
all of the nobility, and every man of rank;
the call went out alike to foot soldiers and squires;
he wished to know the heart of every one of them.

301   When they had all gathered, the Count began to speak,
and any man could see he felt great sorrow:
'My friends, taking counsel is what we now need,
that we may gain some reparation for such violence.

302   No ill did we ever merit from the Navarrese:
we have never done them wrong or caused them insult;
but many are the wrongs we have suffered at their hands,
and we have never had the chance to seek redress.

303   I thought it was their wish to make amends to us,
atoning for those sufferings and wrongs,
but rather what they wish is to redouble our complaint;
they are issuing a challenge, to me and to you all.

304   My friends, let us not tolerate such insult from them!
Let us either find our vengeance or our death there,
rather than bear witness to such pain and great sorrow!
In God's name, my vassals, let us march out against them!

305   In marching out to meet them lies our benefit:
although they have a greater force of knights,
let us not show there any sign of cowardice;
for us to fear them would be base indeed.

306   Know that all men are not equal in battle:
by a mere hundred lances great conflicts are won;
a hundred knights all of one heart have more worth
than three times that number, if not in accord.

307   Ha y buenos e malos,   que non puede al ser:
         los malos que y son   non podrién atender;
         aver s' han por aquéllos   los buenos a vençer;
         veemos muchas vezes   tal cosa conteçer.

308   Muchos son más que nos,   peones e caveros;
         omnes son esforçados   e de pies muy ligeros,
         de asconas e dardos   fazen golpes çerteros;
         traen buena conpaña   de buenos cavalleros.

309   Por esto ha mester   que nos los cometamos:
         si ellos nos cometen   mejoría les damos;
         si ellos entendieren   que nos non los dubdamos,
         dexar nos han el canpo   ante que los firamos.

310   Otra cosa vos digo   e vos la entendredes,
         ferido de pelea   o en quexa m' veredes;
         veré, los castellanos,   cómmo me acorredes,
         menester vos será   quanta fuerça tenedes.

311   Si por alguna guisa   al rey puedo llegar,
         los tuertos que me fizo   cuedo ge demandar.
         No l' podrié ningún omne   de la muerte escapar;
         non avrié, si él muere,   de mi muerte pesar.'

312   Quand' ovo el buen conde   su razón acabada,
         mandó contra Navarra   mover la su mesnada:
         entró les en la tierra   quanto una jornada;
         falló al rey don Sancho   a l' Era Degollada.

313   Quand' el rey vio al conde   venir atán irado,
         enderesçó sus azes   en un fermoso prado;
         el conde castellano,   con su pueblo famado,
         non alongaron plazo   fasta otro mercado.

314   Abaxaron las lanças   e fueron a ferir,
         el conde delantero,   com' oyestes dezir;
         don Sancho de Navarra,   quando lo vio venir,
         con sus azes paradas   salió l' a resçebir.

307   There are good men and bad there, inevitably so;
the bad men there would be unable to stand firm,
and through them the good men will meet their defeat;
time and again we see this pattern recur.

308   They dwarf us in numbers of infantry and knights;
they are spirited men who are very fleet of foot,
and strike certain blows with their spears and their darts;
and they bring a fine company of horsemen of skill.

309   This is why we must take the role of the aggressor,
for if they attack first, then we cede the advantage;
if they understand that we are not at all afraid,
they will yield the battlefield before we strike a blow.

310   One thing more I tell you that you will understand:
I will be hit in battle; you will see my distress;
and I, my Castilians, will see what aid you give me;
you will be in need of all the strength you possess.

311   If by some means I can get close to King Sancho,
I will seek redress for the wrongs he has done me;
no man would be able to save him from death,
and if he meets his end, I shall not grieve my own.'

312   When the good Count had come to the end of his speech,
he ordered his troops to set out against Navarre,
and took them a day's march into that kingdom;
he found King Sancho at the Era Degollada.*

313   When the King saw the Count come stoked with such anger,
he drew up his forces in a beautiful meadow;*
the Castilian count, with his celebrated army,
did not delay their business and await a later day.

314   They lowered their lances and rode out to battle;
the Count led the charge, as you have heard tell;
King Sancho of Navarre, when he saw him come,
rode out to meet him, his battle lines ready.

315   Ferié entre las azes   que fronteras estavan:
        en la parte qu' él iva,   todos carrera l' davan;
        los unos e los otros   firme mientre lidiavan;
        navarros con la muerte   lidiavan e lazravan.

316   Tan grand' era la priessa   que avién en lidiar,
        oyé omne a lexos   las feridas sonar;
        non oirién otra voz   si non astas quebrar,
        espadas reteñir   e los yelmos cortar.

317   Nonbravan los navarros   a '¡Pamplona!', '¡Estella!',
        los firmes castellanos   nonbravan a '¡Castiella!';
        nonbrava 'l rey don Sancho,   a las vezes '¡Castiella',
        com' algunos françeses   a vezes echan pella.

318   El buen cond' e el rey   buscando s' andodieron
        fasta que un' a otro   a ojo se ovieron;
        las armas que traían   çerteras las fizieron,
        fueron se a ferir   quant' de rezio pudieron.

319   Entramos un' a otro   tales golpes se dieron
        que fierros de las lanças   a l' otra part' salieron;
        nunca de cavalleros   tales golpes se vieron:
        todas sus guarniçiones   nada non les valieron.

320   Cuitado fue el rey   de la mala ferida;
        entendió que del golpe   ya perdiera la vida;
        la su grand valentía   luego fue abatida;
        man' a mano del cuerpo   el alma fue salida.

321   El conde fue del golpe   fiera miente llagado,
        ca tenié grand lançada   por el diestro costado;
        llamava '¡Castellanos!',   mas ningún fue uviado;
        de todos sus vassallos   era desanparado.

322   Tovieron castellanos   qu' eran muy falesçidos,
        todos sus buenos fechos   qu' eran por y perdidos;
        con quexa castellanos   andavan muy marridos,
        porque en muy grand yerro   eran todos caídos.

315   He struck at the men in Castile's front lines,
and where he went, they all gave way to him;
men on both sides showed resolve in their fighting,
the Navarrese fighting and suffering with death.

316   So great was the zeal they brought to the battle,
that from a great distance the blows could be heard;
no sound could be heard but the shattering of lances,
the clashing of swords and the cleaving of helms.

317   The Navarrese called on 'Pamplona!', 'Estella!'
and the resolute Castilians gave their cry of 'Castile!';
King Sancho, too, sometimes cried out 'Castile!',
just as some Frenchmen at times act in jest.*

318   The good Count and the King sought each other on the field,
until they each set eyes upon the other;
the weapons that they bore they made unerring,
and so they moved to strike with all their strength.

319   Each of them struck the other blows of such force
that the iron-tipped lances passed right through the body;
no knight was ever seen to deal blows such as these,
and all their armour served them not at all.

320   The King was much troubled with that cruel wound,
and knew that the blow had already cost his life;
in an instant his powerful strength was laid low,
and his soul was departed from his body at once.

321   The Count had been terribly injured by the blow,
with a great lance-wound in his right-hand side;*
he called out 'Castilians!' but none came to help him;
the Count was forsaken by all of his vassals.

322   The Castilians felt they had suffered grave harm,
and that all their great deeds were thus rendered as nought;
the Castilians felt terribly distressed and in grief
at how they were all fallen so deeply into error.*

323 Tanto tenié cad' uno en lo suyo que ver
que non podién ningunos al conde acorrer;
fizo les la vergüença tod' el miedo perder
e ovieron por fuerça las azes a ronper.

324 Sofriendo grandes golpes al conde allegaron;
antes que y llegasen a muchos derribaron.
Muy maltrecho, sin duda, al buen conde fallaron;
de una part' e d' otra muchas almas sacaron.

325 Llegaron castellanos, al conde acorrieron;
luego que y llegaron sobre todos firieron.
A los navarros por fuerça a fuera los fizieron;
temién que era muerto e grand miedo ovieron.

326 Alçaron le de tierra, la ferida le vieron,
todos que muerto era bien ansí le tovieron;
por poco con pesar de seso non salieron;
commo si fuesse muerto, muy gran duelo fizieron.

327 Firieron en navarros, del conde los tiraron,
sobre un buen cavallo a su señor alçaron;
la sangre de su cara toda gela linpiaron;
todos commo de nuevo a llorar començaron.

328 Cuitaron los afirmes, davan lit presurada,
reteñién en los yelmos mucha buena cuchillada;
daban e resçebían mucha buena lançada,
daban e resçebían mucha buena porrada.

329 Non vos queremos más la cosa alongar:
ovieron los navarros el canpo a dexar;
ovo el rey don Sancho muerto y a fincar;
mandó l' luego el conde a Navarra levar.

330 Dexemos a don Sancho – ¡perdon' l' el Crïador! –,
los navarros maltrechos llorando su señor;
avién de vengar se todos fuerte sabor;
salieron al buen conde todos por su amor.

323   Each man had such pressing concerns of his own
        that none of them could go to the aid of the Count;
        but shame at this caused them to shed all their fear
        and they managed to shatter the battle lines by force.

324   Though enduring cruel blows, they reached the Count's side,
        and they cut down many men along the way;
        they found the good Count in a bad way indeed,
        and they set loose the souls of many men, all around.

325   The Castilians arrived and brought aid to their Count;
        at once they launched attacks on all his enemies.
        The force of their attack drove the Navarrese away;
        they feared he was dead and were all much afraid.

326   As they raised him from the ground and saw his wound,
        they were all of them convinced that he was dead;
        in sorrow, they all but took leave of their senses,
        and deeply lamented as though he had died.

327   They drove the Navarrese from the Count with their blows,
        and on a fine horse they then mounted their lord;
        they wiped away clean all the blood from his face,
        and they all began to weep for him afresh.

328   Their attack was a fierce one, the battle intense,
        and many fine sword blows rang out on the helms;
        many fine lance thrusts were given and received,
        and they gave and received many more struck by clubs.

329   No further do we wish to draw out this account:
        the Navarrese were forced to leave the battlefield,
        King Sancho to remain there, his life now lost;*
        the Count at once ordered he be taken to Navarre.

330   Let us leave Sancho – may the Creator forgive him –;
        the Navarrese were downcast in weeping for their lord;
        a hunger for vengeance ran deep in them all,
        all confronting the good Count for love of their lord.

331   El conde de Piteos   e conde de Tolosa
    – parient' era del rey,   esto es çierta cosa –
    tomó de sus condados   conpaña muy fermosa;
    movió pora Castiella   en ora muy astrosa.

332   El conde non uvió   por a la lid llegar,
    pero quando lo sopo   non quiso detardar;
    al buen rey de Navarra   bien cuidó lo vengar;
    al puerto de Getárea   ovo de arribar.

333   Los navarros al conde   todos a él llegaron;
    cómmo fue la fazienda   todo gelo contaron:
    quántos fueron los muertos,   quántos los que fincaron;
    cómmo a él en antes   dos días l' esperaron.

334   El conde de Tolosa   dio les muy grant esfuerço;
    coidó con esse fecho   con él salir a puerto:
    'Ca me han castellanos   fecho este grand tuerto,
    cuido vengar al rey,   que ellos lo han muerto.'

335   El conde don Fernando   avié lo ya oído:
    cóm' era aquel conde   al puerto ya venido;
    el conde don Fernando,   maguer tan mal ferido,
    atal commo estava   pora allá fue ido.

336   Los vassallos del conde   tenién se por errados;
    eran contra el conde   fuerte miente irados;
    eran de su señor   todos muy despagados,
    por que avién por fuerça   sienpre d' andar armados.

337   Folgar non les dexava   nin estar segurados;
    dizién: 'Non es tal vida   si non pora pecados
    que andan noch' e día   e nunca son cansados;
    él semeja Satán   e nos a sus crïados.

338   Por que lidiar queremos   e tanto lo amamos,
    folgura non avemos   si almas non sacamos:
    los de l' ueste antigua,   aquéllos semejamos,
    ca todas cosas cansan   e nos nunca cansamos.

331   The man who was count of Poitou and Toulouse
        – his kinship to the King is certain truth –*
        gathered from his counties a splendid army
        and marched for Castile at an ill-starred hour.

332   The Count left too late to arrive for the battle,
        but on hearing the news he wished not to delay;
        he dearly wanted vengeance for the Navarrese king;
        he came at this point to the mountain pass of Cize.*

333   The Navarrese all flocked towards the Count,
        and told him all of how the battle fared:
        the numbers of the dead and those left living,
        and how they had awaited him the past two days.

334   The Count of Toulouse gave them encouragement indeed
        – he thought by that means he would achieve his goal –:
        'Since this great wrong has been done me by Castilians,
        I seek vengeance for the King, for they have killed him.'

335   The news had already been heard by Count Fernando
        that that count had arrived at the mountain pass,
        and that man Count Fernando, though gravely wounded,
        just as he was, made at once for that place.

336   The Count's vassals felt they were in error here,
        and conceived a furious anger for the Count;
        they all bore their lord a deep displeasure,
        as they were always forced to go in arms.

337   He did not let them rest or be in safety;
        'This life,' they said, 'is only for those devils
        who labour night and day and never tire;
        he seems like Satan, with us as his minions.*

338   Because we will fight and we bear him such love,
        we never have rest without first taking lives:
        we resemble those soldiers of the ancient host,
        for all things are tiring, but we are never tired.

339   Non ha duelo de nos,   que sofrimos tal vida,
nin lo ha de sí mismo   que tien' tan mal' ferida;
si – ¡mal pecado! – muere,   Castiella es perdida;
nunca tomaron omnes   atán mala caída.'

340   Ovieron su acuerdo   que gelo departiessen,
que lo que bien non era   luego gelo dixessen:
que por gran loçanía   en yerro non cayessen;
que por mala codiçia   su señor non perdiessen.

341   Dixo Nuño Laíno: 'Señor, si tú quisieres,
si a ti semejare   o tú por bien tovieres
que estés aquí quedo   fasta que guaresçieres,
que por mala codiçia   en yerro non cayeres.

342   Non sé omn' en el mundo   que podies' endurar
la vida que avemos   nos e vos a passar;
la vuestra grand codiçia   non nos dexa folgar;
avemos la mesura   por aquí d' olvidar.

343   Non recuden las cosas   todas a un lugar;
deve aver el omne   grand seso en lidiar;
si non, podrá aína   muy grand yerro tomar;
podrié tod' el grand prez   por y lo astragar.

344   Los vientos que son fuertes   veemos los cansar,
la mar que es irada   vemos la amansar;
el dïablo non cansa,   nunca puede folgar,
quiere la nuestra vida   la suya semejar.

345   Dexa folgar tus gentes, a ti mesmo sanar;
tienes muy fuerte llaga,   dexa la tú folgar.
Dexa venir tus gentes   qu' aún son por llegar;
muchos son por venir,   deves los esperar.

346   Tú serás a diez días   del golpe bien guarido
e será el tu pueblo   a es' plazo venido.
Poner t' has en el canpo   con tu pueblo guarnido;
será muerto o preso,   d'esto so bien creído.

339   He bears us no grief for the life that we suffer,
nor grieves for himself, when he has such a wound;
if he dies – God forbid! –, then Castile is lost;
men have never suffered such a fall as that would be.'

340   They came to an agreement to put this to him,
and to say to him at once what was not right:
that great pride should not make them fall into error,
nor evil greed cause them the loss of their lord.*

341   Said Nuño Laíno: 'Lord, if you are willing,*
if you think it fit and consider it is right,
stay here and rest a while, until you recover,
lest you fall into error through evil greed.

342   I know no-one in the world who could endure
the life that we and you both have to suffer;
your ravenous greed leaves us no time for rest,
and we have to forget here our sense of restraint.*

343   To the same point not everything returns,
and a man must show much wisdom in his battles;
if not, he may quickly come into great error,
and bring ruin on the glory he has gained.

344   We see winds that rage fiercely tire and fade,
and we can watch the angry sea grow calm;
the Devil never tires, he cannot be at rest,
and he wishes to make our life like his own.

345   Grant your men respite and allow yourself to heal;
your wound is severe – you must grant it respite;
let your men come who are not yet arrived;
there are many still to come – you must await them.

346   You will be fully healed of the blow in ten days,
and by then all your people will be come here.
You will take the battlefield guarded by your people;
he will be killed or captured, of this I am quite sure.

347   Señor, dicho te he   lo que dezir quería;
       mejor consejo d'este,   señor, yo non sabría.
       Non temas que lo digo   por nulla covardía;
       querría te guardar   commo a alma mía.'

348   Quand' ovo acabada   don Nuño su razón,
       començó el buen conde,   esse firme varón;
       avié grand conplimiento   del sen de Salamón:
       nunca fue Alexandre   más grand de coraçón.

349   Dixo: 'Nuño Laínez,   buena razón dixiestes;
       las cosas commo son   assí las departiestes:
       d' alongar esta lid,   creo qu' ansí dixiestes;
       quisquier' que vos lo dixo   vos mal lo aprendiestes.

350   Non deve el que puede   esta lid alongar;
       quien tiene buena ora   otra quier' esperar;
       un día que perdemos   no l' podremos cobrar;
       jamás en aquel día   non podemos tornar.

351   Si omne el su tienpo   en valde quier' passar,
       non quiere d'este mundo   otra cosa levar
       si non estar viçioso   e dormir e folgar,
       d'éste mueren sus fechos   quand' viene a finar.

352   Viçioso e lazrado   amos han de morir,
       el uno nin el otro   non lo puede foír;
       quedan los buenos fechos,   éstos han de vesquir;
       d'ellos toman ensienplo   los que han de venir.

353   Todos los que grand fecho   quisieron acabar,
       por muy grandes travajos   ovieron a passar;
       non comién quand' quisieron,   nin çena nin yantar;
       los viçios de la carne   ovieron d' olvidar.

354   Non cuentan d' Alexandre   las noches nin los días,
       cuentan sus buenos fechos   e sus cavallerías;
       cuentan del rey Davit   que mató a Golías,
       de Judas Macabeo,   fijo de Matatías.

347   All I wished to tell you, my lord, I have told;
      O lord, no better counsel could I give you than this;
      fear not that some cowardice might lie behind my words;
      I would wish to protect you as I would my own soul.'

348   When Nuño had finished what he had to say,
      the good Count began, that man of great courage;
      of the wisdom of Solomon he had a full share,
      and Alexander never had a greater heart.

349   He said, 'Nuño Laínez, you have spoken good sense,
      and you have set things out just as they are:
      I think you proposed that we put off this battle;
      whoever told you this, you learned it ill.

350   He who has the power must not put this battle off;
      he who has the right moment wants to wait for another;
      a day that we lose we can never take back;
      we can never return to that day once again.

351   If a man wants to spend his allotted time in vain,
      and if it is his wish to take nothing from this world
      except a life of pleasure, and sleeping, and rest,
      then when this man meets his end, his deeds die with him.

352   Men of toil and leisure must both come to die,
      for neither kind of man can escape it;
      but fine deeds remain, and these will live on,
      in which those yet to come find their example.

353   Every man who wished to perform great deeds
      had no choice but to pass through the hardest of trials;
      they ate not as they pleased, at dinner or lunch,
      and the pleasures of the flesh they were forced to forgo.

354   They tell of Alexander not his nights or his days,
      but rather his fine deeds and acts of chivalry;
      so they tell of King David, the slayer of Goliath,
      and of Judas Maccabeus, son of Mattathias.*

355   Carlos e Valdovinos,   Roldán e don Ojero,
Terrín e Gualdabuey,   Arnald' e Olivero,
Torpín e don Rinaldos   e 'l gascón Angelero,
Estol' e Salomón,   otro su conpañero.

356   Éstos e otros muchos   que non vos he nonbrados
....
si tan buenos non fueran   oy serién olvidados;
serán los buenos fechos   fasta la fin contados.

357   Por tanto ha mester   que los días contemos,
los días e las noches   en que los despendemos:
quantos en valde passan   nunca los cobraremos;
amigos, bien lo vedes   que mal seso fazemos.'

358   Caveros e peones   ovo los de vençer:
a cosa qu' él dezía   non sabién responder;
quanto él por bien tovo   ovieron l' a fazer;
su razón acabada,   mandó luego mover.

359   El conde don Fernando   con toda su mesnada
llegaron a un agua   muy fuert' e muy irada
– Ebro l' dixeron sienpre,   ansí es oy llamada –
vieron s' en grand revate   que fues' y su posada.

360   Tovieron la ribera   tolosanos guardada;
non dieron castellanos   por esso todo nada;
dando e resçebiendo   mucha buena lançada,
ovieron much' aína   el agua travessada.

361   Ovieron grand rebato   en passar aquel vado;
ovo de petavinos   grand pueblo derribado:
maguer que no querían,   bebién mal de su grado;
d'ellos se afogavan,   d'ellos salién a nado.

362   Abrió por medio 'l agua   el conde la carrera,
ovieron tolosanos   a dexar la ribera;
ordenó las sus azes   en medio d' una glera;
fue los acometer   d' un' estraña manera.

355 Charles and Baudouin, Roland and Ogier,
    Thierry and Gondebuens, Arnaut and Oliver,
    Turpin and Renaud and the Gascon Engeliers,
    Estout and Salomon, another of his men:*

356 these and many others that I have left unnamed,
    ....
    were they not such fine men, they would now be forgotten;
    but their deeds will be told until the end of time.

357 And so we are obliged to keep count of our days,
    and to note the pursuits of our days and our nights;
    those that pass without profit we shall never take back;
    my friends, you can see our present course is ill-advised.'

358 Both foot soldiers and knights were convinced by his words:
    they could find no answer to anything he said;
    they agreed to do whatever he considered to be right;
    his speech over, he ordered them to strike camp at once.

359 Count Fernando, with all of his army in tow,
    arrived at a river which flowed strong and angry
    – always called the Ebro, it bears that name today –;
    they felt a great danger in halting in that place.

360 The men of Toulouse had the bank well defended,
    but to all that, the Castilians gave no second thought;
    as many fine lance-thrusts were given and received,
    in but a short time they were over those waters.

361 They found a great danger in fording that river,
    and cut down a great number of men from Poitou,
    who were forced into drinking, though all against their will;
    some of them were drowned while others swam to safety.

362 The Count made a path through the midst of the waters,
    and the men of Toulouse had to abandon the bank;
    with his battle lines arranged on the sandy shore,
    he took the fight to his foes with rare ferocity.

363   Quand' ovo el buen conde   el río travessado,
           ferió luego en ellos   commo venié irado;
           al que él alcançaba   much' era de malfado:
           d'él iv' a sus parientes   aína mal mandado.

364   El conde don Fernando,   sabidor acabado,
           firié en pitavinos   e fazié les gran daño;
           ronpié las guarniçiones   com' si fuessen un paño;
           non les valié esfuerço,   nin les valié engaño.

365   Acorrían le luego   los sus buenos varones,
           ca tenía y muchos   büenos infançones;
           d' un lugar eran todos   e d' unos coraçones;
           lazravan tolosanos   e lazraban gascones.

366   Pero com' eran muchos,   ivan los acoitando,
           iva de fiera guisa   la lid escalentando;
           iva s' de omnes muertos   essa glera poblando,
           maltraié los afirmes   el conde don Fernando.

367   Andava por las azes   muy fiera mient' irado,
           por que non los vençía   andava muy cuitado;
           dixo: 'Non puede ser;   maguer pes' al pecado,
           no s' pueden tolosanos   fallar bien d'est' mercado.'

368   Metió se por las açes,   muy fuert' espoleando,
           la lança sobre mano,   su pendón aleando:
           '¿Dó estás, el buen conde?',   ansí iva llamando:
           '¡Sal, sal acá al canpo!   ¡Cata a don Fernando!'

369   Antes que ellos amos   veniessen a feridas,
           las gentes tolosanas   todas fueron foídas;
           nunca ningunas gentes   fueron tan mal fallidas,
           ca fueron en grand miedo   e mal preçio metidas.

370   Fueron todos foídos   por una grand montaña;
           fincaron con el conde   muy poca de conpaña;
           nunca fue 'l tolosano   en quexa atamaña,
           ca el cond' de Castiella   le tenié fuerte saña.

363 When the good Count had crossed over the river,
he fell upon his enemy, driven by rage;
any man he came upon was hapless indeed,
his family soon in receipt of ill news.

364 Count Fernando, a man who had great understanding,
attacked the Poitevins and did them great harm;
he tore through their armour as if it were cloth;
neither bravery nor cunning could avail them.

365 His fine knights came rushing at once to his aid,
for many fine noblemen were numbered in his ranks;
they came all from one place and were all of one heart;
both Gascons and Toulousains suffered at their hands.*

366 But their large numbers brought pain to the Castilians,
and the battle's heat was stoked ever fiercer;
the sands grew thick with the bodies of the dead
in the face of Count Fernando's savage onslaught.

367 He rode through the battle lines in terrible anger,
enraged that his victory was still not achieved;
'It cannot be,' he said; 'though it may grieve the Devil,
the men of Toulouse must not profit from this.'

368 He charged through the battle lines, spurring hard his horse,
his lance in his hand and his pennant a-flutter:
'Where are you, good Count?' he cried out as he went;
'Out, out, to the field! Come look upon Fernando!'

369 Before the two of them could come to blows,
all the men of Toulouse were turned in flight;
no troops had ever given service so poor,
for they were filled full of terror and shame.

370 The men had all fled by a lofty mountain's slopes;
very few of his company remained with the Count;
the Count of Toulouse had never seen such a plight,
for the Count of Castile bore him terrible rage.

371   El conde de Tolosa   mucho fue espantado,
        ca vio a don Fernando   venir mucho irado;
        por non tener la gente   qu' era desanparado,
        con sus armas guarnido   al canpo fue tornado.

372   El conde don Fernando,   omne sin crüeldat,
        olvidó con la ira   mesura e bondat;
        al conde fue ferir   d' ira e voluntat;
        non dudó de ferirlo   sin ninguna piedat.

373   El conde castellano,   guerrero natural,
        ferió al tolosano   de un golpe mortal;
        cuitado fue 'l gascón   de la ferida mal;
        dixo a altas vozes: '¡Santa María, val!'

374   El conde de Tolosa   ansí fue mal ferido,
        fue luego del cavallo   a tierra abatido;
        dezir non pudo nada   ca fue luego transido;
        luego quand' él fue muerto,   su pueblo fue vençido.

375   Caveros tolosanos   trezientos y prendieron,
        muchos fueron los otros   que estonç' y murieron;
        ....
        estonçes castellanos   en grand preçio sobieron.

376   El conde orgulloso,   de coraçón loçano,
        oiredes lo que fizo   al conde tolesano:
        desguarneçió l' el cuerpo   él mismo con su mano,
        no l' fizo menos honra   que si fues' su hermano.

377   Quand' l' ovo desguarnido   e todo despojado,
        lavó le e vestió le   de un xamet' preçiado;
        echó l' en un escaño   sotil mientre labrado;
        ovo lo en batalla   de Almozor ganado.

378   El conde castellano   con todo su consejo
        fizo le ataút   bien obrado sobejo,
        guarnido rica miente   de un paño vermejo,
        de clavos bien dorados   que luzién com' espejo.

371 The Count of Toulouse was now sorely afraid,
for he saw Fernando approach, full of anger;
that his people should not think him helpless,
he rode straight out to battle, in his armour.

372 Count Fernando, a man with no semblance of cruelty,
in his fury forgot moderation and kindness;
he went with anger and purpose to strike at that count,
and he struck him at once, dealing blows with no mercy.

373 The Castilian count, who was a natural warrior,
struck a mortal blow to his Toulousain rival;
the attack left the Gascon in awful distress,*
and he cried out aloud, saying, 'Help me, Saint Mary!'

374 The Count of Toulouse thus received a grave wound,
and was knocked down at once from his horse to the ground;
he had no chance to speak, for he passed on at once;
his people were routed right after his death.

375 Three hundred of the knights of Toulouse were there captured,
and many were the others who then died in that place,
....
from then on the Castilians enjoyed great renown.

376 The Count was a proud man, noble of heart;
you shall hear what he did for the Count of Toulouse:*
with his own hand he took the armour from the body,
and paid him no less honour than if they had been brothers.

377 After taking off the armour, having left the body bare,
he washed him and clothed him in a richly-made gown,
and he set him on a chair that was worked with great skill
which he had won in battle as a prize from al-Mansur.

378 The Count of Castile, in all his great wisdom,
had him made a coffin most intricately carved,
which was richly draped with a deep, crimson cloth
and inlaid with gilded studs that shone like mirrors.

379   Mandó a sus vassallos   de la presión sacar,
         mandó les que veniessen   a su señor guardar;
         a grandes e a chicos   todos fizo jurar
         que d'él non se partiessen   fasta en su lugar.

380   Mortajaron el cuerpo,   commo costumbre era,
         d' unos paños preçiados,   ricos de grand manera;
         dio les que despendiessen   por toda la carrera,
         mandó les dar mil pesos   fechos çirios de çera.

381   Quando ovo el conde   el cuerpo mortajado,
         el ataút fue preso,   de clavos bien çerrado,
         fue sobre un' azémila   aína 'parejado;
         mandó que lo levassen   luego a su condado.

382   Tolosanos mesquinos,   llorando su malfado,
         sus caras afiladas,   pueblo mal desonrado,
         llegaron a Tolosa,   cabeça del condado;
         fue commo de primero   el llanto renovado.

383   Dexemos tolosanos   tristes e desonrados
         – ya eran en Tolosa   con su señor llegados –;
         tornemos en el conde   de los fechos granados,
         cómmo avié oídos   otros malos mandados:

384   que venié Almozor   con muy fuertes fonsados,
         que traié treinta mill   vassallos lorigados;
         non serién los peones   nulla guisa contados;
         estavan çerca Lara   en Muñó ayuntados.

385   Quando fue Almoçor   la otra vez vençido,
         con grand pesar que ovo   a Marruecos fue ido;
         mandó por toda África   andar el apellido
         e fue com' a perdón   tod' el pueblo movido.

386   De turcos e alárabes,   essas gentes ligeras,
         que son por' en batallas   unas gentes çerteras,
         – traién arcos e nervios   e ballestas çerberas –
         de éstos venién llenos   senderos e carreras.

379   He ordered that his vassals be released from their prison,
        and that they should come and watch over their lord;
        young and old alike, he made all of them swear
        not to leave him till he reached his place of rest.

380   They enshrouded the body, according to custom;
        the cloth of great value, as rich as could be;
        he gave them all the money they would need on their way;
        they were to have a thousand pesos' waxen candles.

381   When the Count had wrapped the body in its shroud,
        the coffin was sealed, and was nailed firmly closed,
        and, once raised and set upon a mule without delay,
        returned straight to his county, upon the Count's command.

382   Those wretches of Toulouse, as they wept their ill fate,
        their gloom on their faces, a people dishonoured,
        arrived at Toulouse, the seat of their county,
        and their weeping redoubled, as if newly begun.

383   Let us leave the Toulousains, woeful and dishonoured,
        – they were already come to Toulouse, with their lord –
        and return to the Count, that man of great deeds,
        and other ill tidings of which he had heard:

384   the approach of al-Mansur with a vast force of men,
        bringing thirty thousand vassals armed for battle,
        the number of foot soldiers impossible to reckon;
        they were all assembled in Muñó, near Lara.*

385   When al-Mansur had suffered his earlier defeat,
        in his great dejection he had left for Morocco
        and through all of Africa had sent the rallying-call;
        they had all gone to join him, as if to win pardon.*

386   With the Turks and the Arabs, those fleet-footed men,*
        who are warriors of skill in times of battle,
        bearing taut-stringed bows and crossbows for hunting:
        with these men were the paths and ways all crowded.

387   Venién los almofades   e los avenmarinos;
        traién en sus camellos   sus fornos e molinos;
        venién los moros todos   de oriente vezinos:
        venién de todos éstos   cobiertos los caminos.

388   Venién y d'estas gentes   sin cuento e sin tiento;
        non eran d' un lugar   nin d' un entendimiento;
        más feos que Satán   con todo su convento
        quand' sale del infierno   suzio e carboniento.

389   Quando fueron juntados   passaron allen' mar,
        arribaron al puerto   que dizen Gibraltar;
        coidó se Almoçor   del buen conde vengar
        por amor d' acabarlo   no s' podié dar vagar.

390   Córdova e Jaén   con tod' Andaluzía,
        Lorca e Cartajena   con toda Almaría,
        de muchas otras tierras   que nonbrar non sabría,
        ayuntó Almoçor   muy grand cavallería.

391   Quando fueron juntados   començó a venir;
        bien coidó a España   sin falla conquerir,
        qu' el conde castellano   no s' le podrié foír,
        que l' farié en presión   mala muerte morir.

392   E eran en Façinas   ya la gente maldita;
        todos los castellanos   eran en Piedra Fita;
        el conde – ¡la su alma   de pena sea quita! –
        fue se pora San Pedro,   a essa su ermita.

393   Quando fue al ermita   el conde allegado,
        demandó por su monje,   don Pelayo llamado:
        dixeron le por nuevas   que era ya finado,
        ocho días avía   que era soterrado.

394   Entró en la ermita   con muy grand devoçión,
        fincó los sus finojos   e fizo su oraçión;
        de los ojos llorando   fizo su petiçión:
        'Señor, Tú me aguarda   d' error e d' ocasión.

387 Now there came the Almohads and Marinids,*
who carried on their camels their ovens and mills;
there came all the Moors from nearby in the East,
and with all of these men the roads were covered.

388 From these people came numbers beyond telling or counting;
they were not from one place and were not of one mind;
they were uglier than Satan with all of his coven
when he comes out from Hell, caked in dirt and in soot.

389 When they had all gathered, they passed beyond the sea,
and landed at the port men call Gibraltar;*
al-Mansur planned his vengeance upon the good Count,
and could not rest in his desire to attain it.

390 From Córdoba, Jaén, and all Andalusia,
Lorca, Cartagena, and the whole of Almería,*
and from many other lands that have names beyond my ken,
did al-Mansur assemble his great force of knights.

391 When they were assembled he set out on his march,
in certain expectation of conquering Spain,
sure that Castile's Count could never escape him,
and that he would put him to a cruel death in prison.

392 The accursed people were already in Hacinas,
and the Castilians all assembled in Piedrahita;*
the Count – may his soul be free of suffering! –
went to San Pedro, to that hermitage of his.

393 Once the Count had arrived at the hermitage,
he asked to see his friend, the monk Pelayo;
they replied with the news that Pelayo was dead,
and it had now been a week since his burial.

394 He entered the hermitage showing great piety:
he went down on bended knee and made his prayer;
with tears in his eyes did he make his request:
'Lord, may You keep me from error and harm.

395   Señor, por grand amor   de fer a Ti serviçio,
        passo mucho lazerio   e dexo mucho viçio;
        con est' cuerpo lazrado   fago te sacrifiçio;
        con moros e cristianos   meto m' en grand bolliçio.

396   Los reyes de España   con derecho pavor
        olvidaron a Ti,   que eres su Señor;
        tornaron se vassallos   del moro Almoçor
        e por miedo de muerte   fizieron lo peor.

397   ....
        ....
        Nunca de su conpaña   después ove sabor;
        por fer a Ti serviçio   non quis' más su amor.

398   Finqué yo entre todos   solo, desanparado;
        de muerte non ov' miedo   nin quis' aquel dïablo.
        Quando ellos veyeron   que era apartado,
        luego fui d'ellos todos   muy fuert' amenazado.

399   Llegaron me las cartas   a Muñó esse día,
        venieron mensajeros   çinco en aquel día:
        cómmo m' amenazavan   reyes d' Andaluzía
        por que de los d' España   yo sólo me erzía.

400   Ovieron sus poderes   sobre mí d' ayuntar:
        unos venién por tierra,   otros venién por mar;
        querrién me, si podiessen,   d'este sieglo sacar;
        quesiste m' Tú, Señor,   valer e ayudar.

401   Vençí los, maté los,   Señor, con tu poder;
        nunca fui contra Ti,   segunt mi entender;
        tengo me por pagado   si te fize plazer;
        bien tengo que non has   por qué me falesçer.

402   Por las tus escrituras   que dexó Isaías,
        que a los tus vasallos   nunca los falesçrías;
        Señor, tu siervo so   con mis cavallerías;
        no m' partiré de Ti   en todos los mis días.

395   In my great desire to serve You, O Lord,
I suffer much hardship and shun many pleasures;
with this beaten body I offer You sacrifice:
I enter a great conflict of Christians and Moors.

396   The monarchs of Spain felt a deep-seated dread,
as they forgot You, who are Lord over them;
they made themselves the vassals of the Moor al-Mansur,
and took the worst course of action in terror of death.

397   ....
....
No more did I ever have desire for their company,
and in order to serve You, I shunned their friendship.

398   I was left alone among them all and forsaken;
I had no fear of death – that devil I rejected.
When they saw how I was abandoned and alone,
the cruellest of threats came at once from them all.

399   On that day I received all their letters in Muñó:
five messengers arrived upon that one day,
bringing me the threats of Andalusian kings,
for I alone resisted from among the men of Spain.*

400   They were to unite all their forces against me,
some coming by land, and others by sea,
all with the desire, if they could, to take my life;
Lord, it was Your will to grant me help and support.

401   I overcame and slew them, O Lord, with Your strength,
and I believe I never once went against You;
if I brought You any pleasure, I hold myself content,
and now I trust You have no cause to fail me.

402   We know from Your Scriptures left us by Isaiah*
that Your vassals would never see You fail them;
with my army of knights, Lord, I am Your servant,
and I will never leave You, to the end of my days.

403   Mas he yo menester,   Señor, la tu ayuda:
           Señor, sea por Ti   Castiella defenduda,
           toda tierra de África   sobre mí es venuda;
           anparar non la puedo,   Señor, sin tu ayuda.

404   Por fuerça nin por seso   que yo podies' aver,
           non la podrié por guisa   ninguna defender;
           Señor, da me esfuerço,   e seso e poder,
           que pued' a Almoçor   o matar o vençer.'

405   Teniendo su vegilia,   con Dios se razonando,
           un sueño muy sabroso   al conde fue tomando;
           con sus armas guarnido   assí s' fue acostando,
           la carne adormida,   assí yaze soñando.

406   Non podrié el buen conde   aún ser bien dormido,
           el monje san Pelayo   de suso l' fue venido;
           de paños com' el sol   todo venié vestido;
           nunca más bella cosa   viera omne nasçido.

407   Llamó le por su nonbre   al conde don Fernando;
           dixo l': '¿Duermes o velas?   ¿Cómmo estás callando?
           Despierta, vé tu vía,   ca te crez' oy grand bando;
           vé te por' el tu pueblo   que t' está esperando.

408   El Criador te otorga   quanto pedido l' has:
           en los pueblos paganos   grand mortandat farás;
           de tus buenas conpañas   muchas y perderás,
           pero con tod' el daño   el canpo le vençrás.

409   Aún te dize más   el alto Crïador:
           tú eres su vassallo   e Él es tu Señor;
           con los pueblos cristianos,   lidiarás por s' amor,
           manda te que te vayas   lidiar con Almoçor.

410   Yo seré y contigo,   que me l' ha otorgado;
           y será el apóstol   Santïago llamado;
           enbïar nos ha Cristo   valer a su crïado:
           será con tal ayuda   Almoçor enbargado.

403   But, O my Lord, I have need of Your assistance,
          that by You may Castile be now defended;
          all the land of Africa is now come upon me;
          Lord, I cannot guard her if I do not have Your aid.

404   By no strength or cunning that I could possess
          will I manage to find how to protect her;
          Lord, grant me courage and cunning and might,
          that I may kill or vanquish al-Mansur.'

405   As he kept his vigil, conversing with God,
          the sweetest sleep then slowly overtook him;
          still decked in his armour, he lay down to rest,
          and, as his body slept, he lay there dreaming.

406   The good Count could not yet have been soundly asleep,
          when the monk Saint Pelayo came upon him from above,
          dressed all in cloth which shone out like the sun;
          no fairer sight could any man alive have ever seen.

407   Calling Count Fernando's name, he said to him:
          'Are you sleeping or awake? Why speak you not?
          Wake up! Be on your way! You gain many men this day;
          go and join your troops, for they are waiting for your coming.

408   All that you have asked him the Creator now grants you:
          you will inflict great slaughter on the pagan troops;
          from your fine companies many will be lost there,
          but amidst all this suffering, the field will be yours.

409   The Creator on high has still more to tell you:
          that you are His vassal and He is your Lord;
          with the Christian troops, you will fight for love of Him
          and He commands you go to battle al-Mansur.

410   I shall be there with you: He has granted me this boon;
          and there will be the apostle named Santiago;
          Christ will send us there and give aid to His servant;
          with such help will al-Mansur be overwhelmed.

411   Otros vernán y muchos,   commo en visïón;
        en blancas armaduras   – ángeles de Dios son –;
        traerá cada uno   la cruz en su pendón;
        moros quando nos vieren   perdrán el coraçón.

412   Amigo, dicho t' he   lo que a mí mandaron;
        vo me pora aquellos   que m' acá enbïaron.'
        Dos ángeles fermosos   de tierra lo alçaron;
        faziendo alegría,   al çielo lo levaron.

413   Despertó don Fernando   con derecho pavor:
        '¿Qué puede ser aquesto?   ¡Vala m' el Crïador!
        Pecado es que m' quiere   echar en un error;
        Cristo, yo tuyo so;   guarda me, Tú, Señor.'

414   Estando en el sueño   que soñara pensando,
        oyó una grand voz   que l' estava llamando:
        'Lieva d'end', vé tu vía,   el conde don Fernando;
        Almoçor te espera   con el su fuerte bando.

415   Non tardes, vé tu vía;   si non, tuerto me fazes;
        por tanto que me tardas   en muy grand culpa yazes;
        no l' des ninguna tregua   nin fagas con él pazes;
        de todo el tu pueblo   fazer lo has tres azes.

416   Tú entras con los menos   de parte de oriente,
        entrante de la lid   ver m' has vesiblemiente;
        entre la otra az,   de parte d' oçidente,
        y será Santïago,   esto sin fallimiente.

417   Entre l' otra terçera   de parte d' aquilón,
        vençremos, non lo dubdes,   a est' bravo león;
        farás, si esto fazes,   a guisa de Sansón,
        quando con las sus manos   lidió con el bestión.

418   Non quiero más dezirte,   por ende vé tu vía;
        durará la batalla   fasta terçero día.
        ¿Quieres saber quién trae   esta mensajería?
        Millán so yo por nonbre;   Jesu Cristo m' enbía.'

411   Many others will appear there, as if in a vision,
all clad in white armour: they are angels of the Lord,
each one of them carrying a cross on his pennant;
and when they see us, then the Moors will lose all heart.

412   My friend, I have told you what I was bidden say
and now I go to those who sent me here.'
Two beautiful angels raised him up from the ground
and amid their rejoicing, they bore him to Heaven.

413   Fernando awoke then, much stricken with fear:
'What can this be? May the Creator avail me!
The Devil it is who seeks to cast me into error;
Christ, I am Yours; may You protect me, O Lord.'

414   Fernando, while thinking on what he had dreamed,
then heard a loud voice calling out to him:
'Rise up, Count Fernando, and go on your way;
al-Mansur awaits you with his vast band of men.

415   Tarry not! Go on your way, or you wrong me!
You lie in great censure for delaying me so long.
You must grant him no truce, make no offer of peace;
but take your whole force and draw it up in three lines.

416   You enter from the East with the smallest group of men,
and as the battle starts you will have clear sight of me;
among the other battle line, approaching from the West,
Santiago will be counted: of this you can be sure.

417   From the third direction, whence blows the north wind,
we shall vanquish this wild lion – do not doubt it;
you will act, if you do this, in the manner of Samson,*
when he fought the great beast with his own bare hands.

418   I have no more to tell you; with that, be on your way;
the battle will endure until the third day hence.
Do you wish to know who is the bearer of this message?
Millán is my name, and I have come from Jesus Christ.'*

419   Quand' ovo don Fernando   todo esto oído,
el varón san Millán   a los çielos fue ido;
fue luego de l' ermita   el buen cond' espedido;
tornó s' a Piedra Fita   d'onde 'l fuera salido.

420   Quando llegó el conde   a su buena conpaña,
fablaron sus vassallos   todos con fuerte saña;
maltraían le tanto   que era grand fazaña:
....

421   Com' eran malincónicos   todos con gran despecho,
de chicos e de grandes,   de todos fue maltrecho.
'Fazes,' dixeron, 'conde,   sin guisa grand malfecho;
si algún yerro tomas,   será muy grand derecho.

422   Assí commo ladrón   que anda a furtar,
assí sólo señero   te amas apartar;
quando nos te buscamos   no t' podemos fallar;
abremos sól' por esto   algún yerro tomar.

423   Por que tant' te sofrimos,   por end' somos peores;
pedimos te merçed   non nos fagas traidores,
ca non lo fueron nunca   nuestros anteçessores;
non ovo más leales   en mundo nin mejores.'

424   Quand' a toda su guisa   l' ovieron maltraído,
dixo les don Fernando: '¡Por Dios sea oído!
De quanto que yo fize   non so arrepentido;
no m' devedes tener   ansí por tan fallido.

425   Fui yo a la hermita   por mi amigo ver,
por yo e él en uno   amos aver plazer;
quand' fui allá llegado,   demandé d'él saber;
dixeron me que era   en ageno poder.

426   Sope yo cómmo era   mi amigo finado,
mostraron m' el logar   do yazié soterrado;
rogué a Jesu Cristo,   si él fizo pecado,
por la su grand mesura   que l' sea perdonado.

419   When Fernando had heard all he had to say,
the noble Saint Millán went up to Heaven;
the good Count took his leave of the hermitage at once,
and returned to Piedrahita, whence he had come.

420   When the Count was once again with his fine army,
his vassals all addressed him, their anger running deep;
they hurled such rebukes as to beggar belief:
....

421   Melancholic as they all were with displeasure,
by young and old alike was he abused:
'Count,' they said, 'misguidedly you do a great wrong;
if you come to any harm it will be well deserved.

422   Just like a thief whose intention is to steal
do you delight in going off, quite alone,
and when we seek you out we cannot find you;
through this alone we shall incur some harm.

423   For enduring so much for you, we are the worse off;
we beg of your mercy not to render us traitors,
for our forefathers never turned to treachery;
never in the world were men better or more loyal.'

424   When they had had their fill of such abuse,
Fernando spoke: 'In God's name, may I be heard!
For all I have done, I remain unrepentant;
you must not thus hold me to be at such fault.

425   I went to the hermitage, that I might see my friend,
and each of us have pleasure in that company;
on arriving at that place, I sought news of him,
and I was told that he was in Another's hands.

426   I learned of how my friend had left this life,
and they showed me the place where he lay buried;
I prayed to Jesus Christ that, if he had ever sinned,
then by His great wisdom he might be forgiven.

427   Entrante de la puerta   y fiz' mi oración,
        tal qual me dio Dios seso   e metió 'n coraçón,
        vino a mí el monje,   commo en visïón:
        "Despierta," diz, "amigo: hora es e sazón."

428   Dixo me lo en sueños   e non lo quis' creer;
        desperté e non pude   ninguna cosa ver.
        Oí una grand voz   del çielo desçender;
        voz era de los santos   según mi entender.

429   Ésta es la razón   que la voz me dezía:
        "Conde Fernán González,   lieva d'end', vé tu vía;
        tod' el poder de África   e de Andaluzía
        vençer lo has en canpo   d'este terçero día."

430   Dixo m' que mal fazía,   por tanto que tardava,
        a 'quel Rey de los Reyes   por cuy' amor lidiava;
        que fues' e non tardasse   contra la gent' pagana,
        que ¿por qué avié miedo,   pues qu' Él me ayudava?

431   Otras cosas me dixo   que me quiero callar:
        serié grand alongança   de todo lo cantar;
        mas vos aver lo hedes   aína de provar;
        fasta que lo provedes   aver m' he de callar.

432   En aquella ermita   fui bien aconsejado
        del monje san Pelayo,   siervo de Dios amado,
        que por el su consejo   Almozor fue rancado;
        fui le buscar agora   e fallé l' soterrado.

433   Fasta que lo sepades   com' yo lo fui saber,
        por end' non me devedes   por fallido tener:
        aguardar vos querría,   a todo mi poder,
        de por mengua de mí   en yerro non caer.

434   De Dios e de los omnes   mester nos ha consejo;
        si non los afincamos   fernos han mal trebejo;
        trae 'l rey Almozor   muy grand poder sobejo,
        mas nunca en su vida   ayuntó tal conçejo.

427   On passing through the door, I made my prayer there,
just as God showed me in my mind and my soul,
and the monk came towards me, as if in a vision:
"Awaken, friend," he told me, "for now is the time."

428   He told me in my dreams, and I would not believe it;
I awoke, and before me saw nothing at all.
I heard a loud voice come ringing down from heaven;
it was the voice of the saints, as I believe.

429   These are the words that the voice spoke to me:
"Count Fernán González, rise up! Be on your way!
All the power of Africa, and of Andalusia,
you will vanquish on the battlefield, upon this third day."

430   It told me I did wrong, in delaying for so long,
to that King of Kings, for whose love I was fighting;
that I should go at once to attack the pagan peoples;
and why was I afraid, since He gave me His aid?

431   Other things it told me I do not care to mention,
for it would be a long tale if I sang of it all;
but you will very quickly show the truth of what I say,
and until you do so I shall hold my tongue in silence.

432   In that hermitage I was indeed well counselled,
by the monk Saint Pelayo, dear servant of God,
through whose counsel al-Mansur was defeated;
I have just gone to seek him, and found him interred.

433   Until you have learnt this, as I went to learn it,
you must not think me at fault over this;
I would wish to do all that I could to protect you
from falling into error through failings of mine.

434   We have need of counsel both from God and from men;
if we do not pursue them, they will do us great harm;
King al-Mansur brings a most powerful army;
he assembled no greater in all of his life.

435   Mil ha y pora uno,   esto bien lo sabemos;
        dicho es qu' ha mester   que consejo tomemos;
        maguer fuïr queramos,   fazer lo non podemos;
        ansí commo los peçes   enredados yazemos.

436   Aragón e Navarra,   todos los pitavinos,
        si en quexa nos vieren,   non nos serién padrinos:
        non nos darién salida   por ningunos caminos:
        mal nos quieren de muerte   todos nuestros vezinos.

437   Si nos – ¡por mal pecado! –   fuéremos arrancados,
        los nuestros enemigos   serán de nos vengados;
        seremos nos cativos,   fanbrientos e lazrados;
        serán los nuestros fijos   de moros cativados.

438   Los fijos e las fijas   que nos tanto queremos
        ver los hemos cativos,   valer non los podremos;
        do nos mandaren ir,   por fuerça y iremos;
        nuestros fijos e fijas   jamás nunca veremos.

439   Desanparado es   de tod' bien el cativo;
        mas dize muchas vezes   que no querrié ser vivo;
        dize: "Señor del mundo,   ¿por qué m' eres esquivo
        que me fazes vevir   lazrado e perdido?"

440   Ligera cosa es   la muerte de passar;
        muerte de cada día   mala es d' endurar:
        sofrir tanto lazerio   e ver tanto pesar,
        ver los sus enemigos   lo suyo heredar.

441   Contesçe esso mismo   con la gent' renegada:
        heredan nuestra tierra   e tienen la forçada;
        mas dreçar s' ha la rueda   que está trestornada:
        serán ellos vençidos,   la fe de Crist' onrada.

442   No es dicha fortuna   por ser en un estado:
        uno ser sienpre rico   e otro ser menguado;
        camia estas dos cosas   la fortuna prïado:
        al pobre faze rico   e al rico menguado.

435   We know well that they number a thousand to our one;
it has been said already that our need is for counsel;
even if we wish to take flight, we cannot do so:
as if we were fish, we lie caught in their nets.

436   Aragón and Navarre and all the Poitevins,*
on seeing us suffer, would not give us protection;
they would open no paths to allow us escape,
for all our neighbours bear us deadly hatred.

437   If, for our sins, we should meet with defeat,
then our enemies will take their vengeance on us;
we shall be prisoners, hungry and ill-treated,
and our children will be captives of the Moors.

438   The sons and daughters that we love so dearly
we shall see as captives, powerless to help them;
wherever we are told, we shall go, because compelled,
and never look again upon our daughters and our sons.

439   The captive is deprived of every pleasure
and often states his preference not to live,
saying, "Lord of the world, why treat me so harshly,
and force me so to live amid suffering and despair?"

440   It is an easy thing to suffer death,
but death each day is painful to endure:
to suffer so much pain and see so much torment,
while watching your enemies inherit what is yours.

441   This very thing befalls alike the renegade peoples:
they inherit our land and now hold it by force;
but the wheel now spun low will aright itself again;
they will be defeated as Christ's faith is honoured.

442   It is not called Fortune for remaining in one state,
with one man always rich and another always poor;
Fortune is quick to reverse these two states:
it makes the poor man rich and the rich man needy.

443   Quiere fazer las cosas   ansí el Crïador,
de dar e de quitar   Él es el fazedor,
por entender qu' Él es   sobre todos mejor;
el que suel' ser vençido   será el vençedor.

444   A tal Señor com' éste   devemos nos rogar
que por su grand mesura   nos quiera ayudar;
en Él nos está todo,   caer o levantar,
ca sin Él nulla cosa   podemos acabar.

445   Amigos, lo que digo   bien entender devedes:
si fuéremos vençidos,   ¿qué consejo prendredes?
Morredes commo malos,   la tierra perderedes;
si esta vez caedes   non vos levantaredes.

446   De mí mismo vos digo   lo que cuedo fazer:
nin preso nin cabtivo   non me dexaré ser;
maguer ellos a vida   me quisieren prender,
matar me he yo antes   que ser en su poder.

447   Todo aquel de vos   que del canpo saliere
o con miedo de muerte   a presión se les diere,
quede por alevoso   qui tal fecho fiziere:
con Judas en infierno   yaga quando moriere.'

448   Quando esto oyó   el su pueblo cruzado,
todos por una boca   fablaron muy prïado:
'Señor, lo que tú dizes   de nos es otorgado;
el que fuyere yaga   con Judas abraçado.'

449   Quando ovo el conde   dichas estas razones
– antes tenían todos   duros los coraçones –
fueron muy confortados,   caveros e peones;
mandó cómmo fiziessen   essos grandes varones.

450   Mandó que fuessen prestos   otro día mañana,
fuessen puestas las azes   en medio de la plana;
todos fuessen armados   a primera canpana;
darían lid canpal   a essa gent' pagana.

443   Thus does the Creator wish to enact things,
       for it is He who gives and it is He who takes away,
       that He may be seen to be supreme above all others;
       the one accustomed to defeat will be the victor.

444   We must pray to such a Lord and ask of Him
       that in His great mercy He should help us;
       on Him depends our all: to rise up or to fall;
       for without Him we cannot achieve a thing.

445   My friends, what I say you must well understand:
       if we are defeated, what then will be your plan?
       You will die like rogues amid the loss of your lands,
       and if this time you fall, you will never rise up.

446   For myself I tell you the intention that I have:
       not prisoner nor captive will I let myself become;
       even if their wish is to capture me alive,
       I will take my own life before I fall into their power.

447   Any one of you who flees the battlefield
       or gives himself up for prison, fearing death,
       let one who does such deeds be held a traitor,
       and lie in Hell with Judas, when he dies.'*

448   When these words were heard by his people of the cross,
       all with one voice they were quick to cry out:
       'With all that you say, lord, we stand in full accord;
       may any man who flees lie in Judas' embrace.'

449   When the Count had put forward this argument
       – until then they had all been hard of heart –,
       horsemen and foot soldiers alike took great comfort,
       and he set out how those great men were to act.

450   He bade that they be ready on the following morning,
       with battle lines drawn in the middle of the plain,
       and that all should be armed when the first bell tolled;
       they would fight that pagan tribe in open battle.

451   A don Gustio Gonçález,   el que de Salas era,
a él e a sus fijos   dio les la delantera;
con ellos don Velasco   – tanbién d'essa ribera –,
ca por miedo de muerte   non dexarié carrera.

452   Entró Gonçalo Díez   en esta misma az:
era en los consejos   bueno de toda paz,
era por' en faziendas   crudo commo agraz;
quiquier que l' demandasse   fallar lo ie de faz.

453   Dos sobrinos del conde,   valientes e ligeros
– fiçiera los el conde   estonçes cavalleros –
devieran ser contados   éstos en los primeros;
fueron éstos llamados   los lobos carniçeros.

454   Los que Gustio Gonçález   avié d' acabdillar
– dozientos fueron éstos,   caveros de prestar –
éstos mandó el conde   por una part' entrar:
de quáles ellos fueron   no s' podrién mejorar.

455   Dio les seis mill peones   pora la delantera:
omnes de la montaña,   gente fuert' e ligera;
si bien guisados fuessen   commo mester les era,
por tres tantos de moros   non dexarién carrera.

456   Dexemos esta faz   toda bien parada;
non podrié el cabdiello   mejorar se por nada;
serié por nulla fuerça   a duro quebrantada.
Ya era en tod' esto   la otra az guisada.

457   Fue dado por cabdiello   don Lope el vizcaino,
bien rico de mançanas,   pobre de pan e vino;
fueron en essa az   fijos de don Laíno,
otro de la montaña   que dizién don Martino.

458   Avié de buroveses,   otrossí treviñanos,
caveros bien ligeros,   de coraçón loçanos,
de Castiella la Vieja   büenos castellanos
que muchos buenos fechos   fizieron por sus manos.

451   To Gustio González, who hailed from Salas,
together with his sons, was the front line given,
along with Velasco, another man of Salas,*
for no fear of death would ever cause him to give way.

452   Gonzalo Díez entered that same line of battle:*
he was a fine man at council, ever peaceful,
but in battle he was harsh, as an unripe grape,
as any who might test this would quickly discover.

453   Two nephews of the Count, who were nimble and brave,
– the Count had only just then made them knights –
ought to have been counted among the very first;
these men were known as the flesh-eating wolves.

454   Those whom Gustio González was to lead into battle
– two hundred men were these, all knights of great worth –
were commanded by the Count to enter all from one side;
these men were such that none better could be found.

455   He put six thousand foot soldiers in the front line,
men from the mountains, who made strong and agile troops;
if they were well equipped, in the way that was required,
they would not give way to thrice that many Moors.

456   Let us leave this column all drawn up and ready;
there could be no way to improve upon its leader,
and no army could breach it, even at great cost.
Meanwhile, the other column was prepared.

457   Lope of Vizcaya was named as its leader,
a man rich in apples but poor in bread and wine;
among those of that column were the sons of Laíno,
and another mountain-dweller, called Martino.*

458   There were men from La Bureba and more from Treviño,*
knights of great speed and possessed of great hearts;
fine Castilians came from the land of Old Castile,
men whose hands had done many noble deeds.

459   Veníen y de Castro   unas buenas conpañas;
       veníen y con ellos   otras de las montañas;
       fueron y estorianos,   gentes muy bien guisadas:
       muy buenos eran d' armas,   bien conplidos de mañas.

460   Venién estos caveros   en la az medïana:
       éstos fueron dozientos   de la flor castellana;
       todos fueron en canpo   otro día mañana;
       éssa fue pora moros   una negra semana.

461   Dio les seis mill peones   con que los conbatiessen:
       peones con caveros   en uno los partiessen,
       que quando los peones   carrera les abriessen
       entrarían caveros   mejor por do podiessen.

462   El conde don Fernando   de los fechos granados
       ovo veint' escuderos   en esse día armados;
       éstos con el buen conde   en az fueron entrados;
       por todos çincüenta   non más fueron contados.

463   Ruy Cavía e Nuño,   de los d' alfoz de Lara,
       venién y los serranos,   gentes que él poblara
       en una sierra fuerte,   qu' él de moros ganara;
       venién y los Velascos   qu' esse día armara.

464   Venién tres mill peones,   todos de buena gente,
       que por miedo de muerte   non farién fallimiente;
       maguer fuessen buscados   de partes de oriente,
       non fallarién mejores   fasta en oçidente.

465   Consejó les a todos   de quál guisa fiziessen:
       si el día primero   vençer non les podiessen
       que se tornassen fuera   quand' el cuerno oyessen,
       a la seña del conde   todos se acojiessen.

466   Quando ovo el conde   su cosa aguisada,
       sus azes bien paradas,   su gente ordenada,
       sabié bien cada uno   su çertera entrada;
       tornaron a sus tiendas,   cad' un' a su posada.

459   Fine companies of men came there from Castro,*
and with them there came others from the mountains;
Asturians were there, men very well prepared,
who had great skill in arms and extremely sharp minds.

460   It was the central column where these knights would ride,
two hundred men from the flower of Castile;
they all took the battlefield the following morning;
for the Moors it was a black week indeed.

461   He gave them six thousand foot soldiers to fight at their side,
so that together with the knights they might break through,
for when the men who fought on foot had made a path,
the horsemen would then enter where they could.

462   Count Fernando, a man of extraordinary deeds,
had just knighted twenty squires on that day;
these went into line at the good Count's side
– in all they numbered fifty, not one more.

463   Ruy Cavia and Nuño, from the region of Lara,*
and mountain-dwellers came there, whom he had settled
in a savage mountain-range he had won from the Moors;
the Velascos came too, whom he had armed on that day.

464   So too three thousand foot soldiers, all of fine stock,
who would not be found wanting through terror of death,
and even a search that began in the East
could find no better men by the Western extremes.

465   He instructed them all on the way they should act:
if on the first day they could not gain the victory,
they were to turn back at the sound of the horn,*
and all assemble by the standard of the Count.

466   When the Count had his preparations in hand,
his battle lines ready and his troops well arranged,
each man knew for certain where he entered the battle;
they then turned for their tents, each to his own lodgings.

467   Çenaron e folgaron,   essa gente cruzada,
               todos a Dios rogaron   con voluntad pagada
               que y les ayudasse   la su virtud sagrada,

....

468   Vieron aquella noche   una muy fiera cosa:
               venía por el aire   una sierpe raviosa
               dando muy fuertes gritos   la fantasma astrosa;
               toda venié sangrienta,   vermeja commo rosa.

469   Fazié ella senblante   que ferida venía;
               semejav' en los gritos   que el çielo partía.
               Alunbrava las uestes   el fuego que vertía;
               todos ovieron miedo   que quemar los venía.

470   Non ovo end' ninguno   que fues' tan esforçado
               que gran miedo non ovo   e non fue espantado;
               cayó y mucho omne   en tierra desmayado;
               ovieron muy grand miedo   tod' el pueblo cruzado.

471   Despertaron al conde   que era ya dormido;
               ante que él veniesse   el culebro fue ido.
               Falló tod' el su pueblo   commo muy desmaído;
               demandó del culebro   cómmo fuera venido.

472   Dixeron gelo todo,   de quál guisa veniera
               commo cosa ferida   que grandes gritos diera;
               vuelta venié en sangre   aquella bestia fiera:
               se maravillan cómmo   tierra non ençendiera.

473   Quando gelo contaron   assí commo lo vieron,
               entendió bien el conde   que grand miedo ovieron
               qu' esta atal figura   dïablos la fizieron:
               a los pueblos cruzados   revolver los quisieron.

474   A los moros tenían   que venié ayudar;
               coidavan sines duda   cristianos espantar;
               por tal que los cruzados   s' ovieran a tornar,
               quisieran en la ueste   algún fuego echar.

467   They dined and they rested, those troops on crusade,*
and with joy in their hearts did they all pray to God,
that His holy power should there bring them aid,

....

468   That night they saw an extraordinary sight,
as a furious serpent came flying through the air,*
a spectre from the heavens giving piercing screams;
it came covered in blood, stained a rose's vermilion.

469   It gave the appearance of having been wounded,
and seemed from its screams to be rending the sky;
the hosts were alight with the fire that it spewed,
and they all feared its flames would consume them.

470   There was no man among them sufficiently bold
that he felt no great terror or was not afraid;
many men collapsed to the ground in a faint,
and the men on crusade felt a fear great indeed.

471   They roused the Count, who was already sleeping,
but before he could arrive, the snake was gone;
he found all his troops much unnerved by this sight,
and asked them how the snake had made its advent.

472   They gave him full account of how it had appeared,
like a wounded creature giving out great screams;
that remarkable beast came covered in blood:
they were amazed at how the earth had not caught fire.

473   When they told him their tale, just as they saw it,
the Count understood that they held a great fear
lest such an apparition were created by devils
who wanted to trouble the troops on crusade.

474   They believed it had come to bring aid to the Moors,
and doubtless, they thought, to strike terror in Christians;
so that the crusaders would be forced to turn tail,
they had sought to cast a fire upon their army.

475 Mandó a sus varones el buen conde llamar;
quando fueron juntados mandó los escuchar:
qu' él derié qué quería la serpient' demostrar;
luego de estrelleros començó de fablar:

476 'Los moros, bien sabedes, se guían por estrellas;
non se guían por Dios, que se guían por ellas.
Otro Crïador nuevo han fecho ellos d'ellas;
diz que por ellas veen muchas de maraviellas.

477 Ha y otros que saben muchos encantamientos;
fazen muy malos gestos con sus esperamientos
de revolver las nuves e revolver los vientos;
muestra les el dïablo estos entendimientos.

478 Ayuntan los dïablos con sus conjuramentos,
aliegan se con ellos e fazen sus conventos;
dizen de los passados todos sus fallimientos;
todos fazen conçejo, los falsos carbonientos.

479 Algún moro astroso que sabe encantar
fizo aquel dïablo en sierpe figurar
por amor que podiesse a vos mal espantar;
con este tal engaño cuidaron nos tornar.

480 Commo sodes sesudos, bien podedes saber
que non ha él poder de mal a nos fazer,
ca quitó l' Jesu Cristo el su fuerte poder;
veades que son locos los que l' quieren creer.

481 Que es de tod' el mundo en Uno el poder,
qu' a Él sólo devemos todos obedesçer;
ca Él es poderoso de dar e de toller:
a tal Señor com' éste devemos nos temer.

482 Quien este Señor dexa e en la bestia fía,
tengo que es caído a Dios en muy grand ira:
anda en fallimiento la su alma mesquina;
quantos que ansí andan el dïablo los guía.

475   The good Count gave orders for his men to assemble,
       and once they were gathered, he bade that they listen,
       for he would explain to them the meaning of the serpent;
       he launched without delay into speaking of astrologers:*

476   'As you well know, the Moors are guided by stars;
       to them, and not to God, they look for guidance.
       Of the stars, they have made another, new Creator;
       it is said that through them they see many wonders.

477   There are others there well versed in magic arts,
       whose incantations wreak awful, evil deeds:
       stirring up the clouds and whipping up the winds;
       such understanding is fostered by the Devil.

478   The devils come together in casting their magic;
       and are joined by these men, thus forming their covens;
       they tell them all the errors of those who have passed;
       soot-stained and false, they all form their councils.

479   Some despicable Moor who knows how to cast spells
       had that devil transform to resemble a serpent,
       desiring to leave you stricken with dread;
       by such a trick they meant to make us flee.

480   Wise as you are, you are all well aware
       that he has no power to harm us at all,
       for by Jesus Christ was his great power taken;
       behold the folly of those men with faith in him!

481   For power over all the world rests in One alone,
       and to Him and only Him must we all pledge obeisance,
       for with Him lies the power to give and take away;
       a Lord such as this ought to fill us with awe.

482   He who leaves this Lord to put trust in the Beast,*
       I hold that he is fallen into God's great wrath;
       his wretched soul wanders lost in error;
       those on this path have the Devil as their guide.

483   Tornemos en lo al   que agora estamos:
           trabajado avemos,   mester es que durmamos;
           con ellos en el canpo   cras mañana seamos,
           todos en su logar   assí commo mandamos.'

484   Fueron a sus posadas,   s' echaron a dormir,
           començaron las alas   los gallos a ferir;
           levantaron se todos,   missa fueron oír:
           confessar se a Dios,   pecados descubrir.

485   Todos, grandes e chicos,   su oración fizieron;
           del mal que avién fecho   todos se repintieron;
           la ostia consagrada   todos la resçebieron,
           todos de coraçón   a Dios merçed pedieron.

486   Era en todo esto   el día allegado:
           entraron en las armas   tod' el pueblo cruzado;
           las azes fueron puestas   commo les fue mandado;
           bien sabié cada uno   su lugar señalado.

487   Fueron todas las gentes   en un punto guarnidas,
           movieron pora ellos   todos por sus partidas:
           las azes fueron puestas,   mescladas las feridas,
           ovo de cada parte   muchas gentes caídas.

488   El conde don Fernando,   este leal cabdiello,
           paresçié entre todos   un fermoso castiello;
           avié en l' az primera   abierto grand portiello;
           traié en el escudo   muy mucho de cuadriello.

489   Ronpié todas las azes   que fronteras estavan,
           a la parte qu' él iva   todos carrera l' davan;
           los golpes que fazía   bien a lexos sonavan,

           ....

490   Andava por las azes   commo león fanbriento;
           de vençer o morir   tenié fuerte taliento;
           dexava por do iva   tod' el canpo sangriento;
           dava y muchas ánimas   al bestión mascariento.

483   Let us now return to the second point before us:
we have laboured hard, and our need is now of sleep;
in tomorrow's early hours, let us meet them on the field,
with every man in his place, just as we command.'

484   They went to their lodgings and lay down to sleep,
till the cockerels began to beat their wings,
when the men all rose before going to hear Mass,
make confession to God, and reveal their sins.

485   Young and old alike, all the men made their prayer,
all repenting of the evil they had done;
all of them then received the consecrated host,
with a heartfelt plea for the mercy of God.

486   Meanwhile, the day of the battle had arrived,
and the soldiers on crusade all took the field;
the battle lines were drawn up as had been commanded,
with each man sure of his appointed place.

487   The soldiers were all ready when the hour of battle came;
each from his station, they advanced on the Moors;
the columns were arranged, blows were exchanged,
and the fallen numbered many on both sides.

488   That man Count Fernando, his men's loyal leader,
stood out above them all, like a fine castle-turret;
he had made a great breach in the Moors' front line,
a forest of arrow-shafts lodged in his shield.

489   He broke through all the battle lines that faced him,
and where he went, they all gave way to him;
the clash of his blows echoed far in the distance,
....

490   He raged through the lines like a ravenous lion,
and felt a great passion to conquer or die;
everywhere he went, he left the field soaked in blood,
passing over many souls to the hideous Beast.

491   Un rey de los de África   era de fuerça grande
        – entre todos los otros   semejava gigante –
        que al conde buscava   e 'l conde semejante;
        luego quand' vio al conde   fuesse l' parar delante.

492   El conde quando l' vio   tan irado venir
        aguijó el cavallo   e fue l' a resçebir;
        avaxaron las lanças   e fueron se ferir;
        devieran tales golpes   una torre partir.

493   Entramos un' a otro   fueron much' enbargados,
        fueron muy mal feridos,   estavan enbaçados,
        fablar non se podían   tant' eran mal golpados;
        eran de fuertes golpes   amos e dos llagados.

494   El conde don Fernando,   maguer que mal ferido,
        en antes que el rey   entró en su sentido;
        del conde fue el rey   otra vez mal ferido,
        fue luego del cavallo   a tierra abatido.

495   Los vassallos del moro,   quando aquesto vieron,
        çercaron al buen conde,   muy grand priessa le dieron;
        essora castellanos   en valde non sovieron;
        dando grandes feridas,   su señor acorrieron.

496   El conde castellano,   con sus gentes dudadas,
        fueron aquestas oras   fuertemient' esforçadas;
        el cavallo del conde   traié grandes lançadas;
        tenié fasta los pies   las entrañas colgadas.

497   Ovo su buen cavallo   al conde de morir;
        a mayor fuert' sazón   no l' podiera fallir,
        ca non podié tornarse   nin podía foír;
        las coitas que sofría   non las podrié dezir.

498   Estava apeado,   derredor su mesnada,
        escudo contra pecho,   en mano su espada:
        'Vala me,' dixo, 'Cristo,   la tu virtud sagrada;
        non quede oy Castiella   de Ti desanparada.'

491 Among the kings of Africa, one of vast strength
among all the others stood out like a giant;
he sought out the Count, and the Count did the same;
he saw the Count, and went at once to face him.

492 When the Count saw him advance in such anger,
he spurred on his horse and rode out to meet him;
they lowered their lances and went to do battle;
such blows should have sundered a tower in two.

493 The two men were both left reeling from the contest,
both knocked senseless by the blows that they received;
so cruelly were they struck they had not the strength to speak,
the two of them each wounded by the other's savage blows.

494 Badly beaten though he was, that man Count Fernando
was the first of the two to recover his senses,
and the Count once more smote the king a vicious blow;
unseated from his horse, he fell straight to the ground.

495 The vassals of the Moor, when they saw this occur,
had the good Count surrounded and pressed upon him hard;
but this time the Castilians were not to be found wanting,
and they struck fierce blows as they rushed to aid their lord.

496 The Count of Castile and his redoubtable troops
showed at this juncture the peak of their courage;
the horse of the Count bore ill wounds from a lance,
as its entrails hung suspended at its feet.*

497 At this point, the Count's noble horse came to die,
and the time of its dying could not have been worse,
for the Count was unable to retreat or to flee;
the torment he suffered I could not describe.

498 He was left standing, his men gathered round him,
his shield at his heart, and his sword in his hand:
'Christ,' he said, 'may Your holy power protect me;
let Castile not today be abandoned by You!'

499   Los moros eran muchos,   tenién lo bien çercado;
       maguer que el buen conde   estava apeado,
       ferié a todas partes   a guisa d' esforçado;
       los sus buenos vassallos   valieron lo prïado.

500   Dieron l' un buen cavallo,   qual él mester avía;
       dava graçias a Dios,   fazié grand alegría:
       'Señor, merçed tan maña   gradeçer no t' podría
       que tan bien acorriste   a la grand coita mía.'

501   Dexemos nos el conde   mejor de otros reyes,
       faziendo lo que faze   el lobo en las greyes;
       ....
       ....

502   Don Gustïo Gonçález,   que la otra az guiava,
       – corría mucha sangre   por do él aguijava,
       ivan grandes arroyos   commo fuent' que manava –
       fazié grand mortandat   en aquesta gent' brava.

503   Los moros en tod' esto   en valde non yazían;
       en los omnes de pie   grand mortandat fazían.
       Sabet, d' amas las partes   muchos omnes caían;
       a los golpes que davan   las sierras reteñían.

504   Don Dïego Laínez,   con amos sus hermanos,
       ferié de l' otra parte   con otros castellanos;
       fazié grand mortandat   en los pueblos paganos;
       todos caién de vuelta,   los moros e cristianos.

505   Estido la fazienda   en peso tod' el día,
       sobre ganar el canpo   era grand la porfía;
       tenié s' por bien andante   el que mejor fería,
       sobre todos el conde   llevava mejoría.

506   Ferié los don Fernando   de toda voluntad;
       en los pueblos paganos   fazié grand mortandat.
       'Valas me,' dixo, 'Cristo,   Padre de Pïedad;
       sea oy ensalçada   por Ti la cristiandad.'

499   The Moors numbered many, and crowded all around him;
the good Count, although he was now standing on his feet,
struck out on all sides, in the manner of the bold;
those noble men, his vassals, came quickly to his aid.

500   They gave him a fine horse, such as was his need;
he showed his great joy as he gave thanks to God:
'Lord, I could not thank You for a mercy so great
as to bring me such relief from my trouble.'

501   Let us leave the Count, who was the finest of the rulers,
doing as a wolf does when set among the flocks;*
....
....

502   Gustio González, who led the other column
– the spilling of much blood marked the path that he rode,
which flowed in great rivers like a fount gushing forth –
inflicted much slaughter on that fierce tribe of men.

503   The Moors lay not idle while this was occurring,
inflicting much slaughter on the infantry, in turn;
on both sides, I tell you, did many men fall,
and the mountains resounded with the blows that they struck.

504   Diego Laínez, with both of his brothers,*
attacked from the other side with others of Castile,
inflicting much slaughter on the pagan troops;
the Moors and the Christians all fell there, as one.

505   The battle remained in the balance all day,
and great was the struggle for winning the field;
the man with the hardest blows held himself content,
and over all others the Count was supreme.

506   Fernando attacked them with heartfelt conviction;
he inflicted much slaughter on the pagan troops.
'Christ,' he said, 'help me, O merciful Father;
may this day see Christendom exalted by You.'

507   Tenié llenos de polvo   la boca e los dientes,
        que non podié fablar   por confortar sus gentes,
        diziendo: 'Oy sed buenos   vassallos e parientes;
        los buenos en tal día   devedes parar mientes.'

508   Dezié: 'Ferid de rezio,   mis leales amigos;
        avedes muchos tuertos   d'Almozor resçebidos;
        pora vengar nos d'él   set bien mientes metidos,
        menbrad vos que por esso   somos aquí venidos.'

509   El sol era ya puesto,   querié anocheçer;
        nin moros nin cristianos   non se podién vençer.
        Mandó luego el conde   el su cuerno tañer
        e ovieron se todos   a la señ' acojer.

510   Los pueblos castellanos   e las gentes cruzadas
        sacaron a los moros   fueras de sus posadas;
        el conde don Fernando,   con todas sus mesnadas,
        fueron aquella noche   todas bien albergadas.

511   El conde e sus gentes   las posadas tomaron,
        ovieron tal albergue   qual a Dios demandaron;
        quanto mester ovieron   todo y lo fallaron;
        con sus armas guarnidos   toda la noch' velaron.

512   En el día primero   muy grand daño tomaron;
        ¡sean en paraíso   quantos aÿ finaron!
        ....
        ....

513   Otro día mañana   los pueblos descreídos
        estavan en el canpo   con sus armas guarnidos,
        dando muy grandes vozes   e grandes apellidos;
        los montes e los valles   semejavan movidos.

514   El conde don Fernando   con su gente loçana
        todos oyeron missa   otro día mañana;
        fueron todos al canpo   a primera canpana;
        pararon se las azes   en medio de la plana.

507 His mouth and his teeth were so clogged full of dust,
that scarcely could he speak to give comfort to his troops,
saying, 'Be good men this day, my kinsmen and vassals;
you good men on such a day must pay close attention.'

508 He said: 'My loyal friends, put vigour in your blows;
many wrongs have you been done by al-Mansur;
have your minds clear-focused on our vengeance upon him,
and remember we have come here for that reason.'

509 The sun had now set, and nightfall was near;
neither Christians nor Moors could gain victory.
The Count at once ordered his horn to be sounded,
and his men were all to rally to the ensign.

510 The men of Castile and the troops on crusade
forced the Moors to move out from their lodgings,
that man Count Fernando, with all of his forces,
all spent that night most comfortably sheltered.*

511 The Count and his soldiers took over their lodgings,
and had such shelter as they asked of God;
everything they needed, they found in that place;
they spent all the night in vigil, fully armed.

512 On the first day of fighting their losses were severe;
may all those who died there rest in paradise!
....
....

513 The next day's morning saw the unbelieving peoples
standing on the battlefield, their armour all in place,
loud in their roars and tremendous cries of war;
both the mountains and the hills seemed to tremble.

514 Count Fernando, together with his proud band of men,
all went to hear Mass on the following morning;
they all took the field when the first bell tolled,
and drew up their columns in the middle of the plain.

515   Començaron el pleito   do lo avién dexado,
llamando '¡Santïago!',   el apóstol onrado;
las azes fueron vueltas,   el torneo mesclado;
bien avién castellanos   aquel mester usado.

516   Órbita, su alférez,   el que traié su seña,
non sofría más golpes   que si fues' una peña;
nunca mejor la tovo   el buen Terrín d' Ardeña:
Dios perdone su alma,   qu' él yaze en Cardeña.

517   El conde don Fernando,   coraçón sin flaqueza,
señor d' enseñamiento,   çimiento de nobleza,
ferié en los paganos   sin ninguna pereza;
estonç' dixo, 'Caveros,   afán ha en pobreza.'

518   El conde don Fernando,   más bravo que serpiente,
avía la grand fuerça   con el día caliente;
matava e fería   en la mala semiente,
fazié grand mortandat   en pueblo descreyente.

519   Dexemos nos al conde   en grand priessa estar;
nunca nasçió omn' d' armas   que l' podies' mejorar.
Digamos de los otros: non avién más vagar,
ca y les iva todo,   caer o levantar.

520   Los unos e los otros   rezio se conbatieron;
sabet, d' amas las partes   muchos omnes morieron;
la noche fue venida,   de allí se herzieron:
nada non acabaron   por lo que y venieron.

521   Tornaron s' a las tiendas,   fanbrientos e lazrados;
levaron fuerte día,   estavan muy cansados;
avién y muchos omnes   feridos e matados;
çenaron e dormieron   toda la noch' armados.

522   El conde don Fernando,   de fazienda granada,
mandó a prima noche   llamar a su mesnada;
fue a poca de ora   toda con él juntada,
passaron por oír le   aquella gent' lazrada.

515   They picked up the combat from where they had left it,
crying out 'Santiago!' to the honoured apostle,
the battle lines in tumult, the contest underway;
this was a craft that the Castilians knew well.

516   His ensign Órbita, who bore the Count's standard –
had he been a rock the blows would not have pained him less;
good Thierry l'Ardennois never fought a finer battle;
he lies in Cardeña, may God forgive his soul.*

517   Count Fernando, a heart that never weakened,
lord of enlightenment, nobility's touchstone,
struck out at the pagans, his blows never weary,
before saying, 'My knights, great endeavour comes from need.'

518   Count Fernando, raging wilder than a serpent,
was possessed of great strength in the heat of the day;
he struck death-dealing blows to the evil brood,
and inflicted much slaughter on the unbelieving tribe.

519   Let us leave the Count deep in the thick of the battle;
no man of arms was ever born to better him.
Let us tell of the others: their respite was no more,
for here lay their all: to rise up or to fall.

520   The men of both armies were ferocious in battle;
I tell you, many men met their deaths, on both sides;
night was upon them, they withdrew from the field,
with nothing yet achieved of their purpose in coming.

521   In hunger and discomfort, they returned to their tents;
the day had been a hard one, and left them exhausted;
many men among them had been wounded or killed;
they dined and they slept, wearing armour all night.

522   Count Fernando, that man of remarkable deeds,
in the night's first hour bade his men be assembled;
in but a short time they were all gathered round him:
those much-troubled troops went to hear what he said.

523   'Amigos,' dixo 'l conde,   'por Dios que esforçedes;
                 por el muy mal lazerio   que vos non desmayedes.'

....

....

[522–530]
Et quando fue a prima ora en la noche mandó el Conde llamar a todos e díxoles
assí: 'Amigos, por Dios que esforcedes et non desmayedes por el grand lazerio, ca
yo vos digo que cras fasta hora de nona avredes grand acorro en manera que vos
vençredes el campo yl' avredes. Et si vos quisiéredes que venzcamos nos, seamos
cras mañana en el campo ante del sol salido et firamos muy de rezio et de todo
coraçón et non les demos vagar, ca luego nos dexarán el campo por fuerça; et digo
vos que de muertos o de vençudos non escaparán de nos. Et pues que los oviéremos
vençudos et arrancados del campo, fuirán et iremos nos en pos ellos en alcanço
et vengarnos emos d'ellos del mal que nos han fecho. Et seguro so yo de nos que
non seremos vençudos, ca ante nos dexaríemos todos morir que esso fuesse, nin
querríemos dexarnos prender a vida, et bien sé yo que lo mejor faremos.' Pues que
el Conde les ovo dicho esto, fueronse cada unos por sus posadas et dormiron et
folgaron fasta otro día. Et desí levantáronse por la grand mañana et armáronse. Los
moros armáronse otrossí et salieron al campo. Mas los cristianos fizieron la señal
de la cruz ante sus caras et rogaron a Dios de todos sus coraçones que los ayudasse
contra aquellos sus enemigos. Et, su oratión acabada, baxaron las lanças et fueron
ferir en los moros, llamando: '¡Sant Yague!'. Et como quier que ellos estidiessen
muy canssados de la batalla que ovieran ya en los otros días passados, más esforçada
mientre començaron ésta que ninguna de las otras. Et el Conde Fernán González,
como era muy esforçado caballero en armas, fazié en los moros tan grand mortandad
que non avié y ninguno quien se le osasse parar delant.

531   De buen coraçón todos   eran pora lidiar;
                 nin lanças nin espadas   non avién nul vagar;
                 reteñían los yelmos,   las espadas quebrar;
                 ferién en los capiellos,   las lorigas falsar.

532   Los chicos e los grandes,   todos mientes paravan,
                 com' a ángel de Dios   todos a él guardavan;
                 cuando oyén '¡Castiella!'   todos se esforçavan;
                 todos en su palabra   grand esfuerço tomavan.

523   'My friends,' said the Count, 'in God's name, take heart!
             Do not let your spirits be sapped by such hardship.'*

             ....

             ....

[522–530]

And at the first hour of night the Count sent for all his men and addressed them as follows: 'My friends, in God's name take heart, and let not your spirit be weakened by this terrible hardship, for I tell you that tomorrow before the hour of None* you will receive such great aid that you will win the battlefield and hold it. And if it is your desire that we should win this victory, let us be on the field tomorrow before the sun rises and let us strike hard and with all our hearts and give them no respite, for they will be forced to abandon the field to us in an instant, and I tell you that not one of the dead men or the vanquished will escape us. And once we have defeated them and driven them from the field, they will flee and we shall go after them in pursuit, and we shall have our vengeance for the harm that they have done us. And of ourselves I am sure we shall not be defeated, for we would all rather let ourselves die than see that happen, nor would we let ourselves be taken alive, and I know well that we shall act for the best.' Once the Count had told them this, each man went back to his lodgings and slept and rested until the next day came. Then they rose in the early hours of the morning and armed themselves, and the Moors likewise took up their arms and went out onto the field of battle. But the Christians made the sign of the cross before their faces and offered up a heartfelt prayer to God that he might help them against those enemies of theirs. And when their prayer was completed, they lowered their lances and went to strike the Moors, crying out: 'Santiago!'. And although they were much wearied by the battle they had fought in the previous days, they made a more vigorous start to this battle than they had to either of the others. And Count Fernán González, as he was a knight of great valour in arms, inflicted such great slaughter on the Moors that there was no man there who dared to take his stand before him.

531   They were all in good heart for the battle,
             and neither lances nor swords found respite;
             helmets rang out, with the shattering of swords;
             they struck at helms and sliced through coats of mail.

532   Young men and old all paid him close attention,
             and all kept him safe, like the angel of the Lord;
             all strengthened their resolve upon hearing 'Castile!',
             all of them taking great cheer from his word.

533   Don Gustïo Gonçález   – era leal cabdiello –
             avié en los primeros   abierto grand portiello;
             un rey de los de África,   valiente cavallero,
             ferió l' d' una espada   por medio del capiello.

534   Capiello e almófar   e cofia de armar,
             ovo los la espada   ligera de cortar;
             ovo fasta los ojos   la espada passar:
             d' aqueste golpe ovo   don Gustio a finar.

535   Allí do él murió   non yazié él señero:
             un sobrino del conde   qu' era su conpañero
             mató se con un moro   que era buen cavero;
             non avié y de moros   más estraño braçero.

536   Cristianos otros muchos   por ende y morieron;
             ellos en todo esto   en vald' non estuvieron:
             en los pueblos paganos   grand mortandat fizieron;
             fablaron d'ello sienpre   todos quantos l' oyeron.

537   Al conde don Fernando   llegaron los mandados:
             cóm' eran los mejores   de los otros finados;
             los cristanos estavan   tristes e deserrados;
             si los non acorrían   qu' eran desbaratados.

538   Quand' lo oyó el conde,   por end' fue muy quexado;
             aguijó el cavallo,   acorrió les prïado;
             falló de mala guisa   revuelto el mercado:
             presos fueran o muertos   si non fuera llegado.

539   Ferió luego el conde   en los pueblos paganos,
             de los qu' él alcançava   pocos ivan d'él sanos;
             dizié: 'Yo so el conde,   esforçad castellanos;
             ferid los bien de rezio,   amigos e hermanos.'

540   Los cristianos lazrados,   quando aquesto vieron,
             aun qu' eran malandantes,   tod' el miedo perdieron;
             todos con su señor   grand esfuerço cogieron;
             en las fazes paganas   muy de rezio ferieron.

533 Gustio González, that loyal lieutenant,
had made a great breach in their foes' front lines;
a king among the Africans, a valiant knight,
then dealt him a sword-blow flush on his helm.

534 His helm and his chain mail and the cap that lay beneath,
all of these the flashing sword was quick to slice through;
the sword was to cut down as far as his eyes;
from this blow was Gustio to come to his death.

535 In the place where he died, he did not lie alone:
a nephew of the Count, and companion of his,
died fighting with a Moor and a knight of distinction:
among all the Moorish men there, no warrior was greater.

536 Many other Christians died there for that cause;
amidst all of this, they were not found wanting,
inflicting great slaughter on the pagan troops;
all those who heard it would forever tell the tale.

537 Word of all this reached the ears of Count Fernando,
of how the best men of his companions were fallen;
the Christians were overcome with sorrow and confusion;
if help was not forthcoming, they were already lost.

538 When the Count heard the news, it left him distressed;
he spurred on his horse, riding quickly to their aid,
and he found that affairs were much turned for the worse:
they would have been captured or killed, without him.

539 At once did the Count strike out at the pagans,
and of those within his reach, few escaped him unscathed;
he said, 'I am the Count; take heart, my Castilians;
be mighty in your blows, my brothers and friends.'

540 The long-suffering Christians, when they saw this occur,
hard pressed though they were, they lost all of their fear;
their resolve was much strengthened by the coming of their lord,
and they were fierce in their attacks of the pagan lines.

541   El conde castellano,   de coraçón conplido,
        dizié: 'Ferit, vassallos,   que avedes vençido;
        non sé do falle pan   quien oy fuer' retraído;
        mucho le valdrié más   que nunca fues' nasçido.'

542   Non sé omn' en el mundo   que al conde oyesse
        qu' en ninguna manera   aver miedo podiesse;
        nunca podrié ser malo   el que con él se viesse;
        mejor devrié ser d' otro   el que con él visquiesse.

543   El que Gustio Gonçález   essas oras matara
        del conde, si podiera,   de grado se desviara
        – si lo guisar podría,   mejor lo baratara –
        el señor de Castiella   fue s' le parar de cara.

544   El grand rey africano   oyera lo dezir
        que nul omne al conde   non se l' podié guarir;
        por tanto, si podiera,   quisiera lo foír;
        no l' dio vagar el conde   e fue lo a ferir.

545   Firió l' luego el conde   e partió l' el escudo;
        ronpió l' las guarniçiones   con fierro much' agudo;
        de muerte el rey d' África   anparar non se pudo,
        fue del cavallo yuso   a tierra abatudo.

546   Fueron los africanos   d'esto mucho pesantes,
        ca eran del buen conde   todos muy malandantes;
        ferieron sobr' el conde   más de mill cavalgantes;
        el torneo fue vuelto   más firme que de antes.

547   Murieron bien quarenta   de parte de Castiella,
        salié mucho caballo   vazío con su siella;
        avié de sus vassallos   el conde grand manziella;
        cuidó se sines duda   que se perdrié Castiella.

548   Era en fuerte cuita   el conde don Fernando;
        iba, si se l' fiziesse,   su muerte aguisando;
        alçó suso los ojos,   al Crïador rogando,
        com' si fuesse con Él,   ansí l' está llamando:

541   The Count of Castile, a man great of heart,
       said, 'Strike them, my vassals, for victory is yours!
       I know not where the man who here retreats will find bread;
       he would be much better served had he never been born.'

542   I know no man in the world who listened to the Count
       and could have felt any fear, in the slightest respect;
       none who met him could ever be inclined towards evil,
       and any man who lived with him must be of finer nature.

543   The man who had just slain Gustio González,
       would willingly have bolted from the Count, if he could
       – had he managed to do so, he would have fared better –;
       but the lord of Castile went to meet him face to face.

544   That great African king had heard people say
       that no man could fend off the attack of the Count;
       so, had he been able, he would have sought flight,
       but, allowing him no chance, the Count moved to strike.

545   The Count at once struck him and cleaved through his shield;
       he shattered his armour with his razor-sharp steel;
       that African king could not ward off his death:
       thrown down from his horse, he went crashing to the ground.

546   At this, the men of Africa were sorely aggrieved,
       for all suffered much distress at the good Count's hands;
       a thousand knights and more struck out at the Count,
       and the contest became more savage than before.

547   At least forty men died on the side of Castile;
       many horses ran free with their saddles now vacant;
       the Count felt a deep sense of sorrow for his vassals,
       thinking that for certain Castile would be lost.

548   That man Count Fernando now stood in great peril,
       preparing lest his death should overtake him;
       he raised his eyes upwards in prayer to the Creator,
       calling upon Him as if in His presence:

549   'Pues non so venturoso   d'esta lid arrancar,
           quier' qu' escapar pudiesse,   non quiero escapar,
           nin nunca veré yo   más coita nin pesar;
           meter me h' en logar   do m' hayan de matar.

550   Castiella quebrantada   quedará sin señor;
           iré con esta rabia,   mesquino pecador;
           será en cautiberio   del moro Almoçor:
           por non ver aquel día   la muerte es mejor.

551   Señor, ¿por qué nos tienes   a todos fuerte saña?
           Por los nuestros pecados,   ¡non destruyas España!
           perder se por nos ella   semejarié fazaña,
           que de buenos cristianos   non abría calaña.

552   Padre, Señor del mundo,   e vero Jesu Criste,
           de lo que me dixeron   nada non me toviste:
           que me acorrerías   comigo lo posiste;
           yo no te falesçiendo,   ¿por qué me falesçiste?

553   Señor, pues es el conde   de Ti desanparado,
           que por alguna culpa   eres d'él despagado,
           resçebe Tú, Señor,   en comienda 'l condado:
           si non, será aína   por suelo astragado.

554   Pero yo non morré   assí desanparado:
           antes avrán de mí   los moros mal mercado;
           tal cosa fará antes   este cuerpo laçrado
           que quant' el mundo dure   sienpre será contado.

555   Si atanta de graçia   me quesiesses Tú dar
           que yo a Almançor   me pudies' allegar,
           non creo que a vida   me pudies' escapar,
           yo mismo cuidaría   la mi muerte vengar.

556   Todos los mis vassallos   que aquí son finados
           serién por su señor   este día vengados;
           todos en paraíso   conmigo ayuntados,
           faría muy grand honra   el cond' a sus vassallos.'

549   'Since I have not fortune enough to win victory,
       even if I could escape, I do not wish to;
       I will never look again on suffering or sorrow;
       I will place myself where they are sure to kill me.

550   Castile will be broken and left without a lord;
       wretched and sinful, I shall take this fury with me;
       it will be held in bondage by the Moor al-Mansur;
       it is better that I die so as not to see that day.

551   Lord, for what reason do you bear us all such ire?
       Do not destroy Spain on account of our sins;
       for if we cause her loss, then that would seem a sanction
       the like of which good Christians have not seen.

552   Father, the world's Lord and true Jesus Christ,
       You fulfilled nothing of what I was told:
       with me You made a pact to come to my aid;
       as I fail not You, why have You failed me?

553   Lord, since the Count is forsaken by You,*
       as he has displeased You in making some error,
       receive, Lord, this county, which to You I commend;
       if not, it will quickly face total destruction.

554   But I will not yield to death thus forsaken:
       before that, the Moors will find pain at my hands;
       this exhausted body will first do such deeds
       as will be forever told while the world endures.

555   If Your will were to give me such a measure of grace
       to allow me to meet al-Mansur face to face,
       I do not believe he could escape with his life;
       I would seek to be the one to avenge my own death.

556   All of my vassals who have died in this place
       would today have their vengeance by the hands of their lord;
       with all of them gathered in paradise with me,
       the Count would have honoured his vassals indeed.'

557 Querellando s' a Dios el conde don Fernando,
  los finojos fincados, al Crïador rogando,
  oyó una grand voz que l' estava llamando:
  'Ferrando de Castiella, oy te crez' muy grand bando.'

558 Alçó suso sus ojos por ver quién lo llamava,
  vïo 'l santo apóstol que de suso l' estava;
  de caveros con él grand conpaña llevava,
  todos armas cruçadas com' a él semejava.

559 Fueron contra los moros, las açes bien paradas;
  nunca vio omne nado gentes tan esforçadas;
  el moro Almoçor, con todas sus mesnadas,
  con ellos fueron luego fuerte miente enbargadas.

560 Veién d' una señal tantos pueblos armados,
  ovieron muy grand miedo, fueron mal espantados;
  de quál parte venían eran maravillados;
  lo que más les pesava, qu' eran todos cruzados.

561 Dixo 'l rey Almançor: 'Esto non puede ser.
  ¿Dónd' le recreç' al conde atán fuerte poder?
  Cuidava oy sin duda le matar o prender,
  e ha con estas gentes él a nos cometer.'

562 Los cristianos mesquinos, que estavan cansados,
  de fincar con las ánimas eran desfiúçados;
  fueron con el apóstol muy fuerte confortados;
  nunca fueron en ora tan fuerte esforçados.

563 Acreçió les esfuerço, tod' el miedo perdieron;
  en los pueblos paganos grand mortandad fiçieron;
  los poderes de África sofrir non lo pudieron;
  tornaron las espaldas, del canpo se movieron.

564 Quando vio don Ferrando que espaldas tornavan,
  que con miedo de muerte el canpo les dexavan,
  el conde e sus gentes fuerte les aquexavan;
  espuelas en los pies, e azotes tomavan.

557   As Count Fernando lamented to God,
        imploring the Creator on bended knee,
        he heard a loud voice that was calling to him:
        'Fernando of Castile, you gain many men this day.'*

558   He looked up to see who was calling to him,
        and saw the Holy Apostle stood above him;*
        with him he brought a vast company of knights,
        all, thought Fernando, with the cross on their arms.

559   With battle lines clearly drawn, they marched against the Moors;
        no man ever born laid eyes on troops of such resolve;
        the Moor al-Mansur, and all his army with him,
        at once found those men to be a brutal obstruction.

560   Seeing so many armed men all under one ensign,
        the Moors felt great fear and a terrible fright,
        being overcome with wonder at whence these men appeared;
        that they all bore the cross was the Moors' greatest woe.

561   Spoke King al-Mansur: 'Such a thing cannot be;
        whence can such an army come to strengthen the Count?
        Today I thought it certain I would capture him or kill him,
        and now with these troops it is he who will attack.'

562   The hapless Christians, now exhausted from the fight,
        despaired that they would manage to escape with their souls;
        they took great comfort in the coming of the apostle;
        at no other time did they ever feel such courage.

563   Their valour grew greater and they shed all their fear,
        inflicting great slaughter on the troops of the pagans;
        the African armies were unable to endure it:
        turning their backs, they retreated from the field.

564   When Fernando then saw they were turning their backs,
        abandoning the field to them in terror of death,
        the Count and his troops then pressed hard on their tail:
        with spurs on their feet, they made use of their whips.

565   Fasta en Almenar   a moros malfaçaron;
         muchos fueron los presos,   muchos los que mataron;
         un día e dos noches   sienpre los alcançaron;
         después al terçer día   a Fazinas tornaron.

566   Buscaron por los muertos   que espessos yazían
         – com' estavan sangrientos,   a dur' los conoçían –
         los cristianos finados   que los soterrarían,
         cad' un' a sus lugares   que se los levarían.

567   Diz el cond' don Ferrando,   conplido de bondades:
         'Amigos, no m' semeja   qu' en esto bien fagades;
         d' enbargar vos de muertos   nada y non ganades;
         metredes grandes duelos   en vuestras vezindades.

568   Los muertos a los bivos   ¿por qué han d' enbargar?
         Por duelo non podremos   ningún d'ellos tornar.
         Aquí ha un' ermita   que es un buen lugar;
         ternía yo por bien   d' allí los soterrar.

569   Nunca podrién yaçer   en lugar tan honrado;
         yo mismo he mi cuerpo   allí encomendado;
         mando me y llevar   quando fuere finado
         e y quiero fazer   un lugar much' honrado.'

570   Lo que dixo el conde   todos est' otorgaron;
         los cristianos finados   pora y los llevaron;
         mucho honrada miente   allí los soterraron;
         quand' fueron soterrados,   su camino tomaron.

571   Enbió Sancho Ordóñez   al buen conde mandado
         que querié façer cortes   e que fuesse prïado,
         e qu' eran ayuntados   todos los del reinado;
         por él sólo tardava,   que non era uviado.

572   Ovo ir a las cortes   pero con gran pesar;
         era muy fiera cosa   la mano le besar:
         'Señor, Dios de los çielos,   quieras me ayudar
         que yo pued' a Castiella   d'esta premia sacar.'

565   They harmed the Moors and harried them as far as Almenar:*
        many were their prisoners, and many those they killed;
        for a day and two nights they had them firmly in their grasp,
        before returning on the third day to Hacinas.

566   They searched through the dead, who lay thick on the ground,
        so covered with blood they were hard to distinguish,
        to find the dead Christians, and give them their burial,
        taking each one to the place of his home.

567   Then spoke Count Fernando, of goodness replete:
        'My friends, in my eyes you act wrongly in this;
        to burden yourselves with the dead brings no gains,
        but to all your own lands you will bring a deep grief.

568   Why should the dead be a burden on the living?
        We cannot restore any of them to life by our grief.
        Here there is a hermitage, a fine place indeed,
        and I would think it right that we bury them there.

569   They could never lie in a place of such honour;
        I myself have entrusted my body to rest there;*
        I order I be carried there on reaching my death,
        and I wish to endow there a place of great honour.'

570   The words of the Count were agreed to by all,
        and they carried there the Christians who had died;
        they did them much honour as they buried them there,
        and with the burial complete, they returned to their path.

571   The good Count was sent word by Sancho Ordóñez
        that he wished for a parliament and brooked no delay:*
        all the men of the kingdom were already assembled;
        him alone they awaited, who was not yet arrived.

572   He had to attend, though he was much averse:
        to kiss the King's hand he found bitter indeed:*
        'God of the heavens, Lord, grant me Your aid,
        that I may free Castile from this oppression.'

573   El rey e sus varones   muy bien le reçebieron;
       todos con el buen conde   muy grand gozo ovieron;
       fasta en su posada   todos con él venieron;
       entrante de la puerta   todos se despedieron.

574   A chicos e a grandes   de toda la çibdat
       la venida del conde   plaçié de voluntad;
       a la reïna sola   pesava por verdat,
       que avía con él   muy grand enemistad.

575   Avié en estas cortes   muy grand pueblo sobejo;
       después qu' el conde vino   duró les poquellejo,
       ca dio les el buen conde   mucho de buen consejo:
       d'ellos en poridad,   d'ellos por buen conçejo.

576   Levava don Ferrando   un mudado açor:
       non avié en Castiella   otro tal nin mejor;
       otrossí un cavallo   que fuera d' Almançor;
       avié de todo ello   el rey muy grand sabor.

577   El rey, del grand sabor   de a ellos llevar,
       luego dixo al conde   que los querié conprar.
       'Non los venderié, señor,   mas mandes los tomar;
       vender non vos los quiero,   mas quiero vos los dar.'

578   El rey dixo al conde   que non los tomaría
       mas açor e cavallo   que gelos conpraría,
       que d' aquella moneda   mill marcos le daría
       por açor e cavallo   si dar gelos quería.

579   Avenieron se anbos,   fiçieron su mercado:
       puso quánd' gelo diessen   a día señalado:
       si el aver non fuesse   aquel día pagado
       sienpre fues' cada día   al gallarín doblado.

580   Cartas por ABC   partidas y fiçieron,
       todos los juramentos   allí los escrivieron;
       en cabo de la carta   los testigos pusieron
       quantos a esta merca   delante estovieron.

573   The King and his barons received him most warmly,
all delighting in the company of the good Count;
they all stayed at his side right back to his lodgings,
all taking their leave as he stood at his door.

574   Young men and old from all parts of the city
derived great pleasure from the coming of the Count;
the Queen was the only one truly dismayed,*
for she bore him resentment deep-seated indeed.

575   Very many men were attending this parliament,
but once the Count arrived, it was not to last long,
for the good Count did give them a wealth of sound advice,
to some of them in private, to others in full council.

576   Fernando carried with him a hawk that had moulted
– there was none to equal or outmatch it in Castile –
and likewise a horse which had belonged to al-Mansur,*
for all of which the King conceived a very great desire.

577   The King, much desiring to take the two with him
at once told the Count that he wanted to buy them:
'My lord, I would not sell them; but order them be taken.
I have no wish to sell you them; but give you them, I will.'

578   The King told the Count he would not take them,
but would buy from him the hawk and the horse,
and would pay him a thousand marks in that coinage*
for the hawk and the horse, were he willing to give them.

579   The two men agreed and there settled their deal;
a day was appointed for payment to be made;
were the money not paid on that day which they agreed,
the interest would each day double what was owed.*

580   They drew up letters on the spot, divided by ABC,*
on which they recorded all the oaths they had sworn;
at the foot of the letter they put witnesses' names,
all those who were present for this contract of purchase.

581   Assaz avié el rey   buen cavallo conprado,
mas salió l' a tres años   muy caro el mercado:
con el aver de Françia   nunca serié pagado;
por y perdió el rey   Castiella su condado.

582   Fueron todas las cortes   desfechas e partidas:
las gentes castellanas   fueron todas exidas.
Fueron todas las gentes   del rey bien despedidas;
tornaron a sus tierras   d'onde fueron venidas.

583   Antes que él partiesse,   una dueña loçana,
reïna de León,   de don Sancho hermana,
prometió l' al buen conde,   fiço l' fïuzia vana;
cuntió l' com' al carnero   que fue buscar la lana.

584   Demostró l' el dïablo   el engaño aína:
prometió l' casamiento   al conde la reïna;
por que finas' la guerra   le daría su sobrina;
serié el daño grande   sin esta meleçina.

585   Tovo end' el buen conde   que serié bien casado:
otorgó gelo luego   que lo farié de grado.
Enbïó la reïna   a Navarra mandado,
una carta ditada   con un falso ditado.

586   Ésta es la raçón   que la carta deçía:
'De mí, doña Teresa,   a ti, el rey Garçía;
perdí al rey tu padre   que yo grand bien quería;
si yo fues' rey com' tú,   ya vengado l' avría.

587   Oras tú tienes tienpo   por' vengar mi hermano;
por este tal engaño   coger lo has en mano.
Tomarás buen derecho   d' aquel conde loçano;
a vida non le dexes   aquel fuert' castellano.'

588   Quand' oyeron las gentes   d' aqueste casamiento,
todos tenién que era   muy buen ayuntamiento,
que serié de la paz   carrera e çimiento;
mas ordió otras redes   el diablo çeniciento.

581   The King had bought a horse that was fine indeed,
but after three years the deal cost him very dear;
with all the wealth of France it would still not be paid,
and through it the King lost his county of Castile.

582   With that, all the parliament was ended and disbanded,
and all the people of Castile now left that place;
they were all sped warmly on their way by the King,
and returned to their own lands, whence they had come.

583   Before his departure, a lady of disdain,
queen of León and the sister of Sancho,
made the good Count a promise and empty pledge;
his fate was the same as the ram that sought wool.*

584   The Devil moved quickly to show her the deceit:
the Queen pledged the Count the betrothal of a bride:
that the war might be over she would give him her niece,
for much harm would result, were this medicine not taken.*

585   The Count thus considered that he would marry well,
and quickly consented, being happy to accept.
The Queen then sent word to the kingdom of Navarre:
a letter dictated with a mendacious dictation.*

586   These are the words that the letter contained:
'From me, Queen Teresa, to you, King García;*
I lost the King, your father, dear object of my love;
were I a king like you, I would now have avenged him.

587   Now you have the chance to win vengeance for my brother;
through this my deceit, you will have him in your hands.
you will mete out full justice on that arrogant count;
do not leave that mighty Castilian alive.'

588   When news of this wedding was come to the people,
they all thought the union a fine one indeed –
to be the foundation and pathway to peace;
but the cinderous Devil wove different webs.

589 Pusieron su lugar do a vistas veniessen;
    tovieron por bien anbos que a Çirueña fuessen,
    de cada parte çinco caveros aduxessen;
    fablarién e pornién lo que por bien toviessen.

590 Tomó Ferrán Gonçález çinco de sus varones,
    todos de buen derecho e grandes infançones,
    muy grandes de linaje, esforçados varones
    ....

591 Fueron pora Çirueña assí commo mandaron;
    con el cond' de Castiella solos çinco enbïaron;
    el rey e los navarros el pleito falsaron:
    en lugar de los çinco más de treinta llevaron.

592 Quando vio don Ferrando al rey assí guarnido,
    entendió que l' avía del pleito fallesçido:
    'Santa María, val, ca yo so confondido;
    creyendo m' por palabra yo mismo so vendido.'

593 El conde dio grand voz com' si fuesse tronido:
    'Devía ser agora el mundo destruïdo
    con este mal engaño qu' el rey ha cometido;
    lo que me dixo 'l monje, en ello so caído.'

594 Reptando se él mismo de la su malandança,
    non pudiendo tomar nin escudo nin lança,
    fuxo a un ermita, y fue su anparança;
    de man' fasta la noche allí fue su morança.

595 Fiço su escudero a guisa de leal,
    vïo una finiestra en medio del fastial;
    vino pora l' hermita, metió s' por el portal;
    echó les sus espadas, que non pudo fer al.

596 Aquestos escuderos que con el conde fueron,
    quando a su señor acorrer non pudieron,
    todos en sus cavallos aína se cojieron,
    luego con el mandado a Castiella venieron.

589   They agreed on their meeting-place, to which they would go,
and both thought it right that this place be Cirueña,*
and that each party's company be made of five knights;
they would talk, and decide upon what they thought best.

590   Five of his barons did Fernán González take,
all of great integrity and nobles of distinction,
outstanding in their lineage and knights of great valour
....

591   They went to Cirueña, exactly as determined,
just five men the party of the Count of Castile;
the King and the Navarrese broke their agreement:
instead of taking five men, their number passed thirty.

592   When Fernando saw the King thus decked in his armour,
he knew that he had broken the terms of their pact:
'Help me, Saint Mary, for I am deceived;
I put faith in their words, and I now am betrayed.'

593   The Count gave a roar like a great clap of thunder:
'The world at this point should have met its destruction
at this evil deceit which the King has now sprung;
I am fallen into what the monk foretold to me.'

594   Reproaching himself for the error he had made,
and unable to take up his shield or his lance,
he fled to a hermitage, and there found his shelter;*
he remained in that place from the morning till night.

595   His squire then acted as a loyal man should:
on seeing a window in the middle of the gable,
he came to the hermitage and entered the doorway;
he threw them his swords, for no more could he do.

596   Those squires who went in the company of the Count,
when they were unable to give aid to their lord,
leapt astride their horses, and all with great haste,
went at once to bear that news to Castile.

597   Fue del rey don García   la 'glesia bien lidiada,
non la quiso dexar   maguer era sagrada;
non pud' de lo que quiso   el rey acabar nada,
ca tenía el conde   la puerta bien çerrada.

598   El sol era ya baxo,   que se querié tornar;
mandó 'l rey don Garçía   al conde preguntar
si s' querié a presión   sobr' omenaje dar,
que podrié por sól' esto   la muerte escapar.

599   A salva fe jurando   dio se les a presión:
pesó mucho a Dios   fecho tan sin raçón;
oyeron una voz   commo voz de pavón;
partió se el altar   de somo a fondón.

600   Assí está oy día   la iglesia partida,
por que fue atal cosa   en ella conteçida;
cuido que durará   fasta la fin conplida,
ca non fue atal cosa   que sea ascondida.

601   Fue luego don Ferrando   en los fierros metido,
de grand pesar que ovo   cayó amorteçido;
a cabo d' una pieça   tornó en su sentido,
dixo: 'Señor del mundo,   ¿por qué me has fallido?

602   Señor Dios, si quisieres   que yo fues' venturado,
que a mí los navarros   me fallassen armado,
aquesto te ternía   a merçed e a grado
e por esto me tengo   de Ti desanparado.

603   Si fuesses en la tierra,   seriés de mí reptado;
nunca fiz' por que fuesse   de Ti desanparado;
morré de mala guisa   com' omne de mal fado;
si yo pesar te fiçe   bien deves ser vengado.'

604   Dentro en Castro Viejo   al buen conde metieron,
teniendo l' fuerte saña,   mala presión le dieron:
com' omnes sin mesura,   mesura no l' fiçieron;
los vassallos del conde   dexar le non quisieron.

597   King García had the church firmly surrounded:
he would not hold off, even though it was sacred;*
but none of his aims could the King then achieve,
for the Count kept the door of that place firmly closed.

598   The sun was sunk low in the sky, close to setting,
and King García ordered an enquiry of the Count:
if he wished for surrender and prison, on his word;*
for by this means alone could he hope to cheat death.

599   He swore a solemn oath and surrendered to prison:
so unreasonable an act caused the Lord great dismay;
they heard a voice ring out, like the cry of a peacock;
the altar split asunder, from the top to the bottom.*

600   So today does the church remain sundered in two,
because such a event had occurred on that spot;
I believe it will stay so, till the end of days,
for it was not such a happening as may be concealed.

601   Fernando was immediately cast into chains,
and so great was his grief he fell faint on the ground;
a short while passed, and he returned to his senses,
saying, 'Lord of the world, why have You failed me?*

602   Lord God, had Your will been to grant me the good fortune
that the men of Navarre should have discovered me armed,
this I would have thought to be Your mercy and blessing,
and therefore I hold myself forsaken by You.

603   If You were on earth, I would issue You a challenge;
my actions never merited that You should forsake me;
I will die a harsh death as a man of ill fortune;
if I caused You sorrow, You must have full vengeance.'

604   In Castroviejo they imprisoned the good Count;*
they bore him a fierce rage, and treated him cruelly;
as men without measure, they showed him no mercy,
but the vassals of the Count were unwilling to leave him.

605 Dixo al rey Garçía el conde su razón;
'Non has por qué tener ningunos en presión;
habrás por mí señero todos quantos y son;
non les fagas nul mal, qu' ellos sin culpa son.'

606 Soltó los don Garçía, a Castiella venieron;
quando los castellanos el mandado sopieron,
nunca tan mal mensaje castellanos oyeron;
por poco con pesar de seso non salieron.

607 Fizieron muy grand duelo estonçes por Castiella,
mucho vestido negro, rota mucha capiella,
rascadas muchas fruentes, rota mucha mexiella;
tenié en coraçón cad' uno grand manziella.

608 Lloravan e dezían: '¡Somos muy sin ventura!'
Dezién del Crïador mucha fuert' majadura:
'Non quiere que salgamos de premia nin d' ardura,
mas que seamos siervos nos e nuestra natura.

609 Somos los castellanos contra Dios en grand saña
por que nos quiere dar esta premia tamaña;
caímos en la ira de todos los d' España;
tornada es Castiella una pobre cabaña.

610 A otro non sabemos nuestra coita dezir
si non al Crïador que nos deve oír;
con el conde coidávamos d'esta coita salir;
oviemos nos enantes en ella de venir.'

611 Dexemos castellanos en su fuerte pesar,
aver nos hemos luego en ellos a tornar;
juntaron se en uno por se aconsejar;
dexemos los juntados, bien nos deve menbrar.

612 Tornemos en el conde, do l' avemos dexado:
era en Castro Viejo en la cárcel echado;
de gentes de Navarra era bien aguardado;
nunca fue omne nado en presión más coitado.

605 The Count then spoke his piece to King García:
'You have no reason to hold any men in prison;
by holding me alone you will have all of my men;
do not do them harm, for they are blameless in this.'

606 García released them and they came to Castile;
when those of Castile heard the news that they brought,
Castilians had never had a message so grim;
their sorrow almost caused them to be driven from their wits.

607 A great tide of lamenting then spread through Castile:
many black clothes of mourning, many hoods ripped in grief,
many brows being clawed at and cheeks that were scratched;
the heart of each Castilian bore dishonour's great stain.

608 They cried out through their tears, saying 'Ill is our fortune!'
and gave vent to many bruising complaints at the Creator:
'He wants not our escape from oppression and hardship,
but that we and our children should rather be slaves.

609 We Castilians are taken with great fury for God,
because of His desire that we suffer such oppression;
we have incurred the anger of all those in Spain,
and once again Castile has become a tiny hut.*

610 To none other are we able to address our lament
except to the Creator, who must hear us;
with the Count we thought that we would leave this hardship,
but instead we have only just come into it.'

611 Let us leave the Castilians amid their great sorrow –
we shall presently come to return to them;
they gathered together for the purpose of counsel;
let us leave them together; we must keep them in mind.

612 Let us turn once again to the Count, where we left him:
he was in Castroviejo, and thrown into prison;
upon him the men of Navarre kept close guard;
no man ever born suffered crueller imprisonment.

613   Avié en estas tierras   la gente ya oído
         que otro mejor d' armas   nunca fuera nasçido;
         tenié se por mejor   quien l' avié conosçido;
         avié sabor de ver le   quien non le avié vido.

614   Un conde muy onrado   qu' era de Lonbardía
         vino l' en coraçón   de ir en romería;
         tomó de sus vassallos   muy grand cavallería;
         por' ir a Santïago   metió se por su vía.

615   Aquel conde lonbardo,   yendo por la carrera,
         demandó por el conde,   en quáles tierras era;
         dixeron gelo luego,   toda cosa çertera,
         sobre que fuera preso   e sobre quál manera.

616   Demandó él por cierto   todo aquel engaño:
         cóm' avién resçebido   castellanos grand daño;
         levaron le a vistas   a fe e sin engaño,
         en ellas le prendieron,   bien avié ya un año.

617   Preguntó si l' podría   por qualquier cosa ver,
         ca avié grand sabor   de al cond' conosçer;
         que verié si podría   alguna pro tener,
         que tal omne non era   por' en cárçel tener.

618   Fue s' pora Castro Viejo,   demandó los porteros,
         prometió de les dar   muchos de los dineros,
         ....
         que l' dexassen ver 'l conde   con solos dos caveros.

619   Levaron l' al castiello,   las puertas le abrieron,
         los condes un' a otro   muy bien se resçibieron;
         entr' amos en su fabla   grand pieça estovieron;
         la razón acabada,   luego se despedieron.

620   Partieron se entr' amos,   de los ojos llorando;
         fincó en su presión   el conde don Fernando;
         estando en grand coita,   muchas coitas passando,
         que Dios d'end' le sacasse   todavía rogando.

613 The people in those lands had already heard tell
that no man was ever born more skilled in arms;
any man, for meeting him, then thought himself the finer,
and any yet to see him desired to do so.

614 A count of great honour, who hailed from Lombardy,*
conceived the desire to go on a pilgrimage;
he took with him a company of many of his vassals
and set out on the path to Santiago.

615 That Lombard count, as he travelled on his way,
asked of the Count and what lands he was in;
at once he was told the whole truth of the matter:
that the Count was in prison, and how it had occurred.

616 He sought out the truth of the whole of that deceit
and how the Castilians had been done a grave wrong:
they took him to a meeting in candour and good faith,
and there he had been captured, a full year ago.

617 He asked if he could see him, under any pretext,
for great was the desire that he had to meet the Count;
he said that he would see if he could help in some way,
for this was no man to be kept in a prison.

618 He made for Castroviejo and asked for the jailers,
promising to pay them a great sum of money,
....
that they let him see the Count, with just two knights present.

619 They took him to the castle and opened up the gates,
and the two counts received each other warmly;
the two men spent a long time in conversation,
and once it was over, they then said farewell.

620 They made their departure, with tears in their eyes,
and Fernando remained there imprisoned;
he was in great distress and enduring much hardship,
still pleading with God that He free him from there.

621   Aquel conde lonbardo,   quando fue despedido,
        al conde castellano   non l' echó en olvido;
        demandó la donzella,   por que fuera cuntido,
        cóm' el conde oviera   a ser d'ella marido.

622   Mostraron gela luego,   la fermosa donzella;
        vio tan apuesta cosa   que era maraviella;
        fabló luego el conde   de poridat con ella;
        dixo cómmo avía   d'ella muy grand manziella.

623   'Dueña,' dixo el conde,   'eres muy sin ventura,
        non ha de más malfado   en toda tu natura:
        de ti han castellanos   todos fuerte rencura,
        que les vino por ti   este mal sin mesura.

624   Dueña sin pïedad   e sin buen conosçer,
        de fazer bien o mal   tú tienes el poder:
        si al conde non quieres   de muerte estorçer,
        aver se ha Castiella   por tu culpa perder.

625   Fazes muy grand ayuda   a los pueblos paganos,
        ca les quitava éste   a todos pies e manos;
        quitas muy grand esfuerço   a todos los cristianos,
        por end' andan los moros   alegres e loçanos.

626   Eres de tu buen preçio   mucho menoscabada;
        serás por este fecho   por muchos denostada;
        quando fuer' esta cosa   por el mundo sonada,
        será toda la culpa   luego a ti echada.

627   Si tú con este conde   podiesses ser casada,
        tener t' ían las dueñas   por bien aventurada;
        de todos los d' España   serías much' onrada;
        nunca fiziera dueña   tan buena cavalgada.

628   Si eres de sentido,   esto es lo mejor;
        si tú nunca oviste   de cavero amor,
        más deves amar éste   que non emperador;
        non ha omn' en el mundo   de sus armas mejor.'

621   That count from Lombardy, having taken his leave,
did not then forget about the Count of Castile;
he asked about the maiden – the cause of it all –
and how the Count had been intended as her husband.

622   The beautiful maiden was shown him at once;
so fine did she seem that he thought it a wonder;
the Count then moved quickly to speak with her in private,
and he told her of the grievance that he bore her.

623   'My lady,' said the Count, 'you are all without fortune;
there is no-one more ill-starred in all your line;
the Castilians all bear you the deepest resentment,
for on your account this ill beyond measure befell them.

624   Lady with no pity, or proper understanding,
you have it in your hands to do good or do ill:
should you not be willing to free the Count from death,
then Castile is to be lost, and yours the fault.

625   You are giving great assistance to the pagan peoples,
for this man stripped all of them of feet and of hands;
you are robbing all the Christians most dearly of valour,
which leaves the Moorish soldiers full of joy and pride.

626   You have done much discredit to your good reputation,
and this deed will make you reviled by many;
when word of this story has passed across the world,
all the blame will be immediately laid at your door.

627   If you could be joined to this count in marriage,
all ladies would reckon you favoured by Fortune;
the people of Spain would all do you much honour;
no lady would have ever done so noble an act.

628   If you have good sense, this path is the best;
if no knight has ever made you see him with love,
you must love this man above any emperor;
no man in the world can outmatch him in arms.'

629   Despidió se el conde,   con todo fue su vía,
            fue pora Santïago,   conplió su romería;
            enbïó la infante   esta mensajería
            con una de sus dueñas   que ella much' quería.

630   Tornó s' la mensajera   luego con el mandado
            de la coita del conde,   qu' está en grand coidado;
            vino con la respuesta   a l' infante prïado:
            dixo cómmo dexara   al conde muy laçrado:

631   'De lo que m' dixo 'l conde   ove muy grand pesar;
            contra vos al Señor   dio se a querellar,
            que vos sola l' queredes   d'este mundo sacar
            e si vos lo quisiéssedes   él podrié escapar.'

632   Diz la dueña: 'Señora,   por la fe que devedes,
            que vayades al conde   e vos lo conortedes;
            tal conde com' aquéste,   non lo desanparedes;
            si muere de tal guisa,   grand pecado faredes.'

633   Respondió a la dueña   essora la infante:
            'Bien vos digo, crïada,   tengo m' por malandante;
            de quantos males passa,   mucho so d'end' pesante,
            mas venirá sazón   que l' veré bienandante.

634   Quiero contra el conde   una cosa fazer:
            al su fuerte amor   dexar me yo vençer;
            quiero m' aventurar   e ir me lo a ver;
            todo mi coraçón   fazer l' he entender.'

635   La infant' doña Sancha,   de todo bien conplida,
            fue luego al castiello,   fizo en él sobida;
            quando vïo al conde,   tovo se por guarida.
            'Señora,' dixo 'l conde,   '¿quál es esta venida?'

636   'Buen conde,' dixo ella,   'esto faz' buen amor
            que tuelle a las dueñas   vergüença e pavor;
            olvidan los parientes   por el entendedor:
            de lo qu' él se paga   tienen lo por mejor.

629   The Count took his leave and rode off on his way;
he went to Santiago to finish his pilgrimage;
the princess then sent to Fernando this message,
with one of her ladies whom she bore deep affection.

630   Quickly did the messenger return with the news
of the plight of the Count, and his blighted state;
she came quickly with his answer to the princess's side,
saying how she had left the Count sorely hard pressed:

631   'At the words of the Count, I was filled with great sorrow;
he was moved to complain about you to the Lord,
for you alone desire to remove him from this world,
but, if you so wished, he could make his escape.

632   Mistress,' said the lady, 'by the faith you must hold,
go now to the Count, and offer him comfort;
a count such as this one you must not forsake;
if he dies such a death, then your sin will be great.'

633   The princess then made her reply to the lady:
'O nurse, mark my words, I hold myself hapless;
the ills that he suffers weigh heavy on my heart,
but there will be a time when I see his fortunes turn.

634   In regard of the Count, one thing I wish to do:
to allow myself to yield before the strength of his love;
I will venture forth and I will travel there to see him,
and unfold before him all the workings of my heart.'

635   The lady Princess Sancha, possessed of every virtue,
went straight to the castle and climbed up inside;
she set eyes on the Count, and she thought herself saved.
'My lady,' said the Count, 'to what do I owe this?'

636   'Good Count,' she replied, 'I am brought by true love,*
which gives ladies release from their shame and their fear;
they forget about their parents for the sake of their suitor;
for what brings him contentment they have highest regard.

637 Sodes por mi amor,   conde, mucho lazrado;
      ond' nunca bien oviestes   sodes en grand cuidado;
      conde, non vos quexedes   e sed bien segurado;
      sacar vos he d' aquí,   alegre e pagado.

638 Si vos luego agora   d' aquí salir queredes,
      pleito e omenaje   en mi mano faredes;
      que por dueña en mundo   a mí non dexaredes,
      comigo vendiçiones   e missa prenderedes.

639 Si esto non fazedes,   en la cárçel morredes;
      com' omne sin consejo,   nunca d' aquí saldredes;
      vos, mesquino, pensatlo,   si buen seso avedes,
      si vos por vuestra culpa   atal dueña perdedes.'

640 Quand' est' oyó el conde,   tovo se por guarido
      e dixo entre sí: '¡Si fuesse ya conplido!'
      'Señora,' dixo 'l conde,   'por verdat vos lo digo:
      seredes mi muger   e yo vuestro marido.

641 Quien d'esto vos falliere   sea de Dios fallido,
      falesca le la vida   com' falso descreído;
      ruego vos lo, señora,   – en merçed vos lo pido –
      que de lo que fablastes   no l' echedes en olvido.'

642 El conde don Fernando   dixo cosa fermosa:
      'Si vos guisar podiéredes   de fazer esta cosa,
      mientra que vos visquiéredes   nunc' habré otr' esposa;
      si d'esto vos falliere,   ¡falesca m' la Gloriosa!'

643 Quand' tod' esto ovieron   entre sí afirmado,
      luego sacó la dueña   al conde don Fernando:
      'Vayamos nos, señor,   que todo es guisado;
      del buen rey don García   non sea mesturado.'

644 El camino francés   ovieron a dexar,
      tomaron a siniestra   por un grand ençinar;
      el conde don Fernando   non podía andar;
      ovo l' ella un poco   a cuestas a llevar.

637 My Count, your love for me has brought you much distress;
for what never brought you good, you bear much sorrow;
stay your laments, my Count, and here find your comfort:
I will take you out of here, joyful and content.

638 If what you desire is to leave this place at once,
you will swear your loyalty and homage on my hand,
and that you will not leave me, for no lady in the world,
but take blessings and the sacrament with me at your side.

639 If you do not do this, in prison you will die;
as a man without counsel, you will never leave this place;
consider, you wretch, if you have any sense,
whether through your fault you will lose such a lady.'

640 When the Count heard this, he thought himself saved,
and said to himself, 'Would it were already done!'
'My lady,' said the Count, 'I tell you in truth:
you will be my wife, and I your husband.

641 He who fails you in this, let him be failed by God,
and may his life fail him, as a false disbeliever;
I beg you, my lady, – I ask you this mercy –
that you do not forget what you have told me.'

642 Count Fernando then said something very fine:
'If you can find a way to do all that you say,
as long as you live I shall have no other wife;
if I fail you in this, may the Blessed Virgin fail me.'

643 When they had made all this clear to each other,
the lady released Count Fernando at once:
'My lord, let us go now, for all is prepared;
let it not be discovered by good King García.'

644 They came to turn aside from the Road of the French*
and took a left turn through a holm-oak wood;
Count Fernando was unable to continue on foot,
and she had to carry him some way on her back.

645   Quando se fue la noche   día quier' paresçer,
        enant' que ningún omne   los podiesse veer,
        vieron un mont' espesso,   fueron s' y asconder
        e ovieron allí   la noche atender.

646   Dexemos aquí ellos   en la mata estar;
        veredes quánta coita   les quería Dios dar:
        d' un açipreste malo   que iva a caçar
        ovieron los podencos   en el rastro entrar.

647   Fueron luego los canes   do yazién en la mata;
        el conde e la dueña   fueron en grand rebata;
        el açipreste malo,   quando vio la barata,
        plogo l' qual si ganasse   a Acre e Damiata.

648   Ansí commo los vio,   començó de dezir;
        dixo: 'Donos traidores,   non os podedes ir;
        del buen rey don Garçía   non podredes foír;
        amos a dos avredes   mala muerte morir.'

649   Dixo el cond': 'Por Dios   sea la tu bondat
        que nos quieras tener   aquesta poridat;
        en medio de Castiella   dar t' he una çibdat
        de guisa que la ayas   sienpre por eredat.'

650   El falso descreído,   lleno de crüeldat,
        más que si fuessen canes   non ovo pïedat;
        diz: 'Conde, si tú quieres   que sea poridat,
        dexa me con la dueña   conplir mi voluntad.'

651   Quand' oyó don Fernando   cosa tan desguisada,
        non serié más quexado   si le diessen lançada.
        'Par Dios,' le dixo, 'pides   cosa muy desguisada;
        por poco de trabajo   demandas grand soldada.'

652   La dueña fue hartera   escontra 'l coronado:
        'Açiprest', lo que quieres   yo lo faré de grado,
        por end' non nos perdremos   amos e el condado;
        más val' que ayunemos   todos tres el pecado.'

645   As night reached its close and daybreak drew near,
       before they could be seen by the eyes of any man,
       they saw a dense wood and they went there to hide,
       and there lay in wait until nightfall arrived.

646   Let us leave the two of them hiding in the thicket,
       and you will see what pain God wished to give them:
       an evil archpriest, on his way to the hunt,*
       had hounds which now came to set out on their trail.

647   The dogs went at once to their spot in the thicket,
       and the Count and the lady were at terrible risk;
       the evil archpriest, when he saw the deceit,
       was as pleased as if he'd conquered Damietta and Acre.*

648   As soon as he saw them, he began to hold forth,
       saying: 'Traitorous lords, you have nowhere to go;
       you cannot escape the good King, don García;
       the two of you will both die a dreadful death.'

649   Said the Count, 'In God's name, may you be so kind
       that you might be willing to keep this our secret;
       I will give you a city in the middle of Castile,
       so that you may always have it as your legacy.'

650   The false unbeliever, who was brimful of cruelty –
       had they been dogs he might have shown them more pity;
       he said: 'Count, if your wish is for this to be a secret,
       then allow me to fulfil my desire with the lady.'

651   When Fernando heard him speak with such impropriety,
       bearing a lance thrust would have caused him no more pain.*
       He said to him, 'By God! What you ask is wrong indeed;
       you demand a great payment for a trifling task.'

652   In speaking to the tonsured priest, the lady was artful:
       'Archpriest, to your desire I will willingly conform,
       for thus we shall lose neither each other nor the county;
       it is better that all three of us atone for the sin.'*

653   Dixo l' luego la dueña: 'Pensat vos despojar;
       aver vos ha el conde   los paños de guardar,
       e, por que él non vea   atán fuerte pesar,
       plega vos, açipreste,   d' aquí vos apartar.'

654   Quando el arçipreste   ovo esto oído,
       ovo grand alegría   e tovo s' por guarido;
       vergüença no avía   el falso descreído;
       confonder cuidó otro   mas él fue confondido.

655   Ovieron se entramos   ya quanto d' apartar;
       cuidara se la cosa   él luego acabar;
       ovo el açipreste   con ella de travar;
       con sus braços abiertos   iva s' la abraçar.

656   La infant' doña Sancha,   dueña tan mesurada,
       – nunca omne non vio   dueña tan esforçada –
       tomó lo por la barva,   dio l' una grand tirada,
       dixo: 'Don traïdor,   de ti seré vengada.'

657   El conde a la dueña   non podié ayudar
       ca tenié grandes fierros   e non podié andar;
       su cuchiello en mano,   ov' a ella llegar;
       ovieron le entramos   al traïdor matar.

658   Quando de tal manera   morió el traïdor
       – ¡nunca merced le quiera   aver el Crïador! –
       la mula e los paños,   el mudado açor
       quiso Dios que oviessen   más onrado señor.

659   Tovieron tod' el día   la mula arrendada;
       el día fue salido,   la noche omillada;
       quando vieron que era   la noche aquedada,
       movieron se andar   por medio la calçada.

660   Dexemos y a ellos   entrados en carrera
       por llegar a Castiella,   que muy çerca ya era;
       diré de castellanos,   gente fuert' e ligera:
       avenir no s' podían   por ninguna manera.

653   Then the lady said to him, 'Take off your clothes:
        the Count will ensure that your garments are safe;
        and to spare him a sight that will cause him much pain,
        I ask that you take yourself away from this spot.'

654   When the archpriest had heard what she wanted to say,
        he was joyful at having emerged from this well;
        the false unbeliever was devoid of all shame;
        he thought to trick another, but the trick was on him.

655   The two of them retired some distance away;
        the archpriest had thought he would quickly have his way,
        and so he moved forward to take hold of the lady,
        with his arms held open, to clasp her in embrace.

656   Princess Sancha, a lady of judgment so measured,
        – no man has ever seen so courageous a lady –
        took him by the beard and threw him down hard,*
        saying, 'Traitor, on you I will have vengeance.'

657   The Count was unable to give help to the lady,*
        for he wore heavy irons and he could not walk;
        he managed to reach her, his knife in his hand,
        and between them the traitor they managed to kill.

658   When the traitor had met with his death in this way
        – may the Creator never show him mercy! –
        his mule and his garments, his already-moulted hawk,*
        all found, as God willed, a more honourable lord.

659   All the day long they kept the mule on the bridle,
        until the day ended and night was then fallen;
        and, when they saw that the night had settled in,
        they set out on their journey, on the highway.

660   Let us leave that pair here, embarked on their journey
        to arrive at Castile, which was already very near;
        I will tell of the Castilians, a strong and agile race:
        they could not find a path that would lead them to accord.

661   Los unos querién uno,   los otros querién al,
       com' omnes sin cabdiello,   avenién se muy mal.
       Fabló Nuño Laínez,   de seso natural,
       buen cavero de armas   e de señor leal.

662   Començó su razón   muy fuerte e oscura:
       'Fagamos nos señor   de una piedra dura,
       semejable al conde,   d'essa mesma fechura;
       a aquella imagen   fagamos todos jura.

663   Ansí commo al conde,   las manos le besemos,
       pongamos la en carro,   ante nos la llevemos;
       por amor del buen conde   por señor la ternemos:
       pleito e omenaje   nos a ella faremos.

664   La seña de Castiella   en la mano l' pongamos;
       si ella non fuyere,   nos otros non fuyamos;
       sin el cond' a Castiella   jamás nunca vengamos;
       el que antes tornare   por traidor le tengamos.

665   Si el conde es fuerte,   fuerte señor llevamos;
       el conde de Castiella   nos buscar le vayamos.
       Allá finquemos todos   o acá le traigamos,
       tardando esta cosa,   mucho menoscabamos.

666   Al conde de Castiella   muy fuert' onra le damos,
       él puja cada día   e nos menoscabamos;
       semeja que él lidia   e nos nunca lidiamos.
       ¡Don Cristo nos perdone   que tanto nos pecamos!

667   Que veamos qué preçio   damos a un cavero:
       somos más de trezientos   e él solo señero
       e sin él non fazemos   valía d' un dinero;
       pierde omne buen preçio   en poco de mijero.'

668   Quando Nuño Laíno   acabó su razón,
       a chicos e a grandes   plogo de coraçón;
       respondieron le luego   mucho buen infançón:
       'Todos lo otorgamos   que es con grand razón.'

661   Some desired one thing, the rest wished another;
as men with no leader, they could not agree.
Then spoke Nuño Laínez, a man born with wisdom,
a fine knight in combat, and loyal to his lord.

662   He began his remarkable, extraordinary speech:
'Let us carve our own lord from a hard piece of rock,*
to look like the Count, and have just his appearance;
to that image let us all swear our oaths of allegiance.

663   As if it were the Count, let us also kiss its hand,
let us place it in a cart that we carry before us;
for love of the good Count, we shall make it our lord,
and we shall swear to it a pledge, and do it homage.*

664   The standard of Castile let us place in its hand,
and if that does not flee, then neither shall we;
may we never come back to Castile without the Count;
any man who turns sooner, let us hold him a traitor.

665   If the Count is strong, strong too the lord we carry;
let us now set out to find the Count of Castile.
Let us all remain there or bring him back here;
by delaying in this, we deserve great scorn.

666   We pay the greatest honour to the Count of Castile;
he wins glory each day, while we earn discredit;
it seems that he does battle, but we never fight.
May Christ grant us pardon for our sins so great!

667   Let us see what value we place upon a knight:
we are more than three hundred and he is alone,
yet without him we have not the worth of a penny;
a man's good standing is lost in a moment.'

668   When Nuño Laíno had finished his speech,
all men, young and old, had delight in their hearts,
and many fine nobles were quick to reply:
'We all grant it be done, for this course is most sound.'

669   Fizieron su imagen,   com' antes dicho era,
           a figura del conde,   d'essa misma manera;
           pusieron la en carro   de muy fuerte madera;
           sobida en el carro,   entraron en carrera.

670   Todos, chicos e grandes,   a la piedra juraron:
           commo a su señor,   ansí la aguardaron;
           pora ir a Navarra   el camino tomaron,
           en el primero día   a Arlançón llegaron.

671   Desende otro día   essa buena conpaña,
           su señor much' onrado,   su seña much' estraña,
           passaron Montes d' Oca,   una fiera montaña;
           solía ser de los buenos   e los grandes d' España.

672   Caveros castellanos,   conpaña muy laçrada,
           fueron a Bilforado   fer otra albergada;
           qual a Dios demandaron,   ovieron tal posada;
           movieron s' otro día   quando al alvorada.

673   Enantes que oviessen   una legua andado,
           salida fue la noche,   el día aclarado;
           el conde con su dueña   venié mucho laçrado;
           quando vïo la seña   muy mal fue desmayado.

674   La dueña la vio antes   e ovo grand pavor;
           dixo luego la dueña: '¿Qué faremos, señor?
           Veo una grand seña,   non sé de qué color,
           o es de mi hermano   o es de Almonçor.'

675   Fueron en fuerte quexa,   non sabién qué fiziessen,
           ca non veyén montaña   do meter se pudiessen;
           non sabién con la quexa   qué consejo prendiessen,
           ca non veién logar   do guarida oviessen.

676   Eran en fuerte quexa   que nunca fue tamaña;
           quisieran si podieran   alçar se a montaña,
           que se asconderían   siquiera en cabaña;
           fue catando la seña,   mesuró la conpaña.

669 They constructed his image, as had been said,
to resemble the Count, an identical match;
they set it in a cart of the strongest wood,
and when it was installed there, they went on their way.

670 All men, young and old, swore an oath to the rock;
as though it was their lord, so it was honoured;
they set out on the road which led to Navarre,
and on that first day they arrived at Arlanzón.*

671 On the following day, that fine company of men,
their highly honoured lord and their standard so rare,
crossed the Hills of Oca, a remarkable peak,*
that was ever among the finest and greatest in Spain.

672 The Castilian knights, who had endured great hardship,
went on to Belorado to pitch their next camp;*
they found lodgings that were just what they asked of God,
and moved out the next day at the coming of dawn.

673 Before they had managed to cover one league,
the night was departed and the day broke clear;
sorely hard pressed came the Count with his lady,
and on seeing the standard he was struck with despair.

674 The lady saw it first and it caused her great fear,
and at once she said, 'My lord, what shall we do?
I see a large standard, I know not what colour;
it is either of my brother or belongs to al-Mansur.'*

675 They were in great distress, and knew not what to do,
for they could see no forest in which they could hide;
in their worry they knew not the course they should take,
for they could see no place that offered safety.

676 Grave was their distress, they had never seen greater;
were they able, they would have sought refuge in the forests,
in which they would have hidden, if only in a hut;
he studied the standard, appraising the army.

677   Conosçió en las armas   cómmo eran cristianos:
non eran de Navarra   nin eran de paganos;
conosçió cómmo eran   de pueblos castellanos
que ivan su señor   sacar d' agenas manos.

678   'Dueña,' dixo el conde,   'non dedes por end' nada:
será la vuestra mano   d'ellos todos vesada;
la seña e la gente   que vos vedes armada,
aquélla es mi seña   e ellos mi mesnada.

679   Oy vos faré señora   de pueblos castellanos;
serán todos convusco   alegres e loçanos;
todos, chicos e grandes,   besar vos han las manos;
dar vos he en Castiella   fortalezas e llanos.'

680   La dueña, que estava   triste e desmayada,
fue con aquestas nuevas   alegre e pagada;
quando vïo que era   a Castiella llegada,
dio le graçias a Dios,   que la avié bien guiada.

681   En antes qu' el su pueblo   al conde fues' llegado,
fue delant' un cavero   e sopo est' mandado:
cómmo venié el conde   alegre e pagado,
traía la infante   e venié muy cansado.

682   Las gentes castellanas,   quando aquest' oyeron,
que venié su señor   e por çierto l' ovieron;
nunca tan maño gozo   castellanos ovieron;
todos con alegría   a Dios graçias rendieron.

683   Tant' avién de grand gozo   que creer no l' quisieron;
dieron se a correr   quant' de rezio pudieron;
enantes que llegassen,   al conde conosçieron,
llegaron se a él,   en braços le cojieron.

684   Fueron besar las manos   todos a su señora,
diziendo: 'Somos ricos   castellanos agora;
infante doña Sancha,   nasçiestes en buen ora,
por end' vos resçebimos   nos todos por señora.

677 He could tell from their arms that the people were Christians:
they were not from Navarre, and nor were they pagans;
he could tell that the people were come from Castile,
on their way to free their lord from foreign hands.

678 'My lady,' said the Count, 'of this have no fear,
for every one of these men will kiss your hand;
the standard and the troops that you see bearing arms:
that is my standard and they are my army.

679 I will today make you lady of the people of Castile,
and with you they will all be elated and proud;
young and old alike, they will all kiss your hands,
and I will give you fortresses and lands in Castile.'*

680 The lady, whose mood was of sadness and despair,
grew joyful and contented on hearing this news;
when she saw that she had arrived in Castile,
she gave thanks to God who had guided her so well.

681 Before the Count's people had reached where he was,
a knight rode on ahead and learned the news:
that the Count was a man full of joy and contentment,
he was bringing the princess, and his strength was all spent.

682 When the armies of Castile then discovered this news
of the coming of their lord, who was theirs for certain,
no Castilians had ever felt delight such as theirs;
all greatly rejoicing, they gave God their thanks.

683 They felt such delight that they could not believe it,
and pelted towards him as hard as they could;
they recognized the Count before they could reach him,
and on reaching him, they clasped him in their arms.

684 To a man, they all went to kiss the hands of their lady,
saying: 'Now we Castilians are possessed of great wealth.
Princess Sancha, you were born at a favoured hour,
and so do we all now accept you as our lady.*

685   Fiziestes nos merçed,   nunca atal viemos:
        quanto bien nos fiziestes   contar non lo sabriemos;
        ....
        si non fuera por vos   cobrar non lo podriemos.

686   Sacastes a Castiella   de grand cautividat,
        fiziestes grand merçed   a toda cristiandat,
        mucho pesar a moros   – esto es la verdat –
        ¡tod' esto vos gradesca   el Rey de Magestat!'

687   Todos, ella con ellos,   con grand gozo lloravan,
        tenién que eran muertos   e que resuçitavan;
        al Rey de los çïelos   bendezién e laudavan;
        el llanto que fazían   en grand gozo tornavan.

688   Llegaron de venida   todos a Bilforado;
        aquesta villa era   en cabo del condado.
        Un ferrero muy bueno   demandaron prïado,
        el conde don Fernando   de fierros fue sacado.

689   Fueron se pora Burgos   quanto ir se podieron;
        luego que y llegaron   grandes bodas fezieron;
        non alongaron plazo,   bendiçiones prendieron,
        todos, grandes e chicos,   muy grand gozo fiçieron.

690   Alançavan tablados   todos los cavalleros,
        a tablas e escaques   jugavan escuderos;
        de otra part' matavan   los toros los monteros;
        avié y muchas çítulas   e muchos vïoleros.

691   Fazían muy grand gozo   que mayor non podían,
        dos bodas, que non una,   castellanos fazían:
        una por su señor   que cobrado avían,
        otra por que entramos   bendiçiones prendían.

692   En antes que oviessen   las bodas acabadas
        – non avié ocho días   qu' eran escomençadas –,
        fueron a don Fernando   otras nuevas llegadas,
        que venié rey García   con muy grandes mesnadas.

685   You have done us great mercy, we have never seen the like;
all the good you have done us is beyond what we can tell;
....
had it not been for you, we could never have regained him.

686   You have freed Castile from the depths of captivity,
and done a great mercy to all Christendom's lands,
bringing Moors a great sorrow – in this we speak the truth;
may the King of Majesty reward you for all this!'

687   They all, and she with them, then wept with great joy,
for they felt they had been dead and were reborn;*
they gave blessings and praise to the King in Heaven,
and they turned their former weeping to elation.

688   Now they were all arrived back in Belorado,
a town which stood right on the frontier of the county;
a highly-skilled blacksmith was sent for at once,
and from his irons Count Fernando was set free.

689   They set off for Burgos as fast as they were able,
and held a grand wedding as soon as they arrived;
they made no delay in receiving God's blessing,
and all, both young and old, made great rejoicing.

690   The knights were all taking aim at mock castles,
and the squires playing games of draughts and chess;
elsewhere the huntsmen were killing the bulls,
while many played the citole and *vihuela*.*

691   Such was their joy it could not have been greater,
for the Castilians held two celebrations, not one:
one for their lord, whom they now had recovered,
and the other as that couple was married.

692   Before those celebrations reached their close
– not a week had yet passed since they began –
a new report came to Fernando's ears:
King García was coming with a very great army.

693   Mandó luego el conde   a sus gentes guarnir;
        quando fueron guarnidas,   salió l' a resçebir;
        a cabo del condado   ovieron a salir:
        ovieron en el pleito   todos a departir.

694   Las azes fueron luego   paradas tan prïado
        – qual era su mester,   avié lo bien usado –;
        el rey de los navarros   estava bien guisado,
        començaron entramos   un torneo pesado.

695   Segund nos lo leemos,   e dize lo la lienda,
        estovo medio día   en peso la fazienda;
        cansados eran todos   e fartos de contienda;
        tomaron y por poco   los navarros emienda.

696   Llevaron los del canpo   navarro grant partida,
        muchos de castellanos   perdieron y la vida;
        de dardos e de lanças   fazién mucha ferida;
        ovo s' en poca d' ora   mucha sangre vertida.

697   Quando vio don Fernando   castellanos movidos,
        vio los estar cansados   e todos retraídos.
        Fueron de sus palabras   fuerte mient' reprendidos:
        'Por nos pierden oy sieglo   por nasçer e nasçidos.

698   Maguer que vos querades   ansí ser tan fallidos,
        fazer vos he ser buenos   a fuerça o amidos;
        si yo finare, non   querriedes ser nasçidos,
        ca seriedes por ello   traidores conosçidos.'

699   El sosaño del conde   non quesieron sofrir;
        dixeron: 'Más queremos   todos aquí morir
        que don Fernán Gonçález   esto nos fazerir;
        lo que nunca falliemos,   non queremos fallir.'

700   Tornaron en el canpo,   pensaron de ferir
        com' omnes que non han   codiçia de foír;
        fazién muchos cavallos   sin señores salir;
        podrién a grand mijero   bien los golpes oír.

693   The Count at once ordered his troops to be armed,
and when they were ready, he went out to meet him;
beyond the county's limits they then made their way:
in this conflict they would all have roles to play.

694   The battle lines were drawn up at once with such speed
– this was his trade, in which he was well versed –;
the king of the Navarrese was thoroughly prepared,
and the two of them entered a furious contest.

695   According to our reading, and as the text tells us,*
the battle remained half a day in the balance;
every man was tired and weary from the struggle;
the Navarrese came close to gaining vengeance.

696   The army of the Navarrese held the upper hand,
and there many of the Castilians lost their lives;
with darts and with lances many wounds were inflicted,
and in but a little time much blood was shed.

697   When Fernando saw the Castilians giving way,
saw them tired and all driven in retreat,
the harshest rebuke they received from his words:
'Today we harm the living and those yet to come.

698   Although you may wish so to fail in your duty,
I shall make you good men, reluctant or unwilling;
if I should die here you would all regret your birth,
for through it you would all be known as traitors.'*

699   The Count's admonition they wished not to endure,
and said: 'We would rather all die in this place,
than thus bear the censure of Fernán González;
we wish not to err where we never have before.'

700   They returned to the field to mete out their blows
as men who lack any desire to flee;
they left many horses bereft of their lords,
and the blows that they struck echoed far in the distance.

701   El conde orgulloso,   de coraçón loçano,
       vïo a su cuñado   en medio de un llano;
       puso se contra él,   la lança sobre mano;
       dixo: '¡Parta se el canpo   por nos amos, hermano!'

702   Eran uno e otro   enemigos sabudos;
       fueron se a ferir   entramos muy sañudos,
       las lanças avaxadas,   los pendones tendudos;
       dieron se grandes golpes   luego en los escudos.

703   Ferió al rey Garçía   el señor de Castiella;
       atal fue la ferida   que cayó de la siella;
       metió l' toda la lança   por medio la tetiella,
       que fuera del espalda   paresçió la cochiella.

704   Don Fernando por fuerça   ovo al rey prender,
       el pueblo de Navarra   no l' pudo defender;
       ovieron le a Burgos,   essa çibdat, traer;
       mandó l' luego el conde   en los fierros meter.

705   Doze meses conplidos   en fierros le tovieron:
       la presión fue tan mala   que peor non podieron;
       por ningunas rehenes   nunca dar le quisieron;
       non era maraviella,   que negra la fizieron.

706   Tovo lo la condessa   esto por desguisado,
       por ser ella muger   del conde don Fernando
       tener a su hermano   cautivo e laçrado,
       que era tan buen rey   de tan rico reignado.

707   Fabló con castellanos   en aquessa sazón,
       dixo pocas palabras   e muy buena razón:
       'Saquemos, castellanos,   al rey de presïón,
       porque oy los navarros   de mí quexados son.

708   Yo saqué de presión   al conde don Fernando.
       ¿por qué es él agora   contra mi tan villano?'
       ....
       ....

701   The Count felt great pride, and his heart was swelling;
       he saw his wife's brother in the middle of a plain;
       he squared up against him, his lance in his hand,
       and said, 'My brother, let us two decide the battle!'

702   The two foes knew each other intimately well,
       and they rode to do battle, both full of anger;
       their lances were lowered, their pennants aflight;
       great were the blows that they struck each other's shield.

703   King García was hit by the lord of Castile,
       and so fierce was the blow that he fell from his seat;
       the lance of the Count was thrust clean through his breast,*
       and its tip could be seen, having passed through his back.

704   Fernando overpowered the King by force,
       and the people of Navarre could not defend him;
       they took him then to Burgos, that city of renown,
       the Count at once ordering that he be set in chains.

705   They kept him chained in irons a full twelve months,
       and his treatment was as harsh as they could make it;
       there were no hostages for whom they would exchange him:
       little wonder, for they made that time a torture.

706   The Countess considered this action was wrong:
       that while she was the wife of Count Fernando,
       her brother was kept captive and ill treated,
       so great a king was he, his realm so rich.

707   At that point, she then spoke with the Castilians:
       her words were few, but packed with great good sense:*
       'Castilians, let us free the king from prison,
       for the Navarrese now bear me much ill feeling.

708   I freed Count Fernando from his prison;
       why is he now so coarse in treating me?'
       ....
       ....

[708–716]

El capítulo de cómo el conde Fernand Gonçález sacó de la prisión al rey don García
La condessa doña Sancha aviendo grand pesar del padre que yazié preso, fabló con los castellanos et díxoles assí: 'Amigos, vos sabedes de cómo vos yo saqué a vuestro señor el conde de la prisión en que l' tenié mio padre el rey don García, por que él et todos los navarros han muy grand querella de mí, ca tiene que por mí les vino este mal en que hoy están; et agora el conde es muy errado contra mí, que non quiere dar mio padre nin sacarle de la prisión. Onde vos ruego que vos seades tan mesurados que vos que roguedes al conde et travedes con él que me dé mio padre, et yo aver vos he que gradescer siempre; et éste es el primer ruego que vos yo rogué.'

Et ellos dixieron que lo farién de grado et fuéronse luego por' el conde et dixiéronle: 'Señor, pedimos vos por vuestra mesura que nos oyades. Rogamos vos, señor, et pedímosvos por merced que dedes el rey don García a su fija doña Sancha y l' mandedes sacar de la prisión, et faredes en ello grand mesura, et quantos vos lo sopieren tener vos lo han a bien, ca bien sabedes vos quamaño algo fizo ella a nos et a vos, et señor, si al fazedes non vos estará bien.'

Et tanto travaron d'él et tantol' dixieron de buenas razones et debdo que avié y, quel' fizieron otorgar lo que agora dirá aquí la Estoria, et conplirlo; et dize assí: respondió les allí estonces el conde que pues que ellos lo tenién por bien et lo querién, et aunque fuesse mayor cosa, que lo farié muy de grado, et mandól' luego sacar de los fierros. Et d' allí adelant' fizieron muchos plazeres et muchos solazes al rey don García el conde Fernand Gonçález et la condessa soña Sancha, su fija, et los nobles cavalleros de Castiella. Et en tod' aquello guisól' el cuende muy bien a él et a su conpaña de paños et de bestias et de quanto ovo mester, et envió' l pora su regno. El rey don García, pues que llegó a su regno, fuesse por el Estella, et envió por todos los omnes onrados de su regno et fizo y sus cortes; et, desque fueron todos ayuntados, dixo les assí: 'Amigos, vos sabedes cómo yo so desondrado del conde Fernand Gonçález, et la mi desondra vuestra es; et bien sepades que o yo seré d'él vengado o y porné el cuerpo.' Agora dexa aquí la estoria de fablar d'esta razón et torna a contar del rey don Sancho.

[717–720]

El capítulo de cómo el conde Fernand Gonçález fue ayudar al rey don Sancho de León contra los moros
Empós esto el rey don Sancho de León envió sus mandaderos al conde Fernand Gonçález a dezirle de cómo Abderrahmen rey de Córdova era entrado en su tierra

[708–716]

The chapter which tells how Count Fernán González freed King García from prison*

In great regret at the imprisonment of her father,* Countess Sancha addressed the Castilians and spoke these words: 'My friends, you know how I freed your lord the Count from the imprisonment in which he was held by my father King García, as a result of which my father and all the people of Navarre today bear me great resentment, for he holds that it is through me that they have come to suffer this misfortune which they now endure; and now the Count is doing me great wrong in refusing to hand over my father or free him from prison. For this reason I ask you to be so wise as to beg of the Count and insist that he hand over my father to me, and I will have reason to be grateful to you for ever. This is the first request that I have made of you.'

They said that they would willingly do so, and they went at once to the Count and said to him: 'Lord, we ask you in your wisdom to hear us. We beg of you, lord, and ask you as a boon that you give King García to his daughter Sancha and order his release from prison. You will thus be acting with great wisdom, and all those who hear of it will hold it to your credit; for you know well the extent of what she did on our behalf and yours, and, lord, if you do otherwise it will not reflect well upon you.'

So much did they prevail upon him and so many good reasons did they put to him, reminding him of the debt that he owed, that they persuaded him to grant what the History will now recount, and to enact it; and it says this: the Count then replied to them that, since they thought it right and this was their desire, and even though it was a matter of great importance, he would do it most willingly; and at once he ordered that the King be released from his irons. And from then on King García received many pleasures and many kindnesses from Count Fernán González and the Countess, daughter of the King, and the noble knights of Castile. Moreover, the Count equipped him and his company generously with clothes and with animals and with all that he needed, and he sent him on his way, back to his kingdom. King García, on reaching his kingdom, went to Estella and sent for all the noblemen of his kingdom and there assembled his court; and once they were all gathered, he spoke to them thus: 'My friends, you know what dishonour I have suffered at the hands of Count Fernán González, and my dishonour is yours, too; and you should know that I will either be avenged upon him, or die in the attempt.' At this point the story ceases to talk of this matter and once again begins to tell of King Sancho.

[717–720]

The chapter which tells how Count Fernán González went to the aid of King Sancho of León against the Moors

After this King Sancho of León sent his emissaries to Count Fernán González to tell him how Abd al-Rahman, King of Córdoba,* had entered his kingdom with

con muy grand poder de moros, et qu'él rogava mucho que l' fuesse ayudar. El conde Fernand Gonçález, luego que lo oyó, fuesse pora él quanto más aína pudo con aquellos cavalleros que tenié consigo et non quiso más y tardar. Et envió dezir por toda su tierra por cartas et por mandaderos a todos los otros cavalleros que y non eran, que se fuessen empós él. Quando el rey de León vio al conde, plógol' mucho con él et recibiól' muy bien, ca tovo que l'acorrié a muy buena sazón. Desí a cabo de ocho días llegó toda su conpaña al conde, et ovieron su acuerdo que a tercer día saliessen al campo lidiar con los moros, ca mejor serié que non yazer encerrados. Mas pues que los moros ovieron sabiduría ...

721   ....
    cóm' era y el conde con grand cavallería,
    el rey moro de Córdova, luego en otro día,
    desçercó la çibdat e fue se él su vía.

722   Levantó s' de allí, Safagún fue çercar,
    començó toda Campos de correr e robar;
    ovieron estas nuevas al conde de llegar:
    con todas sus conpañas pensó de cabalgar.

723   Conpañas de León, caveros de prestar,
    salieron con el conde, querién lo aguardar;
    non quiso el buen conde e mandó les tornar;
    ovieron leoneses d'esto fuerte pesar.

724   El conde don Fernando, con toda su mesnada,
    vino a Safagunt e falló la çercada;
    dio les un grand torneo, una lid presurada;
    fue luego en est' día la villa desçercada.

725   Avién a toda Canpos corrido e robado;
    llevavan de cristianos grand pueblo cabtivado;
    de vacas e de yeguas e de otro ganado
    tanto llevavan d'ello que non serié contado.

726   Grandes eran los llantos, grandes eran los duelos,
    ivan los padres presos, los fijos e abuelos;
    matavan a las madres, los fijos en braçuelos,
    e davan a los padres muerte con sus fijuelos.

a tremendous army of Moors, and that he was pleading with him to go to his aid. Count Fernán González, as soon as he heard this, went to him as quickly as he could with those knights that he had with him, wishing to tarry no longer where he was. And he sent word through his lands, by letters and emissaries, to all his other knights who had not been present, telling them to follow him. When the King of León saw the Count, he took delight in his arrival and was warm in his welcome, reckoning that he was coming to his aid just in time. Within a week, all the Count's company had arrived and they agreed that on the third day they would go out onto the field to do battle with the Moors, for it would be better not to find themselves pinned down. But once the Moors learned ...

721   ....
how the Count was there, with a great force of knights,
the Moorish king of Córdoba, on the very next day,
abandoned the siege and went off on his way.

722   He left there and went to lay siege to Sahagún,
beginning to make raids and take plunder from all Campos;*
word of these deeds made their way to reach the Count,
who determined to ride out with all his company.

723   The Leonese warriors were fine knights indeed,
and rode out with the Count, for they sought to keep him safe;
the good Count was unwilling and bade them turn back,*
and by this the Leonese were deeply saddened.

724   That man Count Fernando, with all of his army,
came to Sahagún and found it under siege;
he waged a fierce contest, a hard-fought battle,
and at once, on that same day, the siege was lifted.

725   The whole land of Campos they had raided and plundered,
and many Christians had been carried off as captives;
of cows and of mares and of other kinds of livestock
they took so much their spoils could not be tallied.

726   Great was the weeping, and great the lamentation,
with parents, children, and grandparents all captured;
mothers were murdered, with their children in their arms;
both fathers and their sons were put to death.

727 Ivan con muy grand robo alegres e pagados,
non podían andar, que ivan muy cansados;
ovo los el buen conde aína alcançados;
fueron con su venida todos mal espantados.

728 Ferió luego entr' ellos, non les dio nul vagar,
com' águila fanbrienta que se querié cebar;
quand' oyeron los moros a '¡Castiella!' nonbrar,
quisieran si podieran en Córdova estar.

729 Dexaron y la prea, toda a su mal grado;
quien mejor fuir podía tenié s' por venturado.
El rey de cordoveses fincó end' en malfado;
bendizié a Mafómad quand' d'end' fue escapado.

730 El conde don Fernando, de ardides çimiento,
señor de buenas mañas, de buen enseñamiento,
en los pueblos paganos fizo grand escarmiento;
falló e mató d'ellos a todo su talento.

731 Los que avían muertos non los podié tornar;
non dexó de la prea nula cosa levar.
Mandó ir los cativos todos a su lugar;
dezién: '¡Fernán Gonçález, dexe te Dios reignar!'

732 El conde don Fernando, con toda su mesnada,
cuando ovo la prea a sus casas tornada,
por verdat avié fecha muy buena cavalgada;
a León el buen conde luego fizo tornada.

733 Falló los leoneses sañudos e irados;
por que con él non fueran falló los despagados;
los unos e los otros fueron mal denostados;
coidavan sines duda reignar y los pecados.

734 Reïgna de León, navarra natural,
era de castellanos enemiga mortal;
mataran le 'l hermano, quería les grand mal;
de buscarles la muerte non pensava en al.

727   The Moors, with great plunder, were joyful and contented:
their exhaustion was so great that they could not walk;
in a very short time, the good Count had reached them,
and his coming filled each one of them with dread.

728   At once he struck among them and gave them no respite,
like a ravenous eagle in search of its food;
when the Moors heard them send up their cry of 'Castile!',
were it possible, they longed to be in Córdoba.

729   They cast off all their booty, though much against their will,
and he whose flight was fastest then held himself blessed;
the Cordobese king was there left to a bitter fate,
blessing Mohammed when he had managed his escape.

730   Count Fernando, who was the epitome of valour,
a lord of fine conduct, distinguished in learning,
taught the harshest of lessons to the pagan peoples,
as he hunted them down, and he killed them at will.

731   Those who were now dead he could not send back;
he let the Moors take nothing of the booty.
He ordered all the captives go back to their homes,
who cried: 'Fernán González, may God let you reign!'

732   Count Fernando, along with the whole of his army,
once he had let the prisoners return to their homes,
had waged what was in truth a tremendous campaign;
and the good Count turned at once for León.

733   He found the Leonese full of fury and rage,
displeased that they had not been in his company;
each side was bitterly abused by the other;
the devils thought that rule was doubtless theirs.

734   The Queen of León, a native of Navarre,
to the Castilians was the deadliest of foes;
they had killed her brother, and she wished them great ill;
she thought of nothing but of seeking all their deaths.

735   Querié a castellanos   de grado desonrar,
         querié si se l' fiziesse   su hermano vengar;
         avivó leoneses   por con ellos lidiar;
         non la devié por ende   ningún omne rebtar.

736   Era d' amas las partes   la cosa ençendida,
         sopo lo la reïna   e tovo s' por guarida;
         y avié el dïablo   muy grand tela ordida,
         mas fue por el buen rey   la pelea partida.

737   Los unos de los otros   fueron mal denostados,
         fincaron unos d' otros   todos desafïados;
         fueron los castellanos   a sus tierras tornados;
         non fueron por dos años   a las cortes llamados.

738   Enbïó el buen conde   a León mensajeros
         que rogaban al rey   que le dies' sus dineros.
         Dixo el rey don Sancho: 'Allá son mis porteros:
         de commo allegaren,   dar l' hemos los primeros.'

739   Tornaron se al conde,   dixieron l' el mandado;
         que deçía el rey   que los darié de grado,
         mas que aún non era   el su pecho llegado,
         por tanto se l' avía   su aver detardado.

740   Al conde mucho plogo   por que tanto tardava,
         entendié que abría   lo que él codiçiava;
         por que tanto tardaba   el conde y ganava;
         plaçié l' de voluntad   del plaço que passava.

741   El rey Sancho Ordóñez   dio se muy grand vagar,
         ovo después del plaço   tres años a passar;
         ovo en est' comedio   otro tanto pujar;
         todos los de Uropa   non lo podrién pagar.

742   Dexemos Sanch' Ordóñez   en aqueste lugar:
         enbïó sus dineros   al buen conde pagar;
         el conde don Fernando   non los quiso tomar:
         ovo en este pleito   la cosa a dexar.

735   To dishonour the Castilians was her fervent wish,
and to win vengeance for her brother, if she could;
she spurred the Leonese to do battle with them;
on this account, no man could upbraid her.

736   On both sides did the quarrel grow inflamed:
the Queen found out, and thought her aim achieved;
the Devil had spun a vast web in this affair,
but the good King brought the conflict to a close.*

737   Each side was bitterly abused by the other,
and by each other they had both been issued challenge;
the Castilians had turned for their own native lands,
and for two years they were never called to parliament.

738   To León the good Count sent his messengers,
requesting that the King should now settle his debt;
King Sancho said: 'My tax collectors are now on their rounds;
upon their arrival, we shall make the first payment.'

739   Returning to the Count, they gave him the message
that the King said he would willingly pay him,
but, since his taxes were not yet collected,
for that reason had his payment been delayed.

740   The Count took much pleasure in the lengthy delay,
for he knew that he would get what he desired:*
the more the King delayed meant the Count's greater gain,
and deep was his elation at how late it became.

741   King Sancho Ordóñez was very slow in acting:
three years he let pass from the date they agreed;
but such was the increase to his debt in that time,
that all the people of Europe could not have paid it.

742   At this point, let us leave Sancho Ordóñez:
he sent his money to the good Count in payment,
but Count Fernando was unwilling to accept it,
and their pact was thus left uncompleted.

743   Dexemos tod' aquesto,   en Navarra tornemos
           – aún de los navarros   partir non nos podemos –
           allá do lo dexamos,   assí commo leemos:
           en Estella l' dexamos,   allá lo enpeçemos.

744   El rey de los navarros   en las cortes estando,
           a todas sus conpañas   muy fuerte se quexando
           del mal que le fiçiera   el conde don Ferrando,
           ....

745   Dixo les que tal cosa   non querié endurar,
           d' un condeziello malo   tantos daños tomar;
           que con él non quería   otra mient' pleitear,
           mas que querié morir   o se querié vengar.

746   Movió se de Estella   con todo su poder,
           vino pora Castiella,   començó l' a correr;
           essora ovo 'l conde   contra León mover:
           non quedó en la tierra   quien ge la defender.

747   Corrió toda Burueva   e toda Piedralada,
           corrió los Montes d' Oca,   buena tierra provada;
           corrió Río d' Ovierna,   de pan bien abastada;
           a las puertas de Burgos   fiço su albergada.

748   Quesiera, si pudiera,   la condessa levar
           por amor que pudiesse   al conde desonrar;
           la condessa fue ....
           ....

749   Quand' ovo el condado   corrido e robado,
           levaron mucha prea   e mucho de ganado;
           con muy fuerte ganançia   tornó s' a su reinado,
           mas fue a poco tienpo   cara miente conprado.

750   Quando fue don Fernando   a Castiella tornado,
           falló el su condado   corrido e robado;
           de ganados e d' omnes   falló mucho llevado,
           ....

743
Let us leave all of this and return to Navarre
– from the Navarrese we can still not depart –,
there where we left the tale, just as we read it:*
we left off in Estella; there let us begin.

744
While the Navarrese king was in his court,
complaining bitterly to all of his retinue
of the ill he had been done by Count Fernando,
....

745
He told them that he would not endure such a thing
– to be done such harm by a petty little count –,
and that he would deal with him in no other way,
but wished to take his vengeance, or die in the attempt.

746
He marched out from Estella with all of his army,
and came to Castile, which he started to raid;
at that point, the Count was to move on León;*
there was no-one in the land who could defend it from him.

747
He raided all Bureba and all of Petralata;
he raided the Hills of Oca, a fine land of renown;
he raided the Ubierna valley, with its rich stocks of bread,
and pitched his camp at the very gates of Burgos.*

748
He wished, if he could, to carry off the Countess
in his desire to bring dishonour on the Count;
the Countess was ....
....

749
After he had raided and plundered the county,
his army made off with many prisoners and cattle;
returning to his kingdom with valuable gains;
but the price he paid would soon be high indeed.

750
When Fernando returned to the land of Castile,
he found his county had been raided and plundered:
stripped of much cattle, and many of its men,
....

751 Enbïó l' don Ferrando luego desafïar:
    que si lo que levara no l' quesiesse tornar,
    que irié a Navarra sus ganados buscar

    ....

752 Quando al rey Garçía llegó el cavallero,
    recabdó su mandado commo buen mensajero;
    dixo que no l' daría valía d' un dinero,
    de lo al que l' deçía qu' era bien plaçentero.

753 El uno nin el otro alongar no l' quesieron:
    juntaron sus poderes quant' aína pudieron;
    cad' uno de su parte grand gente aduxeron;
    el rey e don Ferrando buscar se andovieron.

754 Juntaron se en uno en un fuerte vallejo,
    buen lugar pora caça de liebres e conejo;
    cojen y mucha grana con que tiñen bermejo;
    al pie le passa Ebro much' irado, sobejo.

755 Valpirre l' diçen todos, e assí le llamaron,
    do el rey e el conde amos se ayuntaron;
    el uno contra 'l otro amos s'endereçaron,
    e la fuert' lid canpal allí escomençaron.

756 Non podría más fuerte nin más brava seer,
    ca y les iva todo, levantar o caer;
    el conde nin el rey non podién más façer;
    los unos e los otros façién tod' su poder.

757 Muy grand' fue la fazienda, mucho más el roído,
    darié el omne bozes e non serié oído;
    el que oído fuesse serié com' grand tronido;
    non podrié oír voçes nin ningún apellido.

758 Grandes eran los golpes, mayores non podían,
    los unos e los otros tod' su poder façían;
    muchos caién en tierra que nunca se erçían;
    de sangre los arroyos mucha tierra cobrían.

751   Fernando at once sent a challenge to the King:
        that, if he was unwilling to return what he had taken,
        then Fernando himself would seek his cattle in Navarre
        ....

752   When the knight had arrived before King García,
        he completed his errand, as befits a good ensign;
        the King refused to give even the value of a penny,
        and said he welcomed all the rest of the message.

753   Neither man wished to let the matter drag on,
        but they gathered their forces with all possible speed,
        as each man assembled a sizeable army;
        the King and Fernando went to seek each other out.

754   The two armies clashed in a deep-sided valley,
        a fine place for hunting for rabbit and hare;
        they gather there much grain to make the red dye,*
        and the torrent of the Ebro does rage at its foot.

755   All call it Valpierre, and so did they then,*
        where King and Count were joined alike in combat;
        each against the other, they both made their stand;
        there was the beginning of the fierce pitched battle.

756   The battle could not have been crueller or more fierce,
        for therein lay their all: to rise up or to fall;
        neither Count nor King could have done a thing more,
        and both sides did everything that lay in their power.

757   The battle was a great one, but dwarfed by the din;
        a man could cry out shouting and still go unheard;
        he who could be heard would have a voice like thunder;
        no shouts could be heard, nor the great cries of war.

758   The blows struck were great, they could not have been greater,
        as men of each army used all of their strength;
        many fell to the ground who would never rise up,
        as rivers of blood covered swathes of the land.

759   Assaz eran navarros   caveros esforçados,
             que en qualquier lugar   serién buenos provados;
             omnes son de grand cuenta,   de coraçón loçanos,
             mas escontra el conde   todos desventurados.

760   Quiso Dios al buen conde   esta graçia façer,
             que moros nin cristianos   non le podién vençer;

             ....

             ....

*El capítulo de cómo el rey de León envió dezir al conde qu'él fuesse a cortes o quel'
dexasse el condado*
Andados VII años del regnado d'este rey don Sancho de León, et fue esto en la Era
de DCCCC et LXXI años, et andava otrossí estonçes el año de la Encarnatión del
Señor en DCCCC et XXXI, et del imperio de Henric Emperador de Roma en XVI.
      El conde Fernán Gonçález, pues que ovo vençudo al rey don García, como
avemos dicho, et fue tornudo a so condado, llegól' mandado del rey de León qu'él
fuesse a cortes o quel' dexasse el condado. El conde, quando ovo leídas las cartas
qu'el rey enviara d'esto, envió por sus ricos omnes et por todos los cavalleros
onrados de Castiella. Et desque fueron venidos a él, díxoles assí:
      'Amigos e parientes, yo so vuestro señor natural et ruego vos que me consegedes
assí como buenos vassallos deven fazer a señor. El rey de León me ha enviado dezir
por sus cartas quel' dé el condado, et yo quiero gelo dar, ca non serié derecho de ge
lo tener por fuerça, por que nos avrié que dezir et retraer a mí et a quantos viniessen
después de mí si yo al ende fiziesse. De más non so yo omne de alçarme con tierra,
et los castellanos tales fechos como éstos non los suelen fazer. Et quando fuesse
sonado por España que nos alçáramos con la tierra al rey de León, todos quantos
buenos fechos fiziemos todos serién perdudos por y. Ca si faze omne cient bienes et
después faze un yerro señero, antes le contarán el un mal fecho que los cient buenos
que aya fechos, et esto nasce todo de envidia. Et nunqua nasció omne en el mundo
que a todos los omnes fuesse comunal. Et por ende dizen a las vezes del grand mal
bien o del bien grand mal: pues nos avemos soffrido grand lazerio et estamos en
estado qual nunqua cuedamos, loado a Dios, et si assí lo perdiéssemos toda nuestra
lazeria serié de balde. Et nos por lealtad nos preciamos de siempre e assí sea pora
siempre, et por ende quiero yo ir a las cortes si por bien lo tenedes, et quando yo
allá fuere non seremos reptados. Amigos e vassallos, oído avedes ya lo que vos
he mostrado, et si vos otro consejo sabedes mejor que éste, ruégovos que me lo
digades, ca si yo errado fuere vos en grand culpa yazedes.

759   Bold men enough were the knights of Navarre
        that their quality would nowhere go unnoted;
        they are men of great worth, who are proud of heart,
        but against the Count, Fortune shunned them all.

760   God wished to bestow on the good Count this gift:
        that neither Moors nor Christians could defeat him

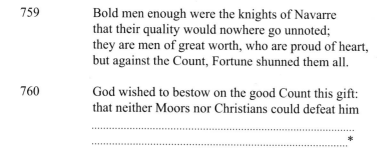

*The chapter which tells how the King of León sent word to the Count that he should attend the parliament or cede to him the county**

Seven years having passed of the reign of this King Sancho of León, in Era* 971, and in the year 981 after the Incarnation of the Lord and in the sixteenth year of the rule of Henry, Emperor of Rome.

Once Count Fernán González had defeated King García, as we have said, and returned to his county, a message reached him from the King of León that he should attend the parliament or cede to him the county. The Count, when he had read the letter that the King had sent him about this, sent for his leading nobles and for all the honoured knights of Castile. And once they had come to him, he spoke to them as follows:

'My friends and kinsmen, I am your natural lord and I ask you to advise me, just as good vassals are duty-bound to do for their lord. The King of León has sent me a written instruction that I cede to him the county, and I am willing to do so, for it would not be right to keep it from him by force, as a result of which he would have cause to make criticism of me and all those who came after me if I reacted otherwise. Moreover, I am not a man to seize land for myself, and that is not the manner in which Castilians are accustomed to act. And, when word went round Spain that we had taken land belonging to the King of León, all the good acts we perform would thereby be rendered as naught. For, if a man commits a hundred good acts and then makes one single error, men will sooner tell of the one wrong action than his hundred good ones, and this is all born of envy. And no man was ever born in the world who was the same to all men. And for that reason at times people speak well of a great ill and very ill of a good: since we have come through great hardship and are in a position we never imagined, thanks be to God, if we were to spoil it in this way, all that we have endured would be in vain. And we have always set great store by loyalty and so may it always be, and therefore I wish to go to the parliament if you consider it right, and when I am there we shall not be open to criticism. Friends and vassals, now you have heard what I have set before you, and if you know of any counsel that is better than this, I ask that you tell me, for if I am in error, then great is your guilt.

Et la cosa que a señor más cumple es buen consegero, ca mucho vale más que aquel que bien lidia por que en el consegero yaze bien e mal. Et el señor ha se de consejar mucho a menudo por que non le ayan los omnes en quel' travar, et puede por mal consegero tomar tal yerro que nunqua, por lidiar que faga, le puede desfazer. E el buen consegero non deve aver miedo nin vergüença al señor, mas dezirle toda la verdad e lo que entiende que es derecho. Mas algunos hay que en logar de ser consegeros son losengeros et non quieren o non osan consejar al señor si non lo entienden quel' plaze, et dizen que aquello es lo mejor. Et estos tales non se pueden salvar que muy grand culpa non han en esto, ca se puede perder un gran omne por mal consegero. Mas el que bien quiere consejar a señor deve primero ver e pensar tod' el fecho que es o a que puede recodir fasta la postremería, e deve guardar en sí mismo que non sea vandero; e non se deve vencer nin por miedo nin por vergüença nin por gran enemistad nin por grand amor nin otrossí por grand desamor nin por dar ni prometer, si consejo derecho quiere dar a señor. Todo esto vos digo por que non menoscabedes del buen prez que avedes, ca si por alguna falla huviades d'él descender, apenas puede ser que lo nunqua podades cobrar. E amigos, sobre todo ha mester que guardedes lealtad, ca, maguer que muere la carne, la maldad que omne faze nunqua muere, et fincan d'él sus parientes con muy mal heredamiento. Assaz vos he mostrado carreras por o seades buenos et vos guardedes de caer en yerro, ca bien sé que antes de pocos días seredes en tal cueita que avredes mester seso et esfuerço. Et vos todos sabedes que el rey me quiere muy grand mal e cierto so que non podré escapar que non sea preso o maltrecho; et allí veré yo cómo me accorredes o qué consejo avredes pora sacar me ende. Et digo vos que, si ir non quisiere a aquellas cortes, que me pueden reptar, et vos bien sabedes que non deve lidiar el omne que tuerto tiene, ca Dios non le quiere ayudar. Et más vale ser muerto o preso que non fazer mal fecho que después hayan a los parientes que retraer. Et esto es lo que yo quiero fazer si vos lo tenedes por bien e quiero me ir luego e ruégovos que aguardedes a García fijo mio.'

Et espidió se estonces d'ellos et fuese de ida, e non quiso consigo levar más de VII cavalleros. Et assí como llegó a León non le salió a recebir omne ninguno, et tóvolo él por mala señal. Otro día fuesse pora palacio et fue por besar la mano al rey, et él no ge la quiso dar, e díxol': 'Tolled vos allá, cuende, ca mucho sodes loçano. Bien ha tres años que non quisiestes venir a mis cortes; de más alçastes me vos con el condado et devedes ser reptado por ende. E sin esto fiziestes me muchos pesares et muchos tuertos et nunqua me los mejorastes; mas fío en Dios que, ante que d' aqui salgades, me faredes ende buen derecho. Pero si todos los tuertos que me avedes fecho me quisiéredes emendar assí como mi corte mandare, dad me buenos fiadores a ello.'

Moreover, what most befits a lord is a good counsellor,* for he is of far worth than the man who fights well in battle, since it depends on the counsellor whether he does right or wrong. And the lord must take advice very frequently so that men have no means of ensnaring him, and through a bad counsellor he may make such an error that, however hard he struggles, can never be undone. And the good counsellor must not be afraid or shy of the lord, but rather tell him all the truth and what he understands to be right. But there are some who, instead of being counsellors, are flatterers, and will not or dare not advise their lord unless they understand that something pleases him, and they say that is the best thing. And such men as these can have no salvation as being without great guilt in this matter, for a great man can be ruined by a bad counsellor. But the man who wishes to give advice to his lord must first see and think through the whole matter as it is or as it might turn out, right through to the end; and he must take care in himself that he is not partisan; and he must not be swayed by fear or embarrassment, by great enmity, great love, or great hostility, and neither by gifts nor promises, if he wishes to give his lord the right advice. I tell you all this so that you will not do damage to the good reputation that you possess, for if through some wrong your esteem should be lessened, it may be unlikely that you will ever recover it. And, my friends, it is necessary above all that you remain loyal, for although flesh dies, the wrong that man does never dies, and his family are left with a sorry inheritance indeed. I have shown you a good number of ways whereby your conduct can be good and you can keep yourselves from falling into error, for I know well that within a few days your troubles will be such that you will have need of both wisdom and valour. And you all know that the King wishes me very great harm and I am sure that I will not be able to escape without suffering prison and ill treatment; and through this I will see how you come to my aid or what plan you will have to free me from there. And I tell you that, if I am not willing to attend that parliament, then I am left open for challenges, and you know well that a man who is in the wrong must not fight, for it is not God's will to help him. And it is better to be dead or imprisoned than to commit a wrong deed which later may be held against your family's account. And this is what I wish to do if you reckon it right; and I wish to go at once, and I ask that you give your protection to my son García.'*

And then he took his leave of them and went on his way, not wishing to take with him any more than seven knights. And when he arrived in León, not a single man went out to meet him, which he took as a bad sign. The next day he went to the palace and made to kiss the hand of the King, who would not give it to him but said: 'Be gone from here, Count, for great is your arrogance. It is three full years that you have been unwilling to come to my parliament, and in addition you stole the county from me, on which basis you must be challenged. This aside, you have caused me much grievance and many wrongs for which you have never made amends; but I trust in God that, before you leave here, you will give me my full due in this affair. But if you are willing to make amends for all the wrongs that you have done me, following the instructions of my parliament,* then give me good guarantors to ensure it.'

Pues que el rey ovo acabada su razón, respondiól' el conde, como omne muy bien razonado et de muy buen seso, mas non le tovo ninguna pro a esta sazón. Et razonó assí el conde: 'Señor, de lo que dezides que me alcé con la tierra, non lo fiz nin vengo de logar por fazer tal fecho, ca por lealdad e por mañas téngome por cavallero complido. Mas fui d' aquí la otra vez muy mal desondrado de los leoneses, et por esto non vinía a las cortes. Pero por una razón si me alçasse con la tierra non faría sin guisa, ca me tenedes mio aver forçado bien a tres años. Et vos sabedes de quál guisa fue el pleito, et cartas hay d'ello entre mí et vos que, si me non pagássades los dineros al plazo, que fuessen cada día doblados. Et vos dadme fiadores otrossí que me cumplades mio aver assí como dize la carta, et yo darvos he fiadores otrossí que vos emiende quantas querellas de mí avedes, assí como vuestra corte mandare.'

El rey fue muy sañudo contra él et mandól' prender allí et echarle en fierros.

El capítulo de cómo el conde Fernand Gonçález salió d'aquella prisión

Quando los castellanos sopieron que el conde era preso, ovieron muy grant pesar et fizieron por ende tamaño duelo como sil' toviessen muerto delant. La condessa doña Sancha otrossí quando lo sopo, cayó amortida en tierra et yogo por muerta una grand pieça del día. Mas pues que entró en su acuerdo, dixiéronle: 'Señora, non fazedes recabdo en vos quexar tanto, ca por vos quexar non tiene pro al conde nin a nos, mas ha mester que catemos alguna carrera por quel' podamos sacar por fuerça o por alguna arte o por qual guisa quier.'

Desí ovieron so acuerdo et fablaron mucho en ello por quál manera lo podrién sacar. Et dizié y cada uno aquello quel' semejava guisado, mas por tod' esso aún non podién fallar carrera por o lo pudiessen fazer. Et por que el coraçón del omne siempre está bulliendo et pensando arte fasta que falle carrera por o pueda complir aquello que ha sabor, non queda, et la fuerte cosa se faze ligera de fazer d'esta guisa, ca el grand amor todas las cosas vence. Et los castellanos tan grand sabor avién de sacar de la prisión a su señor el cuende que su coraçón les dixo quál serié lo mejor. Desí ayuntáronse D cavalleros muy bien guisados de cavallos et de armas, et juraron todos sobre los santos evangelios que fuessen todos con la condesa pora provar sil' podrién sacar. Et desque esta jura fizieron, movieron de Castiella et fuéronse de noche, et non quisieron ir por carrera ninguna, mas por los montes et por los valles desviados por que non los viessen los omnes nin fuessen ellos descubiertos. Et quando llegaron a Mansiella, la del camino, dexáronla de diestro e alçáronse suso contra la somoça et fallaron un monte muy espesso et posaron todos allí en aquel monte.

When the King had finished speaking, the Count answered him, as a man of much good sense and great wisdom, but on this occasion it was of no benefit to him. And the Count put forward this argument: 'My lord, with regard to what you say of how I stole the county, neither did I do so nor do I come from a place where such a thing might be done, for through both loyalty and conduct I consider that I am a knight of high bearing. But on the previous occasion I left here gravely dishonoured by the Leonese, and for that reason I did not attend parliament. However, for one reason, if I were to take the land I would not be acting unreasonably, for you have kept my possessions against my will for a full three years. And you know what the terms of the agreement were and there exists a contract between the two of us such that, if you did not pay me the money by the due date, each day the amount was to be doubled. So you give me guarantors to ensure that you will make payment of my money in line with the contract, and I will do likewise in order that I give you satisfaction for all the grievances that you have against me, following the instructions of your parliament.'

The King flew into a rage against him and ordered him to be arrested there and then and cast into irons.*

The chapter which tells how Count Fernán González was freed from that imprisonment

When the Castilians knew that the Count had been imprisoned, they were deeply troubled and so their grieving was as great as if they had his dead body before them. Likewise, when Countess Sancha learned the news, she fell in a faint to the floor and lay there as if dead for a great part of the day. However, when she recovered her senses, they said to her: 'Lady, you do not act wisely by lamenting so, for your lament does no good to the Count or to us; rather, it is necessary that we devise some way by which we can free him by force, by deception, or by whatever means we can.'

Then, agreeing on this, they talked at length about the matter and about how they could free him. In that discussion each one said what he felt to be wise, but they could nevertheless find no way by which they could achieve it. And since man's heart is always working and scheming until he can find a means by which he can achieve what he desires, it does not remain still, and what is difficult thus becomes easy to achieve, since great love overcomes all things. And the Castilians had such a great desire to release their lord the Count from prison that their heart told them what would be the best thing to do. Thus five hundred knights, very well equipped with horses and arms, assembled and swore on the holy Gospels all to go with the Countess to see whether they could release him. And as soon as they had sworn this oath, they set out from Castile and travelled by night, not wishing to go by any road but through the woodland and valleys off the beaten track, so that no men would see them and they would not be discovered. And when they reached Mansilla* on the Pilgrim Way, they went off to the right and rode up to the hills where they found a very thick wood and in that wood they all rested.

La condessa doña Sancha dexólos estar allí et fuesse ella pora León con dos cavalleros et non más, con su esportiella al cuello et su bordón en la mano como romera. Et fízolo saber al rey de cómo iva en romería a Sanct Yague et quel' rogava quel' dexasse ver al conde. El rey envió l' dezir quel' plazía muy de buena miente, et salió a recebirla fuera de la villa con muchos cavalleros bien quanto una legua. Et desque entraron en la villa fuesse el rey pora su posada et la condessa fue ver al conde. Et quandol' vio fuel' abraçar, llorando mucho de los ojos. El conde estonces conortóla et díxol' que se non quexasse, ca a sofrir era todo lo que Dios querié dar a los omnes, et que tal cosa por reys e por grandes omnes contesçié. La condessa envió luego dezir al rey quel' rogava mucho como a señor bueno y mesurado que mandasse sacar al conde de los fierros, diziéndol' que cavallo travado nunca bien podié fazer fijos. Dixo el rey estonces: 'Si Dios me vala, tengo que dize verdad', et mandól' luego sacar de los fierros.

Et desí folgaron toda la noche amos en uno, et fablaron y mucho de sus cosas et pusieron cómo fiziessen tod' aquello segund que lo tenién ordenado si Dios ge lo quisiesse enderesçar assí. Et levantóse la condessa de muy grand mañana quando a los matines, et vistió al conde de todos sus paños d'ella, et el conde, mudado d'esta guisa, fuesse pora la puerta en semejança de dueña, et la condesa cerca d'él et encubriéndose quanto más et mejor pudo. Et quando llegaron a la puerta dixo la condessa al portero quel' abriesse la puerta. El portero respondió: 'Dueña, saber lo hemos del rey antes, si lo toviéredes por bien.' Dixol' ella estonces: 'Par Dios, portero, non ganas tú ninguna cosa en que yo tarde aquí et que non pueda después complir mi jornada.' El portero, cuedando que era la dueña et que saldrié ella, abrióle la puerta et salió el conde. Et la condessa fincó dentro tras la puerta encubriéndose del portero, de guisa que nunqua lo entendió.

Et el conde pues que salió non se espidió nin fabló por que por ventura non fuesse entendudo en la boz e se estorvasse por y lo que él et la condessa querién. Et fuesse luego derecha mientre pora un portal de cómo le consejara la condessa, do estavan aquellos dos cavalleros suyos atendiéndol' con un cavallo. Et el conde, assí como llegó, cavalgó en aquel cavallo que tenién presto; e començáronse de ir et salieron de la villa muy encubierta mientre et dieron se a andar quanto más pudieron derecha mientre por al logar do dexaran los cavalleros. Et quando llegaron a la somoça fuéronse pora a aquel mont do aquellos cavalleros estavan atendiendo. Et el conde, quando los vio, ovo con ellos muy grand plazer como omne que saliera de tal logar.

Countess Sancha left them there and went to León with only two knights, with her basket round her neck and her staff in her hand like a pilgrim.* And she let the King know how she was going on pilgrimage to Santiago and that she was asking him to let her see the Count. The King sent her word that he would do so with pleasure and went out to meet her a full league outside the city with a large party of knights. And once they had entered the city the King went to his dwelling and the Countess went to see the Count. When she saw him she went to embrace him, with tears streaming from her eyes. The Count then comforted her and told her not to lament, for suffering was all that God wished to give to men, and that such things happened to kings and men of rank. The Countess quickly sent word to the King that she begged him as a good and wise man that he order the release of the Count from his irons, telling him that a tethered stallion could never sire colts. Then the King said: 'May God help me, I hold that she speaks the truth!', and ordered that he at once be released from his chains.

Then the two of them rested together all night, and spoke at length there of their affairs, and set out how they would bring to pass the plans that they had made, if God determined so to guide them. And the Countess rose in the early morning at the hour of Matins* and dressed the Count in all her clothes,* and the Count, so transformed, went to the gate with the appearance of a lady, with the Countess at his side and disguising herself as far and as well as she could. And when they reached the gate the Countess told the gateman to open it. He replied: 'My lady, we must first have word from the King, if you hold that good.' Then she said: 'In God's name, gateman, you gain nothing by my delaying here and then being unable to complete my full day's walking.' The gateman, thinking that it was the lady and that she would be the one leaving, opened the gate to her and the Count went out. And the Countess remained inside behind the gate, keeping herself hidden from the gateman in such a way that he never found out.

And the Count, once he had gone out, neither took his leave nor spoke a word, lest by chance his voice should betray his identity and what he and the Countess desired thereby be thwarted. And he then passed directly through a gateway, just as the Countess had explained to him, where those two knights of hers were awaiting him with a horse. And the Count, as soon as he arrived, mounted that horse which they held ready; and they galloped off and left the city in great secrecy, riding as fast as they could straight to the place where they had left the knights. And when they reached the hills they went straight to that wood where those knights were waiting. And the Count, on seeing them, took great pleasure in their company as would a man who had left such a place.

El capítulo de cómo fizo el rey con la condessa pues que sopo que el conde era ido
Quando el rey don Sancho sopo que era ido el conde e por quál arte le sacara la condessa, pesól' así como si oviesse perdudo el regno. Pero non quiso ser errado contra la condessa, e desque fue ora fuela ver a su posada do albergara con el conde et assentóse con ella a aver sus razones en uno, et preguntóla e díxol' sobre la ida del conde cómo osara ella enssayar tal cosa nin sacar le d' allí. Respondiól' la condessa et dixo: 'Señor, atrevíme en sacar el conde d' aquí por que vi que estava en grand cueita et por que era cosa que me convinié cada que lo yo pudiesse guisar. Et de más, atreviéndome en la vuestra mesura, tengo que lo fiz' muy bien, et vos, Señor, faredes contra mí como buen señor et buen rey, ca fija so de rey e mugier de muy alto varón; et vos non querades fazer contra mí cosa desguisada, ca muy gran debdo he con vuestros fijos et en la mi desondra grand parte avredes vos. Et así como sodes vos de muy buen coñosçer et muy entendudo señor, devedes escoger lo mejor et catar que non fagades cosa que vos ayan los omnes en que travar. Et yo por fazer derecho non devo caer mal.'

Pues que la condessa ovo acabada su razón, respondiól' rey don Sancho d'esta guisa: 'Condessa, vos fiziestes muy buen fecho et a guisa de muy buena dueña, que será contada la vuestra bondad por siempre. Et mando a todos mios vassallos que vayan convusco et vos lieven fasta do es el conde et que non trasnochedes sin él.' Los leoneses fizieron assí como el rey les mandó et levaron la condessa muy onrada mientre como a dueña de tan alta guisa. El conde quando la vio, plógol' mucho con ella et tovo quel' avié Dios fecho mucha merced, et desí fuesse con ella e con toda su conpaña pora su condado.

De cómo el conde Fernand Gonçález envió demandar su aver al rey e de cómol' dio el rey el condado por ello
Enpos esto que dicho es, el conde Fernand Gonçález de Castiella que non sopo estar assessegado et quedo pues que conde fue de Castilla, ca nin le dexaron los moros nin los reys moros nin los cristianos estar en paz, envió estonces dezir al rey don Sancho de León quel' diesse su aver quel' devié por el cavallo et el açor quel' comprara, si non que non podrié estar qu'él non pendrasse por ello. El rey don Sancho non le envió respuesta dond' él fuesse pagado, et el conde ayuntó estonces todo su poder et, desquel' tovo ayuntado, fue et entról' por el regno et corrió le la tierra et levó ende muchos ganados et muchos omnes. Quando el rey don Sancho esto sopo, mandó a su mayordomo tomar muy grand aver et que fuesse al conde a pagarle tod' aquel aver et quel' dixiesse quel' tornasse todo lo qu'él tomara de so regno, ca tenié qu'él non deviera peindrar de tal guisa por tal cosa. El mayordomo

The chapter which tells what the King did with the Countess when he learned that the Count had gone

When King Sancho learned that the Count had gone and the trick by which the Countess had freed him, it grieved him as much as if he had lost his kingdom. But he did not wish to treat the Countess wrongly, and, once it was time to do so, he went to visit her in her dwelling where she had stayed with the Count and sat with her to talk together, and he asked her about the Count's escape and about how she had dared to attempt such a thing or to free him from that prison. The Countess replied to him, saying: 'My lord, I dared to release the Count from this place because I saw that he was in great distress and because, to the best of my judgment, it was the right course of action for me to take. Besides, trusting in your wisdom, I consider that I acted rightly and that you, my lord, will treat me as would a good lord and a good king, for I am the daughter of a king and the wife of a man of very great standing; you should not wish to commit any inappropriate act against me, for I have a great responsibility to your children and you will have a great part in my dishonour. Moreover, as you are a lord of great knowledge and great understanding, you must choose what is best and ensure that you do not do anything that may give men a way of ensnaring you. And I, through doing right, must not suffer misfortune.'

Once the Countess had finished her speech, King Sancho replied to her in this way: 'Countess, you have acted very well and as befits a fine lady, so that people will speak of your goodness for ever. And I command that all of my vassals go with you and escort you to where the Count now is, and that you do not spend a night without him.' The Leonese did just as the King commanded them and escorted the Countess with great honour as befitted a lady of such high standing. When the Count saw her, he took great delight in her and reckoned that God had done him a very great mercy, and at once he returned with her, and with all who accompanied him, back to his county.

The chapter which tells how Count Fernán González sent to the King to demand his money and how the King gave him the county in payment

After the events which have just been narrated, Count Fernán González of Castile, who had not been able to remain still and at rest ever since he had been Count of Castile, for neither the Moors, nor the Moorish kings, nor the Christians allowed him to be at peace, then sent a request to King Sancho of León that he give him what he owed for the horse and the hawk which he had purchased from him; if not, it could not be that he made no payment for it. King Sancho sent him no answer to satisfy him, and the Count then assembled all his troops and, once he had them assembled, he entered the kingdom and ravaged the lands, carrying off much livestock and many men. When King Sancho learned of this, he commanded his steward to take a great sum of money and go to the Count to pay it all to him and tell him to return all that he had taken from his kingdom, for he considered that he should not have

fue al conde por pagarle el aver, mas quando el conde et él vinieron a la cuenta, fallaron que tanto era pujado, aviendo a ser doblado cada día segund la postura, que quantos omnes en España avié que lo non podríen pagar, tan mucho era ya cresçudo sin guisa. Et el mayordomo ovo se de tornar sin recabdo.

El rey, quando esto sopo, tóvose por muy embargado por aquel fecho, ca non fallava quien le diesse y consejo; et, si pudiera, repintiérase d' aquella mercadura de grado, ca se temié de perder el regno por y. Et quando vio que estava por y tan mal parado el pleito et que se nunqua podrié pagar el aver, tan grand era, fablóse con sus vassallos et acordaron quel' diesse el condado en precio por aquel aver, ca nin él nin los reys que empós él viniessen nunqua tanto avrién d'aquel condado et siempre avría y contienda, tan buenos omnes et tan fuertes eran los castellanos et tan catadores de derecho. Et trexieron esta pleitesía con el conde et diol' el rey el condado en precio d'aquel aver. Et el conde falló que mercava muy bien en aquella pleitesía e tomógele de grado. Et de más, tóvose por guarido por ello porque veíe que salié de grand premia, et por que non avrié de besar mano a omne del mundo, si non fuesse al Señor de la Ley, et éste es el apostóligo. Et d'esta guisa que d' aquí es contado salieron los castellanos de premia et de servidumbre et del poder de León et de sus leoneses. ...

to pay for this matter in such a way. The steward went to the Count to pay him the money, but when the Count and he came to reckon up the amount, they found that the sum had increased to such an extent, since the agreement required that it double every day, that all the men there were in Spain could not have paid it, so much had it grown, beyond measure. And the steward had to return without achieving his purpose.

The King, when he learned of this, found this development troublesome indeed, for he could find no-one who could give him advice in the matter; and, if he could, he would willingly have gone back on that deal, for he feared that it might cause him the loss of his kingdom. And when he saw that as a result of this the affair had reached such a serious position and that it would never be possible to pay that sum, since it was so great, he spoke with his vassals and they agreed that he should hand over the county in the place of that money, for neither he nor the kings who came after him would ever have as much as that county was worth, and it would always be a disputed land, for the Castilians were such good and strong men and such close observers of what was right. And they offered this settlement to the Count, and the King gave him the county in the place of that payment. The Count found that in coming to that arrangement he was striking a very good bargain and he accepted it willingly. In addition, he felt that he was safer as a result, as he could see that he was escaping from subservience, and as he would not have to kiss the hand of any man in the world in homage, with the exception of the Lord of the Law, that is to say the Holy Father. And in the way which has here been recounted the Castilians escaped from oppression and from servitude and from the power of León and its people.* ...

COMMENTARY

1 This stanza resembles very closely the opening stanza of Gonzalo de Berceo's *Vida de Santo Domingo de Silos* which was probably composed in about 1236 (see Dutton 1978), and it is highly likely that it was imitated from this source.

to make a rhyme: *prosa*, the term that both Berceo and the author of the *Poema de Fernán González* use to describe their compositions, was widely used in the early Middle Ages to designate a rhythmic poem (see Curtius 1953, 150).

2d from sea to sea: with the capture of Cartagena in 1243 by an army commanded by Prince Alfonso (the future Alfonso X), the Christian kingdoms had extended their control of the Iberian Peninsula to the shores of the Mediterranean. This line is, however, commonly taken as an allusion to the fall of Seville to Fernando III in 1248. The poet repeats the phrase 'from sea to sea', presumably for emphasis, in line 19a, although here the context is that of the Peninsula's conquest by the Goths. See also note to 80bc.

6b King Rodrigo: Roderic, Ruderic, or Rodrigo, the last of the Visigothic kings of Spain (see note to stanza 15), played a key part in the events which led up to the Muslim invasion of the Iberian Peninsula in 711 and figures prominently in accounts written by medieval historians, in legend and in a wide range of literary works composed over the centuries. See also note to line 35d. In the translation we have given him the hispanicized form of his name, Rodrigo, but in the notes we have used the anglicized version Roderic.

9ab Spaniards: here, and in subsequent repeated allusions to 'Spain' and 'Spaniards', the poet is applying appropriately the name of the old Roman province of 'Hispania', which was also used during the period of Visigothic rule; but in this way he also seems to establish a direct link between the Visigoths (see notes to stanza 15 and lines 22bc) and the inhabitants of the Spain of his own day, largely united by their Christian belief and, as he goes on to make clear, under the moral leadership of Castile.

baptism into His law: the Visigoths had adopted Arianism (see note to stanza 15) before arriving in Spain. In Visigothic Spain Nicene Catholicism remained essentially the faith of the Roman community which formed the bulk of the population, whilst Arianism was that of the ruling Visigothic nobility. Tensions increased in the late sixth century, but during the reign of Reccared I Arianism was formally renounced for Nicene Catholicism and denounced as a heresy. The conversion of Reccared himself was announced in 587, soon after his accession to the throne. At a local level changes were probably limited, though the bishops quickly put into practice a programme of forced conversion of Jews. There continued to be resistance to the political implications of the change. For the author of the *Poema de Fernán*

González, as for historians of both the thirteenth century and later periods, it was important to represent the Goths as devout and orthodox upholders of the Christian faith. However, the reality was that the act of rebaptism itself was specifically ruled out by the Third Council of Toledo as Reccared had no desire to emphasize the distinction between Arianism and Catholicism (see Linehan 1993, 23); our poet thus reflects not the practice of the sixth century, but the preoccupations of a later age.

11d   the hideous Beast: the use of this image to describe the Devil is particularly common in the Book of Revelation (see especially chapters 13 and 17). The defeat of the Devil and the punishment of the Beast and the false prophet, together with the reward given to the holy martyrs, is described in Revelation 20:4–10.

12   the first prophets: for a prophecy of the defeat of the Devil as it is described in Revelation, see Ezekiel 38:17–23. There is evidence that Ezekiel was regarded as a fundamental text in early medieval Spain; for example, a commentary on him is known to have belonged to quite a small Galician monastery as early as the ninth century (Collins 2012, 107).

as Saint John confirmed: this is probably an allusion to Saint John's criticism of Herod for his marriage to Herodias, his brother's wife (see, for example, Mark 6:17–18), whose conduct is seen to contrast with the dedication to chastity described in stanza 11.

14c   as the written text says: this is an allusion to the *Liber regum* (*Book of Kings*), a history written in Aragonese dialect in the last decade of the twelfth century or the first decade of the thirteenth century and translated into Castilian in about 1220. This work is a very important source for the first 160 stanzas of the *Poema*.

15   Goths: this Germanic people, originally known as the Theruingi, who originally dominated the fertile territory between the rivers Danube and Deister, began to migrate westwards in the final quarter of the fourth century AD, partly because of the rise to dominance of the nomadic Huns. Initially they petitioned the Emperor to give them lands on which to settle, but, severely exploited, in 378 they revolted and routed the Roman imperial army; steadily they became established within the Empire. The Visigothic people abandoned paganism and adopted Christianity in the form of the Arian heresy (see note to lines 22bc), just when Arianism was being largely eliminated in the Roman Empire. Under Alaric, the Visigoths sacked Rome in 410 and in the following decade they moved into southern Gaul, eventually establishing their own kingdom with its capital in Toulouse. The Visigothic population extended more and more into the Iberian Peninsula and, whereas the Franks ended Visigothic rule in Gaul with a resounding victory in 507, south of the Pyrenees the sixth century was to see the development of a flourishing Romano-Gothic culture; to an increasing extent the Visigothic rulers adopted the culture of their Hispano-Roman subjects.

the line of Magog: the supposed descent of the Goths from Magog was first mentioned by Jordanes in his *Getica*, a Latin history of the Gothic people composed in 551 or 552 AD. Magog is one of the sons of Japheth, mentioned in Genesis 10:2. He is frequently associated with apocalyptic tradition and he is, for example, mentioned in Ezekiel 38:2 and Revelation 20:7 (see notes to line 11d and stanza 12, above). In Spain both Saint Isidore and Apringius of Beja associated Gog and Magog with the Goths (see Nepaulsingh 1986, 85).

18d   the era of Pope Alexander: there is no pope of this name between the second and the eleventh centuries, but Alexander IV was pope from 1254 to 1261, in all probability the period of composition of the *Poema de Fernán González*.

19c   Touraine: this region of west-central France was incorporated into the kingdom of the Visigoths in about 480 AD but after their defeat by Clovis in 507 it passed to the Franks.

22bc   in holy water you have not been baptized: see note to 9ab. In stanzas 20–23 the poet combines two ideas: the conversion of the Goths from paganism on entry to the Roman Empire and the renunciation of the Arian heresy in Visigothic Spain under Reccared.

   heresy: Arianism, based on the teachings of Arius (*c.* 250–336 AD), had been condemned as a heresy by the First Council of Nicaea for its view of the relationship between the three persons of the Trinity and in particular of the nature of the Son of God, whom it saw as subordinate to the figure of the Father.

24c   singled out from among the whole world: it is significant that this point is made just after the mention of Fernán González in 23d. Repeatedly the poet emphasizes the link between the Goths, the Castilians governed by the illustrious count, and the triumphant kingdom of Alfonso X. He makes it clear that all of them share a common destiny as a chosen people whose role is to defend and carry forward the Christian faith; see Introduction, sections 4(iii) and 4(vii).

25d   Reccesuinth: the reading in Spanish text does not enable us to identify the king with certainty, but this is generally believed to be Reccesuinth, who from 649 to 672 ruled over a largely peaceful kingdom and whose most prominent achievement was the introduction of a new law code applied to both Goths and those of Hispano-Roman origin. During his reign the influence of the Church and its bishops in the kingdom increased markedly. It is also possible that the figure alluded to here is Reccesuinth's father Chindasuinth, who reigned from 642 to 653, for part of that time alongside his son.

26   Saint Eugenio (Eugenius II) was Bishop of Toledo from 646 until his death in 657.

   Isidore: Saint Isidore lived from about 560 until 636 and was bishop of Seville (where he was probably born) from about 601; it is evident that he was not a contemporary of either Reccesuinth or Chindasuinth, but the poet's intention here is clearly to reinforce the picture of an age of both political stability and outstanding devotion to the Christian faith. Isidore presided over the Fourth Council of Toledo, at which the Church gave much-needed political backing to the king. He played an important part in turning Visigothic Spain into the most educated part of Western

Europe and for several centuries he was to exercise an immense influence on the development of Spanish education and culture and on the writings of the historians of medieval Spain. His copious writings include a *History of the Kings of the Goths, Vandals and Suevi*, in which he argues that the Goths were the true heirs to Roman culture and which includes a very well known passage in praise of Spain (see note to line 145b, below). His most famous work, however, is the *Etymologiae*, a vast encyclopedia which sought to prove a synthesis of all fields of knowledge, drawing on a wide range of classical as well as Christian authors. Although Isidore was initially interred in Seville, in 1063 his remains were transferred to León, where they were buried in the newly reconsecrated Basílica de San Isidoro.

27d   Wamba: after the death of Reccesuinth in 672, Wamba was elected king by the army, although it seems that, on the grounds of his already advanced years, he was initially reluctant to ascend to the throne. The first years of his reign were marked by a rebellion in the north east of his kingdom and, although he did succeed in bringing peace for a time, he had to deal with a series of conflicts with and among his nobles; there were also a growing number of Muslim coastal raids. During his reign the Eleventh Council of Toledo introduced measures to deal with various ecclesiastical abuses. In 680 Wamba fell victim to a plot which probably involved both his successor and Julian, Bishop of Toledo: it seems that, initially drugged to give the appearance of a fatal illness and declared a penitent, unable now to reign, he was deposed. Wamba spent the final eight years of his life at the Monastery of San Vicente in Toledo.

30b   prudence: the Spanish word used here is *mesura*. It is used several times in the *Poema de Fernán González* and also in other major literary texts of the thirteenth century, notably the *Libro de Alexandre* and the *Poema de Mio Cid*. The concept that it represents – essentially moderation and the avoidance of extremes – is reflected, too, in the moralizing writing of the humanist Diego García de Campos, chancellor of Alfonso VIII. It represents a notion which was clearly of great importance in the Castilian court and Alfonso X includes it among the qualities that he saw as essential in his knights (*Partidas*, 2,21,4). See also Introduction, section 2(vi).

33a   Egica: not, in fact, Wamba's immediate successor, Egica reigned from about 687 to 702 or 703. He enjoys a rather sinister reputation, due in part to his implacable persecution of the Jews. His reign was also marked by conspiracy, led by Bishop Sisbert of Toledo, and by conflict with a section of the nobility, and it also coincided with an outbreak of bubonic plague and with a period of food shortage caused by failure of the harvests.

34b   Wittiza was probably made co-ruler by his father Egica as early as 694 and he was anointed in 700. He reigned until 710 or perhaps even 711. He clearly attempted to address some of the grievances caused by his father's rule, revoking a number of measures taken against some members of the nobility. It seems likely that he attempted to bring about a number of important ecclesiastical reforms and his relationship with the Church seems to have been a positive one. Little is known of the final years of Wittiza's reign, but the nobles appear to have achieved a growing ascendancy over the monarchy and it is possible that Wittiza was assassinated by his successor Roderic or Rodrigo.

35d   through his guilt, the Lord was ill-disposed to him: Roderic or Rodrigo (see also note to line 6b) was in fact a nobleman of obscure origin, although one chronicle records that he was the grandson of King Chindasuinth (see note to line 25d). Having come to power through a coup in which he was aided by both a section of the nobility and probably a number of bishops, Roderic was regarded by some as a usurper. He was faced by opposition from Agila (or Achila) II, according to some sources the son of Wittiza, who was effectively ruling over parts of the north of the Peninsula as a separate kingdom, and he was also confronted by a rebellion by the Basques. In addition he had to deal with raids in the south by the Arabs and Berbers. In early May 711 he received news that a large Arab force had disembarked and, marching south from Pamplona, he is said to have met them in battle on the river Guadalete. He was defeated and never heard of again. In later centuries he came to be surrounded by a body of legend which gave him a moral responsibility for Spain's fall into Muslim hands, and it is to this that the poet is here making a brief allusion. Roderic was said to have raped Florinda or La Cava, the daughter of Count Julian, governor of Ceuta. According to the legend, Julian had entrusted his daughter to Roderic at his court in Toledo and it was in revenge for this act that Julian betrayed his country and gave assistance to the invaders. The earliest mention of this story in a Christian chronicle is in a text which is of Mozarabic origin and dates from the early twelfth century; in this work, curiously, it is Wittiza and not Roderic who is responsible for the rape of Julian's daughter. The legend of sexual misdemeanour and vengeance appears to have Arabic, and probably Egyptian, roots, but it has been suggested that this version of this story had a classical source in Livy's account of the rape of Lucretia, which contributed to the fall of the monarchy in Rome (see Gozalbes Cravioto 2011, 7; Fernández Valverde 2001, 132–134). Literary and historical elements became intertwined and progressively elaborated into the fictitious story of how an act of vengeance came to have immense implications for the future of a nation. Strikingly, as he paints his predominantly positive picture of the Goths in general and of Roderic in particular, our poet places relatively little emphasis on his guilt and lays emphasis on his deception by Julian. The story of La Cava's rape is alluded to only indirectly, perhaps because the poet believes that his public will already be well aware of it; it is deceit – an important theme in the *Poema* – that is evoked as the cause of Spain's fall, and its originator is clearly identified as the Devil (see stanza 68). For a collection of texts dealing with this episode, see Smith (1988, 8–29).

36b   the Shining Mountains: these are the 'Montes Claros', a name for the Atlas Mountains, and they are also mentioned in the *Poema de Mio Cid*, line 1182, where they are likewise associated with a seat of hostile power in North Africa. Roderic did not carry out any African conquests; however, in the sixth century the Visigoths did assert claims to Mauritania Tingitana (now Morocco) (O'Callaghan 2011, 3) and from the middle of that century they had a firm foothold on the north African coast in Ceuta, where legend represents Count Julian as governor (see note to line 42a). On the other hand, the poet here seeks to associate the battle of Roderic and the Goths against the Muslim invaders with the crusading enterprise of his own day (see Introduction, sections 2(ix) and 4(vii)).

41a   No children of Wittiza should ever have been born: Wittiza's sons Alamund, Romulus and Ardabast were probably too young to rule in 711 and seem not to have been given commands by Roderic or to have played a significant part in these events. Some accounts, however, tell of them being given protection by the treacherous Count Julian (see note to line 42a), and some Muslim sources, such as the tenth-century writer Ibn al-Qutiyya, portray the sons of Wittiza as collaborators in the conquest, cunningly betraying Roderic in battle. For an explanation of the poet's comment we could also look to the role played by Agila II, who ruled over parts of the north of the Peninsula (see note to line 35d). Agila was a member of Wittiza's clan and according to some sources was his son. Undoubtedly, the conflict between Agila and Roderic considerably weakened the Visigothic force that faced the Muslim invaders. After Roderic's death a section of the nobility elected Wittiza's brother Oppa as their king, but there continued to be conflicts with other factions, notably with the nobles loyal to Agila. Agila reigned over a reduced territory until his death in about 716.

42a   Count Julian: a Count Iulianus (or Yulyan) is mentioned as governor of Tingitana (Ceuta, an island off the African coast of the Strait of Gibraltar) by both Arabic and Christian sources. However, he is not mentioned in Christian chronicles until the early twelfth century (see note to line 35d). Scholars disagree about Julian's origin, but it is quite likely that he was in fact not Visigothic but the last Byzantine governor of Ceuta. He probably possessed territories on either the Spanish or the African coast. It seems clear that by 709 he had entered an alliance with the Muslim leaders and that he played a major part in facilitating the invasion of 711. He subsequently converted to Islam and was given territories in Spain. For a fuller account of the elaboration of the legend of Count Julian, see Gozalbes Cravioto (2011). Our poet alludes to the collection of tribute (*parias*): *parias* were taxes imposed, from the eleventh century onwards, by the Christian kingdoms on their Muslim tributaries, and it is inconceivable that in the early eighth century the Visigoths could have been collecting such a tax from African territories. Most versions of the story are less specific about the nature of the business which took Julian to Morocco; for example, Rodrigo Jiménez de Rada describes him as being sent by Roderic on a diplomatic mission (*De rebus Hispaniae*, III, 19).

43b   Tāriq ibn Ziyad was the general, believed to have been the governor of the Berbers at Tangier, who led the Islamic conquest of the Iberian Peninsula. He seems to have led an exploratory raid in July 710 and in spring 711 he returned with a force of some 7,000 men who crossed in ships made available by Count Julian. His troops disembarked at the port of Gibraltar (see line 72c). The name 'Gibraltar' is derived from the Arabic phrase *Jabal Tāriq*, meaning 'mountain of Tāriq'.

50 what need have you of arms: this line, together with the following two stanzas, seems to echo at least one of two biblical texts: Isaiah 2:4 and Micah 4:3–4. See Deyermond (1990, 52–53), who points out that both Isaiah and Micah 'present the beating of swords into ploughshares as part of an apocalyptic vision, where earthly history comes to an end.'

57d the like of this province: the kingdoms listed in this stanza did not, of course, exist in the eighth century and they were in no sense a unity in the thirteenth. That they are listed here as parts of a single entity, with a single royal court, can be seen as a reflection of the imperial aspirations cherished by Alfonso X at the time of the poem's composition. The term 'province' could refer back to the Hispania of Roman Spain, but it was also used in Visigothic Spain, to designate the ecclesiastical administrative areas into which the kingdom was divided.

58c pardon: there seems to be an allusion here to the Visigoths' burden of sin (see, for example, 98cd and 113a), which it will fall to them and later generations to expurgate.

59d the Moors, its rulers of old: the Moors had, of course, never inhabited or ruled the Iberian Peninsula before the time of the Visigoths, but this stanza is an excellent example of how the poet identifies these eighth-century Christians with those of his own day. These words would be more appropriate, perhaps, in the mouth of a triumphant Christian ruler such as Alfonso X himself.

63d cast them in the fire: Nepaulsingh (1986, 86) argues that in the burning of the Goths' weapons in a huge fire there is an echo of Ezekiel 39:9.

73a pagans: our poet repeatedly identifies Islam with paganism. This is far from the more nuanced and sensitive approach of the author of the *Poema de Mio Cid* to the depiction of Muslim characters. Indeed, the approach here seems much closer to the crusading zeal which characterizes much French epic and is summed up by Roland's statement that 'Pagans are wrong and Christians are right' ('Paien unt tort e chrestïens unt dreit': *Chanson de Roland*, l.1015).

74a Seville could not have fallen into Muslim hands before Roderic's army had met them in battle, but Muslim sources (see Livermore 1971, 295) show that the invaders understood the importance of this city (then known as Hispalis) as the capital of the Spains before the arrival of the Goths, who had transferred their centre of power to Toledo. In 711, Seville remained an important legal and ecclesiastical centre, but it had few military resources; it was captured after a siege. In the 1250s, however, it will have been remembered as a centre of great political and strategic importance, whose capture in 1248 had marked the high point of Fernando III's military triumphs.

77d foretold by the prophets: Victorio (2010, 60) argues that these are 'false prophecies', which exist in accounts drawn up after the events, re-interpreting signs as premonitions of the events of 711. Others (see Nepaulsingh 1986, 86 and López

Guil 2001, 39) point to biblical sources in Ezekiel and Revelation; the punishment meted out to the land of Magog (Ezekiel 39:6) seems significant here in the light of the linking of the Goths with 'the line of Magog' in line 15c. See also the emphasis on retribution ordained by God in lines 80ab.

78c   Sangonera: the site of the battle is not certain, in spite of much discussion by scholars. Muslim writers place it 'near Sidonia' and it must have been close to the main road from the south to Córdoba; it is generally agreed that it was near the river Guadalete (see Livermore 1971, 286–287). Sangonera is mentioned in some versions, for example in the *Estoria de España*, which describes it as being between Murcia and Lorca. It has been argued that 'Sangonera' may be a deformation of 'Sidonia' (Sánchez-Albornoz 1944, 194ff.).

80bc   put to the sword: there is probably an allusion here to Ezekiel 39:23 (see Nepaulsingh 1986, 86).

she was to be restored: this enigmatic statement can be understood if we bear in mind the poet's close identification of the Visigoths with the crusaders of the poet's own day: in his mind the objectives of both have become fused, in such a way that the Visigoths seem to be a successful warrior people who have already once expelled the Moors against whom they are now once again to be pitted in battle. (See Introduction, sections 2(ix) and 4(vii), and also Armistead 1961, 16–18.)

81d   Him from whom their sins deserve no pardon: the poet implies here that the defeat of Roderic and the consequent suffering endured by the Visigothic people are in keeping with God's wish that through this catastrophe they may fully expiate their sin. In this sense the Muslim invaders, themselves in due course to receive their punishment, are agents of God's will (see López Guil 2001, 167 and also note to line 98a).

82d   it seemed to shake the heavens and the earth: see Ezekiel 38:19–20 (Nepaulsingh 1986, 86) for a possible source.

84a   In Viseu was later discovered his tomb: Viseu is a city in northern central Portugal and is rich in legends associated with the period of the reconquest and notably with the Leonese king Ramiro II, sovereign, ally and for a time antagonist of the Fernán González of history. The existence of Roderic's tomb in the city is mentioned in the Aragonese chronicle the *Liber regum.*

87a   Old Castile: the earliest mention of Castile is to be found in a document of the monastery of San Millán de la Cogolla dating from the beginning of the ninth century, and another document of 852 shows that the area was governed by a count. It seems that the territory that was to form the core of Castile had originally (since late Roman times) been a fortified frontier area under the command of a *dux* or general. Arab chronicles knew this as al-Quilá ('the castles'). Significantly, there is clear evidence of continuity of both population and institutions in this area before and after the Islamic invasion. See the analysis of the evidence for this in Aniano Cadiñanos López-Quintana (2002; summarized on pp. 141–144). The area which came to be known as *Castella Vetula* (Old Castile) was bounded in the south by the

Obarenes Mountains (on the southern limit of the Cantabrian range), in the north by the Atlantic, in the east by the county of Álava and in the west by the rivers Deva and Pisuerga. The picture of an inaccessible mountain enclave painted in this stanza is essentially an accurate one, though by the early tenth century the county of Castile had extended southwards beyond the mountains as far as the banks of the river Duero.

88a The Asturias: in the years which followed the Umayyad invasion, Muslim rule seems to have been effective throughout the Peninsula with the exception of Asturias in the extreme north, where Pelayo (Pelagius), a Visigothic nobleman (see note to line 115a), ruled over a mixture of Asturians, Visigoths and fugitives from the south (see Lomax 1978, 25ff.). Pelayo was able to extend his small kingdom northwards to the coast and both eastwards and westwards through the mountains and eventually to absorb the lordship of Cantabria to the east.

98a Ill-starred was our fate! Deyermond (1990, 53–54) analyzes the poet's treatment in this and the following stanzas of the well known Augustinian concept of the heathen used by God as an instrument of punishment for a Christian people which has erred in its ways and turned its back on God. He points to the existence of numerous biblical parallels and draws attention to the similarity between the presentation here of the Muslim conquest of Spain and the Babylonian conquest of Jerusalem (a parallel underlined by the poet himself in lines 107cd).

101c the written text: the term *ditado* was quite commonly applied to a written text and particularly a poem (on several occasions, for example, in the *Libro de Alexandre*). For the importance of dictation as part of the process of composition, see Bailey (2010, 24; 33; 83–85). The text alluded to here, however, has not been identified. Saint Martin had been bishop of Tours in the fourth century and in the eighth century the basilica in which he was buried was already an immensely wealthy shrine. In 732 the Islamic armies were advancing towards it when they were defeated by the royal army of Charles Martel, an event which put an end to Muslim raids in south west France. The basilica was to become a major stopping point for pilgrims on the road to Santiago de Compostela. Following a fire in 1230 it was rebuilt on an even grander scale but was subsequently destroyed during the French Revolution.

104a al-Mansur (or Almanzor) figures prominently in the *Poema* as an adversary of Fernán González, but the two figures were not contemporaries. When Hisham II succeeded his father as caliph in 976, during his minority Umayyad Spain was governed by his chief minister Mohammed ibn Abi Amir, who, having defeated a rebellion by a jealous general and routed the combined armies of León, Castile and Navarre at Rueda, took the title al-Mansur bi'llah ('victorious through God'). Until his death in 1006 al-Mansur enjoyed a position of almost total dominance throughout the Peninsula, emphasized by his numerous devastating raids deep into the Christian kingdoms of the north. For an account of his career, see Lomax (1978, 46–48). This powerful and notorious Muslim leader has clearly been introduced into the *Poema* to serve as a worthy opponent to Fernán González, the idealized champion of Christian Spain.

105d   Saint Peter in the angry main: it is significant that the list of examples begins with Saint Peter, in view of the poet's connection with the monastery of San Pedro de Arlanza.

For the well-known account of how Saint Peter was saved from drowning in the Lake of Gennesaret or Sea of Galilee, see Matthew 14:24–33. This invocation by the Castilians of divine aid, which lists a series of examples of miraculous intervention, has thirteenth-century literary parallels in Berceo's *Los loores de Nuestra Señora* (stanzas 91–92) and in Jimena's prayer in the *Poema de Mio Cid* (lines 330–365). López Guil (2001, 175) points out that the prayer in the *Poema de Fernán González* is closer stylistically than is Berceo's composition to the prayers of epic but that the differences that separate it from such prayers are nevertheless substantial.

106   Catherine of Alexandria (believed to have lived in the fourth century) was said to have refused marriage with the Emperor as she held herself to be the 'bride of Christ'; according to legend, she was condemned to be broken on a wheel, but the wheel broke down, injuring bystanders; however, she was subsequently beheaded. Saint Catherine was venerated as the patron of young girls, students and the clergy, nurses and craftsmen who worked with wheels; as she was seen as a scholarly advocate and also as the protectress of the dying, her intercession was valued highly (see Farmer 2004, 95). According to the Bible, Queen **Esther**, herself a Jewess, interceded with her husband Xerxes on behalf of the Jewish people, saving them, and presumably herself, from the threat of extermination (see Esther 7:3–4). **Marina** (or Margaret) of Antioch probably never existed as a historical individual but her name appeared in the West in the ninth century and she became famous in the time of the Crusades (Farmer 2004, 344). Legend recounts that, having converted to Christianity, she refused the advances of the governor of Antioch and as a result suffered a series of horrific tortures: these included being swallowed by Satan in the form of a dragon, from which she managed to escape intact because a cross that she bore irritated its insides. She is said to have been a highly persuasive preacher and to have made many converts to Christianity before being beheaded.

107a   David: David recalls how God saved him from the lion as he embarks on the encounter with the Philistine giant Goliath (see 1 Samuel 17:37–58). Three of the stanzas which make up this prayer relate totally or in part to miracles which occurred during the Babylonian captivity (see Deyermond 1990, 53–54) and there can be little doubt that our poet wishes us to bear this parallel in mind as we are told of how Fernán González delivers the Castilians from oppression.

108   Susanna: Daniel 13 (considered apocryphal by Protestants) tells how Susanna, the wife of Joachim, having been falsely accused of adultery and condemned to death, was saved at the last moment by Daniel, the accusers then being put to death. For the account of how **Daniel** was kept safe during his time in the pit of lions, see Daniel 6:16–24. The allusion to **Matthew** is to the apostle ize.

and evangelist who, according to medieval legend (as recounted, for example, in Jacobus de Voragine's *Legenda aurea*) tamed two fire-breathing dragons that had been brought by enchanters.

109   the three children: Daniel 3:1–30 tells of how King Nebuchadnezzar commanded that three young men, Shadrach, Meshach and Abednego, be thrown into a furnace as punishment for failing to worship a gold statue, and how divine protection ensured that they were untouched by the flames. The allusion to **serpents' jaws** is a mystifying one, for it does not relate to the well-known episode in Daniel. The serpent is closely identified in the Bible with the Devil (for example, Revelation 12:9) and the image of being snatched from its jaws could well be used here to suggest spiritual salvation as well as physical protection.

110   Saint John the Evangelist: the story recounted here has been much represented in the visual arts: Saint John was said to have been challenged by the high priest of Diana at Ephesus to drink a cup containing poison which had killed a criminal; when he blessed the cup, the poison rose from it in the form of a serpent. The origin of the story is likely to be in Christ's warning to James and John recorded in Matthew 20:23.

113a   We are in great error: Coates (2008, 211) points out how this confession is associated with penance, 'a vital part of the process of making righteous, enabling the conversion of *homo peccator* to *homo justus*', and that it leads on to the election of Pelayo, thus setting in motion a regenerative process which continues throughout the poem.

115a   Pelayo: see note to line 88a. The origins of Pelayo (Pelagius) are shadowy; it is likely that he was in fact of Asturian descent, but according to Christian chronicles of the late ninth century he had been a nobleman in the court of King Roderic and after the Visigoths' defeat at Guadalete he had fled with his family to the mountains of the north. At this stage, neither his rank nor his lineage had given him the standing to assume leadership. He took part in several raids into Muslim territory but was captured and taken to Córdoba, from where he escaped and returned to Asturias, eventually being elected leader by a popular assembly. Continuing skirmishes provoked a Muslim attack and, after initially suffering heavy casualties, Pelayo's troops withdrew into the mountains, where (probably in 724) their overwhelming victory in what was in reality a fairly minor encounter at Covadonga forced the Muslim troops to retreat. Pelayo subsequently established his capital in Cangas de Onís and devoted himself to consolidating his monarchy. He died in 737. The military importance of Pelayo's victory at Covadonga has undoubtedly been exaggerated. Moreover, it is unlikely that Pelayo would have been aware of any religious differences between himself and the Muslim conquerors; it was 'a subsequent ideological rewriting of history' which was to see Pelayo as creating a new line of Christian monarchy born out of this episode (see Collins 2012, 63); but Pelayo's victory is nonetheless significant in that it represents a first step in the long process of the Christian recovery of the Peninsula. (See, for example, Collins 1995, 182; 225–226; Lomax 1978, 25–26.)

118d **I fancy that you will have heard tell of it before:** the poet seems to suggest here that this legend is very well known in oral tradition, but there are also quite close parallels in learned sources, for example in a fifth-century account of how the enemies of the emperor Theodosius were wounded by their own arrows (Castro 1958, 98–99; West 1983, 67).

122b **Fáfila** (Fávila) was Pelayo's son and successor and ruled for only two years, before being killed by a bear; very little is known of Fáfila's reign but our poet follows his source, the *Liber regum*, which describes this king as being of base character.

123c **Alfonso:** Pelayo's daughter Ermosinda married Alfonso, son of Peter, *dux* or duke of Cantabria, the region which bordered on Asturias from the east. On the death of King Fáfila in 739, Alfonso, his brother-in-law, was chosen to succeed him. He ruled as Alfonso I until 757 and came to be known as 'Alfonso the Catholic'. Some Asturian chronicles present him and his father as direct descendants of the Visigoths, although this may not be an authentic claim. During Alfonso's reign the Asturians raided several towns in Galicia and across the plateau (including those mentioned in lines 124a–c). They did not seek to hold the cities permanently as the *Poema* suggests but destroyed their fortifications, slaughtered their Muslim inhabitants and carried off their Christian populations, thus creating a largely depopulated area which served as a kind of buffer zone between the small Christian kingdom in the north and Umayyad Spain. (See Collins 1995, 182; 226–228; Lomax 1978, 26–28.)

124d **Amaya** is a peak in the north west of the present province of Burgos which rises to a height of 1377 metres; at its foot is a settlement of the same name, and this was the site of an ancient (probably in origin pre-Roman) fortification. Amaya had been one of the principal strongholds controlled by the dukes of Cantabria, strategically situated at an important point of access to their territory. However, in the years following the Islamic invasion, Duke Peter (see note to line 123c) was driven back into the mountains. Although the Muslim inhabitants were driven out during the reign of Alfonso I, it was not in fact until the second half of the ninth century that the area was eventually repopulated. It was in 854 that, as part of a more general programme of expansion under Ordoño I of León, Amaya was resettled and refortified.

125c **Fruela:** Alfonso's son Fruela I (757–68) was known as 'the Cruel'. Probably his most significant achievement was to force the withdrawal of the Berber garrisons in Galicia by means of a brutal campaign of harassment. His reign was also, however, marked by the suppression of a rebellion of the Basques in Álava, and, having murdered his brother, he was to meet a violent death at the hands of his own followers (see Collins 1995, 227).

126 **Alfonso ... 'the Chaste':** initially unpopular, after his father's death Alfonso was twice passed over in favour of rival pretenders to the throne. However, when he did finally become king in 791 as Alfonso II, he proceeded to reign for

51 years, in spite of a rebellion in 801–802 which temporarily confined him to a monastery. Alfonso moved the court of the Asturian monarchy to its definitive location in Oviedo and set about imitating Visigothic tradition and re-establishing the organization of the Goths, both secular and ecclesiastical. (See, for example, Collins 1995, 182; 229–230; Collins 2012, 65–70; Lomax 1978, 29–30.) Alfonso created a new bishopric in Oviedo and a complex of ecclesiastical buildings was built during his reign to incorporate the basilica founded by Fruela I; this cathedral of **San Salvador** was rebuilt in the Romanesque style in the late eleventh and the early twelfth century and the present-day gothic building dates from a century later. Alfonso 'the Chaste', who died without leaving an heir, is said not to have had a sexual relationship with his wife Berta; though his nickname may also derive from the fact that he introduced the observance of chastity into the Asturian church.

127b King Charles: Alfonso II did have some dealings with Charlemagne, but their nature is not known. There is no reason to suppose that there was hostility between them. Charlemagne or Charles the Great was King of the Franks from 768 to 814 and Emperor of the West from 800 to 814. The lands under his control expanded to take in most of Western Europe. Moreover his military, administrative, political and cultural achievements were so great that his posthumous reputation grew to immense proportions and is widely reflected in medieval art and literature. His venture into Spain in 777–778, however, ended in disaster: encouraged to cross the Pyrenees by the Muslim governor of Saragossa, who sought help against the emir of Barcelona, Charlemagne received offers of surrender from Barcelona and Gerona but failed to take Saragossa itself (see Lomax 1978, 32–33). As the Frankish army returned rapidly to deal with a rebellion in Saxony, their rear-guard was ambushed in the Pass of Roncevaux or Roncesvalles and suffered heavy casualties; the dead included Duke Roland of Brittany, later to be presented in Frankish legend as the battle's hero and most famously depicted in the *Chanson de Roland*, an epic poem dating from the end of the eleventh century. The historical ambushers were probably principally Basques, but the *Chanson* describes Roland's adversaries as Saracens.

129d to take it in five years: this seems to be an allusion to the opening lines of the *Chanson de Roland*, which claimed that Charlemagne had conquered Spain in seven years; the claim was well known in thirteenth-century Spain, for it is also mentioned by Rodrigo Jiménez de Rada (see López Guil 2001, 183).

132ab Bernardo del Carpio is the fictitious hero of numerous ballads that have come down to us and also, it is generally agreed, of a nationalistic epic poem, now lost, which we know to have existed by the 1230s, when its contents were incorporated into the histories of both Lucas de Tuy and Rodrigo Jiménez de Rada; subsequently, together with other related material, it was to become part of the *Estoria de España*. According to the two earlier chronicles, Bernardo was a Leonese nobleman who was in conflict with his king, Alfonso II (the ballads make him Alfonso's rightful heir), partly because of Alfonso's connections with the

Franks. Among the feats that Bernardo was said to have achieved was his victory over Charlemagne's nephew Roland at Roncesvalles (see note to line 127b). The *Poema de Fernán González* introduces three new elements into the account (see Chalon 1970, 61–67): crucially, it makes Bernardo Castilian rather than Leonese; it represents him as fighting against the French on his own account rather than at the behest of the Leonese Alfonso II; and it shows him fighting two battles against them, at Fuenterrabía and the pass of Aspe, rather than just one.

There is no evidence for the existence of **Fuenterrabía** as early as the eighth century when these events are said to have taken place. On the other hand it is known to have been quite a well developed settlement by the late twelfth century; in 1200 this strategically important town, which stands on the estuary of the river Bidasoa, was captured by the Castilians from the Navarrese and three years later Alfonso VIII granted it a charter. Fuenterrabía, now officially known as Hondarribia, is situated on the frontier between France and Spain. It would probably have been known to the poet for its military importance. It is not, however, near to Roncesvalles, where the battle in which Roland is said to have died took place, and it is not clear why our poet mentions this port unless it is in error (probably caused by confusion of the two meanings of *portus* in his Latin source – 'mountain pass' and 'port').

134b   as the written text says: this is probably (see Marden 1904, 180) the *Historia Turpini*, Book IV of the *Codex Calixtinus*, also known as the *Pseudo-Turpin Chronicle*; the *Codex* is essentially a guide for pilgrims following the road to Santiago de Compostela and it exists in an elaborately illuminated manuscript of the mid-twelfth century. Book IV tells of the achievements of Charlemagne and includes (chapter 21) an account of his campaign in Spain and the battle at Roncesvalles.

135d   Marseilles: there seems here to be confusion between the name of the French port and that of the Muslim general, Marsile or Marsirius, who figures in both the *Chanson de Roland* and works derived from it, including the *Historia Turpini*.

138b   the mountain pass of Cize: the *Codex Calixtinus* (see note to line 134b) describes the height known as the Portus Cisereus or Port de Cize as 'the gateway to Spain'. It goes on to explain how just to the south is situated the valley of Roncesvalles where Charlemagne's army suffered its disastrous defeat.

139b   the passes of Aspe: the Vallée d'Aspe is situated in the central Pyrenees and rises to the Somport (or Aspe) Pass which marks the frontier with Spain.

142   Marsile (see note to line 135d) is the fictitious pagan king of the Saracens who plays a prominent role as Roland's adversary in the *Chanson de Roland*. His character was based on the historical figure of Abd al-Malik, a highly successful general under Abd al-Rahman I, emir of Córdoba; Abd al-Malik became governor in turn of Seville, Saragossa and, in 772, of the whole of eastern Spain. Bernardo's appeal to Marsile is perhaps surprising in the light of the crusading zeal that characterises the *Poema*, but it is nevertheless in tune with the work's heavily nationalistic emphasis: Castile is to be seen as possessing heroes whose prestige can eclipse that of French warriors like Roland. In kissing Marsile's hands, Bernardo is not presenting himself as his vassal but simply making a request (López Guil 2001, 188) to be allowed to display the courage and military prowess of the Castilians. The **Twelve Peers** (who included Roland) were essentially a literary creation: they were Charlemagne's foremost warriors, a group of noblemen who represented the height of Christian military prowess; they play a prominent role in the *Chanson de Roland* and other epics and their exploits were much elaborated in later literary tradition. In the twelfth century Louis VII instituted a system of peers and by 1228 their number had been adjusted to the traditional number of twelve. In the *Chanson*, all the Peers die in battle.

145b   the land in which you live: the ultimate source of the following panegyric is the passage in praise of Spain (*De laude Spaniae*) which appears at the beginning of Saint Isidore's work *History of the Kings of the Goths, Vandals and Suevi*, written in about 624. This passage includes, for example, mention of the wealth of the land, the richness in mines and rivers and the abundance of livestock and horses; by 'Spain', of course, we are to understand the whole of the Iberian Peninsula. Lucas of Tuy, composing his *Chronicle of the World* (*Chronicon mundi*) in about 1236, likewise includes a section towards the beginning of his work in which he dwells on Spain's great natural wealth and qualities, but he also mentions a series of great men who were born or lived in the Iberian Peninsula; the list of these begins with the Apostle James, Santiago, through Spain's association with whom – according to both Lucas of Tuy and our poet – God intended to set her above other nations. The *Chronicon mundi* may well have been a direct source for this section of the *Poema de Fernán González*. However, in the context of what is effectively an *aition* or 'founding myth', what distinguishes this passage from those in these earlier histories is its narrow concentration on the virtues of Castile; this feature was not taken up in the similar passage of praise which was subsequently to be included in Alfonso X's *Estoria de España*.

150d   the source of their salt: salt-workings in northern Spain are documented from the early ninth century. By the mid-thirteenth century the exploitation of the sources of salt, vital as part of the diet and as a preservative, was a royal monopoly and a highly lucrative source of income for the Crown. In many cases, monasteries received privileges which gave them the right to obtain salt either free or at reduced prices.

151b   grain, to make the scarlet dye: kermes was much used from Roman times for the production of red dye. It is obtained from an insect which lives on the sap of certain trees such as the kermes oak, common in parts of Spain. Many Western European languages referred to the substance as 'grain', as a result of the resemblance which the dried eggs bore to grains of wheat or sand. Cochineal was of Mexican and South American origin and unavailable in Europe until the sixteenth century.

152b   her quality of horse: Spain was widely associated with fine horses, and praise for them is to be found in a number of texts of the twelfth and thirteenth centuries, among them the *Historia Turpini* (see note to 134b). In the *Libro de*

Alexandre the gift sent to the Emperor by the people of Spain is a magnificent stallion. (See Hernando Pérez 2001, 57–58.)

153cd   let us not pass over the honoured Apostle: it came to be widely believed that Saint James the Apostle, brother of Saint John, preached in Spain and that after his death in Jerusalem his body was brought back to Galicia, where it was buried near Iria Flavia. According to tradition, in 813 Bishop Theodemir claimed to have discovered the saint's body. A series of churches were built on the site of the discovery and at the end of the eleventh century, when the shrine was already attracting swelling numbers of pilgrims from all over Christendom, the episcopal see was moved to Santiago. Saint James became the patron of the whole of Christian Spain and he was to be credited with a host of miracles, notably associated with his guise of *Matamoros* or *Moor-killer*. There is in fact no evidence from the Roman or Visigothic periods for Saint James' association with Spain (except for a single mention in a poem by Aldhelm of Sherborne) and information about the early development of the cult is mainly derived from the *Historia Compostelana*, a history commissioned in the mid-twelfth century by Diego Gelmírez, archbishop of Santiago de Compostela.

154c   above England and France: the poet is here pressing the Spanish claim to outdo its English and French rivals, turning a blind eye to the inconvenient point that Santiago de Compostela is associated with the kingdom of León rather than with Castile; indeed he is to go on to claim in a central part of his poem that Santiago lent highly visible support to the Castilians. The French monarchy possessed a wealth of relics: several of the treasures of the Basilica of Saint Denis, for example, dated back to the Merovingian and Carolingian periods (including relics that Charlemagne was said to have brought back from a mythical visit to the Holy Land), and the Sainte-Chapelle, consecrated in 1248, had been commissioned by Louis IX to house his collection of Passion Relics, including what was believed to be the Crown of Thorns. In England, the cult of Saint Thomas of Canterbury grew rapidly in popularity in the thirteenth century, but the most important tomb discovery had been of a different kind: in 1193 Henry II had directed the monks of Glastonbury to carry out excavations which had led to the discovery of what were believed to be the bodies of King Arthur and his queen, immensely important because of the associations with Arthur claimed by the Plantagenets and also on account of the potential link with the Holy Grail.

(For the cultural significance of the interest shown in Arthur by Henry II and his wife Eleanor of Aquitaine, see Introduction, section 2(v)).

157a   it is Castile that bears the palm: for discussion of the poet's emphasis on the development and the role of Castile, see Introduction, section 4(iii). Up to this point, the poet has repeatedly alluded to Spain as a whole, but from now on his concern is to be essentially with the destiny of Castile and its people, with Navarre and León mentioned mostly in the context of rivalry or dispute.

163b   two men of great prudence: there is no known historical basis for the existence of these two judges, who nevertheless were to figure prominently in chronicles and legend. Laín Calvo first appears in the *Historia Roderici*, composed in about 1180, where he is listed as the first of the ancestors of the Cid (see note to 165d). Nuño Rasura's first mention in any written text is as the grandfather of Fernán González and is in the *Crónica najerense*, a work more or less contemporary with the *Historia Roderici*. The role claimed for the two judges, first mentioned in a text composed between 1157 and 1194, was to be significantly elaborated by the historians of the thirteenth century. Indeed, West (1983, 29) points out that, according to Alfonso X's *Estoria de España*, on Nuño's death, Gonzalo's election by a popular vote was 'equatable to kingship'. See also Introduction, section 2(vii), and for an analysis of the process by which the roles of Nuño Rasura and Laín Calvo were invented, Peña Pérez (2005, 53–65) and Martínez Díez (2005, 1.280–290).

165d the Cid: Rodrigo Díaz de Vivar (1043–1099) is the most famous of Castile's epic heroes: a minor nobleman brought up in the Castilian royal household, he became royal standard bearer for Sancho II and fought for him in the war against Sancho's brother Alfonso VI of León. After Sancho's death Rodrigo became Alfonso's vassal but was subsequently exiled and embarked on a series of enterprises which demonstrated his outstanding military abilities and won him, from his Muslim enemies, the honorific title of 'Cid' or 'Lord'. Defeating some Christian adversaries but most famously the formidable Almoravid invaders, he established himself as lord of Valencia which he held and governed until his death. One of his two daughters married the *infante* of Navarre, the other the Count of Barcelona. El Cid's career was much celebrated in chronicles and in a wide range of literary works, notably the *Poema de Mio Cid*, composed in about 1207 (see Such and Hodgkinson 1987). The epithet *Campeador* (Champion, Great Warrior), used in the Spanish text, was a further honorific title already applied to the historical Cid in his own lifetime.

167a–c Gonzalo Núñez: the name conventionally attributed to Fernando's father is almost certainly an invention whose purpose is to link the hero closely to the invented but imposing figure of Nuño Rasura. It is likely that the real name was Gonzalo Fernández, an individual who appears in a number of documents with the title of 'count' in the early tenth century (Martínez Díez 2005, 1.297–303) and who played an important part in re-establishing the town of Lara as a strategic centre (García González 2008a, 197). This Gonzalo did not have **three sons**: it seems clear that Fernán González had just one brother, Ramiro, younger than himself, who is recorded as fighting at the head of frontier troops in 936 (*ibid.*, 295–297). The figures of Diego and Rodrigo are almost certainly invented. There are many parallels for the representation of the youngest of three brothers as the one to succeed in a quest or epic task; see López Guil (2001, 197) and West, who comments that this detail 'appears to be much closer to the fantasy world of the folk tale than to the world of the heroic epic' (1983, 37). The **men of noble birth** mentioned here are *infançones* (*infanzones*), the least prestigious group of the nobility, linked to the emerging village communities; this social group first emerged in the later tenth century (see Álvarez Borge 1996, 34–35). The status of the *infanzones* was defined both by their legal rights and privileges and by their military role, and any *infanzón* would by definition be a horseman. By the time of the *Poema*'s composition there was quite a sharp distinction between the relatively small group of families that made up the upper nobility (*ricos hombres*) and on the other hand the lower nobility that included the *infanzones* (*ibid.*, 136–137).

171   no more then than a tiny little corner: for a description of the small area originally covered by 'Old Castile', see note to line 87a. We should be aware, however, of how the poet exaggerates in order to emphasize the extent of his hero's achievement. By 912, two years after Fernán González's birth, the territories of the Castilian counts had extended south of the mountains as far as the line of the Duero. The area was not a single, unified one but was made up of several small counties. Moreover, the movement southwards was already creating difficulty by increasing the size of the frontier with Islamic Spain in an area which was uncomfortably far removed from the Asturian-Leonese capital (see García González 2008a, 199ff.). The **Hills of Oca** are part of the range to the east of Burgos which divide Castile from Navarre. The present-day **Itero del Castillo**, in the Middle Ages a fortified town, lies on the banks of the River Pisuerga which marked the frontier in the west with León. As the river valley broadens, the old town of Itero was situated on the flood plain. **Carazo** is situated about 60 kilometres south east of Burgos and just seven kilometres to the east of the monastery of Santo Domingo de Silos. It seems clear that the poet is not accurate when he says that **Carazo was still held by the Moors** when Fernán González's career began, as it is some 40 kilometres north of the Duero and was one of a series of defensive fortifications and towers which had been erected as the Christians had occupied the land from the River Arlanza to the Duero (Martínez Díez 2005, 1.230); this process was effectively complete by 912, just after our hero's birth. There is convincing evidence that the poet has chosen to transfer to Carazo a later victory won by the Count at Osma in about 934 (Serrano 1943, 20–21). Christian and Muslim sources differ considerably in their accounts of the outcome of this battle but Christian chronicles present it as a significant victory of the Christian troops of Ramiro II and Fernán González over a powerful raiding party led by Abd al-Rahman III (see Martínez Díez 2005, 1.322–326). In addition, Hernando Pérez (2001, 117) suggests a parallel between the dramatic function of this early display of prowess by the young count and a similar episode in the career of the hero of the *Libro de Alexandre*. **Line 171c** is missing in the manuscript but editors have reconstructed it from the Argote de Molina text (see Introduction, section 1(ii); Menéndez Pidal 1951, 56).

**173   **This account of the development of Castile in three stages has a parallel, for example, in the story of the foundation of Rome in the *Aeneid*. There is no suggestion of a direct borrowing, but for discussion of the significance of this detail see Introduction, section 3(v). In reality, the final stage in the development described in this stanza was only brought about by Fernando I in 1037, almost 70 years after the Count's death.

175c **he brought wide new lands:** essentially, the achievement of the historical Fernán González can be summarized as creating a strong and powerful single county of Castile, bringing under his control the group of Castilian counties which had previously existed; and in the course of this process of unification or concentration of power he also extended his authority to the east over what was then the county of Álava. See Martínez Díez (2005, 1.443–445), and, for further discussion of the achievement of Fernán González, Introduction, sections 1(iii) and 2(ii).

177c **a poor man, a worker of charcoal:** the burning of wood, usually formed into conical piles, to produce charcoal was an ancient trade and was a common one in the Middle Ages. Although we have evidence of Fernando's noble birth and his family's connection with the monastery of Santa María de Lara is clearly recorded in a document of 929, there is no other reliable information about our hero's early years. The 1344 Portuguese *Crónica geral de Espanha* describes how Fernando was sent away beyond the Cantabrian mountains to be educated by a good knight. However, the tale of the charcoal burner which appears in the *Poema de Fernán González* is the first written evidence of a tradition which subsequent accounts were to elaborate with a growing wealth of details. (See Martínez Díez 2005, 1.304–305.) West (1983, 39) suggests a correspondence between this worker of charcoal, *carbón*, and the term *carboniento* applied to both Satan and the Islamic invaders in line 388d; however, there does not seem to be any real evidence to attribute evil or violent intent to this individual, or to back up West's suggestion that we might see the charcoal burner as a kind of devil figure. Various literary parallels have been suggested with our poet's account of Fernán González's childhood: for example Keller (1990, 50–51) discusses a possible link with a French *Life of Saint Eustace*; Deyermond (1960, 35–37) suggests the *Liber regum* as a source, but he also (1990, 54–55) points to an Old Testament association. West (1983, 40) also suggests a parallel with the description *bufa-tizo* ('ash-blower'), applied to a lazy or reluctant hero by the Provençal poet Marcabrú. There is undoubtedly in this episode an echo of the account of the upbringing of Paris in the *Libro de Alexandre* (stanzas 346–61) and this is one of numerous examples of how our poet uses this source to lend a sense of epic grandeur to his narrative. Essentially, it seems that our poet, by including this tale, is seeking to make Fernán González part of a tradition, both biblical and secular, associated with individuals whose deeds were to prove of immense significance for their nation.

180b **the wheel that turns at random:** our poet uses this image on three occasions (see also lines 74cd and stanzas 441–445). Deyermond (1990, 63–65) points out that this cycle of fall and recovery is of fundamental importance in the historical books of the Old Testament and argues that Fernán González, like Christ, is to bring an end to this cyclical pattern. The classical topos of the Wheel of Fortune was immensely popular with medieval writers and was of central importance, for example, in Boethius' *Consolation of Philosophy*, a highly influential work composed in the sixth century AD. Our poet will certainly have come across its use in the *Libro de*

Alexandre, to which the idea of the constantly shifting nature of Fortune is central; see, for example, stanzas 1652–1655, in which Darius talks to his troops of how her wheel will turn so that their present misfortune will soon be transformed into triumph.

185d   her suffering of old: Deyermond (1990, 57) points out that, although the allusion here is not explicitly linked to the Fall and the expulsion from Eden, given the way in which the overthrow of Visigothic Spain has been represented in the *Poema*, these words 'are enough to trigger recollections of an ancestral disaster and its Biblical counterpart.'

190d   escape her oppression: it is not clear to which kind of 'oppression' this applies. Lines 186b and 191c, for example, indicate that the poet has the Muslims in mind, and this is backed up by the fact that Fernando immediately launches a campaign against them. On the other hand, line 188d seems to suggest that the concern is with the Castilians' subjection to León, and, indeed, it is the achievement of Castile's independence from its neighbours that is to be represented as his ultimate triumph. The different adversaries of the Castilian people are blurred into one single weight of oppression which the hero will struggle to overcome. More specifically, in this passage the poet may well have in mind the depiction in the *Libro de Alexandre* of the young warrior's determination to put an end to the suffering endured for generations by his people (stanzas 21ff.). There are several such parallels (see also, for example, note to line 177c).

192d   a difficult stronghold set high in the hills: Carazo (see also note to stanza 171) is also mentioned by Gonzalo de Berceo in *La vida de Santo Domingo de Silos*, where it is described as 'una cabeça alta, famado castellar' ('a famed stronghold, high and prominent'; see Dutton 1978, 64); the similarity between the two descriptions suggests a direct borrowing or possibly a borrowing from a common source, and the two of them have the ring of an epithet drawn from the language of epic. Dutton (1961, 198–199) argues that this is evidence that the two poets will have had a common source in a lost epic and points out that Berceo's account suggests that Carazo will already have been well known to his public. The description which appears in the two variant forms is an accurate one, as the castle of Carazo was built to take advantage of a rocky and steep-sided hill which formed a natural fortification.

193b   noble lords: see note on the 'men of noble birth' in 167a–c.

199c   Almería, situated in the extreme south east of the Iberian Peninsula, was founded as a city in about 955 by Abd al-Rahman III. It developed into the most important port of al-Andalus, famous in particular for the export of silk, and was the base of the Umayyad navy. It was reconquered by Alfonso VII for a short time in the mid-twelfth century, but subsequently, as part of the kingdom of Granada, it was not to fall into Christian hands until 1489. Both here and in 390b, the poet seems to view Almería as a large territory, perhaps confusing it in his mind with the whole of al-Andalus.

200b Muñó: this town and its castle, situated on the left bank of the River Arlanza and dominating the surrounding area, were named after Munio Núñez, one of the counts responsible for the repopulation of the area north of the Duero in the years leading up to 912 (Martínez Díez 2005, 1.193–194). From 929 Muñó was the seat of a bishop (García González 2008a, 240) and at that time it was a fortress superior to Burgos (Serrano 1943, 21). We know that it still enjoyed considerable prestige in the thirteenth century: it was in Muñó that in 1224 Fernando III, in front of both Queen Berenguela and his leading noblemen, proposed the launching of the new and crucial campaign into Andalucía. Moreover, it has been suggested (Hernando Pérez 2001, 117) that the prominence of Muñó in the *Poema* is related to the upbringing of Alfonso X, who spent part of his childhood in the area controlled by its castle.

202a Gonzalo Díaz: Luciano Serrano (1943, 28) believes that this individual was a nobleman in Fernán González's court and that of his son García Fernández, and identifies him with the Count's *alférez* or lieutenant Gómez Díaz, named in a document of the monastery of Cardeña in 932 (see also Martínez Díez 2005, 1.291). Once again, however, there is a clear parallel between the narrative here and that of the *Libro de Alexandre*. Gonzalo Díaz's caution angers his leader just as the counsel of the general Parmenio repeatedly meets a cold response from Alexander and leads him to lecture his troops on the need for valour and firmness of purpose (see, for example, the advice given in stanzas 1272–1279 and the reaction in 1280–1286). Nuño Laíno (or Laínez) receives a similarly cold response when he likewise advises caution in stanzas 341ff., and that response also clearly reveals a debt to the *Libro de Alexandre* (see note to stanza 354).

205d hew off all our heads: decapitation was indeed a common fate inflicted on the enemy of Islam: *Sura* 47:3 of the Qur'an enjoins the faithful to strike off the heads of unbelievers when they are encountered on the battlefield.

209–224 The Count's harangue, urging his troops to imitate the heroic deeds of their predecessors in the struggle against Islam, is as applicable to the mid-thirteenth century as it is to the first half of the tenth century. See Introduction, section 4(vii).

214c to lower their worth: the term used in the Spanish text (*menos valer*) is a legal one, designating a degree of infamy which is considered to be just below treason and which disqualified an individual from holding any kind of official position. Alfonso X devotes to it a section of the *Siete Partidas* (7,5); see also Duggan (1989, 44–45).

215c they thought it their duty to die before their lords: the emphasis placed in the *Poema* on the duty of the people to protect and honour their lord and their king, both physically and in terms of his fame and honour, corresponds closely with the ideas developed at length by Alfonso X, as in the *Siete Partidas* (see, for example, 2,13,26). Alfonso explains that this is an obligation, recognized by ancient peoples, towards the king as representative of God on earth. See also Introduction, section 4(iv).

225d Lara: situated just over 40 kilometres to the south east of Muñó, Lara had been re-established as a Christian settlement during the 860s and under Gonzalo Fernández (almost certainly Fernando's father – see note to 167a–c) it acquired considerable strategic importance and became the centre of one of the Castilian counties which were to be united under Fernando. The only solid historical fact that is known about Fernando's childhood concerns his family's link at that time with the convent of Santa María de Lara (see note to line 177c) and it is likely that he exercised power as count of Lara from 929 (see Martínez Díez 2005, 1.308 and García González 2008a, 296–297). Today the castle of Lara continues to dominate the surrounding landscape, but it is a ruin, and the villages which originally made up its *alfoz* or area of jurisdiction have fallen sharply in population.

226cd   in pursuit of a boar: the boar is indeed an appropriate animal for the Count to pursue at this stage, for it is associated in the Bible with the wild animals that attacked the Lord's vineyard in Psalm 80:13–15, an image which is generally taken to stand for the attacks by the dangerous enemies of the chosen people. On the other hand numerous parallels have been suggested for the folkloric elements of such a hunt – see, for example, Deyermond (1968, 86–87) and West (1983, 26–31; 49ff.). West points to the great frequency with which the hunt figures in Celtic lore and argues (p. 50) that 'the hunt and prophecy motif has become bound to the foundation legend of the monastery of San Pedro de Arlanza' and that (p. 51) '[i]n our Christianized epic, the fairy of the forest or the giant of the castle becomes the monk of a hidden hermitage'. She goes on to suggest (p. 56) that 'Fernán González's accidental entry into the hermitage may be mythologically explained as a symbolic death and resurrection experience'. We have pointed in the introduction to the importance of the hunt in courtly literature and have also discussed the way in which this image runs throughout the *Poema de Fernán González*, binding the work together (see section 4(ix)). Scholars have pointed to close similarities in our poet's depiction of this episode with Marie de France's tale *Guigemar* (composed in the late twelfth century) and with the French *Life of Saint Eustace* (see Keller 1990, 62–63; West 1983, 52–53; and also note to line 177c, above). There is also a particularly important parallel in the legend of the foundation of the cathedral of Palencia by Sancho Garcés of Navarre, and Deyermond's analysis of the two accounts (1968, 82–92) leads him to conclude that there is a very likely source for this passage of the *Poema de Fernán González* in Rodrigo Jiménez de Rada's *De rebus Hispaniae*. In addition, Hernando Pérez (2001, 218) points to a similarity with the way in which in the *Libro de Alexandre* the heroic warrior in battle is likened to a huntsman riding in pursuit of his prey.

Las Quebañas: the original reading in the text is 'Vasquebañas': this place name has not been identified; López Guil (2001, 216) suggests a possible connection with the area around the lagoon of Sanguesuela, which is documented as existing in the twelfth century in the area between Muñó and Lara. However, in adapting the reading in both text and translation, we have followed Hernando Pérez (2001, 113; 218) who suggests a deformation of Las Quebañas/Las Cabañas, the name of a farm belonging to the prestigious monastery of Bujedo and situated some 10 kilometres from the area of Lara where the Count's troops were camped.

228d   San Pedro was the name: this is the first mention in the poem of the Benedictine monastery of San Pedro de Arlanza which, in the *Poema* at least, is to play an important role in the hero's career and with which the poet undoubtedly has a close connection. For discussion of the question of whether the monastery was founded by Fernán González and of its association with the composition of the poem, see Introduction, section 2(viii). San Pedro de Arlanza is situated on the banks of the River Arlanza between the villages of Covarrubias and Hortigüela, some forty-five kilometres to the south east of Burgos. It was less than ten kilometres from Lara (see note to line 225d). From 1037 the monastery took the name of San Pelayo, after the pious hermit who plays such an important role in the *Poema*. Already in the tenth century the monastery was a significant landowner, largely on account of decisions taken by the counts (see Álvarez Borge 1996, 106) and in the eleventh century it benefited considerably from the patronage of Fernando I. The present monastery church, of which only ruins now remain, was begun in 1080. The poet here describes how his hero comes not to this later church but to a cave, situated high above the river, which was the site of the original hermitage (see Pérez de Urbel 1945, 1.418). The hermitage, which has passed through numerous stages of construction, from pre-Romanesque to Baroque, survives today. Scholars have commented on how the description given in the *Poema* does not reflect accurately the situation of the monastery or even of the original hermitage, but this is probably the result of the poet's desire to exaggerate the steepness and difficulty of the path that his hero has to follow (see Hernando Pérez 2001, 116).

233c   Pelayo: although we are told later that this good monk (Pelayo or Pelagius) has on his death become a saint, there is clearly no connection between him and the well-known Saint Pelagius of Córdoba (San Pelayo mártir), who was said to have been executed as a boy at the Caliph's command in 926. More significant is the close parallel that our poet seems to be establishing between this monk and the figure of King Pelayo (see notes to lines 88a and 115a) and in turn between them and Fernán González. Deyermond (1990, 55) points out that 'stanzas 114–16 and their echoes later in the poem bind King Pelayo, the monk Pelayo, and Count Fernán González together in a network of associations, a kind of secular prefiguration. Fernán González is shown to be Pelayo's rightful heir both through narrative patterning and by divine approval mediated through the prophecies of the second Pelayo.'

240a   Before the third day: the parallel that the poet establishes with Christ is an obvious one, but this is one of many occasions in the *Poema* when the number three is clearly significant (see also Keller 1990, 11–21 and Introduction, section 3(v)). For a discussion of the allusions in the *Poema* to both the Old Testament and the New Testament and their significance for the work's interpretation, see Introduction, section 4(vii).

247bc   my whole fifth share: the principle of reserving a fifth share of booty for the lord is also, for example, reflected in the *Poema de Mio Cid* (see lines 494, 515, 805, *etc.*) and in fact has its origin in the similar Muslim custom of paying a fifth of the spoils of war to the caliph as prescribed in the Qur'an. (See Menéndez Pidal 1969, 1.199.) The value of such a donation would have been immense and it represents a considerable act of self-denial on the part of the Count (for discussion of the value of such booty see Keller 1990, 26ff.). It should be pointed out, however, that the fifth share belonged specifically and exclusively to the king (*Siete Partidas* 2,26,5; see also Lacarra 1979, 41–43). This detail is very revealing with regard to the poet's attitude to his hero. It is unlikely that he sees him as here usurping the right of his lord, the king of León, but rather he views him as a successor to King Roderic and a precursor to Alfonso X, a man with the stature and rights of a king.

   to have my burial here: Fernán González and his wife were indeed buried at San Pedro de Arlanza and their tombs remained there until, on the monastery's closure in 1841, they were transferred to the collegiate church in the nearby town of Covarrubias where they can still be seen today.

249d   their weeping and their wailing turned to joy: Fernando's lone adventure which has separated him from his followers and brought him back to them equipped with a new insight, supernatural in origin, is considered by some scholars to be a kind of 'symbolic death and resurrection' experience (see, for example West 1983, 58), which he shares with a number of other famous epic heroes. The supernatural element is to be all the more powerful when he pays his second visit to the hermitage before his battle with the Muslims.

255a   Puente Fitero was the name given to the bridge which crossed the River Pisuerga at Itero del Castillo, a point which marked the western frontier of Castile (see note to stanza 171). López Guil (2001, 226) points to the existence in the mid-twelfth century of the place-name Ponfitero, though this has now disappeared. The episode of the horseman who is swallowed up by the ground has biblical parallels, on which the poet has probably drawn, notably in Numbers 16, where the rebellious Korah, Dathan and Abiram similarly disappear into a chasm. This biblical passage is also alluded to in the *Libro de Alexandre* (line 1243d), and in addition it is the basis of an anathema which appears in some public documents, calling down punishment on any who should not fulfil the contract (see Hernando Pérez 2001, 228).

   The manuscript includes an extra line, almost certainly the result of a scribal error, between the first and second lines of this stanza; this has caused editors much difficulty.

Lacuna between stanzas 255 and 262: we have included at this point the text of the *Estoria de España* (see Introduction, section 1(ii)) which gives a clear picture of the content of the missing text. Some editors (see, for example, Victorio 2010, 96–98) have used material from this chronicle to reconstruct the passage which is missing at this point.

   Gustio González, singled out here for praise for his valour, could well be indentified (see Álvarez Borge 1996, 78) with the grandfather of the seven young noblemen whose death through treachery is recounted in the *Estoria de España* and other chronicles, in versions which are believed to be based on a lost epic poem, *Los siete infantes de Lara/de Salas* (*The Seven Noblemen of Lara/of Salas*). The *siete infantes* are also extensively commemorated in ballad tradition.

263a   Velasco: this is the name of another distinguished Castilian family, believed to have been descended from Nuño Rasura (see note to 163b, above). In the parallel passage in the *Estoria de España*, 'Velasco' is named as Roy Blásquez, presumably the same figure as the Ruy Velázquez whose family feud with the Lara lies behind the betrayal at the centre of *Los siete infantes de Lara/de Salas*. Serrano (1943, 28), however, identifies this individual as Velasco González, lord of Huerta de Arriba o de Abajo in Vallegimeno, situated in the region of Salas.

263b–d lacuna: the copyist has probably omitted more than just the three lines of this stanza. Chronicle accounts seem to make it clear that stanza 264 relates to help being given to the Count, but there is nothing to lead into this in what has gone before.

275d   the poor municipality: the wording here recalls directly that used in 173c (and also 172a), in which the poet describes the stages by which Castile rose to greatness. The poem's public is clearly expected to remember and note such details. Our attention is thus drawn to the way in which the transformation is achieved – a heroic struggle in battle against the unbeliever.

277d   Alexander and Porus: repeatedly in the *Libro de Alexandre* there is emphasis on the vast amount of booty gained by Alexander and his followers in the course of their conquests. The Indian ruler Porus is one of Alexander's principal antagonists; he is depicted as being so fine a warrior that, after defeating him in a duel, Alexander rewards him by allowing him to remain in control of a large empire. The spectacular wealth of his palace and its unusual features are the subject of a distinctive descriptive passage (stanzas 2117–2142).

279d   displayed upon its altar: there was fierce competition among monasteries to impress visitors and potential visitors by the wealth of relics that it possessed. Hence, for example, the comparison between Silos and Arlanza that Gonzalo de Berceo makes in the *Vida de Santo Domingo de Silos* (*Life of Saint Dominic of Silos*), stanzas 264–286.

283b   the city of Burgos: Burgos is generally considered to have been founded by the Castilian count Diego Rodríguez Porcelos as a fortification on the right bank of the River Arlanzón; its strategic position led to its continuing growth and by 899 it became the seat of a county. From 899 to 931 the counties of Burgos and Castile were essentially separate (Martínez Díez 2005, 1.197), although at times both were governed by the same person. We know that Gonzalo Fernández, our hero's father, was count of Burgos at various points during this period. When in 932 Ramiro II gave Fernán González power over an extensive terrain made up of a number of previously existing counties, Burgos became established as the seat of his authority and, well defended and situated in a fertile valley, it was to expand rapidly (García González 2008a, 227–228).

285c   the king of the Navarrese launched an attack: the picture which the *Poema* gives of almost constant warfare between Castile and Navarre does not correspond to historical reality; this attack by the Navarrese did not actually take place and Fernán González did not defeat or kill in battle the neighbouring kingdom's monarch. Sancho Garcés I of Pamplona died a natural death in 925 and his son and successor García Sánchez reigned from 925 to 970, throughout all of Fernando's recorded career, albeit as co-ruler in the early stages. Indeed, the title of King of Navarre was not used before 987. The origin of the story of conflict between the two figures probably relates to an episode which occurred in 961, as the result of Fernando's entanglement in León's dynastic conflicts: with Muslim assistance, King García captured the Count at Cirueña and held him prisoner for some months. Even here, commonly accepted accounts of the episode must be treated with care (see Martínez Díez 2005, 1.416–419). For discussion of the thematic importance in the *Poema* of this Navarrese conflict, see Introduction, sections 2(ix) and 4(v).

289a   the Count sent a message: the exchange of messages between King Sancho and Fernán González contains clear echoes of the correspondence in the *Libro de Alexandre* between the young Alexander and King Darius who, like King Sancho, mocks what he sees as his young adversary's overconfidence (see the exchange of letters between Alexander and Darius in stanzas 780–819).

292b   friendship with the pagan nations: the *Estoria de España* elaborates on this, accusing King García of Navarre of assembling 'muy grandes huestes de los suyos et de agenos, gascones et moros' ('great forces made up of his own people and of others, both Gascons and Moors'). This certainly seems to involve an allusion to the French support received by the Navarrese monarchy of the House of Champagne in the mid-thirteenth century and it seems highly likely that the mention of the Gascons relates to this period. See Introduction, section 2(ix). However, the poet's original comment certainly appears also to reflect the blood links of the early rulers of Pamplona with the Islamized Banū Qasī clan and Navarre's connection with Muslim Spain in the lifetime of Fernán González, when Queen Toda placed her realm directly under the protection of the caliph. (It is also just possible that the poet is here alluding to the pact made by both Navarre and León with the Almohads after the battle of Alarcos in 1195, for this would clearly be entirely consistent with the picture that is painted in the *Poema* of the Castilians standing alone and threatened by Christian foes and by Muslims alike; and it would have endured for many years in the Castilians' memory.)

293c   those frontier lands: the term used in the Spanish text is 'Estremadura', a term which, rather than designating the present-day region of Extremadura, was applied to the lands on and beyond the southern frontiers of the Christian kingdoms, so that the area that it was considered to cover continuously changed.

312d   the Era Degollada has been identified with the stony plain and hills of

Valpierre which lie between Nájera and Briones (see López Guil 2001, 242 and Zamora Vicente 1978, 92). Valpierre is also mentioned in stanza 755 as the site of the later battle between Fernando and Sancho's son García. There is no evidence, however, of any such battle actually taking place.

313b   in a beautiful meadow: there is a further echo here of the *Libro de Alexandre* where the topic of the *locus amoenus*, a set-piece description of a place of beauty, is used (in stanzas 935–40) to precede a battle scene which depicts the horrors of war. This tradition of juxtaposing idyllic peace and beauty with the apparatus of war is at least as old as Homer's detailed description of the scenes forged as decoration on Achilles' shield (*Iliad* 18.478–608).

317   Pamplona! Having been an important administrative centre under both the Romans and the Visigoths, in the early years of the ninth century the Basque city of Pamplona was turned by a local chieftain called Íñigo Arista into the capital city of an independent kingdom, although in the early stages it would depend closely on collaboration with Muslim rulers. It would be normal in battle for troops to shout the name of their nation or city, and this practice is widely represented in Spanish epic (López Guil 2001, 243). However, it would be surprising if contemporaries of Fernán González were to invoke the same of **Estella!**, as this city was only founded under this name, near to the older settlement of Lizarra, in 1076 (see Martín Duque 1990, 317ff.). Situated on the pilgrim route to Santiago de Compostela, Estella thrived as a trading centre and reached its height of prosperity in the thirteenth century. Here, then, we have one further detail which links the description of battle scenes in the *Poema* with a period significantly later than that of the events being recounted.

some Frenchmen at times act in jest: it has been pointed out that this detail of the Navarrese king's conduct, which seems to have been rejected by the authors of the chronicles, belongs rather more to the world of the *juglares* (López Guil 2001, 243 and Muñoz Cortés 1946, 211–214). In mentioning 'Frenchmen' in this essentially mocking context, the poet is probably alluding to the very close association which existed at the time of the *Poema*'s composition between Navarre and France under the House of Champagne. In fact Thibault II of Navarre was resident in France for most of his reign and only visited his kingdom on five occasions in order to inspect the procedures of government (see García Arancón 1985, 46–47 and also Introduction, sections 2 (ix) and 4(v)).

321b   a great lance-wound in his right-hand side: this is the first of a number of details whose function is to associate Fernán González in the agony of battle with the suffering of Christ on the cross.

322d   fallen so deeply into error: the Castilians' concern that they are seriously at fault reflects the emphasis on the overriding duty of the people to protect the person of their lord which is to be found in the legal works of Alfonso X, for example in *Partidas* 2,13,26.

329c   his life now lost: Fernán González certainly did not kill any Navarrese monarch in battle. It seems likely (see, for example, Serrano 1943, xxiii) that there is an echo here of the defeat and death of King García Sánchez of Navarre at the battle of Atapuerca in 1054. On this occasion the victor was the Castilian monarch Fernando I, but it seems entirely plausible that tradition came to associate this victory with his earlier namesake. See also notes to 695a and 703c.

331ab   the man who was count of Poitou and Toulouse: the Spanish text perhaps suggests that the copyist believed the two counts to be separate individuals, but it seems clear that this is in fact an allusion to one man who held both titles. Our translation reflects the latter interpretation. It has been argued (see Keller 1990, 95–98, and López Guil 2001, 18–19 and 247) that this could be Guillaume VII of Poitou, who on two occasions was also count of Toulouse, fought in Spain and achieved great fame as a troubadour; better known as Guillaume IX of Aquitaine, he was also an ancestor of Alfonso X. It seems to us much more likely, however, that the figure that our poet has in mind in creating this fictional episode is Alphonse of Poitiers (or Poitou) and Toulouse, brother of the French king, Louis IX, during whose absence on crusade from 1249 to 1254 he governed France as regent. Alphonse had a clear Castilian connection, for, as the son of Blanche of Castile, he was the cousin of Fernando III and uncle of Alfonso X. He was also the great-grandson of Blanche of Navarre (*c.*1181–1229), countess of Champagne, and thus indeed related to the Navarrese monarchy, tied by **kinship to the King**. There can be no doubt that our poet knew of Alphonse's prominent role and that he was well aware too of the close links which bound the Navarrese monarchs to France; he may have known, too, of Alphonse's personal acquaintance with Thibault IV of Champagne, Teobaldo I of Navarre (Ducluzeau 2006, 33). Significantly, Alphonse, as regent, was a major figure in the confrontation over Gascony which occurred with Alfonso X in 1253 and his international prestige may well have been increased by his role as a protector of poets, among them Rutebeuf, the most important *trouvère* of his day (Ducluzeau 2006, 110–12; 174–77; see also Introduction, section 2(ix)).

332d   Cize: see note to line 138b. The poet probably wishes his audience to be aware of the parallel here between the arrival of the two French armies at this pass: that of Charlemagne and that of the Count of Poitou and Toulouse, both destined to suffer defeat at the hands of the Castilians.

337d   he seems like Satan: such a comparison seems highly surprising in view of the number of details in the *Poema* which suggest a Christ-like aspect to the hero's role. The criticism levelled here, however, is a further reflection of the influence exerted on the poet by the *Libro de Alexandre*, where the hero who is driven by pride and by an insatiable desire to conquer – and, in this case, also to discover – and as a result is at times likened to the devil (see, for example, line 1186b and stanza 1725) and shown to place himself in serious danger of damnation. There seems in the complaint of Fernán González's followers to be a clear reflection of that expressed by those of Alexander (stanzas 2265ff.) when he, likewise recovering from a serious injury, decides to press on with his campaigns. The essential difference is that Alexander's troops were motivated here by concern for their leader's welfare.

340cd great pride ... nor evil greed: it would be difficult to argue that Fernán González is really characterized by either of these vices, but the response that the poet attributes to the Castilians once again illustrates how far his account has been influenced in by the *Libro de Alexandre*. In the earlier poem the hero is driven on to seemingly endless campaigns by a great desire for both material gain and for knowledge and it is both this greed and, above all, his pride that are constantly highlighted as the causes of his inevitable downfall. Criticism for the same failings has here been projected onto the Count, even though in his campaigning he seeks essentially the good and the safety of his people and he is not marked by Alexander's fatal flaw.

341a Nuño Laíno: in stanza 349 Nuño is given a different surname – Laínez. The existence of various Castilian noblemen of this name is documented, but there are none that are associated with Fernán González. Given that this individual is to appear to be a good counsellor, it is fitting that his name should contain elements of both of the legendary judges, Nuño Rasura and Laín Calvo (see note to line 163b). Nuño is again to come to the fore when the leaderless Castilian people are in search of guidance (line 661c) and here again his role seems to be linked to that of the judges.

342cd The quality which Nuño contrasts with **greed** is *mesura*, moderation or **restraint**, which is of great importance in both the *Libro de Alexandre* and the *Poema de Fernán González* (see note to line 30b).

354 They tell of Alexander: there is a direct allusion here to the *Libro de Alexandre*, stanza 2288, where the hero talks of the importance of the renown which is achieved through valour and endeavour (see Such and Rabone 2009, 46):

> I do not count my life in years or in days
> but by great deeds and acts of chivalry.
> Homer did not set down in his allegories
> the months Achilles lived, but his acts of valour.

Judas Maccabeus was a son of the Jewish priest **Mattathias** and is renowned as one of the greatest warriors in Jewish history. He led a lengthy successful revolt against the Seleucid empire and eventually died in battle in 166 BC. The two books of Maccabees, which contain the history of the Jews under his leadership, are part of the Catholic canon of the Scriptures but are omitted in the Protestant Bible. He was also commonly depicted in medieval art as a hero of the Old Testament.

355 Having given examples of memorably valiant conduct taken from both the history of the pagan world and the Bible, the poet now draws on more recent examples of heroism as recounted in the account of the destruction of Charlemagne's rearguard at Roncesvalles (see note to line 127b). The knights that he mentions here are all among those who, according to legend, took part in Charlemagne's expedition into Spain. It is certainly not necessary for us to assume from this list that the poet had first-hand knowledge of the *Chanson de Roland*: he seems to have had access to the *Historia Turpini* (see note to line 134b), where he would have found listed all the names that he includes here (see Latin text in Castets 1880, 17–19).

365d Gascons: Gascony is the region of south west France which extends southwards and eastwards from Bordeaux, reaching as far as the Pyrenees. In the east it reaches close to the city of Toulouse, but it would not have been part of the territory of the Count of Poitiers and Toulouse. There were Gascon expeditions against Muslim Spain in the ninth century (see Lomax 1978, 36), but there is no reason at all why Gascon troops would have been fighting against Fernán González. On the other hand, over two centuries later involvement in Gascony was to play a significant part in Castile's foreign policy. In 1169 Henry II of England gave his wife's possessions in Gascony to their daughter Eleanor as her dowry on her marriage to Alfonso VIII. In 1205 Alfonso attempted to exert his right to Gascony, mounting a military campaign which ultimately proved unsuccessful. Although he then abandoned his claim to the region, his great-grandson Alfonso X had his right to it much in mind when he came to the throne, and the dispute over Gascony, closely involved with the conflict with Navarre, was much at the fore at the time when, almost certainly, the *Poema de Fernán González* was composed.

373c the Gascon: the Count was not a Gascon (see note to line 365d), but it is significant that our poet again seeks to establish his link with this disputed territory and to emphasize the relationship between what he presents as historical fact and a contemporary issue.

376b you shall hear what he did: this entirely fictional episode gives the poet an opportunity to draw attention to the magnanimity and generosity which his hero shows towards an enemy defeated in battle. Once again it seems clear that he is taking the idea from a passage in the *Libro de Alexandre*, in this case the description of the burial of King Darius (stanzas 1772ff.) and also the treatment of Darius' wife Stateira, who dies whilst Alexander's prisoner (stanzas 1235ff.).

384d near Lara: Muñó (see note to 200b) is in fact situated at some distance (over 40 kilometres) from Lara and it has been argued that this statement is evidence that the poet's knowledge of local geography was shaky and thus he may well not have been a native of the area in question (Serrano 1943, 44; Hernando Pérez 2001, 117).

385 Morocco: following the arrival of Islam in the form of the Umayyad armies in the late seventh century, Berber resistance was steadily overcome; the Arabs' new province of Ifriqiya was established and eventually pacified to the extent that the expedition of 711 could be launched into Spain. Under the Idrisid Dynasty (from 780 AD), Morocco, which had originally been a subsidiary province of Ifriqiya, became an important centre of learning and a major military power. From the eleventh century, a series of powerful Berber dynasties ruled Morocco, and under in turn the Almoravids and the Almohads, Morocco dominated the Maghreb and Muslim Spain. In the tenth century, in the heyday of the Caliphate of Córdoba, there is no reason to see al-Mansur as basing his power in north Africa, the situation which this stanza seems to depict. On the other hand, in the context of the early years of the reign of Alfonso X, Castilian attention was very much directed towards Morocco, in the light of the King's plans to launch a crusade (see Introduction, section 2(ix)).

as if to win pardon: the poet is here suggesting that the Muslim troops were motivated by the same belief which inspired the Christian crusaders – the promise that for those who died in battle there would be absolution and remission of their sins. The *jihad nil Sahif* or struggle to defend and expand the Islamic state was seen as a fundamental duty of the Muslim, but it would not have been identified in the same way with the winning of forgiveness.

386a **Turks:** Fernán González will certainly not have found himself fighting against Turks. It seems significant, however, that the poet is aware enough of their importance to include them here. The Turks may well have been adversaries for Alfonso X as raiders of Spain's Mediterranean coast, and it is known that in 1246, after the capture of Jaén, his father Fernando III had held a council of war to debate whether he should now attack Seville, Salé or the Turks of Asia Minor (Lomax 1978, 150).

387a The **Almohads** were essentially a highly organized religious movement which was initiated in the early twelfth century by iban Tumart, a member of a Berber tribe from the Atlas mountains, and eventually came to dominate all of the Maghreb (north west Africa) and al-Andalus. It was against Muslim armies under the Almohads that Alfonso VIII suffered a crushing defeat at Alarcos in 1195 but went on to win his overwhelming victory at Las Navas de Tolosa in 1212. Subsequently the Almohads hung on to power in the Maghreb but their territory was progressively lost in a series of revolts. Their principal adversaries were the Banū Marīn or **Marinids**, in origin another Berber tribe, who were engaging the Almohads in battle as early as 1145. It was almost a century later, however – in 1244 – that they took Fes and made it their capital; by 1269 they had conquered Marrakech and taken control of most of the Maghreb. They subsequently extended their influence into the kingdom of Granada and attempted to secure control of the Straits of Gibraltar. By the early years of Alfonso's reign, as he prepared his fleet for a probable invasion of Morocco (see O'Callaghan 2011, 11ff.), the Castilian king was well aware of the opposition that he would face from both the fading power of the Almohads and the newly emerging dynasty of the Marinids, and it is evident that our poet was informed about them too.

389b **Gibraltar** is about three miles long and a quarter of a mile wide and is linked to the Spanish mainland by a low-lying narrow strip of land. It served for several centuries 'not as a barrier severing Europe from Africa but as a bridge between the two continents' (O'Callaghan 2011, 3). It had been strategically important during the invasion of 711 (see note to 43b), but its mention here looks forward as well as back: it seems likely that the objective of Alfonso's proposed crusade (O'Callaghan 2011, 23–25) was Ceuta, situated fourteen miles away directly across the strait; in the anticipated attack by Alfonso's crusaders Gibraltar would be a vital point of embarkation.

390ab   From the mid-eighth century **Córdoba** had become the seat of the Umayyad emirate and had developed into a cultural, political and economic centre of immense importance, one of the most advanced cities in the world. In the age of Fernán González it was the capital of the caliph, Abd al-Rahman III, and subsequently the base from which al-Mansur exercised power over much of the Peninsula. Some two and a half centuries later, Fernando III reconquered the city in 1236. **Jaén,** situated about ninety kilometres to the north of Granada and seventy-five kilometres to the south of the site of the battle of Las Navas de Tolosa, was a flourishing city throughout the period of Muslim domination, and was particularly important as an agricultural and manufacturing centre. It was centred on a formidable hill-top fortress and withstood fierce sieges by Fernando III in 1225 and in 1230 but eventually was handed over to him after a pact in 1245. For the remainder of the Middle Ages, Jaén was to retain considerable strategic, and therefore political, importance. **Lorca** is situated in the south east of Spain occupying a strategically important position near to the coast, reinforced by its imposing castle whose defensive structures made it virtually impregnable. From 1042 Lorca was the seat of an independent kingdom, whose power extended as far as Jaén. From 1172 it was in the hands of the Almohads, but in summer 1244 it was captured by a Christian army under the command of Prince Alfonso, later to become Alfonso X. **Cartagena,** also situated in the south east of the Peninsula, was one of the most important ports of Muslim Spain. It fell, probably a year after Lorca, to a campaign conducted at land and sea by Alfonso. These were conquests of which the future Castilian monarch could justifiably feel proud (González Jiménez 2006, 29–30). For **Almería,** see note to 199c.

392ab   **Hacinas** is today a small village situated more or less mid-way between Burgos and Soria, 13 kilometres from the monastery of Santo Domingo de Silos. Its castle, constructed during the ninth century, is evidence of the strategic importance of its position during the conflicts between Castile and Navarre, but it has never been the scene of a major battle. The immensely important Christian victory over the Muslim armies in which Fernán González did participate, though not as overall commander of the Christian armies and not against al-Mansur (see Introduction, section 1(iii)), was fought outside the walls of Simancas; this small town is situated some way further west, in the present-day province of Valladolid. **Piedrahita:** this is Piedrahita de Muñó, situated very close to Hacinas and to Santo Domingo de Silos. Today it is a tiny village of about 20 inhabitants. Piedrahita is situated close to the site of the battle of Atapuerca, a famous Castilian triumph over the Navarrese (see note to line 329c).

399d   **I alone resisted:** Fernán González was not, of course, resisting alone, as he was fighting as a vassal and ally of the king of León, Ramiro II. On the other hand, this sense of isolation in the face of an immensely powerful Muslim enemy does seem to evoke the situation of the Castilians under Alfonso VIII, at least as they will have viewed it. In the disastrous conflict at Alarcos in 1195 the Castilians engaged the enemy with only token Portuguese support; even the great victory at Las Navas de Tolosa was, in Castilian eyes, seen as won virtually without assistance: the Leonese and the Portuguese were not involved at all, almost all the French knights defected before the battle, and in his report to the Pope Alfonso describes the kings of Navarre and Aragón as bringing only very small numbers of knights (see Linehan 2008, 53–55). The view of Castile as a nation which by steadfastness in adversity and firm adherence to its beliefs achieves glory for itself and triumph on behalf of all Christendom is, of course, entirely consistent with that of a people working out a destiny especially allotted to it by its Christian God (see note to 402a).

402a Isaiah: the prophet repeatedly foretells how the Lord will reward and protect those of His chosen people who have remained faithful through adversity, and how He will defeat and punish their idolatrous enemies; for examples of His many assurances to Israel, described as God's servant, see for example Isaiah 41:8–13 and 42:1–13. For an analysis of how the *Poema de Fernán González* likens the struggle of the Castilians, a chosen people, to those of the people of Israel, see particularly Deyermond (1990).

417c Samson: God granted Samson supernatural strength to help him begin the task of rescuing the people of Israel from the Philistines. Judges 14:5–6 recounts how he wrestled a lion with his bare hands.

418d Millán is my name: Saint Millán or Saint Aemilianus was a hermit priest who lived in the mid-sixth century and is said to have founded the monastery of San Millán de la Cogolla. The monastery, situated to the south of Nájera and some 40 kilometres from Logroño, was to benefit considerably from the generosity of the kings of Navarre. It is closely identified with the early development of written Castilian, and Gonzalo de Berceo, who is known to have worked for the monastery as a notary, included amongst his substantial literary output a life of Saint Millán. Berceo's poem was composed at some point between 1228 and 1246 and certainly before the composition of the *Poema de Fernán González* (see Dutton 1967, 6). Berceo represents the saint as supporting Fernán González in this crucial battle and intervening directly alongside Santiago – which he conspicuously fails to do in the *Poema de Fernán González*. Significantly, according to this account it is the monastery of San Millán de la Cogolla and not that of San Pedro de Arlanza which is to benefit financially from the Christian victory; for the importance of these different accounts, see Introduction, section 2(viii). It is believed to have been after the battle of Simancas that Saint Millán was made patron saint of Castile.

436a Aragón: the existence of the county of Aragón – of Frankish origin – was first documented in 828; it was linked to the kingdom of Navarre until 1035, and in this sense it is not surprising to see the Aragonese named here alongside the Navarrese and the Poitevins. However, it is probably once again to the political situation in 1254 – see Introduction, section 2(ix) – that we need to look to explain the involvement of the Aragonese at this point. On top of a long-standing situation of mutual mistrust, the Anglo-Castilian treaty of that year left the Aragonese, like the Navarrese, feeling threatened, and they responded by signing at Monteagudo in Navarre an agreement of friendship and mutual support. Tension on the frontier between Castile and Aragón rose to a dangerous level. (See González Jiménez 2004, 75–79.)

447d lie in Hell with Judas: there is an echo here of a legal formula found in monastic documents of the twelfth century. See also, for example, *Libro de Alexandre* line 1911d.

451a–c Gustio González: see note to lacuna between stanzas 255 and 262. **Velasco:** see note to line 263a. **Salas** is situated near to the monastery of Santo Domingo de Silos and very close to Hacinas, where our poet set his account of the battle. It was in fact founded in 974 by García Fernández, Fernando's son, and later came to be known as *Salas de los Infantes* after the legendary figures of the young noblemen whose death was widely commemorated in both oral tradition and later chronicles. It is striking that both Gustio González and Velasco are figures intimately associated with this legend.

452a Gonzalo Díez: this will have been common enough name, both in the tenth century and at the time of the *Poema*'s composition, but it is not possible to identify any specific contemporary of Fernán González to whom the individual named here relates.

457 Lope of Vizcaya: our poet is probably basing this figure on the lords of Vizcaya, extremely influential figures in thirteenth-century Spain. Lope Díaz de Haro, señor de Vizcaya, had been the king's *alférez* or lieutenant until his death in 1237, when his son Diego took over the position. By summer 1254, however, he was in dispute with King Alfonso, and he took refuge in Navarre. **Laíno** and **Martino** are not identifiable individuals, although there has been an attempt to relate the latter to Martín González, who, according to the legend incorporated in later chronicles, was responsible for bringing up the young count (see, for example, López Guil 2001, 284; Martínez Díez 2005, 1.305).

458a La Bureba or Burueba is a district in the north east of the present-day province of Burgos, an area of level land surrounded by mountains; centred on the town of Briviesca, it was strategically important in the Middle Ages, lying on the route from the north east of Spain onto the Castilian meseta. **Treviño** is today a small enclave belonging to the province of Burgos but surrounded by land which is part of Álava. Its foundation by Sancho VI of Navarre is mentioned in a document of the monastery of San Millán de la Cogolla. At the end of the twelfth century it was conquered from Navarre by Alfonso VIII of Castile. It is mentioned by Rodrigo Jiménez de Rada in the *De rebus Hispaniae* and was awarded its *fuero*, or charter of rights, by Alfonso X in 1254.

459a Castro: this is Castrojeriz, situated about 40 kilometres to the west of Burgos, on the pilgrim route to Santiago de Compostela. It was repopulated in 882/883 by Munio Núñez, possibly an uncle of Fernán González (Martínez Díez 2005, 1.329–330). It was awarded its *fuero* in 974 by Fernán González's son, Count García Fernández, and this is believed to be the earliest such charter granted in Castile. The Castros were one of the great families of Castile in the twelfth and thirteenth centuries.

463a **Ruy Cavia** cannot be identified with any specific individual of the tenth or the thirteenth century. The village of Cavia, however, is situated about twenty kilometres south west of Burgos and it is certainly possible that a man by this name did exist: by the first half of the fourteenth century the Señor de Monzón y Cavia had risen to high office under Alfonso XI. **Nuño** is a name too common to allow identification. For the close link between Fernán González and **the region of Lara**, and also for consideration of the significance of the role played by the Lara family in the mid-thirteenth century, see note to 225d and also Introduction, sections 2(ii) and 2(ix), with note 13. The *alfoz*, or administrative district, of Lara was an extensive one, taking in, for example, the monasteries of San Pedro de Arlanza and Santo Domingo de Silos and several of the places named in the poem such as Carazo, Hacinas and Salas de los Infantes.

465c **at the sound of the horn:** it seems likely that there is an allusion here to the *Chanson de Roland*, according to which it is because of the French hero's refusal to blow his horn to sound the retreat that the huge slaughter is made inevitable. There is, however, no clear justification for assuming that the poet has first-hand knowledge of the epic poem: the sounding of the horn also plays a plays a part, albeit a rather different one, in the *Historia Turpini*, to which we know that he had access (see notes to stanzas 134b and 355).

467a **those troops on crusade:** the theme of the crusade runs throughout the poem; the Goths (as in 79d), the troops of Fernán González and the celestial army which supports them (411c) all fight in the name of the Cross. The triumph that Fernando is about to achieve, wiping out the stain of sin and avenging the Goths' defeat, will offer encouragement to the Christian troops of the poet's own day who are about to embark on a new crusade across the Straits of Gibraltar (see, for instance, notes to lines 387a and 389b). It is interesting to compare with this Rodrigo Jiménez de Rada's depiction of the campaign leading up to Las Navas de Tolosa as a crusade, in an account which places considerable emphasis on the apparently miraculous role of the cross in the battle itself (Pick 2004, 43–46). Strikingly, too, the first recorded use of the Spanish word 'cruzada' dates from some years after that battle and it was Alfonso X in the 1250s who was the first Spanish monarch to make systematic use of the notion of the crusade (see Luis Fernández Gallardo 2009, 17–19).

468b **a furious serpent:** this episode may well be related to an actual historical event, the almost total solar eclipse which occurred on 6th August 939, just before the battle of Simancas. By the thirteenth century, the accounts given in chronicles of this event (which lasted almost an hour) had been exaggerated to such an extent that we read of a flame that emerged from the sea, consuming towns, cities, men and beasts (Martínez Díez 2005, 1.342). The eclipse and what seems to be the appearance of a comet are mentioned by Berceo in *La Vida de San Millán de la Cogolla* (stanzas 378–384), but both Berceo and the author of the *Poema de Fernán González* omit the more extravagant details that appear in the chronicle accounts. Dutton (1961, 199–202) suggests that there may be an allusion, in the Berceo version at least, to a source in an oral narrative. On the other hand, there is a parallel to be found in the *Libro de Alexandre* in the account of Darius's dream (stanzas 951–954), a phenomenon close to the one being described by our poet, and the *Alexandre* also contains a description and explanation of an eclipse (see note to 475d).

475d   speaking of astrologers: West (1983, 58–64) argues that the interpretation of mysteries or riddles should be seen as one of the tests by which a hero asserts his leadership. The model which the poet has in mind here, however, could well be a more precise literary one: in the *Libro de Alexandre* the soothsayer Aristander is summoned to allay the fears of Alexander's army by explaining in detail the principle of an eclipse (stanzas 1209–1232), and the hero takes advantage of this intervention in order to allay his troops' fears and move his men out to battle. Eclipses and other phenomena involving celestial bodies have long held a great sense of wonder and there is a long tradition of individuals winning distinction by explaining them, going back to the time of the Greeks Thales and Anaxagoras. In the case of the *Alexandre*, the poet is at pains to demonstrate the value of scholarship. In the *Poema de Fernán González*, however, the nature of the explanation given for the alarming natural phenomenon is of a very different kind, itself hinging on superstition and really demonstrating an ability to think clearly under pressure. Nevertheless, it is striking that once again our poet includes an episode whose purpose is to increase his hero's stature and which has a parallel in the earlier work.

482a   the Beast: on several occasions in the *Poema*, the Muslims are identified with the Devil, whose machinations had led Christian Spain to fall into their hands (see note to line 11d and also Deyermond 1990, 53–57). Our poet was certainly not alone in seeing the Muslims as the agents of the Devil: the struggle of the warrior of Christ against the Beast as embodied in the threat of Islam was a very common one in both the visual arts and the historiography of medieval Spain (Monteira Arias 2012, 329ff.).

496d   its entrails hung suspended: in this gruesome detail there is a close parallel with the description of the death of Alexander's horse Bucephalus in the *Libro de Alexandre* (stanza 2088). Like Alexander, Fernando is quickly given a horse, an example of the emphasis placed in both poems on the importance of selfless loyalty shown to the leader and feudal lord.

501ab   the finest of the rulers: editors are divided on the reading for the final word of the line, which appears to be either 'reyes' (kings) or 'leyes' (laws). The difficulty in the reading that we have adopted is, of course, that Fernán González was never a king, even though his role is in some respects presented as that of a monarch and he is closely identified with later Castilian rulers.

as a wolf does when set among the flocks: this is a simile common in classical and medieval epic and also with Biblical parallels (for example, Acts 20:29). Nevertheless, it should be observed that the battle descriptions have a great deal in common with those of the *Libro de Alexandre*. In this case the resemblance in phrasing is a very close one (see *Alexandre* 1055b) but there are many more stylistic parallels with the earlier poem (see Introduction, section 3(iv)).

504a Diego Laínez: this is a name of a well-known Castilian nobleman, but from a later age: he was the father of Rodrigo Díaz de Vivar, the Cid (see note to 165d). The *Historia Roderici* tells how his father had seized from the Navarrese a number of castles, probably on the occasion of the death of King García in battle at Atapuerca in 1054.

510d comfortably sheltered: there is a sense here that the poet has some idea of the realities of campaigning. There is just an echo of the way in which the Christian troops, having achieved victory in the battle of Las Navas de Tolosa, at the end of the day are reported to have slept in comfort in the tents of their defeated enemies (Salvador Martínez 2012, 347).

516 Órbita: this does not seem to be an identifiable individual, but there could here be an echo of the importance of the role played by Alfonso VIII's standard at Las Navas de Tolosa as recorded in the chronicles (see, for example, O'Callaghan 2002, 50).

Thierry l'Ardennois: it has been claimed (see, for example, López Guil 2001, 300 and Victorio 2010, 138) that this individual is one of Charlemagne's Twelve Peers who, according to the Chanson de Roland, died at Roncevaux/Roncesvalles. Some scholars take this allusion as clear-cut evidence that the author of the *Poema de Fernán González* had direct knowledge of the *Chanson de Roland*. In fact, the link with the *Chanson de Roland* is a more indirect one: the character in question is called Thierry d'Anjou, is not listed as one of the Peers, and does not die in the battle. He is the knight who defeats the champion of the traitor Ganelon in judicial combat at the end of the poem. However, it is in later versions of the story, for example in the Latin account in the *Historia Turpini* (see notes to line 134b and stanza 355), which our poet certainly knew, that this figure comes to be included in the list of those killed. The name Terrín de Ardeña appears in other Spanish versions such as the *Cantar de Roncesvalles*, which probably dates from the late thirteenth century and of which just a short fragment survives. Ardeña is a region now in north east Spain in the province of Gerona. There is, then, no evidence here that the poet was directly acquainted with the French epic.

The monastery of San Pedro de **Cardeña** is situated about fourteen kilometres south east of Burgos and quite close to the pilgrim route to Santiago de Compostela. It was founded in 899 as the Christian kingdoms extended their territories southwards towards the line of the river Duero, but in 934 it was the victim of a savage Muslim raid and its two hundred monks were all slaughtered. It is known that Fernán González's family had connections with Cardeña: for example, in 935 his mother is known to have made a donation to the monastery. However, Cardeña's closest link with Castile's legendary heroes is with the Cid, as the author of the *Poema de Mio Cid* (probably composed in 1207) is very keen to emphasize. After the Cid's death in 1099, his body, with that of his wife, was eventually taken from Valencia to Cardeña, where a tomb-cult grew up, involving the collection of relics but also the generation of a significant body of legend. The elaboration of this legendary material was to continue until the mid-thirteenth century and much of it was to be incorporated into Alfonso X's *Estoria de España*. San Pedro de Cardeña possessed a significant collection of other relics, including the head of San Esteban, abbot at the time of the massacre; but it was highly unlikely to have possessed the tomb of the French knight, whose identity in the *Poema de Fernán González* seems to be much in doubt. It is possible that in (d) the poet is telling us about Órbita and not Thierry, but as has already been seen, nothing is known of him as a historical individual.

Lacuna between stanzas 523 and 531: at this point it seems that seven and a half stanzas are missing from the manuscript, but we have included the corresponding section of the *Estoria de España*, which almost certainly closely reflects their content. For an attempted reconstruction of the missing text, see Victorio (2010, 139–140).

the hour of None: this is one of the canonical hours of prayer in the Church day, originally appointed for about 3.00 in the afternoon. Its name comes from the Latin *nonus*, ninth: according to Roman custom, the day began at sunrise and ended at sunset, and this period was divided into twelve hours (their lengths varying with the time of year). Thus the ninth hour will fall in mid-afternoon. (See Such and Rabone 2009, 682.)

553a   forsaken by You: possibly unintentionally, this statement prefigures the three anguished cries that the Count is to make on being taken prisoner (601d, 602d, 603b), echoing Christ's words from the cross (see Deyermond 1990, 59–60).

557d   Fernando of Castile: this title has the ring of royalty – the Count is here portrayed as a ruler closely identified with his land. However, we may also be reminded here of two later bearers of this title: Fernando I, victor at Atapuerca in 1054, under whom Castile was really to become an independent kingdom; and Fernando III, the great conqueror of the thirteenth century and father of Alfonso X.

558b   the Holy Apostle: accounts of the appearance of Santiago in battle are not restricted either to essentially literary sources or to major battles. For example, the Christian chronicles tell us that, during a minor battle in 1231 between a small Christian force led by Fernando III's brother, Alfonso de Molina, and a larger Muslim army, the Muslims themselves were convinced that they saw Santiago, mounted on a white charger, in the midst of the fray (see Salvador Martínez 2012, 697). On this occasion, as in the *Poema de Fernán González*, this appearance seems to have been brought about in part by the invocation of the saint's name and that of Castile.

565a   Almenar: this is almost certainly the village of Almenar de Soria, situated about 110 kilometres south east of Hacinas.

569b   entrusted my body to rest there: see note to lines 247bc.

571ab   Sancho Ordóñez: this is King Sancho I of León, known as 'el Craso', 'the Fat', on account of his extreme obesity. The correct name should be Sancho Ramírez, and the poet's error was probably caused by his failure to realize that

Ordoño, Sancho's predecessor as king, was not his father but his brother. Sancho was remembered above all for his obesity and his ineptitude, and he is thus an ideal figure to be cast as the man whose stupidity causes him to lose the county of Castile: hence his prominence in the *Poema*. In reality, however, for much of Fernán González's career the Leonese monarch was Ramiro II, a very effective, if ruthless ruler. It was alongside Ramiro that Fernando fought at the battle of Simancas and for several years the relationship between them was a harmonious one. However, on Ramiro's death in 951, the political situation became much more complicated: having once conspired with the king of Pamplona against the legitimate heir in favour of Sancho, the Count subsequently supported Sancho's cousin, who reigned very briefly as Ordoño IV. It was after a lengthy troubled period that Fernán González made his peace with Sancho and swore allegiance to him. The relationship between the king and his count could never have been an easy one. For further consideration of these events, see Introduction, section 2(ii). In view of the similarity between their names, it is, of course, important that we distinguish clearly between Sancho of León and the two rulers of Navarre mentioned in the *Poema*: Sancho Garcés and his son García Sánchez.

parliament: the term *Cortes* or *Cortes generales* (also *curia plena*) relates to a gathering of the representatives of the kingdom. The first time that the term is used in a royal document is in 1254 (see O'Callaghan 1993, 46) and by the mid-thirteenth century such an assembly would be attended by the monarch and his immediate family, the nobility, members of the clergy (who would include archbishops, bishops and the masters of the military orders) and also representatives of the cities. The origins of this institution seem to have been Leonese rather than Castilian and it is generally considered that the first meeting of a 'curia plena', involving all three of the estates, took place in the Basilica of San Isidoro in León in 1188. It would be wrong to view such a parliament as a sign of democracy, though attempts have been made to attribute to it a considerable importance in this respect (Keane 2009, 171–180). The *Cortes* had no legislative power, though it was clearly possible for powerful groups to exert influence on the king. Combined Leonese and Castilian *Cortes* met after the union of the kingdoms in 1230, and under Alfonso X the body met with increased frequency; in the early years of Alfonso's reign there were *Cortes* in Seville (1252), Toledo (1254), Burgos (1254) and Palencia (1255). (For a full account of the development of the *Cortes*, see Procter 1980.) No such institution existed in the times of Fernán González, although it could be possible to see this episode as essentially just a summons to the king's court.

572b   to kiss the King's hand: the act of homage would involve both the swearing of an oath, probably in the presence of relics and sacraments, and also the performance of ritual gestures, in this case including the kissing of the lord's hand. This constituted a formal act of submission to the lord, which involved a pledge of fealty and the acceptance of an obligation to convene at the lord's residence to conduct official business, to perform military service and to give material or financial assistance as the lord required. The significance of this act, in terms both of its symbolism and of the practical commitment that it implied, was therefore very great. A famous example of the consequences of this act is the deep resentment which was to remain with Alfonso IX of León as a result of finding himself obliged to perform an act of homage to his cousin Alfonso VIII of Castile at Carrión in 1188 (see Salvador Martínez 2012, 126–129).

574c   the Queen: according to our poet, this Queen Teresa of León was sister of King Sancho of Navarre – whose death at the hands of Fernán González during the battle of La Era Degollada is recounted in stanza 320 – and aunt of Sancho's successor, García Sánchez I. For a fuller explanation of her hatred for the Count, see stanzas 734–735. The name that the poet gives her is historically accurate; however, the Teresa of history had no Navarrese connection and the historical King Sancho Ramírez of León was in fact married to Teresa Ansúrez, daughter of Ansur Fernández, count of Monzón. The extensive territories of the county of Monzón stretched from the limits of Cantabria in the north as far as the north west of the present-day province of Segovia in the south. Ansur Fernández is recorded as holding the office of count of Castile during the time that Fernán González fell from favour with the King of León and was imprisoned, so it is possible that this historical rivalry between the two families is reflected in our poet's narrative.

576a–c   a hawk that had moulted ... a horse: these two items could indeed have been of immense value. There are parallels in the *Poema de Mio Cid*, for example, in the mention of the moulted hawks confiscated by the king (see Such and Hodgkinson 1987, 41) and of horses won in battle (*ibid.*, ll.1573; 2011). There is a record, for example, of such animals being accepted in the eleventh century in exchange for a monastery (see Pitollet 1902, 158), though García Gallo (1984, 275–289) argues that what is being described in the offer of the horse and the hawk may in fact have originated in a kind of voluntary offering made in response to a grant or concession, in this case that of the right to govern the county independently. García Gallo suggests that our poet transformed the situation from one in which both parties gave something of their own volition into a sale by contract. The horse and hawk are clearly the signs of an individual of valour who has been victorious in battle, however, and as such at this point in the poem they represent much more than financial value; there is a further parallel, for example, in the *Libro de Alexandre* when Thalestris, also in search of something of great importance for her kingdom, presents herself to Alexander riding a fine horse and (stanza 1872) carrying a seven times moulted hawk (see Hernando Pérez 2001, 107); a hawk plays a prominent and extended part in the lost epic of *Los siete infantes de Lara* (see Montgomery 1998, 53–54). There are examples in the visual arts of the hawk being used as a symbol of authority and possession, as in a painting at Chinon which seems to show Eleanor of Aquitaine handing over to her son and heir a falcon which represents lordship over her territory (Flori 2004, 163), or in the Bayeux tapestry, which shows King Harold bearing a hawk at the outset but the victorious King William doing so as the battle reaches its conclusion. The origin of the episode of the horse and the hawk in the *Poema de Fernán González* has been much debated and for some scholars it is the key piece of evidence for the antiquity of the oral tradition on which the *Poema de Fernán González* is based. It has been suggested that there is a close parallel in a detail to be found in the sixth-century *Historia Getica*, a work dealing with the early history of the Goths, and some scholars have seen this as evidence for a link between the Spanish epic and Gothic tradition (see Entwistle 1924, but also for a reappraisal of the evidence, Harvey 1976). Deyermond and Chaplin (1972, 48) have emphasized the folkloric nature of the episode; they are inclined to include it within a 'deceptive bargain' category (though it could be argued that, as it is the king who insists on making the purchase, it is not really made clear at this stage in the *Poema* that Fernán González does indeed set out to deceive). On the other hand, Harvey and Hook (1982) point to Arab versions of the Moorish Conquest of Spain in 711 which involve deals – leading to the loss of Spain – including either just hawks or horses and hawks. One of these accounts, by Ibn al-Qūtiyya, was composed before 977. Such a version could certainly have entered Christian tradition long before the composition of the *Poema*, and our poet would surely see it as appropriate indeed for his hero to gain independence for Castile in a manner which both reflects and redeems the error through which Spain had been lost by his ancestors. Weiss (2006, 174–177) suggests that this episode has a broader symbolic significance: in the horse and hawk, 'noble symbols of the warrior ethos are degraded, by being treated as mere merchandise' and the king's initial failure to recognize the contract in effect gives justification to the inevitability of violence. 'From this perspective, the endlessly proliferating value of the horse and the hawk comes to symbolize the unpayable debt to war' (p. 176).

578c   a thousand marks: one mark was equivalent in value to eight ounces of gold or silver, so the sum of money involved is very large. It is, for example, equivalent to the amount that the Navarrese monarchy brought from Champagne to pay for a potential war at the time of the conflict over Gascony (García Arancón 1985, 252). In the *Poema de Mio Cid* one hundred marks are considered ample payment to the monastery of Cardeña for providing for the Cid's family and their ladies for a year (see Such and Hodgkinson 1987, 50). In fact the monarchs of Castile and León did not mint their own coins until after the capture of Toledo in 1085; and in the thirteenth century it would be more usual to express a payment in *maravedíes* and *sueldos* (see, for example, Ruiz 2004, 155).

579d   the interest would each day double what was owed: the normal penalty for non-completion of such a contract would probably have been simply for the amount to be doubled (see García Gallo 1955, 666). The penalty might have been increased by the addition of periodic fines but the principle followed here would not have corresponded to any accepted medieval legal or financial practice. García Gallo suggests that there is an explanation of such principles in Arabic mathematical works and also points to a well-known story of Indian origin about the reward requested by the inventor of the game of chess (*ibid.*, 667). Our poet's grasp of the implications of compound interest suggests a reasonably sophisticated understanding on his part of financial processes.

580a letters ... divided by ABC: these were legal documents in which two copies were made on the same parchment with, in the centre, an inscription usually in the form of a sequence of letters. The document (and the set of letters) was then divided in two and the authenticity of one of the copies could be demonstrated by showing that the two parts matched exactly. See also, for example, the *Libro de Alexandre* 1537b and 2525b. It has been argued that this legal device was less used after the first quarter of the thirteenth century and by 1250 would have been anachronistic (Hernando Pérez 2001, 83; see also, for further notes on anachronism, Serrano 1943, 32), but it could also be a detail that has been imitated from the *Alexandre* itself.

583 queen of León and the sister of Sancho: see note to 574c.

the ram that sought wool: the allusion is to a popular expression, listed by Covarrubias and others and meaning 'to be deceived': 'como al carnero que va a buscar la lana agena e viene d'allá trasquilada la suya' ('like the ram which goes in search of other sheep's wool and returns shorn of its own').

584 the betrothal of a bride: this is the first mention in the *Poema* of the lady who was to become Fernán González's wife and bear him seven children. The poet blurs two stages in his hero's career and probably the identities of two different women (see below), but it is undoubtedly Fernando's first wife Sancha that he has in mind here. The name that she is given in the *Poema* is historically accurate: she was Sancha Sánchez of Pamplona, daughter of Sancho Garcés I of Navarre and Toda Aznárez. This was Sancha's third marriage – her first two husbands were King Ordoño II of León and the Alavese Count Álvaro Herramélliz, both of whom had died. Her marriage to Fernando probably took place in 932 or 933. It is worth noting that the network of royal relationships was a tight and intricate one: Sancha's two sisters, Oneca and Urraca were married to Alfonso IV and Ramiro II of León respectively, whilst her mother, Toda, was aunt to the Caliph, Abd al-Rahman III. Without doubt the historical Sancha, sister of the queen of León and daughter of the king of Navarre, will have remained an influential figure even during her husband's imprisonment by Ramiro and it is plausible that, one way or another, she will have played a role in securing his release. On the other hand, the account of Fernando's confinement by the king of Navarre on which our poet is now embarking relates to an event which is said to have taken place almost two decades later, after Sancha's death. The explanation probably lies in the fact that the historical Count actually married twice: at some point between 959 and 964 he married Urraca, daughter of King García Sánchez of Pamplona and niece of his first wife Sancha. Confusingly, the order of the Count's two periods of imprisonment has been inverted in the *Poema* and here, as in accounts in the chronicles, the roles of two women have been fused into one.

that the war might be over: this is a rather surprising comment, given that

Castile has not been shown at this point to be at war either with León or with Navarre. There is perhaps an echo here of an actual clash between Fernán González and King García of Pamplona in 960 (see Martínez Díez 2005, 1.418–419), but the comment could also be seen as a reflection of the historical importance of such unions as a means of putting an end to the constant warring between Christian kingdoms during the late twelfth century and the early decades of the thirteenth century; probably the most famous case of this would be the highly contentious marriage between Berenguela of Castile and Alfonso IX of León in 1197.

her niece: the Queen Teresa of history had no Navarrese connection (see note to 574c) and this relationship with Sancha is evidently a fictional creation.

585d   dictated ... dictation: the *ars dictaminis* was indeed the term applied in the Middle Ages to the art of letter writing and it would have been common to dictate a letter aloud for a scribe to copy (see Murphy 1974, 194ff.).

586b   King García: this is García Sánchez I, the son of King Sancho Garcés who, according to the *Poema* though not in history, had been slain in battle by Fernán González. García Sánchez I ruled Navarre throughout the entirety of the Castilian count's military and political career and was the father of his second wife Urraca (see note to stanza 584).

589b   Cirueña is a village in the province of Logroño, south east of Santo Domingo de la Calzada and close both to the monastery of San Millán de la Cogolla and to the pilgrim route. The *Poema de Fernán González* coincides with the twelfth-century *Crónica najerense* in citing Cirueña as the place where the Count was captured.

594c   and there found his shelter: the hunter has now become the hunted. There is a clear parallel between what the Count does here and the way in which the boar seeks refuge in a hermitage in stanza 227, and this is underlined by specific verbal echoes. We are reminded of the Count's respectful conduct on that occasion and of the protection which God has extended to him as a result of his virtuous conduct.

597b   even though it was sacred: there is an evident contrast here with the Count's own conduct when the boar that he was hunting took refuge in a sacred place (see stanza 230 and Introduction, section 4(ix)).

598c   on his word: the Spanish term used here, 'omenaje' (or 'homage'), is one which implies total submission to the captor; for the usual implications of 'homage' paid to a feudal lord, see note to line 572b. It is perhaps significant that this is soon to be replaced by another, very different kind of 'homage', this time to a courtly lady (see line 638b).

599   and surrendered to prison: it is known for certain that Fernán González suffered a period of imprisonment at the hands of Ramiro II of León in 944–945; in addition, convincing evidence of his later period of imprisonment in Pamplona by King García Sánchez of Navarre (believed to have taken place in about 960) is to be found in an account of Islamic origin composed in the fourteenth century. This later episode does appear in the *Crónica najerense*, composed in the late twelfth century. According to this source, in 960 Fernán González was freed from his imprisonment at the hands of the Navarrese on agreeing to marry Sancha; but serious factual inaccuracies make such an account very hard to believe (see Martínez Díez 2005, 1.415–419). What seems clear is that there were indeed two historical imprisonments and that their order has been reversed in the *Poema*, probably in order to increase the focus on Fernán González's relationship with León as the poem approaches its climax. Some scholars are inclined to believe that the poet actually inverted the original order in which he had intended the two episodes to appear within the poem (see, for example, Keller 1990, 136–146) whilst others suggest that a single event has been divided into two, perhaps because of the original episode's popularity (Deyermond and Chaplin 1972, 47–48; Irizarry 1983, 60).

like the cry of a peacock: this detail has been shown to be derived from the *Libro de Alexandre* and it is also beyond doubt that the poet will here have had in mind associations of the peacock as set out in the medieval bestiaries. These include the warnings by the preacher of the ultimate punishment which awaits us for our sin and also the need to beware of the sin of arrogance (see Lugones 1977, 31–32). There is a strong link between Fernán González's loud cry (described both here and in line 593a) and Christ's cry from the Cross. The allusion here is made clearer still by the statement that **the altar split asunder, from the top to the bottom**, with the verbal parallel between the Spanish text 'de somo a fondón' and the biblical text 'a summo usque deorsum' an extremely close one; (see Matthew 27:46 and 50–51; cf. Mark 15:34 and 37–38). Deyermond (1990, 59–65) provides a masterly analysis of the biblical parallels in this episode and of their significance, concluding that '[h]e is not a Christ figure, but as Christ is to sacred history, so Fernán González is to the secular history of Spain' (*ibid.*, 65).

601d   why have You failed me? See also notes to line 553a and stanza 599. The wording is different here but there is nevertheless an echo of Christ's expression of despair; with the accusation repeated in stanzas 602d and 603b, the poet achieves considerable dramatic effect as well as forcing us to consider the nature of the parallel between the fate suffered here by the *Poema*'s hero and that of Christ.

604a   Castroviejo is a village in the province of Logroño, south of Nájera and about 20 kilometres south east of Cirueña. Deyermond (1990, 60) tentatively suggests a resemblance between this imprisonment (see particularly stanza 612) and the entombment of Christ as described in Matthew 27:66 and also points to further possible biblical parallels for this passage, for example between the lamentation described in stanza 607 and the account of the weeping for Christ in Luke 23:48.

609   the anger of all those in Spain: the poet again represents the Castilian people as standing alone, at best without assistance and at worst prey to attacks from all other parts of Spain, Christian or Muslim. For the relevance of this to the Spain of the thirteenth century, see note to line 399d.

a tiny hut: there is a precise parallel here with the word, literally meaning a mountain hut, used by Fernán González in line 181a as he embarks on his initial campaigns; the suggestion seems to be that the wheel has come full circle (see Weiss 2006, 159).

614a   A count ... who hailed from Lombardy: in the thirteenth century Lombardy was famed for its wealth and its highly developed commercial and financial activities. See, for example, the allusion in the *Libro de Alexandre*, line 91c. This individual, then, will be associated with wealth and power. His status as a pilgrim will be a guarantee of rectitude and fair-mindedness. However, in addition there is a striking parallel with the statement in the *Razón de amor* (*Speech about Love*, which dates from the early thirteenth century) that it was composed by a scholar who 'moró mucho en lombardia | pora aprender cortesía' ('dwelt for a long time in Lombardy | to learn the art of courtly love'); see López Guil (2001, 81), who also argues that the poet establishes a close relationship between the pilgrim's journey along the road to Santiago and the love that he helps to develop between Fernando and Sancha. It is worth noting that, according to the *Estoria de España*, the second time that Sancha sets off to rescue her husband from prison, she too goes in the guise of a pilgrim. The image of the lover as a pilgrim is much used by courtly love poets (see also Introduction, section 3(vi)).

636a   I am brought by true love: the mention of 'buen amor' ('true love') sets the developing relationship between Fernando and Sancha within the framework of courtly love, just as the use of the term 'entendedor' in 636c defines the Count as a lover accepted as such by his lady. Sancha depicts herself as in the grips of a passion which takes away her sense of responsibility to all but her lover (636c), and in this sense she does not act like a conventional courtly lady. Nevertheless, this passage is heavily influenced by the ideas and imagery of courtly love: Sancha is presented as the cause of her lover's suffering and his imprisonment in this context inevitably suggests the prison of love. In line 638b Fernando is required to swear loyalty and homage on Sancha's hand, a direct parallel with the process through which the vassal attested to his relationship of fidelity to his feudal lord; this is an image central to the depiction of courtly love in the poetry of the troubadours. For further discussion of the depiction of secular love in the *Poema*, see López Guil (2001, 79–85), and, for the influence of the world of the troubadours in the Castilian court, Introduction, section 2(v) and note 7, and Salvador Martínez (2012, 384–385; 401–404).

644a   the Road of the French: of the routes which led to Santiago de Compostela (see note to lines 153cd), the one which passed across northern Spain was by far the busiest. Four established pilgrim routes from starting points in France and beyond converged in the western Pyrenees. From there a combined track crossed northern Spain, passing through, for example, Pamplona, Logroño, Nájera, Burgos, Sahagún, León and Lugo. Along the road there was considerable French cultural influence and there developed numerous communities of Frankish origin.

646c   an evil archpriest: this episode combines a number of folkloric motifs: notably that of the hunter who encounters human quarry and that of the man of low moral standards whose lust leads to his own punishment – here we can infer that he is stabbed with his own hunting knife. There is an implication that the archpriest is a man of considerable wealth (as in the detail of the moulted hawk; see note to lines 576a–c) and there is a sharp contrast between the requirements of his religious calling (emphasized, for example, by the detail of his tonsure in line 652a) and the absence in his conduct of any sense of true Christian belief, charity or self-restraint (stanza 650). It has also been pointed out that it was specifically forbidden for an archpriest to hunt with dogs and hawks (Toro-Garland 1973; Keller 1990, 120). This is the third occasion in the *Poema* on which the role of the hunter has been prominent, and through this sequence our attention is inevitably drawn to the difference between the lecherous archpriest's abuse of his position and the true Christianity displayed by the hermits at San Pedro de Arlanza.

647d   Damietta and Acre: Acre is an ancient coastal city in northern Israel, of great strategic importance. It was the main port of the area under the Umayyad and Abbasid caliphates and developed into the most important port of the eastern Mediterranean. It was famously recaptured from Saladin during the Third Crusade in 1191 and three years later became the capital of the remnant of the Kingdom of Jerusalem. The final stronghold of the crusaders, it was to fall to the Mamluks of Egypt in 1291. **Damietta** was likewise a port and major commercial centre, which is also mentioned as synonymous with great wealth in the *Libro de Alexandre* (line 860d). It is situated on the Nile delta and was the object of an extended siege and was eventually taken during the Fifth Crusade. It was again besieged in 1249 when Louis IX of France had led the Seventh Crusade to Egypt, and on this occasion it was quite quickly captured. Louis' aim was to use Egypt as a base for an attack on Jerusalem, but the flooding of the Nile caused a lengthy delay. For some time the crusaders enjoyed the great wealth of the city, but they subsequently suffered from both hunger and disease. After their defeat at the battle of Mansourah and the capture of virtually the entire Christian army, Damietta had to be used as the ransom for King Louis, who then sailed on with his barons to Acre, leaving the wounded at Damietta to be massacred. In 1254 King Louis returned to France at the end of a campaign which had begun in triumph and ended in almost total failure. Keller (1990, 93–95) views the poet's mention of these cities, in the context of the archpriest's apparent amorous triumph, as ironic, implying that early success will rapidly be followed by a grim outcome. However, although this interpretation is convincing in the case of Damietta, there is no reason why the poet should have such a view of Acre. What seems most significant is the fact that he has some understanding of the contemporary importance of the two ports and of the wealth that was associated with them.

651b   a lance thrust: this is the second occasion in the *Poema* that we are told of the Count enduring a lance wound. On the previous occasion (see stanza 321) it had been a physical wound in his side suffered in the combat with King Sancho, but here it is a metaphorical one, inflicted by the treacherous cleric. We cannot be sure of the poet's intention here, but, in the light of the number of allusions which emphasize the parallels between Fernán González's role and that of Christ, there is a strong possibility that here too the intention is to use a biblical parallel to heighten our sense of outrage at the Count's betrayal.

652d   that all three of us atone for the sin: the Spanish text uses the phrase 'to fast for the sin', that is, to do penance. Zamora Vicente (1979, 193) argues that the suggestion of the penance being shared implies that the sin is an excusable one or has beneficial consequences.

656c   by the beard: this act is a particularly significant one: law codes of medieval Castile impose very strong penalties for grabbing a man by the beard, an act which brought considerable dishonour, and the penalties were especially severe if the victim was a married man (see Serra Ruiz 1965, 84–85). There are numerous mentions in the *Poema de Mio Cid* of the Cid's beard, for example the hero's exclamation at the *Cortes* of Toledo that it has never been caught or plucked (see ll.3280–3287). Some editors, following the reading in the *Estoria de España*, prefer to emend 'barba' in the Spanish text to 'boruca', which, it has been suggested (Pattison 2007, 19–20), can have the meaning of 'testicles'.

657a   The Count was unable to give help to the lady: it has been argued that in her courage, prodigious stamina and, above all, her ability and readiness to take the initiative when men are unable to do so, Sancha shows many of the classical qualities of the Amazon woman (as embodied, too, by Thalestris in the *Libro de Alexandre*). See Irizarry (1983, 57–59).

658c   his mule and his garments, his already-moulted hawk: perhaps there is a grim parody here of the theme of the horse and the hawk which is to be of such great significance in the final part of the *Poema*.

662b   carve our own lord from a hard piece of rock: there is a sense of a pagan ritual here and similarities have been suggested in Mediterranean and Germanic tradition. However, Deyermond (1990, 61–62) points out that there is no question of this being a graven image or of the Castilians incurring divine wrath by their action. Rather, he draws our attention to a conspicuous New Testament parallel in Matthew 16:18: 'tu es Petrus, et super hanc petram aedificabo ecclesiam meam'; just as Christ has His representative on earth, the rock or stone on which His Church is built, so Fernán González is represented by this figure of solid stone, to which his Christian people pledge loyal service.

663d   homage: for the significance of this act, see note to 572b.

670d   Arlanzón is situated close to the road to Santiago, some twenty kilometres east of Burgos. Initially this fortified settlement had an essentially military role but it became the centre of a group of villages and monasteries. In the late twelfth century it became the property of the royal convent of Las Huelgas.

671c   Hills of Oca: these hills marked the eastern extremity of Castile (see note to stanza 171). Their highest point is the peak of Valbuena (1,162 metres).

672b   Belorado stands on the road to Santiago, just under fifty kilometres east of Burgos. It had existed since the Roman period, and in the Middle Ages it gained military importance as a bulwark of Castilian power. It was to have connections with the Cid and was favoured, for example, both by Alfonso VIII and by Alfonso X, who, during stays in the town, made it substantial gifts. Still today Belorado claims that its right to hold a market on Mondays is the result of a concession granted by Fernán González in gratitude for being freed of his chains.

674d   my brother: the historical Sancha Sánchez was indeed sister of King García Sánchez of Pamplona. For **al-Mansur**, see note to line 104a.

679d   I will give you fortresses and lands: this would constitute the *arras*, or gift that was made to the bride as part of the marriage settlement. Such arrangements could be of considerable political importance in the Spain of the twelfth and thirteenth centuries, for example when in 1199 Alfonso IX of León handed over lands and 30 castles as part of the arrangements for his marriage to Berenguela of Castile; the memory of the complications caused by Alfonso's gift is known to have been very much alive in the mid-thirteenth century (see Salvador Martínez 2012, 452) and it is likely that at this point both the poet and his public will have had such well-known features of recent political history firmly in mind.

684   to kiss the hands of their lady: this is as ritual gesture which relates to the paying of homage (see notes to lines 572b and 636a). It is striking and unusual that the Castilians perform this act to Fernando's future wife. It is possible to see here an echo of the extremely significant occasion in 1217 when the representatives of the Castilian towns paid homage to Alfonso X's grandmother Berenguela, pledging their support to her in the face of the claim to the Castilian throne of Alfonso IX of León. Alfonso X was intensely aware of the importance of this episode, devoting to it a whole chapter of the *Estoria de España* (see Salvador Martínez 2012, 516; 520). Significantly, Leonese (or Navarrese) law would not have allowed a woman to succeed to the throne, and the acceptance of the legitimate (and legitimizing) role of a female ruler was a specifically Castilian tradition. For discussion of the distinctive role of women in the Castilian royal dynasty in the twelfth and thirteenth centuries and its reflection in both historical texts from the *Crónica najerense* and the *Poema de Fernán González*, see the illuminating study by Georges Martin (2009).

you were born at a favoured hour: there is a clear echo here of the kind of laudatory expression typical of the language of epic; this formula which was much applied to the hero of the *Poema de Mio Cid* (see, for example, Álvar Fáñez's greeting in 1.379). For the significance of its application here to Sancha, see Introduction, section 3(iii).

687b   reborn: the image of resurrection is applied not just to the Count but also to his people, with whom he and his fate are very closely identified.

690   mock castles: a construction of wood and scaffolding, perhaps in the form of a castle, was set up and knights attempted to knock it down by throwing a kind of dart. This form of entertainment at times of celebration was very popular in the thirteenth century: it is also mentioned, for example, in both the *Poema de Mio Cid* (see ll.1602; 2249) and the *Libro de Alexandre* (711c; 1961b) and it was such a competition which caused conflict to break out in the lost epic of *Los siete infantes* *de Lara/Salas.* A **citole** is a plucked instrument which appeared in Europe in the late twelfth century, probably having derived from the classical cithara, a kind of lyre. It is known to have been very popular among court entertainers in thirteenth-century Spain, and one musician in the court of Alfonso X was known simply by the name of the instrument, Cítola (Paredes Núñez 2010, 52). The medieval *vihuela* is a bowed instrument probably derived from the Byzantine lyre. It is depicted in the visual arts from the tenth century and its use in the court of Alfonso X is evident from illustrations which accompany the *Cantigas de la Virgen* (see G. Menéndez Pidal 1986, 240).

695a   as the text tells us: we do not know what this text is, but the poet could not be clearer in telling us that here (unlike, perhaps, in the previous episode) he is following a written source. His reliance on this source is again emphasized in line 743c. On the other hand, there is no known historical account of any serious confrontation between Fernán González and the Navarrese, except the brief narratives of the clash at Cirueña which led to his imprisonment. It is certainly possible that the allusion here is to a now lost juglaresque account of the Count's deeds, although if so it will have been a written one. It is perhaps possible, too, that, just as the *Poema* seems to include several echoes of Castilian history and tradition, here we have a reflection of a Castilian triumph from a different age: Fernando I's victory over García Sánchez III at Atapuerca in 1054 (see also note to 329c). A major difference is that in this battle the Navarrese monarch was killed rather than imprisoned, but there are certainly some (albeit quite predictable) similarities with the account in the *Crónica najerense* (Book III, 5), including the emphasis on the desire for vengeance, the wish to capture the king alive, the sounds of battle, the amount of bloodshed, and the hand-to-hand fighting, with specific mention of both darts and lances.

698d   traitors: this is literally the case. For the emphasis in Alfonso X's law codes on the absolute duty of every individual to protect the person of the king, see Introduction, section 4(iv).

703c   thrust clean through his breast: this is a standard epic description of a mortal wound but in the following stanza we learn that García is alive and taken prisoner. This apparent contradiction seems to indicate (see West 1983, 151–152) that two versions of this legend existed, one involving the death of the Navarrese monarch and the other his imprisonment. On the other hand, it could well be that this episode and the description of the death of King Sancho of Navarre earlier in the poem are both elaborations of the same source, very possibly the account of the battle of Atapuerca from the *Crónica najerense* (see note to 695a, above).

707b   great good sense: our poet is not alone in contrasting brevity of expression with perceptiveness of content. The author of the *Libro de Alexandre* (line 330d), likewise using the term *razón*, praises the same skill as an example of scholarship.

Lacuna between stanzas 708 and 721: approximately thirteen stanzas of the text are missing from the manuscript, but we have included the corresponding section of the

Estoria de España (see for example the similar lacuna between stanzas 523 and 531). For an attempted reconstruction of the missing text, see Victorio (2010, 170–173).

her father: historically, Fernando's wife Sancha was the sister of King García, and not his daughter, and that is how our poet presents her. On the other hand, his second wife, Urraca, was indeed King García's daughter and the authors of the chronicle may well have her in mind at this point (see note to stanza 584 for an explanation of how in the *Poema* the Count's two wives have been merged into one character).

Abd al-Rahman, King of Córdoba: whilst the *Poema* uses the formidable figure of al-Mansur as the Count's Muslim adversary, the chronicle is more historically accurate: Abd al-Rahman III (891–961) was, from 929, the first Umayyad caliph of Córdoba, under whose reign the city entered a period of great wealth and splendour. Abd al-Rahman's achievements include the building of the great palace complex of Medina Azahara outside Córdoba. However, his most fundamental success was in establishing firm control over both al-Andalus and an area of north Africa. The defeat inflicted on him in 939 by Ramiro II, supported by Fernán González, stood out as a major failure for a ruler who styled himself 'the Victorious'.

722ab   Sahagún: the royal monastery of San Benito de Sahagún was situated some seventy kilometres south east of the city of León and was to become one of the most important monasteries in Spain, reaching the height of its importance as a centre of Cluniac reform in the mid-eleventh century under Alfonso VI. It is mentioned, for example, in the *Poema de Mio Cid* as the place where the Cid's messenger visits Alfonso in his court. It still played a very prominent role at the time of our poem's composition: in March-April 1255 Alfonso X stayed there for a month (Salvador Martínez 2010, 118–120). The monastery had been founded at the beginning of the tenth century through a donation by Alfonso III of León and it went on to acquire lands which extended as far as Segovia. It suffered an infamous raid by al-Mansur in 988 when its buildings were destroyed, and it is possibly to this event that the poet is here making an allusion. **Campos**, in its full form 'Tierra de Campos', is the name given from the late thirteenth century to an extensive area which forms part of the present-day provinces of León, Zamora, Palencia and Valladolid. Having been a frontier zone between Islamic Spain and the Christian kingdoms, it was steadily repopulated under the Leonese monarchs in the second half of the ninth century. It was a rich agricultural area, but it was to become the scene of long-lasting disputes and conflicts between the kingdoms of Castile and León.

723c   bade them turn back: by stanza 733 the sorrow which this produces will have been transformed into 'fury and rage'. The Leonese knights have been humiliated by being considered unnecessary in this battle against their enemies, and it is justifiable to see in this a jibe by the poet aimed at the Leonese on account of their failure to support the Castilians in major battles fought by Alfonso VIII: the defeat at Alarcos in 1195 when both the Leonese and the Navarrese troops were late in arriving, and most conspicuously the great Castilian triumph at Las Navas de Tolosa in 1212.

736d the good King: it is striking that King Sancho of León is depicted at this point as essentially a good man; we later see him filled with anger and casting the Count into prison, but this is partly offset by his magnanimous treatment of Sancha after she has freed her husband. Sancho is shown here to promote unity whilst it is his wife, closely identified with Navarre rather than León, who does all within her power to introduce discord and conflict. It is significant that, in spite of the evident tensions and although Fernán González is shown as outwitting his lord and monarch, he is never seen as coming into open conflict with him. We must bear in mind, too, that when the *Poema de Fernán González* was composed, Castile and León had for some time been a united kingdom and the poet was undoubtedly seeking to show that, if there was hostility, it came from outside that kingdom, from Navarre.

740b he would get what he desired: it may not have been clear initially that the Count had set out to deceive King Sancho, but it now becomes apparent that he has always had an understanding of the potential consequences of the conditions of the deal. The poet has very skilfully shown his hero to be a man of great intelligence, whilst placing the emphasis on the King's naivety rather than on any sense of underhanded conduct.

743c just as we read it: see note to 695a.

746c move on León: the Spanish text suggests that the Count was attacking León, but in fact at this point he had gone to aid King Sancho against the marauding Muslim forces.

747 For La **Bureba** see note to 458a. The area was dominated by the castle of **Petralata** (or Piedralada) which stood on a crag rising to a height of 1,200 metres. The oldest evidence for the existence of the castle is from 1040 and it was abandoned at the end of the thirteenth century. The **Ubierna** river is a tributary of the Arlanzón and flows to the north of Burgos. Today the area is still important for its agriculture.

754c grain to make the red dye: see note to 151b. In this stanza the poet is using a powerful combination of images to evoke the nature of battle: the cruelty of the hunt (a parallel that he has used on a number of occasions in the poem), the anger represented by the raging torrent of the river, and the outpouring of blood suggested by the bright red colour of the dye.

755a Valpierre: see note on La Era Degollada in line 312d. The town of Briones, for example, in the north of the area, stands on a steep hill which overlooks the river Ebro.

760cd In the sentence which corresponds to these two missing lines, the chronicle tells us simply that 'In that place King García was defeated, together with all his forces'.

Lacuna after stanza 760: to judge from the corresponding passage in the *Estoria de España*, the missing section seems to have been of approximately 80 stanzas, and it is this section that is given here. However, the Portuguese *Crónica geral de Espanha*, which dates from 1344, includes a significantly longer section which tells how, when Sancho fails to keep his bargain, hostilities escalate until the Leonese and the Castilians are on the brink of war; in this account it is thanks to mediation by the abbot of Sahagún that Sancho is eventually persuaded that Castile must be given its freedom.

Era: the *anno domini* system of dating was not adopted in Castile until the late fourteenth century. Probably starting in the third century AD, a different system was introduced in both the south of France and the Iberian Peninsula and used in documents, inscriptions and chronicles: the starting point for this Hispanic Era was 1st January 38 BC (the year following the completion of the process of pacification of the province of Hispania by Octavian). To convert a date from the Hispanic Era to the *anno domini* system, it is, therefore, necessary to subtract 38 years.

a good counsellor: we cannot, of course, be sure that all of the following lengthy section on the responsibilities of the king's counsellors reflects the content of the *Poema*. However, it is clear that the subject was a major concern of Alfonso, and a similar set of principles is to be found in the *Siete Partidas*, 2,9,5.

my son García: Sancha in fact bore the Count four sons (Gonzalo, Sancho, Munio and García) and at least three daughters (Urraca, Muniadonna and Fronilde). It is known that Gonzalo survived until adulthood; he is recorded as being married by 959, but he seems to have died soon afterwards. Sancho and Munio appear to have died young, but it was García Fernández who was to prove a worthy successor to his father, governing the county of Castile with a high level of autonomy until his death in 995 and continuing to extend the frontiers of Castile into Islamic territory. One of Fernando's daughters, Urraca, was to be a queen three times, marrying, in turn, both Ordoño III and Ordoño IV of León and Sancho II of Pamplona.

following the instructions of my parliament: for the nature and role of the *Cortes*, see note to lines 571ab. This remark, later ironically echoed by Fernán González, appears to shift the responsibility for King Sancho's actions onto his advisers. The *Cortes* really had no legislative role and they were in no sense a democratic institution. Nevertheless, it is clear that under Alfonso X, in the period when the *Poema* was being composed, they were being summoned with increased frequency and the poet will have seen them as an increasingly important feature of the system of government; the *Cortes* of Castile and León still met separately. We have not been told of any conduct of the Count which would explain the wrongs of which he is accused here, for the poet has been at pains to depict him as scrupulous in the observance of his duties towards his king and lord, but the implication seems clearly to be that the effect of his abilities as a warrior and leader of his people has been all too apparent and that he has steadily been asserting Castile's independence.

cast into irons: this actually corresponds to the first occasion on which the historical Fernán González was imprisoned: as is recounted, for example, in the *Crónica de Sampiro*, composed in the early eleventh century, the Count conspired against Ramiro II and as a result spent some months in prison from 944 to 945 before being reconciled with his monarch. See also note to stanza 599 and Introduction, section 2(ii).

Mansilla: this small town is situated about 20 kilometres south east of León. It has had several names, including Mansilla del Camino, as we are told by the text, but today it is known as Mansilla de las Mulas. From the tenth century it was an important settlement on the pilgrim road, marking the point where its route converged with the old Roman road. It was also the crossing point for the river Esla and as such it is mentioned in the pilgrim's guide which forms part of the twelfth-century *Codex Calixtinus* (see note to 134b). Mansilla's substantial walls date largely from 1181 when the town was repopulated by Fernando II. The Spanish text mentions 'la somoza', which some have taken as a proper name, but in fact this word is likely to be a more general description of the hilly area approaching the mountains which lie to the north and are clearly visible from Mansilla. The allusion here could not possibly be to the area now known as La Somoza which is situated a long way to the west and would have involved travelling some way beyond the city of León. Certainly, however, Sancha's knights will have made a significant detour into difficult countryside in order to escape detection.

like a pilgrim: disguise as a pilgrim is a well-established folk-motif (Deyermond and Chaplin 1972, 47–48). However, this detail also relates the second time that the Count is freed from prison with the first, when the intermediary was an actual pilgrim, and reinforces the link between the love between Fernando and Sancha and the pilgrimage (see also note to line 614a).

Matins is the first of the canonical hours of prayer in the Church day. It would have begun at first light and continued until dawn; in practice this would vary from about 2.30 a.m. in midsummer to about 6.30 a.m. in midwinter.

dressed the Count in all her clothes: this account of the freeing of the Count by the use of disguise exploits another common folk-motif (Deyermond and Chaplin 1972, 48). Injecting a strong comic note at a critical point in the narrative, it serves to increase the dramatic power of the narrative and will, no doubt, have been very effective in performance. It also serves to emphasize still further the role of Sancha and in particular her courage, her resourcefulness and her readiness to take the initiative amidst a violent and essentially masculine world.

the Castilians escaped from ... the power of León and its people: it has been suggested that the missing section of the poem would have gone on to recount further episodes, including another triumph over Muslim armies (Lacarra 1979, 13–14), but there is no firm evidence to support this. The 1344 Portuguese *Crónica geral de Espanha* recounts the death of Fernán González in Burgos and his burial at San Pedro de Arlanza, and some scholars are inclined to see this as a prosified version of the end of the *Poema*, presenting the monastery essentially as a shrine to the hero's glory (see West 1983, 77–79). The suggestion seems a plausible one, but once again there is no solid basis for assuming a continuation beyond the events related in the *Estoria de España*. Indeed, it seems fitting for the poem to end with Fernan González achieving what is presented as the liberation of Castile. The poet's depiction of his career began with an expression of his determination to bring an end to the oppression suffered at the hands of the Muslims. The focus has shifted onto liberation from domination by the Leonese, but what remains the same is the exhilaration at the emergence of a free people with previous centuries' errors now fully redeemed. The historical fact, however, is that Fernán González did not turn Castile into an independent political unit and the counts of Castile remained subject to the authority of the kings of León. During his lifetime Castile did become a lordship which for several generations was to be firmly linked to one family enjoying a range of rights and exemptions. Ironically, the king who was to put an end to the existence of such hereditary counties was King Fernando I of León and Castile, the great-grandson of Fernán González.